TABLE of CONTENTS

Section Two (subjects of interest)   PAGE

Preface

For the best part of my life, I have been trying to acquire, a deep understanding of the doctrine of the Church of Jesus Christ of Latter Day Saints. This effort has been like trying to work a jigsaw puzzle that is lying face down on a table. Each time there is a talk given from the pulpit, a passage of scripture read, sitting through a lesson of some kind, or reading an article in a church magazine, someone is turning over a small piece of the puzzle, and this piece-by-piece effort reoccurs throughout our lives. The problem is, when turning over these puzzle pieces, they are often, so disassociated these pieces seldom give us enough information to see just where and how they fit into the whole of the puzzle. Since the puzzle is upside down on the table, it is difficult, if not impossible, to see how it all fits together in a doctrinal way. Now everyone knows, a one hundred-piece puzzle is easier to work than a thousand-piece puzzle, but the gospel is like a million-piece puzzle. The puzzle has serious implications in our lives and behavior; the behavior God prescribes, represents our understanding of doctrine. It is imperative, members make every effort to study and understand the doctrine as presented by the Mormon Church. This very doctrine provides behavioral guidance, and gives assurance; the kingdom of Heaven is reachable. If our doctrinal understanding is uncertain, the operation of our behavioral guidance is inadequate. It is important to understand, all *true religious information* springs from only two sources, scriptural and prophetic. All research on any religious matter is a product of amassing as much doctrinal information as can be found from as many reliable and authoritative sources as possible. No doctor of divinity, theologian, religious scholar, doctrinal historian, nor bible researcher has any propriety rights or exclusivity to their published material because it all comes from the same two sources named above. If their material does not come from scriptural or prophetic utterances then it is not authoritative, After all these years there is not very much, in the way of doctrine, that scholars have not examined in a hundred different ways in thousands of different publications. My sole objective is to take the considerable amount of information I have researched on any given subject, and connect the dots in the best way I can. Thereby fitting as many small pieces of any doctrinal subject together, making each a larger piece, so this huge doctrinal puzzle is easier to understand. I do not claim to possess any new or revelatory information; I do not speak from or with any authoritative right; nor do I expect any reading of my material to be take it as the final word on any subject. In fact, I encourage the reader to research all references included with the text. Start a research project of their own seeking out other related references, and when they feel satisfied they have given the subject as much effort as possible, learned as much as they can, then, involve themselves in prayer to receive a reassuring response from the Holy Ghost. Then and only then will they know the truth.

ISBN 978-0-692-99559-4

SECTION ONE

Eternal Laws of God

Over the years, many hours have been spent studying the Eternal Laws of God, but when discussing this field of enquiry with other members of the Mormon Church it became evident most members have limited understanding and almost no interest in the subject. This section of the book is to trying to provide an understanding of the Eternal Laws of Gods. To define what the Eternal Laws of God are, and determine the scope and influence of these laws. Since the Church believes in Eternal Laws of God, explain how these laws pertain to us. The list of laws, as presently known are,

- Law of Aggression
- Law of the Fast,
- Law of Tithing
- Law of Adoption
- Law of Eternal Increase
- Law of Unity
- Law of Chastity
- Law of Attraction
- Law of Consecration
- Law of Eternal Progression
- Law of Repentance
- Law of Forgiveness
- Law of Eternal Increase
- Law of Self Reliance
- Law of Election
- Law of Justice

- Law of Mercy
- Law of Natural Law
- Law of Retaliation
- Law of War
- Law of Being
- Law of Free Grace
- Law of Sacrifice
- Law of the Church
- Law of the Harvest
- Law of Fulfillment
- Law of Multiple Fulfillment
- Law of Sufficient Reason
- Law of Common Consent
- Law of Witness
- Law of Retribution
- Law of Light

The Doctrine and Covenants teaches, "All kingdoms have a law given; and there is no space in which there is no kingdom" (*D&C 88:36–37*). Thus, it is clear; all things in the vast immensity of space are under the influence of law. All the elements of this universe are controlled, governed, and upheld by law— nothing is exempt. Nothing is arbitrary or left to chance. The same unvarying result always flows from the same cause. The principles of eternal law are immutable, eternal, and everlasting." (*McConkie, Mormon Doctrine, p. 433*) These Eternal Laws cause and maintain order in the universe; they are mortal as well as spiritual. The creators of the universe, the founders of this nation and the Prophets who restored the Mormon religion used these laws in their endeavors, and these laws are still used in the ongoing spiritual administration of the world.

Natural Law is the secular term for the Eternal Laws of God, which is often referred to as God's Laws. When someone says Gods Law, the average person thinks, "ah, commandments", so it is necessary to group Gods Rules into two categories, for purposes of clarity. The first category is Eternal Laws of God, which are of course, God's Rules, and they are always eternal. The second category is Commandments, which are also God's Rules, but oft times mistakenly called Eternal Laws of God. The correct terminology for commandments is Devine Laws of God. The key to understanding Eternal Laws of God is they cannot, under any circumstances, be changed, or broken. Although commandments are laws also coming from God, they differ from Eternal Laws of God because the number of commandments can change; it seems the count always increases, never decreases. Note the change in the Word of Wisdom, from a non-commanded code of conduct, to a non-stated commandment where, conformity is required in many instances in church. Gods Laws have always existed, and it is by understanding, or coming into compliance with them, humanity is able to achieve the outcome they most desire, and the desired outcome is their eternal joy and happiness. All temporal commandments are spiritual because their source is the Eternal Laws of God; all Eternal Laws of Gods are spiritual and eternal therefore; they are in full force here in mortality. This close association of Eternal Laws of God to commandments is why people sometimes think Eternal Laws of Gods and commandments are the same thing, and they can break the Eternal Laws of Gods in the same way commandments are broken. This section will continue to address Eternal Laws of Gods and leave the explanation of Devine laws of God for another time.

According to the doctrine of the Church of Jesus Christ of Latter Day Saints, God took some unorganized intelligences from chaos and gave them the law. If they agreed to obey these laws, they could become His spirit children. These eternal laws govern everything, and God organized His creation based on these laws. It also means, these eternal laws have always been in existence, and these laws govern God Himself. "The light which is in all things, which giveth life to all things, which is the law by which all things are governed, even the power of God who sitteth upon his throne, who is in the bosom of eternity, who is in the midst of all things" (*D&C 88:13*). Here it clearly says the Law of Light governs everything, even God. The clearest illustrative examples of Eternal Laws of God are the laws governing the universe, such as the law of gravity, which is the primary force used to accomplish the creation. Mortals simply cannot break the law of gravity. Flying an airplane is not breaking the law of gravity; flying is still 100% in compliance with gravity. A metal object lifted by a magnet does not break the law of gravity, the metal object is simply responding to the greater applied force, not in opposition to gravity but in concert with it. Another example, which is a little more difficult to understand, is The Law of Eternal Progression, a law found in religious tenets, given by God. The facts are, mortals cannot stop themselves from progressing. It is not possible to stop, alter, abolish, repeal, or break this law in any way. All are born into the spirit world traversed into this mortality, and will continue into the eternal realm, on the path toward a reward in heaven, whatever that may be, and the process cannot be stopped. Every person will receive their reward, or lack there-of, no matter what they do while on this earth. Lacking knowledge or understanding of any of these laws does not lessen their impact in any way. The truth is, all Eternal Laws of Gods exist independent of knowledge or understanding, and whether understood or not, mortals must live within their structure or suffer the consequences. If a person does not believe it, and builds themselves a set of wings, then jumps off the roof in an effort to fly and they will soon understand, they cannot defy God's Eternal Law of gravity.

The first time in recorded history, the concept of Eternal Laws of God was documented was in the writings, was a Roman political writer, Marcus Tullius Cicero (106-43 B.C.) who rejected the plurality of gods the Roman Empire worshiped, but believed in a single God, being the Supreme Creator. Cicero, in his writings, On the Republic, and On the Laws, projected the grandeur and promise of some future society based on Eternal Laws of God.

Cicero spoke of building a society on principles of Eternal Laws of God by recognizing and identifying the rules of *right conduct* as the laws of the Supreme Creator of the universe. He recognized the "brilliant intelligence of a Supreme Designer with an ongoing interest in both human and cosmic affairs … once the reality of the Creator is clearly identified in the mind, the only intelligent approach to government, justice, and human relations

3

would be in terms of the laws which the Supreme Creator has already established. The Creator's order of things is called Eternal Laws of God" (*Cicero 106–43 B.C*).

Cicero defined Eternal Laws of God as *right conduct* according to the laws established by the Supreme Creator. "Eternal Laws of God is right reason in agreement with nature; it is of universal application, unchanging and everlasting ... It is a sin to try to alter this law, nor is it allowable to repeal any part of it, and it is impossible to abolish it entirely. Citizens cannot be freed from its obligations by senate or vote of the people. One eternal and unchangeable law will be valid for all nations and all times, and there will be one master and ruler, which is God, over all, for He is the author of this law" (*Cicero 106–43 B.C*).

Sir William Blackstone (1723-1780) was an English judge and law professor who authored the four-volume Commentaries on the Laws of England, and there in explains Eternal Laws of God. These law books became the second most frequently invoked political authorities of the Founders of the United States, The Origins of American Constitutionalism, 1988. By the way, the Bible came in first. In these law books, Blackstone said… "Man, considered as a creature, must necessarily be subject to the laws of his Creator, for he is entirely a dependent being…And consequently, as man depends absolutely upon his Maker for everything, it is necessary, he should in all points conform to his Maker's will. This will of his Maker is called the law of nature or Eternal Laws of God. This law of nature, being coeval (coexistent) with mankind and dictated by God Himself, is of course superior in obligation to any other. It is binding over the entire globe, in all countries, and at all times; no human laws are of any validity, if contrary to this" (*Blackstone 1723-1780*).

Therefore, Blackstone said, the laws of nature are the will of God for man.
Blackstone continued: "And if the reasons were always clear and perfect, the task would be pleasant and easy; there is not a need for any other guide, but the law of nature. However, every man now finds things contrary in his own experience, his reason is corrupt, and his understanding full of ignorance and error. This has given manifold occasion for the benign interposition of Divine Providence, which…hath been pleased, at sundry times, and in diverse manners, to discover, and enforce its laws by an immediate and direct revelation. The doctrines thus delivered, called, and revealed as divine law, and found only in the Holy Scriptures." (*Blackstone 1723-1780*)

Summarizing Blackstone's second phrase, *the laws of nature* are the reveled laws of God, found in the Holy Scriptures. Blackstone's conclusion

4

couples these two phrases: "Upon these two foundations, the law of nature, and the law of revelation (the law of natures or Eternal Laws of God), depend all the human laws; that is to say, no human laws should be suffered to contradict these" (*Blackstone 1723-1780*).

The first time many people heard anything about the Eternal Laws of God was in high school, while studying U.S, History and Civics, and more particularly The Constitution, The Declaration of Independence, and The Bill of Rights.

The first paragraph of The Declaration of Independence, says. "When in the course of human events it becomes necessary for one people to dissolve the political bands which have connected them with another and to assume among the powers of the earth the separate and equal station to which the laws of nature and of nature's God entitles them, a decent respect to the opinions of mankind requires that they should declare the causes which impel them to the separation" (*Declaration of Independence*).

Violations of these laws, the laws of nature, and of nature's God, caused the Founders to declare they must separate themselves from Great Britain, and due to the Law of Nature; they were entitled to establish themselves among the powers of the earth as a separate and equal station.

The second sentence of The Bill of Rights, a statement of Eternal Laws of God and human rights says; "We hold these truths to be self-evident, that all men are created equal, that they are endowed by their Creator with certain unalienable Rights, that among these are, Life, Liberty and the pursuit of Happiness" (*Bill of Rights*).

This sentence has been referred to as, one of the best-known sentences in the English language and the most potent and consequential words in American history

God created all people equally in the following three ways under the terms of Eternal Laws of God:

1. Equal before God.

2. Equal before the law.

3. Equal in rights.

Life, liberty and the pursuit of happiness are only three of the 28 Principles of Freedom the Founding Fathers that every person must understand. The remaining 25 are contained in the text below.

In addition, The Bill of Rights is the collective name for the first ten amendments to the United States Constitution, which limit the power of the U.S. Federal Government. These limitations serve to protect the natural rights of liberty and property including freedoms of religion, speech, a free press, free assembly, and free association, as well as the right to keep and bear arms.

The Bill of Rights uses the term, unalienable rights, meaning, these rights cannot to be transferred, or taken away, because of being protected by law, and then explains what these rights are, and asserts, these rights are obtained through natural Law, which was given by God... A majority of the community hath an indubitable, unalienable, and indefeasible right to reform, alter, or abolish the government... All men are, by nature, Eternal Laws of God, equally free and independent and have certain inherent rights from God, of which ... they cannot divest; namely, the enjoyment of life and liberty, with the means of acquiring and possessing property, and pursuing and obtaining happiness and safety. The government should not have the power of suspending, or executing laws, without consent of the representatives of the people. A legal defendant has the right to be "confronted with the accusers and witnesses, to call for evidence in his favor, and to a speedy trial by an impartial jury of his vicinage, and may not be compelled to give evidence against himself. Individuals should be protected against cruel and unusual punishments, baseless search and seizure, and be guaranteed a trial by jury. The government should not abridge freedom of the press, or freedom of religion, all men are equally entitled to the free exercise of religion. The government should be enjoined against maintaining a standing army rather than a well-regulated militia" (*Bill of Rights*)

Therefore, it is obvious, the founding fathers, who are often called the framers of the Constitution, intended this country, governed by Eternal Laws of God, and these rights were never to be altered. How did the Founding Fathers, understood these concepts and applied these principles? Here is a few of their statements.

"All laws, however, may be arranged in two different classes. (1) Divine. (2) Human...But it should always be remembered that this law, natural or revealed law, made for men or for nations, flows from the same Divine source: it is the law of God...Human law must rest its authority ultimately upon the authority of that law which is Divine" (*James Wilson, 1804, Signer both the Declaration of Independence & the Constitution, and a U.S. Supreme Court Justice*).

"The law...dictated by God Himself is, of course, superior in obligation to any other. It is binding over the entire globe, in all countries, and at all times. No human laws are of any validity if contrary to this" (*Alexander Hamilton Feb 23, 1775*).

"The 'Law of nature' is a rule of conduct arising out of the God's relations of human beings established by the Creator and existing prior to any positive precept (human law) ...these...have been established by the Creator and are, with a peculiar felicity of expression, denominated in Scripture, "ordinances of heaven" (*Noah Webster, America's schoolmaster, Author of 1st American English Dictionary, authored Art. 1 Section 8 of U.S. Constitution*).

"Our citizens should early understand that the genuine source of correct republican principles is the Bible...particularly the New Testament, or the Christian religion" (*Noah Webster, America's schoolmaster, Author of 1st American English Dictionary, authored Art. 1 Section 8 of U.S. Constitution*).

"The education of youth should be watched with the most scrupulous attention. It is much easier to introduce and establish an effectual system...than to correct by penal statutes the ill effects of a bad system...The education of youth... lays the foundations on which both law and gospel rest for success" (*Noah Webster, America's schoolmaster, Author of 1st American English Dictionary, authored Art. 1 Section 8 of U.S. Constitution*).

"It cannot be emphasized too strongly or too often that this great nation was founded, not by religionists, but by Christians; not on religions, but on the gospel of Jesus Christ. For this very reason peoples of other faiths have been afforded asylum, prosperity, and freedom of worship here" (*Patrick Henry, 5 times Governor of Virginia*).

The last quote comes from the Father of this Country, George Washington's famous promise, and is the key to political prosperity from his farewell address. The greatness of this country depends upon two principles, religion, and morality:

"Of all the dispositions and habits which lead to political prosperity, religion and morality are indispensable supports. In vain, would that man claim the tribute of patriotism, who should labor to subvert these great Pillars of human happiness, these firmest props of the duties of men and citizens? The mere Politician, equally with the pious man ought to respect and to cherish them. A volume could not trace all their connections with private and public felicity. Let it simply be asked, where is the security for property, for reputation, for life, if the sense of religious obligation and oaths, which are the instruments of investigation in Courts of Justice? In addition, let not anyone with caution indulge the supposition that morality can be maintained without religion. Whatever may be conceded to the influence of refined education on minds of peculiar structure reason and experience both forbid people to expect that national morality can prevail in exclusion of religious principle. Tis substantially true, that virtue or morality is a necessary spring of popular government. The rule indeed extends with more or less force to every species of free Government. Who that is a sincere friend to it can look with indifference upon attempts to shake the foundation of the fabric" (*George Washington, Farewell Address*).

Nowadays, when speaking of the laws of nature law, many people think this means doing whatever comes naturally, or perhaps whatever the animals might do. There seems to be little reverence to absolute truth, or respect for Eternal Laws of God. To some modern philosophers, man's law is supreme. Everything is evolving, and many people, most legislatures, and the courts do not seem to be concerned with consequences now, or in the hereafter of their disregard for Eternal Laws of God. In spite of these people, legislatures, and the courts, there is another group of people who are very much concerned with the Laws of God and spend a considerable amount of time and energy living up to the expectations of God, because the Laws of God are an integral part of their religion. All principles, tenets, and doctrines of the Church of Jesus Christ of Latter Day Saints exemplify the Laws of God. As come to know, from reading the New Testament, the Savior taught his Apostles the Laws of God, but how did Joseph Smith become an expert on the Laws of God? Many people in the Church know the Prophet Joseph Smith, the founder of the Church of Jesus Christ of Latter Day Saints, was also taught the Laws of God through direct revelations from God, and it is because of this teaching he was able to reveal the most correct Doctrines and Laws of God to the world.

The Prophet Joseph Smith taught the United States was a country specially set apart by God, the Founding Fathers. The formation of the government was nothing short of God's inspiration in the application of Eternal Laws of God, in documents, such as the Constitution, Bill of Rights, and The Declaration of Independence as outlined above. The general population of the church understands they have an obligation to defend the principles of the Constitution under circumstances where iniquity, or moral decay, may devastate the concepts of the Eternal Laws of God.

Joseph Smith predicted the "U.S. Constitution would one day hang by a thread and the elders of the Church would, at some critical juncture, be instrumental in saving it" (*Discourse Delivered by Joseph Smith, July 19, 1840*).

Church President John Taylor seemed to go further when he prophesied, "When the people shall have torn to shreds the Constitution of the United

States the Elders of Israel will be found holding it up to the nations of the earth and proclaiming liberty and equal rights to all men" (*Journal of Discourses 21:8*).

Because the Priesthood of the Church of Jesus Christ of Latter Day Saints has been called by God to save the Constitution in these times of constitutional peril, the elders of the church themselves might well require wisdom at least equal to that of the men raised up to found it. The lack of knowledge or understanding of the Laws of God does not lessen its impact on, or the responsibility given to, these priesthood holders in any way. For when the time comes, and the laws of man have so corrupted the Laws of God, the very freedom of the people is in jeopardy, the priesthood holders will be expected to respond in ways, such as, using every public forum available to alert, and educate the citizens. Involving themselves in public service, voting the culprits of corruption out of office, forming and/or supporting political candidates that represent their views, and in other diverse manners it will become self-evident, it is time to restore the Laws of God back to this nation.

Law of Adoption

All of the children of God are heirs to the gospel and the priesthood because of the covenant God made with Abraham. Few of the Lord's servants hold a position of prominence equaling to Abraham. Along with Christians, Jews, and Muslims, Latter-day Saints consider Abraham the father of the faithful and the exemplary ancestor of those who serve God. There are millions of men worldwide, named after this great patriarch, attesting to the legacy of his life and deeds and to the honored memory in which his descendants hold him.

Abraham has a well-deserved place in history. The books of Genesis and Abraham record his faith and diligence in serving the Lord (Abr. 1–3; Gen. 11:26–25:10) The sacred records show, he committed himself to do all God commanded, even being willing to sacrifice, in response to God's command, what was most precious to him—his son (Gen. 22:1–18; Heb. 11:17–19). Of all men on earth, the Lord chose this faithful man to become the father of a covenant people. Through his direct lineage and his adopted descendants, the blessings of the gospel are available to all men and women. For the members of the Church of Jesus Christ of Latter-day Saints, Abraham is a focal point of the churches covenant history, and faithful Saints rejoice to be among his descendants and seek to follow his example of righteousness.

A covenant is an agreement in which two parties make commitments to each other. Each party takes upon himself, as part of his acceptance of the covenant, certain obligations pertaining to the relationship. In a gospel covenant, it is necessary to enter into sacred agreements with God, promising obedience to his will. In turn, he has promised glorious blessings if His followers obey and serve him.

The Patriarch Abraham committed himself unwaveringly to the Lord's service and was therefore, privileged to enter into a covenant with him. The Bible describes the blessings the Lord promised Abraham because of his faith and obedience. The following are the four promises: Recorded in Genesis.

Promise 1: "Lift up now thine eyes, and look from the place where thou art northward, and southward, and eastward, and westward: For all the land which thou seest, to thee will I give it, and to thy seed forever" (*Gen. 13:14–15*).

Promise 2: "And I will make thy seed as the dust of the earth: so that if a man can number the dust of the earth, then shall thy seed also be numbered" (*Gen. 13:16*).

Promise 3: "I will establish my covenant between me and thee and thy seed after thee in their generations for an everlasting covenant, to be a God unto thee, and to thy seed after thee" (*Gen. 17:7*).

Promise 4: "In thy seed shall all the nations of the earth be blessed" (Gen. 22:18).

Abraham's and Sarah's son and grandson, Isaac and Jacob, received similar promises and became subject to the same covenants and obligations Abraham had received. (Gen. 26:3–4; Gen. 28:13–14; Gen. 35:11–12) The Lord renewed this covenant at Mount Sinai with the descendants of these three men of the house of Israel. (Ex. 19:1–8). By inheritance, those who descend from that lineage receive the same blessings and enter into the same obligations as their great ancestors. In modern times, the Lord has renewed this covenant with his Saints. (D&C 84:33–40, 48; D&C 110:12) Thus, Latter-day Saints today can rightly perceive the covenant of the Patriarchs as being a covenant between God and themselves.

The passages cited above, along with other scriptures, point to four major aspects of the Abrahamic covenant.

1. A Promised Land

The Lord gave the land of Canaan as a blessing to Abraham, his wife Sarah, and his covenant children. Later revelations reveal, the Lord has designated other promised lands—the Americas as an inheritance to the children of Joseph, for example (3Ne. 15:13; 3Ne. 16:16; Ether 13:8).

Yet, the scriptures clearly states, the promise was only effective, depending upon the people's righteous behavior. In the Old Testament, God postponed the promise of the land when his people refused to serve him. First, the ten northern tribes were taken from the land because of their unworthiness (2 Kgs. 17), and then, the tribes of Judah, and Benjamin were similarly taken (2 Kgs. 24–25). The Lord denied ancient Israel the blessing because its people had failed to earn it, fulfilling the Lord's word; inheritance in the land can only be had on the condition of faithfulness (Deut. 4:25–27; Deut. 28:15, 62–64).

Since a promised land is the blessing of a sacred covenant, the covenant people can receive it only by fulfilling the stipulations of the covenant. When the scattered tribes of Israel again accept the ancient Abrahamic covenant, the Lord will gather them fully, in peace, to their lands of promise. (2Ne. 6:11; 2 Ne. 10:7–8)

2. A Great Posterity

Perhaps the best-known blessing of the Abrahamic covenant is of a vast posterity. The Lord promised Abraham, his descendants would be as numerous as the stars. Today, one can see this promise partially fulfilled in the many millions who look upon Abraham as their ancestor. Millions of Arabs acknowledge Abraham as their lineal parent, as do millions of Jews. More than seven million Latter-day Saints hold him as their predecessor, while more than one billion other Christians and Muslims consider Abraham to be their father in a symbolic sense. These figures show the impressive fulfillment of God's promise to his noble servant.

The ultimate realization of the Lord's promise, however, will come in a different way. Modern revelation testifies of a heavenly fulfillment: "Abraham received promises concerning his seed, and of the fruit of his loins ... which were to continue so long as they were in the world; and as touching Abraham and his seed, ... both in the world and out of the world should they continue as innumerable as the stars; or, if ye were to count the sand upon the seashore ye could not number them" (*D&C 132:30*).

The Abrahamic promise of countless descendants pertains to the eternal world as well as to descendants on earth. (See Bruce R. McConkie, The Millennial Messiah, The Second Coming of the Son of Man, Salt Lake City: Deseret Book Co., 1982, pp. 262–64, 267) Even with the understanding of exaltation, eternal families, and the nature of God and his work, it is difficult to envision the magnitude of the promise the Lord made to Abraham.

3. Priesthood and Gospel Blessings

Among the promises of the Abrahamic covenant is the one whereby faithful heirs will possess the gospel and the power of the Lord's priesthood. Covenant descendants of Abraham and Sarah have a right, by virtue of their inheritance, to these blessings. However, as with other covenantal blessings, they actually realize the blessings of their birthright only based on personal worthiness.

A key passage of scripture teaches about that right. "In thee (that is, in thy Priesthood) and in thy seed (that is, thy Posterity), for I give unto thee a promise that this right shall continue in thee, and in thy seed after thee (that is to say, the literal seed, or the seed of the body) shall all the families of the earth be blessed" (*Abr. 2:11*).

Thus, the priesthood will continue with Abraham and Sarah's descendants. However, there have been periods of apostasy in, which the gospel and the priesthood were not available to the world. It remained hidden from Abraham's lineage until the modern day restoration, where the priesthood was renewed. Joseph Smith was given this same priesthood promise in the following scripture,

"Thus saith the Lord unto you, with whom the priesthood hath continued through the lineage of your fathers— "For ye are lawful heirs, according to the flesh, and have been hid from the world with Christ in God— Therefore your life and the priesthood have remained, and must needs remain through you and your lineage until the restoration of all things spoken by the mouths of all the holy prophets since the world began" (*D&C 86:8–10*).

4. A Mission of Salvation to Others

The scriptures teach, through the covenant family of Abraham and Sarah "shall all the families of the earth be blessed, even with the blessings of the Gospel, which are the blessings of salvation, even of life eternal" (*Abr. 2:11*). Foremost among the blessings that the family of Abraham brought about is, the atoning sacrifice of Jesus Christ.

Jesus, who was a descendant of Abraham and Sarah, blesses all people through His atonement. Because of Him, the bands of death through resurrection are broken; and all but the few who commit the unpardonable sin will receive an eternal inheritance in a degree of glory.

The second aspect of the Abrahamic ministry of salvation is a calling Abraham's covenant children have received: to take the gospel and its blessings to the rest of God's children. The Lord has called the house of Israel to carry the gospel to the world. He explained the following to Abraham concerning his descendants: "In their hands they shall bear this ministry and Priesthood unto all nations" (*Abr. 2:9*).

Since the days of Abraham, Isaac, and Jacob, when gospels blessings have been on earth, they are available through the house of Israel. Thus, Abraham and Sarah's descendants are the Chosen People. They are the chosen, not because they have an easier path to salvation, nor because God loves them more than He loves other people, but chosen to serve, in the same sense individual Latter-day Saints are chosen for callings in the Church. When considering the House of Israel has chosen status to be a calling to serve—like any other calling in the gospel—the saints can keep the calling in proper perspective.

The Abrahamic covenant blesses those who are not of Abraham's lineage in a very direct way. The house of Israel is the family of the Lord's Saints. According to the scriptures, those who accept the gospel and join in the Abrahamic covenant become members of the family of Israel, even if they are not Abraham's literal descendants. The Lord taught Abraham concerning the nations of the earth who would not be his physical offspring:

"I will bless them through thy name; for as many as receive this Gospel shall be called after thy name, and shall be accounted thy seed, and shall rise up and bless thee, as their father" (*Abr. 2:10*).

Paul taught the same doctrine about non-Israelites, adopted into the family of Abraham: "For as many of you as have been baptized into Christ have put on Christ" (*Gal 3:27*).

"There is neither Jew nor Greek [in other words, neither Israelite nor non-Israelite], there is neither bond, nor free, there is neither male nor female: for ye are all one in Christ Jesus. And if ye be Christ's, then are ye Abraham's seed, and heirs according to the promise" (*Gal. 3:29*).

The Book of Abraham in the Pearl of Great Price adds additional insight into the covenant promises Jehovah made to Abraham:

"And thou shalt be a blessing unto thy seed after thee, that in their hands they shall bear this ministry and Priesthood unto all nations; And I will bless them through thy name; for as many as receive this Gospel shall be called after thy name, and shall be accounted thy seed, and shall rise up and bless thee, as their father; And I will bless them that bless thee, and curse them that curse thee; and in thee (that is, in thy Priesthood) and in thy seed (that is, thy Priesthood), for I give unto thee a promise that this right shall continue in thee, and in thy seed after thee (that is to say, the literal seed, or the seed of the body) shall all the families of the earth be blessed, even with the blessings of the Gospel, which are the blessings of salvation, even of life eternal" (*Abraham 2:9-11*).

The Doctrine and Covenants teaches the crowning blessing Abraham received was celestial marriage, which qualified him for exaltation and enabled him to become like God (D&C 131:1–4; 132:29–32, 37). Elder Bruce R. McConkie wrote, when, "married in the temple for time and for all eternity, each worthy member of the Church enters personally into the same covenant the Lord made with Abraham" (*Mormon doctrine, Genisis17:7*).

The principle of adoption brings those who are not Abraham's descendants, but who accept the gospel, into his family. The Lord accounts them heirs of the covenant with its blessings and obligations; they become members of the house of Israel. Members learn of their lineage through a patriarchal blessing. Thus, there is no distinction between the literal seed of Abraham and his heirs through adoption, for they are all one in Christ Jesus.

In the last days, the Lord has called the covenant children of the ancient patriarchs, "a light unto the Gentiles, and through this priesthood, a savior unto my people Israel" (*D&C 86:11*). The twofold missionary calling of the latter-day children of Abraham, Isaac, and Jacob is,

(1) To gather others of the house of Israel back to the covenants that God made with their forefathers, and

(2) To gather all others who desire to become one with them.

The Lord has restored the gospel in modern times for the blessing of all people. Every faithful man and woman can receive its blessings to the fullest degree, by accepting baptismal and temple covenants and by living righteously. When covenant blessings are available among the Lord's Saints, all people of the earth benefit. What a marvelous opportunity, and a great responsibility to make those blessings available to all of Father's children.

Joseph Smith was exceedingly anxious to have the Saints sealed— since few of the Church members had ancestors within the young Church, they often chose to seal themselves to prominent Church leaders such as Joseph Smith, or Brigham Young. The key understanding was, an unbroken chain of sealing was required, to bind the whole world into a single human family. To have a better understanding of this subject, read the chapters, Sealing, and Families can be Together Forever.

President Wilford Woodruff explained how he and other Church presidents had felt about the matter:

"I have not felt satisfied, neither did President Taylor, neither has any man since the Prophet Joseph who has attended to the ordinance of adoption in the temples of God. We have felt that there was more to be

14

revealed upon the subject than we had received. Revelations were given in the St. George Temple, which President Young presented to the Church of God. Changes were made there, and we still have more changes to make, in order to satisfy Heavenly Father, and satisfy the dead and ourselves. I will tell you what some of them are. I have prayed over this matter, and my brethren have. We have felt as President Taylor said, that we have got to have more revelation concerning sealing under the law of adoption" (*Wilford Woodruff, General Conference April 1894*).

President Woodruff then announced to the April 1854 General Conference, and particularly to the presidents of the four temples in Utah, he had gone before the Lord to know who he should be adopted to, and the Spirit of God instructed him, he should be sealed to his natural father. Prior to this time, it was the practice, to seal worthy members to the prophets and apostles in the Church. President Woodruff now pronounced the prior practice, an incorrect procedure, and called upon the membership of the church to accept, as a revelation, this announcement, which incidentally he had previously presented to his counselors and to the Quorum of Twelve Apostles.

The house of Israel, in a spiritual and eternal perspective, will finally include all who are the true followers of Jesus Christ. Although those of the direct blood lineage of the house of Israel are genealogically the sheep of God's fold, they must fulfill all the spiritual conditions of discipleship. Those not of the blood of Israel can become Israel through adoption (cf. Rom. 8:14; Gal. 3:7, 29;4:5-7; Matt. 3:9; JST Luke 3:8; Abr. 2:10), through the principles, and the ordinances of the gospel: faith in the Lord Jesus Christ; repentance of sins; baptism by water and reception of the Holy Ghost; and enduring to the end.

In a larger sense, it is necessary that everyone to be adopted into the family of God in order to enjoy the fullness of his blessings in the world to come. As the Only Begotten of the Father in the flesh, Jesus is the only natural heir and therefore the only one whose birthright is the kingdom of his Father. If others are to qualify as joint-heirs with Christ in his Father's kingdom, they must be adopted, and can only be adopted, by God, through the ordinances of the New and Everlasting Covenant.

The adoption process is, in the Prophet Joseph Smith's words, "a new creation by the Holy Ghost" (*TPJS, p. 150*). As summarized in the Doctrine and Covenants, individuals who enter into the covenant and magnify their calling are "sanctified by the Spirit unto the renewing of their bodies. They become the sons of Moses and of Aaron and the seed of Abraham, and the church and kingdom, and the elect of God" (*D&C 84:33-34*).

An important aspect of ordinances is the power given to man to become sons of God. Thou being the spirit offspring of God, because of the fall, their heir ship have been lost, and those who have sinned are doomed to inherit the consequences of their fallen condition. However, through the ordinances of the gospel of Jesus Christ, all can become heirs of God again. For as many as are led by the Spirit of God, Paul wrote, they are the sons of God. They become free from the bondage of sin. "For ye have not received the spirit of bondage again to fear; but ye have received the Spirit of adoption, whereby we cry Abba, Father" (*Rom. 8:14-15*).

This adoption applies to all mankind, not just to the Jews. Elder Bruce R. McConkie explained: "By the law of adoption those who receive the gospel and obey its laws, no matter what their literal blood lineage may have been, are adopted into the lineage of Abraham (*Ab. 2: 9-11*). "The effect of the Holy Ghost upon a Gentile is to purge out the old blood, and make him actually of the seed of Abraham. Such a person has a new creation by the Holy Ghost," (*Teachings, pp. 149 150*). Those who magnify their callings in the Melchizedek priesthood are promised, "They will be sanctified by the Spirit unto the renewing of their bodies, they become the sons of Moses and of Aaron and the seed of Abraham" (*D. & C. 84:33 34*). Indeed, the faithful are adopted to the family of Christ. "Because of the covenant which ye have made ye shall be called the children of Christ, his sons, and his daughters; for behold, this day he hath spiritually begotten you; for ye say that your hearts are changed through faith on his name; therefore, ye are born of him and have become his sons and his daughters". (*Mosiah 5:7*). Paul explained the doctrine of adoption by saying, "As many as are led by the Spirit of God, they are the sons of God," because they receive the Spirit of adoption, being or becoming Israelites, "to whom pertaineth the adoption" (*Rom. 8:14 24; 9:4; Gal. 4:5; Eph. 1:5*). Again, he wrote, "Because of the atonement and by obedience to gospel law men have power to become the sons of God in that they are spiritually begotten of God and adopted as members of his family. They become the sons of God and joint heirs with Christ of the fullness of the Father's kingdom" (See *D. & C. 39:1 6; 76:54 60; Rom. 8:14 17; Gal. 3:1 7; 1 John 3:1 4; Rev. 21:7*).

An important aspect of ordinances is the power given to man to become sons of God. All of the spiritual offspring, of God, because of the fall, have lost their heirship, and are doomed, to inherit the consequences of their fallen condition, and through the ordinances of the gospel of Jesus Christ, can they become heirs of God again. "For as many as are led by the Spirit of God," Paul wrote, "they are the sons of God." They become free from the bondage of sin. "For ye have not received the spirit of bondage again to fear; but ye have received the Spirit of adoption, whereby we cry Abba, Father" (*Rom. 8:14-15*).

Law of Agency

In this discussion, there are four different ways, the law of agency, will be discussed.

1. Agency, as a precursor to the creation and all the way to judgement, meaning, from the very beginning, during the pre-mortal existence and all the way through mortality and up until judgement, the use of agency determines, for the most part, the reward received at the time of judgement.
2. Agency, as the workaday concept.
3. Agency, as a freedom.
4. Lastly, a couple of concepts concerning agency that are interesting. One is the term *free agency,* and the other is the term *moral agency.*

To start with, agency and the creation, while it is known, there was agency (the ability to choose) from the very beginning (See *Moroni, 7; 16*) it is unknown what agency looked like prior to receiving the Light of Christ, nor is there any understanding of the essence of agency during the early part of the preexistence. All unorganized intelligences, from the very beginning, could choose to obey God's laws, or not. If they declined God's offer, they continued as unorganized intelligences. Obviously, there was some kind of agency in play since there was the ability to make a choice. However, there is nothing known about how it worked. When disorganized intelligences, chose to receive the Light of Christ, and become organized, they experienced a change of sphere. Meaning, there was a change made, from being a disorganized intelligence, residing in outer darkness, to becoming an organized intelligence, living within the domain of God. If their obedience was sufficient, they became spirit children of God. According to President Young, this was a movement from one sphere to another, thus, when intelligences were starting to move through the layers of the Plan of Salvation, there were deaths, and rebirths involved. There was also covenants made to follow the Laws of God, and that, within itself, caused the first instance of agency to change, it is unknown what that change entailed. This change, though not clearly understood, reveals that any time a person makes a covenant with God; there is a change in their agency. Do not be confused, after making a covenant with God, the ability to make choices still exists, but the timing of those choices is more refined, and the options become somewhat limited. In addition, the timing of those choices can have an effect on everything when standing at the judgement bar. Take baptism as an example, many things done prior to making the baptismal covenant, can be overlooked, (timing) but after baptism, that all changes, (limited options). This premortal agency awareness and the knowledge of things being diverse from sphere to sphere, comes from statements made by President Young (Discourses of Brigham Young) and interpretations of the Doctrine and Covenants. "All truth is independent in that sphere in which God has placed it, to act for itself, as all intelligence also; otherwise there is no existence, Behold, here is the agency of man, and here is the condemnation of man; because that which was from the beginning is plainly manifest unto them, and they receive not the light" (*D&C 93:29-30*). Some say, in the pre-mortal existence, before God's children chose sides, there was indeed free agency. Meaning, agency was unrestrained until the War in Heaven, during, which all were required to choose between Satan's plan, and Jesus' plan, but once the choice was made, agency again changed, and became limited to only a choice between good or evil, thus it was no longer unrestrained agency. It seems this, change in agency, is correct because, whatever agency was, prior to the War in Heaven, there was not a Satan, or a Savior so there had to be a change in the substance of agency. However, the assumption that, at one time there was total unrestrained agency is somewhat incorrect, there is not enough information about prior agencies to know what is correct. This idea of agency being transformed, as movement is made from sphere to sphere is also exemplified when talking about the stages of creation. In the scriptures, the creation is not just related by just saying, God created everything, but is all spelled out by saying, each element, or part of the creation was created independently and separately. This is seen in first chapter of Genesis, where the creation of the separate stages of earth are laid out, and in the D&C, where details the creation of the universe is explained. Furthermore , the intelligences and the process of them receiving the Light of Christ, as related in (*D&C, 88:7-13*), is representative of all the material used in the process of creating the universe by Christ including the formation of the earth. That is to say, the planets, making up the universe are one type of matter used in the creation, and were intelligences that received the Light, and these intelligences stay in their respective shapes, and orbits in obedience to the will of God. The earth and its contents, rocks, trees, oceans, animals, etc. represent this same type of matter, as intelligences recipient of the Light of Christ. They also stay in their respective shapes, and are being obedient to the will of God, but obedient on a higher level than the matter of the universe. Mortals fall into the same category of matter, they also stay in their respective shapes, and their mortal circumstances remain as such by being obedient to the will of God, again, on a higher level of obedience than other earth related objects. It seems, all of these created objects have been placed in a different sphere, and are described in singular situates in the scriptures, and therefore "each was created with its own independent truth" (*D&C, 93:29-30*). Thus, each sphere is unique from the other in terms of agency, matter, truth, and law. This scripture discloses, all things created will act for its self and judged accordingly. It is obvious; not all these different levels of creation can, nor should, receive judgement by the same rules or truths, therefore D&C 93:29-33 makes sense. "Man was also in the beginning with God. Intelligence, or the light of truth, was not created or made, neither indeed can be. All truth is independent in the sphere in which God has placed it, to act for itself, as all intelligence also; otherwise, there is no existence. Behold, here is the agency of man, and here is the condemnation of man; because that which was from the beginning is plainly manifest unto them, and they receive not the light. And, every man whose spirit receiveth not the light is under condemnation. For man is spirit. The elements are eternal, and spirit and element, inseparably connected, receive a fullness of joy" (*D&C 93:29-33*).

A workaday concept of agency

Mortals understand agency as a necessary part of the Plan of Salvation, and agency makes life on earth a period of testing. In Abraham 3:25, God said, "We will prove them herewith, to see if they will do all things whatsoever the Lord their God shall command them". This language of testing, or proving, links up with Alma's sermon, "And thus we see, that there was a time granted unto man to repent, yea, a probationary time, a time to repent and serve God" (*Alma. 42:4, 4*). People's understanding is, during this time of probation, and this time of repentance, agency is opened up precisely between the two divine words—Atonement and Resurrection, perhaps particularly because the atonement and resurrection opens onto the rest of eternity. This seems to mean, the entrance into this test called mortality, is irreversible. If one understands the "Law of Eternal Progression", this makes sense. In Abraham, the question of one's *nature* or *character* is a question of willingness to do all God commands, and seems only to be concerned with obedience to commandments, but in fact, when linked to the scriptures in Alma, the entire experience of mortality is a test of ones use of agency. Without agency, none would be unable to show Heavenly Father whether they would do all He commanded. To speak of one's, agency, is ultimately to speak of one as an, agent. Moreover, to be an agent, strictly speaking, is not to be free from commitments. To become an agent is to be a commissioned representative of some person or organization, and to be one who has the freedom to handle things however, one sees fit. This understanding of the word agent saturates the Doctrine and Covenants; therein the word, agent, most often appears as the Saints being a representative of the Lord. In Mormon theology, there is this presumption, everyone has agency, and members recognize this phrase to be as important as what it implies. The implication is, as Jesus explained His mission to the apostles, upon His death, all who took upon themselves His name, inherited His mission as Disciples of Christ. His followers then assume the responsible for His mission, from here on they must satisfy their responsibility by using their agency correctly. To be a free agent is to determine, where one would like to make one's commitments. However, do not confuse the act of being a free agent with the term free agency. Here, acting for oneself, one has the absolute freedom to decide how and when to represent themselves, or to act entirely for oneself (*Moses 6: 56*). It is easy to think of exercising agency as freely making unrestrained choices; one can do anything one wants, but since having agency is the covenant, which makes us a representative of the Lord, it is clear, making these choices places us in a position of responsibility, and any choices made have liability attached, therefore the choice is never free. The trick is not to think of Agency as free. Agency is ultimately the play between the freedom, in light of the atonement, to elect whatever agency is wanted and the freedom, within the elected agency, to fulfill one's commission however one sees fit, with the understanding, the outcome governs their reward in heaven. A scripture in Helaman clearly explains this. "And now remember, remember, my brethren, that whosoever perisheth, perisheth unto himself; and whosoever doeth iniquity, doeth it unto himself; for behold, ye are free; ye are permitted to act for yourselves; for behold, God hath given unto you a knowledge and he hath made you free. He hath given unto you that ye might know good from evil, and he hath given unto you that ye might choose life or death; and ye can do good and be restored unto that which is good, or have that which is good restored unto you; or ye can do evil, and have that which is evil restored unto you" (Helaman 14:30-31).

Agency as a freedom

It is interesting to examine agency from a different perspective, which is Agency as a freedom. Agency was one of the principal issues to arise in the pre-mortal Council in Heaven. It was one of the main causes of the conflict between the followers of Christ, and the followers of Satan. Satan said, "Behold, here am I, send me, I will be thy son, and I will redeem all mankind, that one soul shall not be lost, and surely I will do it; wherefore give me thine honor" (*Moses 4:1*). In saying, give me thine honor, thus, causing refutation of his offer, "he rebelled against God and sought to

20

destroy the agency of man" (*Moses 4:3*). One wonders what Satan could have meant by, I will redeem all mankind, and one soul shall not be lost. Scholars usually assume, mortals would live the entire Plan of Salvation without agency, this means Satan was going to force everyone into righteousness, and thus, force everyone back into the presence of God. However, Joseph Smith, in the King Follett discourse, suggests the story was more complicated. In the middle of talking about the sons of perdition, about how they have to become worthy of the celestial glory before they can become doomed to outer darkness through their absolute betrayal, Joseph explains the following: "The contention in heaven was, Jesus said there were certain man would not be saved and the devil said he could save them. He rebelled against God and was thrust down" (*Moses 4:1*). It is quite clear from this passage, Satan was after God's honor, and if his plan been accepted, there would not be any test, nor would there be any agency since all mortals would be in bondage to Satan. In (2 Nephi chapter 2) Nephi says, without agency nothing would have ever existed, for there would not be any point. This sheds a much more serious light on Satan's plan, than just being argument over who gets God's honor. It is unknown what agency was like in the pre-mortal sphere, but when speaking of agency, here in mortality, all choices made are between Satan's bondage, and the free will of Christ's plan. Although, while in mortality, Satan still has the opportunity the lure mortals into his program, by tempting them with alternatives in opposition to the way of life offer by Christ. When following the temptations of Satan, mortals find their options become limited, in terms of salvation. It is necessary to ask, is this disobedience affecting anything other than a single choice? The following example suggests how this works. Imagine seeing a sign on the seashore reading, Danger—whirlpool. No swimming allowed here. Some might think to themselves, ah, another restriction, but is it? There, are still many choices a person can make, but it is clear, some of these choices are in opposition with each other. Everyone has the choice to swim somewhere else, to walk along the beach, pick up seashells, watch the sunset, or just go home. However, if the choice made is to ignore the sign and swim in the dangerous waters, once the whirlpool has a person in its grasp, and is pulling them under, there are very few choices left. If calling for help does not work, and swimming against the strength of the whirlpool is not an option, then one may drown. This example has application in Mormon life. Every member has only two choices; either, they obey the sign, or not, there is not a third choice, this is the way testing was set–up for this mortal probation, God allows Satan to oppose the good. God said of Satan: "I caused that he should be cast down; and he became Satan, yea, even the devil, the father of all lies, to deceive and to blind men, and to lead them captive at his will, even as many as would not hearken unto my voice" (*Moses 4:3-4*). It becomes relatively clear; the necessity of opposition in agency is complex. It is more than simply painting a picture in which there are two categorically opposed possibilities, and the freedom to choose whichever of the two one desires, is their right by ownership of agency. It is more like a mortal scenario in, which it seems, Satan has mortals cornered, and it is immensely difficult to choose anything other than what Satan wants them to do. It is only through the correct use of agency, a kind of freedom comes to their aid; here it seems, members must understand how to make the correct use of their agency, in order to free themselves from Satan's grasp. When choosing to live according to God's plan, people gain a strengthening of agency. Making right choices increases the power to make choices that are more appropriate, and it is this power, which delivers freedom. Agency is the remarkable power and when combined with faith, it becomes the ability—an almost paradoxical ability—to break free of the clutches of the, fall, and all of the repercussions that comes from the activities of Satan.

Free agency

Members of the church often use the term free agency, though, in truth, this is an illusionary term, since all agency deals with the natural sequences of cause-and-effect. Once understood, it is easy to make the point that any act of agency is a question of natural consequences. While on this earth, mortals have the freedom to act, but not have the freedom to choose the consequences for their actions. Even though, they have the freedom to choose their course of action, the consequences of choices often have repercussions beyond control. The consequences, whether good or bad, follow as a natural result of any choices made; therefore, agency is not unilaterally free but is constrained in many ways. Most of the time, people do not actually choose to do something right or wrong, choosing good over evil, liberty over captivity, but by allowing themselves to act in a certain inappropriate way; they are, by default, making a choice. By this inadvertent action, they come to realize, some choices are not made freely, although the cause-and-effect is the same, and these choices carry the same personal responsibility to the law. In short, there are always consequences, and often the person cannot choose what those consequences are, or whom their actions will hurt or help. However, the function of the law, in drawing lines between what should or should not done, is precisely what allows Satan to step in, and to begin his work, and these particular consequences are often the last thing one thinks about, or sometimes even knows about. The point is, people ought not to obey God because they rationally recognize the negative consequences of every action, but one should be obedient because they love God, and have faith in Him. So the upshot of all this is, there is no such thing as free agency and the term should be removed from the Mormon lexicon, since any decision made has consequences and the end results, whatever they might be, are not free. God has clearly said, through His prophets; mortals are free to choose between good and evil. The freedom to choose between good and evil and to act for oneself is referred to the use of agency, never the less, *free to choose*, does not translate into, *free agency*.

Moral agency

There are only two places in the scriptures where this phrase (moral Agency) is used. One is in D&C. 101:78, and a talk given by President Boyd Packer, where he makes an important statement concerning agency, using the D&C scripture as his base. In a talk given by President Packer in 1992, under the heading, No Free Agency, he says--- "the phrase free agency does not appear anywhere in scripture. The only agency spoken of there is moral agency, which, the Lord said, every man may act in doctrine and principle pertaining to futurity, according to the moral agency which I have given unto him, that every man may be accountable for his own sins in the Day of Judgment" (*President Packer quoting from D&C 101:78*). One cannot be entirely sure what to make of this change or shift in the concept of agency, but it is significant because President Packer's talk brings up more questions than answers. The most drastic change is this: the term free agency, surprisingly replacing the term moral agency. While it is certainly true, the term free agency does not appear in scripture, it is equally true, the term moral agency only appears once, and in a highly specific context. The one and only appearance is in D&C 101:78, where it serves to clarify the relationship between Mormons and, of all things, the United States Constitution. The following is the complete scripture. "And again I say unto you, those who have been scattered by their enemies, it is my will that they should continue to importune for redress, and redemption, by the hands of those who are placed as rulers and are in authority over you according to the laws and constitution of the people, which I have suffered to be established, and should be maintained for the rights and protection of all flesh, according to just and holy principles; That every man may act in doctrine and principle pertaining to futurity, according to the moral agency which I have given unto him, that every man may be accountable for his own sins in the day of judgment" (D&C.101:76-78).

23

It is crucial to draw a distinction between moral agency, which is highly specified and categorically secular, and other kinds of agency— particularly, the kind of agency most LDS members are used to dealing with. However, the passages where President Packer deals directly with the concept of free agency certainly seem to attempt to suggest all agency is replaced with moral agency. Hopefully, he is making clear; the non-scriptural notion of free agency should not be used to counter what the Lord has actually said about moral agency. If this is his assertion then his point is well taken, but, after closer examination, it is difficult to understand his point. However, when he says the only agency spoken of in the scriptures is moral agency, some investigation is necessary. There are only six places in the scriptures where the word agency is spoken of; (D&C101:78, D&C 93:31, D&C 64:18, D&C 29:36, Moses 4:3, and Moses 7:32). In five of these six cases, the discussion of agency does not have, nor is there any suggestion of moral overtones. Over all, the scriptures suggest God's children have always have had, still do have agency, and will always have agency. One of the components of agency, during mortality, though secular, is precisely this question of moral agency. Since Brother Packer has made his declaration, church members have to decide if all agency is moral agency, or does just the term free agency mean moral agency, or, did he mean something completely different? Honestly, when a man of such stature in the Mormon religion expresses something like this, even though his discussion may not be, completely, understood by many, the world need to pay a lot of attention to his words.

Law of Aggression

Many modern religious people think wars are unproductive, and unnecessary, but as all have seen, when law and order breaks down, unrest arises. If this unrest leads to war, law and order further breaks down. However, even war, cannot be conducted successfully in a total state of anarchy, or chaos. Therefore, to a greater or lesser extent, all civilizations accept, and employ certain laws, rules, or practices to govern behavior toward an adversary, before war is declared, and then a different set of laws, and rules to govern behavior against an enemy during times of war. In ancient Israel, and in Book of Mormon times, this was also the case.

This article is an attempt to reconcile the apparent paradox between having, and upholding the rules of war while, at the same time, following God's commands. Along this path, the goal is to try to find some method of reconciliation, or some rationale, to understand how all people, since Adam and Eve, have supported war while, at the same time, believing it is wrong to initiate force against another individuals, thus, denying them their agency. Moreover, all the time they are trying to live the doctrine, known simply as the Golden Rule: Do unto others, as you would have them do unto you. In modern times, this same paradox exists with the US Constitution, wherein, as most LDS people believe, God inspired man's agency and yet the Constitution still contains articles of war.

Although no code of conduct governing the act of war has survived from the era of the New Testament, the Old Testament texts have survived, and clearly show there were some laws, and social rules regulating both the domestic, and international aspects of war in ancient Israel, and in fact all around the eastern Mediterranean. The main sources regarding martial law, under the Law of Moses, are in the Old Testament book of Deuteronomy 13:12-16; 20:10-14, 19-20; 21:10-14; 23:1-14; and 24:5. One may also extract from the narrative in the Old Testament, there were certain rules, and principles designed to regulate conduct during times of war, although some of them may seem foreign to people today. One may further conclude, Christians, living during the New Testament times, often were influenced by the Old Testament obligations, previously set forth among, and by the Israelites. Additionally, the Book of Mormon, Doctrine, and Covenants provide support to the concept, declaring war does not violate the Rules of God, providing the rules, as contained in Law of Aggression, (*D&C 98:23-48*), be strictly followed. The rules of war, laid out in the scriptures, may seem to be harsh, and in some cases hard to understand, but modern-day readers have to take into consideration the time, situation, and environment that contributed to the law being given. In all cases, the scriptural text forbids entering into war for the gaining of wealth, domination, power, or retribution. It seems self-defense, is the main reason conflict is justified.

Now is the time to set up a test case, apply the Law of Aggression, and see how all this works. I have chosen the critique of the Nephi/Laban encounter as the litmus test for all other recorded battles, since this is one of the most disputed events in all scriptures. If this one event can pass the test, surly the others can. The complete story of Nephi and Laban is in Book of Mormon, 1st Nephi chapter 1, verses 3&4, and briefly goes as follows:

Lehi's four sons, Laman, Lemuel, Sam, and Nephi were reluctant to obey their father's orders to return to Jerusalem, and go to the house of Laban to obtain a set of, family owned, brass plates on deposit there. They were fearful of Laban's power. and ruthless reputation. However, Nephi vowed, he would obey his father. and accordingly, with some trepidation, the four sons of Lehi set out for Jerusalem. First, Laman, the oldest son, went to Laban alone to request the records, but Laban cast Laman out of his house, and threatened to kill him. Next, Nephi, and his brothers offered all of their valuables to Laban in return for the brass plates. Laban took the boys valuables, then, refused to keep his end of the deal, ordering his men to slay Lehi's sons. The four boys fled Jerusalem fearing for their lives. After fleeing Jerusalem, the elder brothers Laman, and Lemuel were angry with their father Lehi, and their younger brothers Sam, and Nephi, so Laman and Lemuel commenced beating Sam and Nephi with rods. Suddenly, an angel appeared, commanding the elder duo to desist, and ordered all of them to return forthwith to the city, where Laban would fall into their hands. Though Nephi encouraged his brothers by reminding them of God's might, it was only with great reluctance they agreed to press on. Undaunted, Nephi, after leaving his three brothers at the edge of the city, slipped back into Jerusalem alone at night, where he soon found Laban lying unconscious in a drunken stupor. The Spirit of God told Nephi to kill Laban with his own sword, and seize the records, saying "It is better one man should perish than a nation should dwindle and perish in unbelief" (*1Nephi 4:13*). After complying, Nephi disguised himself as Laban, and entered his house. There he found one of Laban's servants, Zoram, whom he commanded to retrieve the brass plates and to follow him out of the city. Zoram obeyed and after gathering up his family, joining Nephi, and the three brothers, they all left Jerusalem with the brass plates, and subsequently reunited with rest of Lehi's family, in their journey to the New World.

The two sides of the disagreement are these: was Nephi justified in killing Laban or not? Some say Laban was incapacitated, and did not offer any threat to Nephi, nor his brothers. Therefore, Nephi could have taken the plates, and left the city unharmed. These folks say, there are many commandments saying not to kill if it can be reasonable avoided, and this is one of those cases. Additionally, they say, the Lord always requires mortals to follow His given laws unless there is some compelling reason for noncompliance. This reason v/s revelation is a very valid point, and addressed in a statement by Joseph Smith, in the last paragraph of this article. Others say, Laban, though passed out drunk, would soon regain his sobriety and would give orders to his men to follow the boys, kill them, and regain the plates. In defense of Nephi, they turn to the words of Joseph Smith concerning the subject of divine intervention. "That which is wrong under one circumstance may be, and often is, right under another. God said, *Thou, shalt not kill*; at another time He said, *thou shalt utterly destroy*. This is the principle on which the government of heaven is conducted—by revelation adapted to the circumstances in which the children of the kingdom are placed. Whatever God requires is right, no matter what it is, although we may not see the reason thereof till long after the events transpire" (*Teachings of the Prophet Joseph Smith, p. 256*).

26

To resolve this dilemma, turn to the Law of Aggression, as found in the 98th section of the Doctrine and Covenants, and see if Nephi's actions justifiably corresponded to the law as given. It is important to note, that verse 32 of section 98, is the same directive given to all of the ancient apostles and prophets. It follows, the self-same brass plates being contended over, contained this very law, and presumably Nephi, and his brothers were familiar with this law, since these were their plates and portions of this law is recorded and referenced to many times later in the Book of Mormon.

"Now, I speak unto you concerning your families—if men will smite you, or your families, once, and ye bear it patiently and revile not against them, neither seek revenge, ye shall be rewarded; But if ye bear it not patiently, it shall be accounted unto you as being meted out as a just measure unto you. Again, if your enemy shall smite you the second time, and you revile not against your enemy, and bear it patiently, your reward shall be a hundredfold. Again, if he shall smite you the third time and ye bear it patiently, your reward shall be doubled unto you four-fold; and these three testimonies shall stand against your enemy if he repents not, and shall not be blotted out. And now, verily I say unto you, if that enemy shall escape my vengeance, that he be not brought into judgment before me, then ye shall see to it that ye warn him in my name, that he come no more upon you, neither upon your family, even your children's children unto the third and fourth generation. And then, if he shall come upon you or your children, or your children's children unto the third and fourth generation, I have delivered thine enemy into thine hands. And then if thou wilt spare him; thou shalt be rewarded for thy righteousness; and also thy children and thy children's children unto the third and fourth generation. Nevertheless, thine enemy is in thine hands; and if thou rewardest him according to his works, thou art justified; if he has sought thy life, and thy life is endangered by him, thine enemy is in thine hands and thou art justified. Behold, this is the law I gave unto my servant Nephi, and thy fathers, Joseph, and Jacob, and Isaac, and Abraham, and all mine ancient prophets and apostles. And again, this is the law that I gave unto mine ancients, that they should not go out unto battle against any nation, kindred, tongue, or people, save I, the Lord, commanded them. And if any nation, tongue, or people should proclaim war against them, they should first lift a standard of peace unto that people, nation, or tongue; And if that people did not accept the offering of peace, neither the second nor the third time, they should bring these testimonies before the Lord; Then I, the Lord, would give unto them a commandment, and justify them in going out to battle against that nation, tongue, or people" (D&C 98:23-36).

When analyzing the statement above, with the understanding that all laws, and commandments are designed, not only to direct acceptable behavior, but also to teach virtue. The instruction, contained in the law of aggression, given to Nephi, if your enemy smites you a second and a third time, be patient, Jesus conveyed this same instruction to Christians, in the New Testament. Turn to verses D&C 98:23-27, which point out the importance of the commandment, turn the other cheek, which Christians properly recognize as the justice of God. These scriptures also demonstrate the importance of not exacting retribution on someone, who has wrongly aggressed against you—even three times! This is to learn patience, and not have revenge in one's heart. The Lord even says, there will be a reward given if there is aggression the fourth time, and the injured party does not seek revenge. In D&C 98:27-31, a fuller explanation of the law as given. It is required to warn the aggressor, in God's name, to cease his hostility for four generations to come. If this warning does not put off the provoker, the Lord will delivered the aggressor into the hands of the injured party, and he is justified in dealing with the situation as required, to reward the provoker for his good works, or go into battle, or defense. In D&C 98:32–33 The Lord tells us, as He has told the ancients, the law forbids, going into battle without receiving a commandment, to do so. In D&C 98:34-36 the Lord is even clearer regarding aggression on a grand scale, speaking of wars between nations, He says, if any aggressor nation wants to proclaim war, it is necessary to first, make a peace offering to the opposing nation at least three times, to reconcile the problems. If these peace offerings fail, then the aggressor nation must to go to the Lord in prayer, and inquire of His will. If the Lord desires He will issue a commandment, which will justify the proclamation of war or not. However, it is also justified to reward the enemy, according to his works, although, the law does not make this action the preferential method of resolution, it would be to the credit of all if these kinds of situations were defused through negotiations rather than by confrontation. These verses point out, the Lord approves of wars of self-defense, but not wars of aggressions instigated to dominate.

Now, it is proper to say, Nephi was justified in his killing of Laban. This means Laban did not only endanger Nephi's life, and his families, since Laban had threatened them at least three times previously. Although Nephi, while being prompted by righteous indignation, had a full awareness the law, was still reluctant to kill Laban. Yet, he was not initiating an act of aggression, indeed he tried to defuse the situation and make peace by buying the plates. This is very clear, as indicated in the story, Laban had initiated the act of aggression—not Nephi. Verse 31 provides the proper context, and shows Nephi was following an anciently known law, and his actions were in accordance to the law. Also, conclusively shown; Nephi was justified in killing Laban, and was not initiating any act of aggression. In its ancient legal context, the slaying of Laban makes sense, both legally and religiously, as an unpremeditated, undesired, divinely prompted, and justifiable killing, something very different from what people today normally think of as justifiable homicide.

An alternate view of this law would be to frame this last section, regarding Nephi's exploit, in a reason vis-à-vis revelation analysis. The reason part would include the non-aggression principle, it is wrong to initiate force against another individual thus, denying them their agency, while the revelation part includes the command from God to Nephi, and the quote from Joseph Smith about revelation. Now, can, or does revelation ever violate the reason? This is the place, where a good knowledge of doctrine, the ability to interpret scriptures precisely, and a sound background in religious teachings will work, in the effort to gain understanding.

The careless reader, without a proper exegesis of the Prophet's statement T PJS, p.25 may assume, God's decrees are arbitrary, or future commandments could violate previous ones. The reader, whether devout or not, would then be on shaky ground, never sure of what commands to hold onto, not knowing, which ones may change. This position, without careful analysis, appears to state, all is relative except the constancy of following whatever God decrees. In short, this is a rationalist's nightmare. Yet, fortunately, Joseph Smith was only highlighting the intricacies involved in understanding and interpreting God's revealed word, and of being receptive to revelation through the Holy Ghost. This, however, does not lead to the false dichotomy between reason and revelation—where reason takes a back seat to revelation. Joseph Smith explicitly states it is necessary to follow revelation, the true reason, though not understood at the time, will always reveal itself later. The solution of the conflict between Nephi and Laban, while warranted by revelation, was also, based on reason, as demonstrated through laws existing in Nephi's day. Importantly, such laws did not contradict the non-aggression principle, it is wrong to, arbitrarily, initiate force against another individual. The non-aggression principle merely states, an individual cannot initiate aggression but an individual can respond in self-defense. Self-defense can include a host of measures such as, all-out battle, preemptive strikes, spying, and acts of sabotage, etc. Indeed, the War in Heaven was itself, fought to secure man's eternal agency. The ability to freely choose, and not forced to choose by others, has to be balanced between reason and revelation. People, picking and choosing, which commandments they will, or will not obey, for purposes of satisfying their own selfish reasons, causes this unbalancing. Nephi's encounter with Laban is further proof of the importance of the non-aggression principle, and Nephi's action was in no way contradictory, when properly contextualized, both historically, and through additional scriptures. The non-aggression principle is the counterpart to agency, and thus cannot be contradicted, broken, or abused by a Just God. In answer to the question, does God's commands ever violate the law, is, no!

The Law of Being
(Righteous Thought)

The Law of Being simply says, during any level of existence, the innermost thoughts of a person define who they are, what they are, or will become. The Law of Being arises as an inherent condition of thought itself. Thought is associative with all things created by anyone at any time. Therefore, this Law combined with the Law of cause and effect establishes a person as a being. For the purpose of this section, the focus will be on people and how they magnify their station through thought. The more a person focuses on something, the more that thing is magnified in their being. If people desire to a have more righteousness in their life, change their thoughts and they will become a righteous being to the extent of their clarity of thought. An old adage states, *I think therefore I am. I am therefore I have.* For anyone to have something, they must be in a compatible mental and emotional state before they can have it.

All mortals are born with two identities, one is spiritual (often referred to as the soul) and the other is mortal (often referred to as temporal beings), both housed in earthly bodies. In this dual identity one is righteousness and mortal is one of a carnal, sensual and devilish nature (Mosiah 3; 3), referred in the scriptures as the *natural man*. These two identities are often in conflict with each other. Starting at birth the soul comes to its own and through every step of its earthly pilgrimage alongside it's human counterpart and they attract those combinations of conditions and circumstances which are the reflections of their own purity or impurity, their strength or weakness and their righteousness or unrighteousness which, thereby, gauges their progression through eternity.

As maturity grows, it is normal to desire to be better people and try to be more in harmony with their spiritual side. In order to satisfy these desires, it becomes necessary for people to alter their lives, and become righteous. A good number of people wonder why they never seem to attain all they desire; no matter how much they try. Of course, they are good people, trying to do their best, why do they continue to experience these problems. The problem is thinking, or in other words, the quality of their thoughts, either righteous or unrighteous. It is important to understand thoughts, and character are same, and one's true character can only manifest and discover itself through its exposure to environment and circumstance. The environment where character dwells is in thoughts and those thoughts control actions, which contribute to, and control, the circumstances of life. The harmonious conditions of a person's life transpire, not to the individual's outward appearances, but to his innermost thoughts. The person's present circumstances are so intimately connected, with those vital thoughts within himself, as long as those thoughts remain dominate, they are indispensable to his development. In order to improve the conditions of life, one's thoughts must change, since thoughts govern the entire being. Wise men have said, *men do not attract something they want, but something they are*. Man's outward ambitions develop at every step only because his inmost thoughts and desires are either righteous or unrighteous. His ambitions are furthered if his righteous thoughts are in harmony with his ambitions, thwarted if not. Man finds his ability to progress impeded only by himself, his lack of self-control over his thoughts. Thoughts and actions are the gatekeepers of circumstances. They can be the angels of freedom or the chains of imprisonment. "Not what he prays for does a man get, but what he justly earns" (D&C 130; 20). His wishes and prayers are only gratified and answered when they harmonize with his thoughts and actions.

Some think, circumstances control the condition of their lives, not so! Take for example, three children from the same family, born into an underprivileged situation. One becomes ever more deprived, and falls into poverty, while the state of affairs of the second remains the same and the third gains wealth and prosperity. If circumstances were the only controlling factor, the situation and conditions of each of these children would remain parallel. It has been demonstrated in case after case, similar circumstances rarely produce similar results, so it is obvious, something is controlling conditions in people's lives other than circumstances. Every man is where he is by the law of his being. The thoughts by which he has built his character have brought him there, and in the arrangement of his life, there is no element of chance, but all is the result of a law, which cannot err. This is just as true of those who feel out of harmony with their surroundings as of those who are contented with them. Circumstance does not make the man; it reveals him to himself. Conditions, such as descending into vice and suffering are the results of vicious inclinations, while, ascending into virtue and pure happiness is the cultivation of virtuous aspirations. In addition, man, therefore, as the lord and master of thought, is the maker of himself, the shaper, and author of his environment.

Law, not confusion, is the dominating principle in the universe. Justice, not injustice, is the essence and substance of life. Moreover, righteousness, not corruption, is the molding and moving force in the spiritual government of the world. This being so, man has but to right himself to find, the universe is right; and during the process of putting himself right, he will find, as he alters his thoughts toward things and other people, things and other people will alter their behavior toward him. The proof of this truth is in every person, and it reveals itself by systematic introspection and self-analysis. Let a man radically alter his thoughts, and he will be astonished at the rapid transformation it will effect in the material and spiritual conditions of his life. Men imagine their unrighteous thoughts can be kept secret, but they cannot. Unrighteous thoughts immediately become words, which rapidly crystallize into action, and action solidifies into habits of sensuality, thus, defining your character, which solidify into circumstances of misery, which becomes a pattern of behavior, which, further solidifies into adverse circumstances in one's life. Is this who you are? On the other hand, beautiful thoughts crystallize into habits of grace and kindliness, which solidify into genial and sunny circumstances. Pure thoughts crystallize into habits of temperance and self-control, which solidify into circumstances of repose and peace. Thoughts of courage, self-reliance, and decision crystallize into manly habits, which solidify into circumstances of success, plenty, and freedom.

"Change your thoughts, for they become words; your words become your actions; your actions become your habits; your habits become your character; your character effects your behavior; your behavior, defines who you are; and who you are, surely controls your destiny" (*Frank Outlaw 1977*).

Man is a thought being, his life and character, is formed by the thoughts in which he habitually dwells. By practice, association, and habit, thoughts tend to repeat themselves with greater and greater ease and frequency, and so the character becomes *fixed*, in a given direction by producing an automatic action called, habit. It is by dwelling on pure thoughts; a man forms habits of pure enlightened actions and well performed conduct. By the ceaseless repetition of pure thought, he at last becomes one with his thoughts, and is a purified being, manifesting his attainment in pure actions, in a serene and wise life.

The majority of men live in a series of conflicting desires, passions, emotions, and speculations, thereby felling restlessness, uncertainty, and sorrow. When a man begins to train his mind, he gradually gains control over his inward conflict and outward circumstances by bringing his thoughts to focus upon a central principle. In this way old habits of impure and erroneous thought and actions, are broken up and there is an increase in harmony and insight where-by new habits of pure and enlightened thought and action can be formed, allowing growing perfection and peace to become the dominate part of the character of man.

There are ten thought disorders a person must be deal with to control thought.

1. Extreme thinking,
2. Over generalization,
3. Personalization,
4. Magnification/minimization,
5. Jumping to conclusions,
6. Selective focus,
7. Concrete thinking,
8. Actor V/S observer bias.
9. Closed thinking,
10. Emotional Reasoning.

This task of controlling thoughts is not easy and it takes some a lifetime to complete. The example of a child learning to write illustrates the level of difficulty. In the beginning, it is common for a child to hold the writing instrument incorrectly. This is the first and easiest of many obstacles mastered, but it is through training and considerable trial and error, mastery is accomplished. The next obstacle to appear is the alphabet, and then spelling, sentence structure and grammar. Once these are somewhat in hand, the next challenge is to compose with fluidity of thought and clarity. As the child ceaselessly and repeatedly continues his pursuit, he finds he can function with greater and greater ease and precision. Controlling ones' thoughts, overcoming old habits and the transformation of one's character is this same process of education, trail, and error, accompanied by a copiousness amount of patients.

As man embarks on a lifelong pilgrimage of self-discipline and purification, he travels more toward his inward identity. Thus, becoming swayed less by the passion, grief, pleasure, and pain inherent with his outward identity. By achieving success in the management of his own mind, he increasingly lives a more joyful, steadfast, and virtuous life, moving closer and closer to Godliness, thereby magnifying his being as a child of God.

LAW OF COMMON CONSENT

To begin this discussion about the Law of Common Consent, start with this question: Can any person hold any administrative office in the church, set any new policy, introduce any new scripture, or even hold the priesthood without the consent of the people?

"No man can preside in this Church in any capacity without the consent of the people. The Lord has placed upon the membership, the responsibility of sustaining by vote those, called to various positions of responsibility. No man, should the people decide to the contrary, could preside over any body of Latter-day Saints in this Church, and yet it is not the right of the people to nominate, to choose, for that is the right of the priesthood" *(Smith, Doctrines of Salvation, 3:123).* Here are some scriptures supporting the claims made above.

"And the LORD said unto Samuel, Hearken, unto the voice of the people in all that they say unto thee: for they have not rejected thee, but they have rejected me, that I should not reign over them" *(1 Samuel 8:7).*
Mosiah said, "Now it is not common that the voice of the people desireth anything contrary to that which is right; but it is common for the lesser part of the people to desire that which is not right; therefore, this shall ye observe and make it your law—to do your business by the voice of the people" (Mosiah 29: 26).

There is additional information contained in Mormon Doctrine: Elder Bruce R. McConkie explained, "Administrative affairs of the Church are handled in accordance with the law of common consent. This law is that in God's earthly kingdom, the King Counsels what should be done, but then he allows his subjects to accept or reject his proposals. Unless the principle of free agency is operated in righteousness men, do not progress to ultimate salvation in the heavenly kingdom hereafter. Accordingly, church officers are selected by the spirit of revelation in those appointed to choose them, but before the officers may serve in their positions, they must receive a formal sustaining vote of the people over whom they are to preside" *(D &C 20:65–67; 26:2; 28; 13 38:34; 41:9–11; 42:11; 102:9–10; 124:143–144, Mormon Doctrine, pp. 149–50).* "No person is to be ordained to any office in this church, where there is a regularly organized branch of the same, without the vote of that church" *(D&C. 20:65-67).* "And all things shall be done by common consent in the church, by much prayer and faith, for all things you shall receive by faith. Amen." *(D&C. 26:2).* "The Lord said, "For all things must be done in order, and by common consent in the church, by the prayer of faith." *(D&C. 28:13).* "And now, I give unto the church in these parts a commandment, that certain men among them shall be appointed, and they shall be appointed by the voice of the church" *(D&C. 38:34)*. "And again, I have called my servant Edward Partridge; and I give a commandment, that he should be appointed by the voice of the church, and ordained a bishop unto the church, to leave his merchandise and to spend all his time in the labors of the church" *(D&C. 451:9)*. "And again, I say unto you, that my servant Edward Partridge shall stand in the office whereunto I have appointed him. And it shall come to pass, that if he transgresses another shall be appointed in his stead. Even so. Amen. -- Again I say unto you, that it shall not be given to anyone to go forth to preach my gospel, or to build up my church, except he be ordained by someone who has authority, and it is known to the church that he has authority and has been regularly ordained by the heads of the church *(D&C.42:10-11)*. "The president of the church, who is also the president of the council, is appointed by revelation and acknowledged in his administration by the voice of the church" *(D&C. 102:9-10)*. "The above offices I have given unto you, and the keys thereof, for helps and for governments, for the work of the ministry and the perfecting of my saints. -- And a commandment I give unto you, that you should fill all these offices and approve of those names which I have mentioned, or else disapprove of them at my general conference" *(D&C. 124:143-144)*.

It is clear; the membership the church has the final vote when it comes to accepting those called to an administration position in the church. It is necessary for all Church officers, to receive a sustained vote by common consent; this same principle also operates for policies, major decisions, acceptance of new scripture, and other things in the religious lives of the Saints. The Lord said, "And all things shall be done by common consent in the church, by much prayer and faith, for all things you shall receive by faith. Amen" (D&C 26:2). The overriding reason for the Law of Common Consent has to do with agency. It is not possible for members to be fully responsibility for their actions if any situation or person holds an authoritative station over them without their consent. If this were not so, everyone would be able to excuse their bad behavior by claiming somebody made them do it. The sustaining vote, which is an act of agency, is the stipulation, placing members in a responsible position, just as it is when Satan is involved in their lives.

In Latter-day Saint sacrament meetings, there is time is allotted for ward business. Part of the procedure with items of business is an invitation to the congregation to sustain fellow Church members in their callings by raising their right hand. If members are opposed to the proposed action, they can also make it known in the same manner. This practice, formally known as the law of common consent, is not only a noticeable part of meetings but also an essential principle in proper gospel government and personal progression. Unfortunately, the practicing of the law of common consent, during a meeting, is occasionally, viewed by many members, as nothing more than a postscript to a business agenda. Perhaps because of the frequency of the event, the application of the law of common consent may become an automated raising of a hand in mechanical approval. Some say, the law of common consent is too common and therefore they feel it is a commonplace occurrence in the Church and it signifies more of a tradition than actual function. Many members simply do not realize the significance of their sustaining vote and all it entails. Although common consent is familiar to Church members, it is anything but common. President J. Reuben Clark Jr. taught, "It is clear, the sustaining vote by the people is not, and cannot to be regarded as, a mere matter of form, but on the contrary a matter of the last gravity."

Perhaps this important gospel principle has become a matter of form to some not because of familiarity with it but because of a lack of familiarity. For example, some members may understand the proper procedure but have never learned, or have forgotten, the purposes of the principle. Others may be acquainted with the purposes and practices of common consent but have failed to see the doctrinal significance as emphasized in the Doctrine and Covenants and throughout Church history. As the Saints learn about the law of common consent, it becomes anything but common. Obviously, it requires more than raising a hand on Sundays to become familiar with the law of common consent. To develop a deeper familiarity with this practice, it is helpful to obtain a basic understanding of Christ's government in His kingdom. Next, a historical overview of common consent reveals its historical precedence and underscores its importance and necessity. With this background, it is easier to understand the proper practice or procedure of this principle. When understood correctly, common consent becomes a meaningful rite of worship for the Saints, which ultimately brings them closer to the Savior.

To understand common consent, it is important first to understand the workings of the government of God. It can be described the government of the kingdom of God as a theocracy but also "something like a democracy." This description is a simple clarification of a seemingly complex and often misunderstood organization. There are two significant pillars in the Lord's government: theocracy and democracy. The first pillar, theocracy, accents Christ's undeniable position as head of the kingdom–the sole proprietor. The second pillar, democracy, emphasizes the people's opportunity to participate in their government. This combination of terms, however, immediately raises questions from traditional political sciences.

Is a theocracy the same as a democracy? On the surface, these terms not only seem incompatible but also provoke a jealous power struggle. A democracy does not seem to fit with a theocracy because of the world's understanding and definition of democracy. However, thankfully, when the population understands this term properly, the powerful second pillar not only fits but seen for the essential principle in gospel government and doctrine it is. The pillar of democracy described in the Lord's kingdom was something like a democracy. In a traditional democracy, the people, vested with power, hold important participatory rights. The role of the people under a conventional theocracy, on the other hand, is being part of the kingdom rather than of its governmental process and procedure. The Lord's kingdom, unlike a conventional theocracy, allows the members to participate in its government. A unique combination in which all power, vested in the Lord (theocracy) with the participation of the people (democracy) is thus, called a Theo democracy. In this form of government, the decisions for the kingdom of the Lord are His decisions but His people have the opportunity to exercise their presence in His kingdom. Members of the Lord's kingdom exercise their democratic presence through the principle of common consent.

Now, how much power does this law give the people of the church? It is surprising, how difficult it is to decide what is correct and what is incorrect, when conflict over a sustaining vote arises. Here are some scenarios:

Scenario #1: The bishop calls Brother Smith to be the new teacher's quorum adviser. A vote is called for and 51% of the people raise their hand in opposition. Does Brother Smith become the new teacher's quorum adviser?

Scenario #2: The bishop calls Sister Jones to be the new relief society president. 30% of the people raise their hands in approbation. 10% of the people raise their hands in opposition. 60% of the people do not raise their hands, at all. Does Sister Jones become the new relief society president?

Scenario #3: The president of the church claims to have received a new revelation from the Lord, which he reads in general conference. The contents are controversial. The President calls for a sustaining vote to approve of the revelation and add it to the scriptural canon. 60% of the people raise their hand in opposition. Will the revelation added to the scriptural canon, or not?

Scenario #4: The members of the Green Leaf 3rd Ward are tired of their tyrannical bishop. They feel he is exercising unrighteous dominion as he attempts to micromanage everything. They want to remove him and decide, amongst themselves, to take a vote in sacrament meeting to that end. One member volunteers to propose the vote. During the next sacrament meeting, at some point in the voting portion, Brother Carlson suddenly stands up and asks, a vote be taken to determine whether bishop Young should be removed from his position over them. At the protest of the bishopric, brother Tenney stands up and seconds the motion of Brother Carlson. The results of the sustaining vote are; 70% of the people vote to remove the bishop (dissolve the bishopric.) Will the bishopric automatically be dissolved or not? Is anything going to happen to brother Carlson and Tenney for their actions?

Scenario #5: during the same sacrament meeting, just after the ward has voted on the removal of the bishopric, Brother Humphrey stands up, presents the name of Brother Johnson as the new bishop, and calls for a vote. Brother Johnson is a likable fellow, and, nearly unanimously, is voted in as the new, un-ordained, bishop. The people of the ward are adamant, they only want Brother Johnson as their Bishop, and when the Stake President arrives, to set matters straight, chaos is the results. Every non-brother Johnson bishop, presented, is voted down. Must the Stake President accede to the wishes of the people, like Samuel, and ordain Brother Johnson or not?

Here in scenario #5 is time when it is necessary to understand the Law of Common Consent. In the first place, some of the ward members are making a defacto calling by their insisting Brother Johnson be the Bishop. This is a violation of the Law of Common Consent, since Brother Johnson may not be suitable to the Lord as a bishop, for reasons unknown to the membership. The process is the leadership, who holds the proper priesthood keys, under the influence of the Holy Ghost, and commanded, by the Lord, must present names, for the purpose, of filling these positions by inspiration. "The above offices I have given unto you, and the keys thereof, for helps and for governments, for the work of the ministry and the perfecting of my saints.-- And a commandment I give unto you, that you should fill all these offices and approve of those names which I have mentioned, or else disapprove of them at my general conference" (D&C. 124:143-144). The ward members do not hold the keys and in this circumstance are using their sustaining power incorrectly and irreverently to manipulate the situation. Now add to the confusion the principle of calling and election made sure. The following procedure of the Law of Common Consent makes any appointment, both called (by the priesthood leadership) and elected (by the people's sustaining vote) sure. The requirement is there must be both a calling and an election; otherwise, there is no surety. The Lord does the calling (through his appointed servants) and the people do the electing (voting). During the Council in Heaven, when God called Jesus to be the Savior, this calling was followed by a vote, in which the majority sustained him. Had the majority said, No, to Jesus, he would not have been the Savior. The first word is God's, but the final word is God's subjects. Ultimately, it appears the individual members of the kingdom, as a voice, meaning a majority voice, have been granted the right to decide what happens. Members have both the sustaining and veto powers. Do they have more than that? Do they have the calling power? This question posed in scenario #5. If the voice of the people call Brother Johnson to be their bishop, do they or do they not have the right or power to do so. If they do have such a power or right, then the Stake President should do as Samuel and hearken unto them. If he does not hearken unto them, when they are legitimately exercising one of their rights, then he is a usurper. If they do not have this power, then they are usurpers.

Of course, in a Zion world, persons are of one heart and one mind, and so, presumably, the situation discussed would not occur. However, this is clearly a telestial rather than a celestial sphere so anything can happen. Now, it is frequently taught or assumed, members are to sustain Church leaders unquestioningly, the idea of giving this decision prayerful consideration rather than just an automatic, robotic response quite intriguing, and in keeping with the Law of Consent. This brings to the forefront member's responsibilities when sustaining others, whether it is a robotic act or a prayerful response, the level of accountability, since it is an act of agency, is the same.

Elder Loren C. Dunn explained the responsibilities that accompany the sustaining process: "When we sustain officers, we are given the opportunity of sustaining those whom the Lord has already called by revelation. ...The Lord, then, gives the members opportunity to sustain the action of a divine calling and in effect express themselves if for any reason they may feel otherwise. To sustain is to make the action binding on the membership to support those people whom they have sustained. When a person goes through the sacred act of raising his arm to the square, he should remember, with soberness, which he has done and commence to act in harmony with his sustaining vote both in public and in private." (*Ensign, July 1972, p. 43*)

"When you vote affirmatively you make a solemn covenant with the Lord that you will sustain, that is, give your full loyalty and support, without equivocation or reservation, to the officer for whom you vote" (*Harold B. Lee*).

When Should a Person Cast a Negative Vote? "I have no right to raise my hand in opposition to a man who is appointed to any position in this Church, simply because I may not like him, or because of some personal disagreement or feeling I may have, but only on the grounds that he is guilty of wrong doing, of transgression of the laws of the Church which would disqualify him for the position which he is called to hold" (*Smith, Doctrines of Salvation, 3:124*).

The Law of Consecration

The purpose of this section is not to explain the United Order or the law of tithing but to address some of the myths plaguing Latter-day thinking concerning the interplay between the Law of Consecration, Tithing, and The United Order. Here are some of the myths,

1. Members are not living the Law of Consecration now because the law was rescinded, but are living a lessor law, The Law of Tithing.
2. The United Order must be restored in the latter days.
3. The Law of Consecration (meaning the United Order) must be restored in fullness before the second coming of Christ".

Counter point to #1--- It is true the Church is not practicing the united order today, but this has no bearing on whether or not members can live the law of consecration, because the law of consecration is a law for an inheritance in the celestial kingdom. God, the Eternal Father, His Son Jesus Christ, and all holy beings abide by this law. It is an eternal law and has nothing to do with any temporal order. The Law of Consecration does not need restoring since it never was rescinded and the requirement of the Mormon Church, in terms of financial remittance, at this time, requires the members to pay a full tithing. Tithing is not, in any way, a lessor law. If you recall it was given to Adam, "A tithe of everything from the land, whether grain from the soil or fruit from the trees, belongs to the Lord; it is holy to the Lord, (Leviticus 27:30) and given to Abraham, "And praise be to God Most-High, who delivered your enemies into your hand. Then Abram gave him a tenth of everything." (*Gen. 14:20*) and then restored by Joseph Smith in 1838, "And this shall be the beginning of the tithing of my people. And after that, those who have thus been tithed shall pay one-tenth of all their interest annually; and this shall be a standing law unto them forever, for my holy priesthood, saith the Lord. Verily I say unto you, it shall come to pass that all those who gather unto the land of Zion shall be tithed of their surplus properties, and shall observe this law, or they shall not be found worthy to abide among you" (*D&C, 119:3-5*). Therefore, in spite of the united order not being practiced or restored, the second coming is right on schedule, and those worthy saints who will receive an inheritance in the Celestial Kingdom are on the right track.

Counter point to #2--- None of the revelations in the Doctrine and Covenants rescinds, suspends, or revokes the law of consecration. The law was revealed to Joseph Smith in February 1831, and the law itself simply has been, and will be in effect forever. Consecration is the law of the celestial kingdom, and section 78 teaches, no one will receive an inheritance there, who has not obeyed the law. The *United order* refers to the cooperative enterprises established in LDS communities of the Great Basin, Mexico, and Canada during the last quarter of the nineteenth century. Designed to promote unity and to reduce dependence on non-Mormon merchants and traders, When President Young died in 1877, most of the united orders had already failed, a few functioned successfully for a decade, and a very few continued in some form into the 1890s. The united order was never intended to replace, or even to be the complete fulfillment of the Law of Consecration. There is not a single scripture saying the united order, as a temporal enterprise, has to be restored for any reason.

Counter point to #3--- One of the common misconceptions concerning the law of consecration is, people often conflate this law with the united order. Thinking these two are the same thing causes difficulties understanding each of them. The united order is not the law of consecration, although the principle governing the united order falls under the doctrine of the Law of Consecration... Some view the united order as merely an economic alternative to capitalism or the free enterprise system, others as an outgrowth of early communal experiments in America. Whatever your view of the united order may be, it is important to know the difference between the united order and the law of consecration. The law of consecration is the celestial law of obedience, not an economic experiment. With regards to the implementation of the Law of Consecration, Orson Pratt taught, "There is nothing laid down in revelation requiring us to take a particular method over another" (*Journal of Discourses 1881*).
The law of consecration does not rely on the united order to function. Other modes and means can be used to live the main tenets of this law. The principles of the law of consecration may be lived by each of anyone today, and involves much more than material possessions.

In addition to these three items discussed above, there are some members of the Mormon Church, who feel, there are two kinds of consecrations. The consecrating of oil, used for the healing of the sick, is one kind of consecration, and material consecrations, offered to and in the church from time to time, is a different kind of Consecration, with governance in the lives of mortals. This thinking is flawed, to consecrate anything, an object, or even yourself, is to set something apart and dedicate it for a holy purpose. These ideas are the same. There is not any difference between consecrating a bottle of oil for the purposes of God and consecrating your life to the service of God, even though latter is substantially more difficult than the former.

The issue of consecrating their temporal lives and their tangible possessions for spiritual purposes seems to be an issue for some people. Always remember, while living in a mortal existence, the grasp of spiritual things is tainted by this mortal reality. A veil was drawn over memory and though knowledge of spiritual things may be known, any clear comprehension of the spiritual circumstances of this and other worlds has been withheld. However, as mortals, there has to be a way to glorify God. Now, surely, God does not need worldly possessions, so how does this work? The old adage *you reap what you sow* or *you get what you give* is leading people in the right direction when it comes to the Law of Consecration. The lord has told His children, God has reserved a place in His kingdom and is willing to dedicate to them, all He has if they will obey the Law of Consecration. Remember---when God says all He means all. It follows then, when there is a receiving of all there must a giving of all, even though all anyone has, at this time, is the things associated with mortal existence, including self. This act of giving, and the willingness to give is far more important than the items given, even though they are given within the framework of love. This demonstration, through covenant, of love toward God and each person's level of faith and obedience is one of the ways mortals can glorify God. The only other way is through dedicated service towards mankind. So when it is all boiled down to its lowest common denominator;

1. What is substance of consecration? ---Service and obedience.
2. What is the essence of consecration? --- Love.
3. What is the mechanics of consecration? --- Covenants.

Members covenant to live the Law of Consecration. Until one abides by the laws of obedience, sacrifice, and the requirements of the gospel, he cannot abide the law of consecration, which is the law pertaining to the celestial kingdom. "For if you will that I give you place in the celestial world, you must prepare yourselves by doing the things which I have commanded you and required of you" (D&C 78:7). The saints need to stop thinking of consecration only as yielding up personal or material possessions, because the law of consecration is not primarily material in scope. Quite the contrary, it includes all things. However, the ultimate consecration is the yielding up the spiritual side of oneself to God heart, soul, and mind. These were the encompassing words of Christ in describing the first commandment, which is constantly, not periodically, operative (Matt. 22:37). If kept, then performances will in turn, be fully consecrated for the lasting welfare of the soul. (*2nd Ne. 32:9*).

42

Law of Election and Grace

There seems there is some consternation among the members of the church when the subject of, Election and Grace, comes up. Members have difficulty with the idea that some people are born with a greater opportunity than others are, they want the playing field to be even from the start, and it does not seem fair, especially, when someone that they know is born into challenging circumstances that are so tough, they simply cannot ever overcome them. It seems to them, God is choosing winners and losers and to these members, this is very troublesome. So what can be said, to those members, to appease their misgivings and restore buoyancy in their lives? It is questionable, that   in a discourse such as this; their buoyancy can be fully restored. It is a lifetime endeavor to finally, start to understand the laws of God, and only then can the Holy Ghost offer assurances and comfort. What does the scriptures, and the prophets, have to say about this subject?

A Letter from the Prophet Paul to the Church in Rome, written about 57 A.D. somewhere in or around Corinth, while Paul was on his third mission journey, is in the scriptures as the Book of Romans and in (Romans 9: 1-33) he explains the Law of Election and Grace. (Warning to the reader); The Prophet Paul's writing style, the contextual differences and the vernacular of his day is so different, it is hard to comprehend all he writes.

"For the children being not yet born, neither having done any good or evil that the purpose of God according to election might stand, not of works, but of him that calleth" (*Romans 9:11*). Paul here tells how the election of grace fits in to the gospel scheme, saying that, for us and even for children yet unborn, no matter if you have done any good or evil, and no matter what good works you might have done, the purpose of God and His election will apply to those who have been called to their probation in mortality.   His Roman readers knew what he was talking about because they already understood the doctrine of election. Since the sectarian world of today has little or no comprehension of pre-existence and eternal progression, or the doctrines on which elections are based, it is no wonder these and other teachings of Paul are so completely misconstrued.

"This doctrine of the election of grace is as follows: 'As part of the new song the saints will sing when they see-eye-to-eye and the millennial era has been ushered in will be these words, "The Lord hath redeemed his people, Israel, according to the election of grace, which was brought to pass by the faith and covenant of their fathers" (*D&C. 84:98–102; Rom.11:1–5*). This election of grace is a very fundamental, logical, and important part of God's dealings with men through the ages. The doctrine of the election of grace is the process of bringing the most valiant of spirit children into

43

mortality, foreordained to bring to pass the salvation of the greatest possible number of his spirit children the Lord, in general, sends the most righteous and worthy saints to earth through the lineage of Abraham and Jacob. This course is a manifestation of his grace or in other words his love, mercy, and condescension toward his children. "God chose Jacob over Esau while the two were yet in Rebecca's womb and before either, as far as the works of this life are concerned, had earned any preferential status. Why? It is a pure matter of pre-existence. Jacob came into the world with greater spiritual capacity than Esau; he was foreordained to a special work; he was elected to serve in a chosen capacity" (*McConkie*).

"This election to a chosen lineage is based on pre-existent worthiness and is made according to the foreknowledge of God" (*1 Pet. 1:2*). Those so grouped together during their mortal probation have more abundant opportunities to make and keep the covenants of salvation, a right which they earned by pre-existent devotion to the cause of righteousness. As part of this election, Abraham and others of the noble and great spirits were chosen before they were born for; the particular missions assigned them in this life, Abr. 3:22–24, Rom. 9, McConkie, DNTC 2:273–74. Paul's teachings also show, although someone may be born into a favored lineage or a family of great faith, he or she cannot receive the blessings of gospel covenants without being obedient to God's commandments. Similarly, a Latter-day Saint, of today, obtains salvation only through individual faith and obedience. Elder Russell M. Nelson of the Quorum of the Twelve Apostles taught: "The development of faith in the Lord is an individual matter. … Each of us is born individually; likewise, each of us is 'born again' (*John 3:3, 7*), individually. Salvation is an individual matter" (*Salvation and Exaltation," Ensign or Liahona, May 2008, 8*).

"As it is written, Jacob have I loved, but Esau have I hated" (Romans 9:13). Did the Lord actually Hate Esau?

While it is likely the names Esau and Jacob stood for the nations sprung from these two brothers, namely, Edom and Israel, it still seems strange, God should choose one to hate and one to love. However, while the Greek (miseo) word used here does mean hate, in the same sense it is used today; Paul is quoting a phrase from (Malachi 1:3). In Hebrew the verb (sânê) translated to hate carried many shades of meaning, including rejection, strong displeasure, or, very commonly, loving less than. The important point in Paul's discussion is the acceptance of Jacob and rejection of Esau was based on personal righteousness during their time in the pre-existence, not on some arbitrary judgment.

"God chose Jacob over Esau while the two were yet in Rebecca's womb and before either, as far as the works of this life are concerned, had earned any preferential status. Why? It is a pure matter of pre-existence. Jacob was coming into the world with greater spiritual capacity than Esau was; he was foreordained to a special work; he was elected to serve in a chosen capacity. Then through the lineage of Jacob, God sent those valiant spirits, those noble and great ones, who in his infinite wisdom and foreknowledge he knew would be inclined to serve him. Through Esau came those spirits of lesser valiance and devotion. Hence, in the very nature of things, many of Jacob's seed were righteous in this life, and many of Esau's were wicked, causing Malachi to say in the Lord's name, some fifteen hundred years later, God loved the house of Jacob and hated the house of Esau" (*Mal. 1:2–3, McConkie, DNTC, 2:277*).

People, who belong to the family of Israel by inheritance or adoption, may lay claim to every blessing reserved for Israel. Although not all their current blessings are the result of conduct in this world, some go back into the beginning with God. Review the following scriptures and carefully study the dialogue between David and John.

(Romans 9:11, 12) Did God bestow the same favors on Jacob and Esau? Was mortal performance the basis for God's favoring Jacob over Esau— had there been opportunity for either child to do either good or evil at the time of the indication of favor?

(Romans 9:14) Does, in fact, God favoring Jacob over Esau even at the time of birth mean, God arbitrarily selects those upon whom his favors will be bestowed without reference to their worthiness or obedience?

(Romans 9:18–20) Looking at God's dealings with men from a purely mortal perspective it is difficult to see why He gives to one blessings and withholds from another. The questions in verse 19 are the questions asked by those who do not understand premortal life. Is it appropriate to challenge God, or to suggest he is not fair in placing mortals in the stations occupied in this world? If two souls are born into this world in seemingly unequal circumstances, and God is just, what had to occur to justify Gods placing them in unequal circumstances?

Hopefully, the reader will get a lot out of those scriptures on first reading but it takes years of study to fully understand them, although, they are very enlightening. All of the concepts Paul was trying to convey, will now be addressed in a conversational style, as if it was held today. There are two people selected for this conversation, one to ask questions (David) and another (John) to provide answers.

David --- If some of the circumstances in which I find myself are based upon my conduct before, where did I begin? When did I start?

John --- Well, first, there is an eternity of spirit matter. "Our spirit matter was eternal and co-existent with God, but it was organized into spirit bodies

45

by our Heavenly Father" (*Kimball, Miracle of Forgiveness, p. 5*). "All men were first born in pre-existence as the literal spirit offspring of God our Heavenly Father. This birth constituted the beginning of the human ego as a conscious identity. By the ordained procreative process our exalted and immortal Father begat his spirit progeny in pre-existence" (*McConkie, Mormon Doctrine, p. 84*). "All men and women are in the similitude of the universal Father and Mother, and are literally the sons and daughters of Deity" (*The First Presidency [Joseph Smith, John R. Winder, and Anthon H. Lund], "The Origin of Man," Improvement Era, Nov. 1909, p. 78*).

David --- If I was born in the premortal world, what experiences did I go through there that provided God with a basis to favor or restrict me in this world?

John --- We lived there in the home of our Father in heaven.

He is a resurrected and holy and perfected man, and we are his offspring. We are his spirit children. He lives in the family unit. We are members of his family. We lived in this premortal life with him for an infinite period. We were on probation; we were being schooled, tested, and examined; we were given the laws and the circumstances so we could progress and advance.

"This system was given to us, and for an infinite period of time, we advanced and progressed and did things enabling us to go along the course leading to exaltation and dominion and godhood. In this prior life, this premortal existence, this pre-existence, we developed various capacities and talents. Some developed them in one field and some in another. The most important of all fields was the field of spirituality, the ability, the talent, the capacity to recognize truth" (*Bruce R. McConkie, as cited in When Thou Art Converted, Strengthen Thy Brethren, A Study Guide for the Melchizedek Priesthood Quorums of the Church, 1974–75, pp. 8–9*).

"Our spirit bodies went through a long period of growth and development and training and, having passed the test successfully, were finally admitted to this earth and to mortality" (*Kimball, Miracle of Forgiveness, p. 5*).

"Preexistence is not some remote and mysterious place. All of us are but a few years removed from the Eternal Presence, from him whose children we are and in whose house we dwelt . . . We know we had friends and associates there. We know we were schooled and trained and taught in the most perfect educational system ever devised, and by obedience to his eternal laws we developed infinite varieties and degrees of talents . . . When we come into mortality, we bring the talents, capacities, and abilities acquired by obedience to law in our prior existence" (*Bruce R. McConkie in CR, Apr. 1974, pp. 101–3*).

David --- Am I to understand, when I was born as the spirit son of God in heaven, I lived there with my Father and mother in heaven and with my spirit brothers and sisters, and I had opportunities to learn, to be tested, and to develop talents and abilities?

John --- Correct. Some accounts we have of the premortal life teach, we "were on the same standing" (*Alma 13:5*), and we were "innocent" in the beginning (*D&C 93:38*). "We were given laws and agency, and commandments to have faith and repent from the wrongs that we could do there. ". . . Man could and did in many instances, sin before he was born . . ." (*Smith, The Way to Perfection, p. 44*).

"God gave his children their agency even in the spirit world, by which the individual spirits had the privilege, just as men have here, of choosing the good and rejecting the evil, or partaking of the evil to suffer the consequences of their sins . . . Some even there were more faithful than others in keeping the commandments of the Lord. . . .The spirits of men . . . had an equal start, and we know they were all innocent in the beginning; but the right of free agency which was given to them enabled some to outstrip others, and thus, through the eons of immortal existence, to become more intelligent, more faithful, for they were free to act for themselves, to think for themselves, to receive the truth or rebel against it" (*Smith, Doctrines of Salvation, 1:58–59*).

Many responded to the spirit of God there. They were favored and foreordained to receive privileges.

". . . And it was on account of their exceeding faith and repentance, and their righteousness before God, they choosing to repent and work righteousness rather than to perish; therefore, they were called after this holy order, and were sanctified, and their garments were washed white through the blood of the Lamb" (*Alma 13:10, 11; compare (McConkie, Mormon Doctrine, p. 477*).

"Now this is the doctrine of foreordination; this is the doctrine of election. This is the reason why the Lord has a chosen and favored and peculiar people on earth; and this is why he said: 'My sheep hear my voice, and I know them, and they follow me'" (*Bruce R. McConkie in CR, Apr. 1974, p. 103*).

David --- But what of those in pre-mortality who rejected the Spirit of God and did not exercise exceeding great faith and repentance and righteousness before God?

John --- They were not able to "enjoy the great privileges that others were foreordained to receive" (*Alma 13:4*). They "did not show the loyalty to their Redeemer that they should" (*Smith, Way to Perfection, p. 43*).

David --- But weren't they allowed to come into the world innocent, too?

John --- Yes. "They were innocent at the time of their mortal birth" (*D&C 93:38*). Elder Joseph Fielding Smith said this: "Their sin was not one that merited the extreme punishment which was inflicted on the devil and his angels. They were not denied the privilege of receiving the second estate, but were permitted to come to the earth-life with some restrictions placed upon them . . . Yet, like all other spirits who come into this world, they come innocent before God so far as mortal existence is concerned, and here, under certain restrictions, they may work out their second estate" (*Way to Perfection, pp. 43, 44*).

Hence, some in this world receive great privileges and opportunities to receive the gospel because they chose to do good in preexistence. Others are limited here because they were not as "noble and great" (*Abraham 3:22*).

David --- And how does the concept of Israel enter into this?

John --- The family of Jacob is somehow involved in preexistence.

"Israel is an eternal people. Members of that chosen race first gained their inheritance with the faithful in the premortal life. Israel was a distinct people in pre-existence. Many of the valiant and noble spirits in that first estate were chosen, elected, and foreordained to be born into the family of Jacob, to be natural heirs of all of the blessings of the gospel. It was to their pre-existent status that Moses alluded when, in speaking to mortal Israel, he said, "Remember the days of old, consider the years of many generations: ask thy father, and he will shew thee; thy elders, and they will tell thee. When the most High divided to the nations their inheritance, when he separated the sons of Adam, he set the bounds of the people according to the number of the children of Israel. For the Lord's portion is his people; Jacob is the lot of his inheritance" (*Deut. 32:7–9*). Those of mortal Israel who walk uprightly in this second estate shall have eternal inheritance with Israel in the world to come" (*McConkie, DNTC, 2:284*).

David --- So the fact that I am here now and receiving blessings and opportunities means I have already passed the test, under different circumstances and conditions?

John --- Yes. Moreover, if you succeed here in this second estate, you shall not only be entitled to advantages in the world to come (D&C 130:19), but you "shall have glory added upon [your head] for ever and ever" (Abraham 3:26).

David --- Does birthright by itself secure your eternal destiny? In addition, will Israel be saved just because they are of Israel?

John--- The answer is found in Romans 10:11–13.

Of course, the gentiles in Paul's day had not had the same opportunities to receive the gospel as had members of the house of Israel. However, did members of the house of Israel receive the rewards of the gospel just because they had the advantage of hearing about the gospel before the gentiles?

"The house of Israel was a distinct people in pre-existence; that is, by obedience and devotion, certain of the spirit children of the Father earned the right to be born in the lineage of Abraham, of Isaac, and of Jacob, and of being natural heirs to the blessings of the gospel. However, some of them, after such a favored birth, after being numbered with the chosen seed, turn from the course of righteousness and become children of the flesh; that is, they walk after the manner of the world, rejecting the spiritual blessings held in store for Israel. They are disinherited; they shall not continue as children in the family of the prophets when the chosen race continues as a distinct people in the eternal worlds. Thus they are descendants of the prophets in this life but shall not inherit with the sons of God in the life to come" (*McConkie, DNTC, 2:276–77*).

"There are many among us who because of their faithfulness in the spirit world were 'called' to do a great work here, but like reckless spendthrifts they are exercising their free agency in riotous living and are losing their birthright and the blessings that were theirs had they proved faithful to their calling." (*Lee, Youth and the Church, p. 172*).

Now what of you? For all has been said of Israel applies to you. You were vitally interested and personally involved there. What shall you do, and what shall you be, here? You came from God, and you have been given great privileges and blessings here because of your faithfulness. Nevertheless, you will go back one day, and you will answer for all these blessings, for as Paul wrote, "Every one of us shall give account of himself to God" (*Romans 14:12*).

"And so you see, all have come, and each with a program of divine appointments keyed into his immortal soul, appointments that act and react throughout the sojourn of his tenure in this world, that whisper of friendships long since forged and of associations and relationships and communion that death itself will never defeat. That is what membership in the family of Israel is—an eternal privilege that commenced in the pre-mortal realms, that continues even now, and that shall continue, if you are faithful, forever and without end" (David O. McKay).

Conclusion,

There has always been a divine tapestry in people's lives, the threads from the distant past will merge sometime in the future to form the intricate patterns, and this will be their identity forever. Long ago, in a far better land, while existing with Father in Heaven, there was friendships made, and strengthened through ages of an infinite existence; and through those friendships, trust and mutual help, bonds of love were forged. These bonds of love, though unbeknownst to us while in mortality, form the essence of the eternal family. Since all things brought forth and cultivated in an eternal setting, shall ever be eternal, unchanging, and everlasting. All of Gods children were and are part of that. All were there "when the morning stars sang together, and all the sons of God shouted for joy" (*Job 38:7*).

The Law of Eternal Increase

When the leadership of the church talks about Eternal Increase, for the most part, they are talking the circumstance or event wherein exalted beings participate in birthing of spirit children in the Celestial Kingdom, often referred to as Celestial Procreation. The purpose of this section is to further the conversation on this subject and try to interrelate information about how this event influences lives in mortality. The Law of Eternal Increase is the means put in place as a system wherein God can accomplish His eternal calling. "Behold, this is my work and my glory-to bring to pass the immortality and eternal life of man" (*Moses 1:39*). Simply put, this process takes place as organized intelligences reach the point of readiness and need to move from the sphere where they reside, into the sphere of the preexistence where they will become spirit children of God. While the process of becoming a spirit child of God facilitated by those exalted Priests and Priestesses residing in the highest kingdom of the Celestial Kingdom, and holding the Holy Order of the Patriarchal Priesthood, they calling, is to insure God an eternal supply of spirit children. This spherical movement, I.E. moving from an intelligence to a spirit child of God, requires a circumstance of death and rebirth. To further explain, this birth and death issue, there is a place in the Discourses of Brigham Young where he explained, each time an entity moves from one sphere to another it is necessary for a death and a rebirth to take place. These deaths and rebirths are an essential part of the eternal journey because they provide the locomotion needed to traverse through the different layers of the Plan of Salvation. For example, when these entities move from the preexistence (spirit world) into mortality, there is a death in the spirit world and a birth in mortality. There is empirical evidence this is true. Then when making the move from mortality into the afterlife there is a death in mortality, which mortals have witnessed many times and a rebirth in the eternal realm. In fact, the spirit children of God have already and will continue to experience multiple deaths and rebirths before reaching the end of their eternal journey. During mortal probation, the opportunity to participate in mortal pro-creation, which is also a necessary part of God's established plan. It is through this mortal birthing process and then later the Celestial birthing

50

process, the Law of Eternal Increase is satisfied. When hearing or reading about this kind of thing, it is easy to think of it as something happening far away and a long time from now, but if you think about it, all spirit children were the recipient of this exact process. Some exalted couple was responsible for enabling an intelligence to become a spirit child of God, and saints living worthy can do the same done for others.

LDS Apostle, Orson Pratt said it this way. "As soon as each God has begotten many millions of male and female spirits, and his Heavenly inheritance becomes too small and too uncomfortable to accommodate his great family, he, in connection with his sons, organizes a new world, after a similar order to the one which we now inhabit, where he sends both the male and female spirits to inhabit tabernacles of flesh and bones" (*The Seer, p. 37*).

Additionally, when worthy saints reach a certain point in the Celestial Kingdom they will become Gods, having no end and continuing from everlasting to everlasting according to D&C 132. Therefore, as they help those intelligences to start on their path of increase, it seems, they will also experience, for themselves, everlasting existence. "Then shall they be gods, because they have no end; therefore, shall they be from everlasting to everlasting, because they continue; then shall they be above all, because all things are subject unto them. Then shall they be gods, because they have all power, and the angels are subject unto them. Verily, verily, I say unto you, except ye abide my law ye cannot attain to this glory. For strait is the gate, and narrow the way that leadeth unto the exaltation and continuation of the lives, and few there be that find it, because ye receive me not in the world neither do ye know me" (*D&C 132:20&22*). (In this 20th verse the words, *continuation of the lives,* is referring to the birthing of spirit children).

Another scripture explains the process that is required to be exalted to the highest level in the Celestial Kingdom. "Abraham received concubines, and they bore him children; and it was accounted unto him for righteousness, because they were given unto him, and he abode in my law; as Isaac also and Jacob did none other things than that which they were commanded; and because they did none other things than that which they were commanded, they have entered into their exaltation, according to the promises, and sit upon thrones, and are not angels but are gods" (*D&C 132; 37*).

This is where it is easy to start to develop some confusing thoughts, like, if all these exalted beings are gods, what does it mean when someone says, there is only one God? Moreover, often, If God is our Heavenly Father, and there is a Heavenly Mother, who is also a God, is there any scriptures, actually saying, these exalted beings are, in fact, responsible for the birth of spirit children? If not, how is this reconciled?

To gain understanding to the first question it becomes necessary to understand the Jewish Adage of *Seven Heavens*. It is common to hear someone say, their living in seventh heaven when things are going right for them. This is referring to an old Jewish adage. To find those passages concerning seven heavens read the apocryphal testament of Levi, where Levi learns, he would soon die, and he is explaining the gospel to his sons. Let's read Levi's words and compare them to Mormon theology of degrees of glory as outlined by the Prophet Joseph Smith in the 76th section of the D&C, *Outer Darkness, Telestial Kingdom, Terrestrial Kingdom, and the three stations or levels in the Celestial Kingdom* are in italics and set in place to match Levi's testament.

Testament of Levi: starting with verse three.

Hear, then, concerning the seven heavens.

The first or lowest is for this cause more, gloomy; it is near all the iniquities of men (*outer darkness*).

The second hath fire, snow, and ice, ready for the day of the ordinance of the Lord, in the righteous judgment of God: in it are all the spirits of the retributions for vengeance on the wicked (*Telestial Kingdom*).

In the third are the hosts of the armies, which are ordained for the Day of Judgment, to work vengeance on the spirits of deceit and of Beliar (*Terrestrial Kingdom*).

And the heavens up to the fourth above these are holy, for in the highest of all dwelleth the Great Glory, in the holy of holies, far above all holiness (highest degree of the *Celestial Kingdom*).

Fifth, in the heaven next to it are the angels of the presence of the Lord, who minister and make propitiation to the Lord for all the ignorance's of the righteous; and they offer to the Lord a reasonable sweet-smelling savor, and a bloodless offering (*middle degree of the Celestial Kingdom*).

Sixth, in the heaven below this are the angels who bear the answers to the angels of the presence of the Lord, and in the heaven next to this are thrones, dominions, in which hymns are offered to God (lowest degree of the Celestial Kingdom, ministering angles). Therefore, whenever the Lord looks upon us, all creation is shaken, yea, the heavens, and the earth, and the abysses, are shaken at the presence of His majesty; but the sons of men, regarding not these things, sin, and provoke the Most High.

There are six heavens talked about so far, and they cover all heavens recorded in the 76th section of the D&C. so, what is the seventh? This is what answers the first question, the seventh heaven is the one who has Majesty and is Most High, God, who has received the calling of

GODHOOD. Even though these exalted beings are Gods they have yet to receive Godhood. Much the same with the Apostles of the Mormon Church, they are all prophets but only one called to be The Prophet. Therefore, when reading or hearing about a plurality of Gods it is easy understand what it means, knowing Heavenly Father is the Supreme God.

The next confusing thing is this Father and Mother in Heaven issue. Researchers cannot find, anywhere in the scriptures, a single statement remotely suggesting, all mortals who have been born on this earth from Adam and Eve up to today, with all of their spiritual components, are the product of a single mother and Father, and if someone did suggest it, it would not be believed. However, what is found in the scriptures is in all of Gods dealing with His children, He delegates the work to those children who are the most faithful, starting with Jehovah and the creation. It is reasonable to believe, the same pattern of behavior would be extend right up to the Celestial Kingdom. Are all mortals the off springs of Heavenly Father? Of course they are. Is there a Heavenly Mother? Sure there is. However, this does not equate to the belief that God and His Wife did all of this by themselves. Similarly, Did God create the heavens and the earth? Of course He did. Did He have help? Of course He did, He employed Jehovah along with a bunch of Archangels.

The Law of Eternal Progression

The concept of eternal progression is a significant feature of the gospel teachings of the Church of Jesus Christ of Latter Day Saints and is readily distinguishable from all other traditional Christian theology. The traditional Christian view holds, those entering heaven pass into "a state of eternal, inactive, bliss, and joy. While in the presence of God they worship him and sing praises to him eternally, but nothing more" (*Widtsoe, p. 142*). Latter-day Saints, however, constantly seek personal and righteous improvement not only by establishing Zion in this world, but also by anticipating the continuation of progressing eternally. This attitude, perpetuated through the Latter-day communities is because of their understanding of a law given to mankind through the prophets in these latter days called The Law of Eternal Progression. Part of Latter Day Saints understanding of this law comes from the statement "As man is, God once was; as God is, man may become" (*Lorenzo Snow*). If the Law of Eternal Progression were not in place, this statement by the Prophet Lorenzo Snow, never could have been given.

The law of eternal progression cannot be precisely defined or comprehended, yet it is fundamental to the LDS eternal view. It embodies many concepts taught by Joseph Smith, especially in his King Follett discourse. The phrase eternal progression first occurs in the discourses of Brigham Young. "It is based on the proposition, there is no such thing as principle, power, wisdom, knowledge, life, position, or anything imagined during this mortal probation, that remains stationary" (*D of B Y*). All personal accomplishments, or the lack thereof will either lead one to be closer to God or push one further away from God, and all personal righteousness must either increase or decrease. One cannot stand still. A person's attitude about eternal progression will largely determine his philosophy of life. The believer will find himself exalting, increasing, expanding and extending broader and broader until "we can know as we are known, see as we are seen" (*B.Y. Teaching of the Prophets*). However, the disbeliever will surely go the opposite way since he does not have the philosophical basis to advance toward righteousness and thus, his eternal progression, is forever, arrested.

For us this all started when Christ began the process of creation by taking disorganized intelligences (D&C 88:5-14) from disorganized space and organize them in order for them, through their acceptance of the Laws of God and their obedience, to become spirit children of God and live in organized space. Once the spirit children of God, voted in the Counsel in Heaven to follow Christ, the Plan of Salvation, which was an eternal plan, was set into motion and the spirit children of god were then able to continue their eternal advancement by receiving bodies in mortality. Once this great eternal process had started and there is no turning back for those having received, the Light of Christ and made covenants. The law of eternal progression, a law governed by the Law of Light, which also governs all things, even God, cannot be broken, cannot stop, alter, abolish, repeal, or break this law in any way. The facts are mortals cannot stop themselves from progressing. Once born into this mortality, mortal beings are on the path toward their reward in heaven (whatever it may be), and they cannot stop their process. All will receive their reward, or lack there-of, no matter what they do while on this earth, since everything has a direct bearing on their reward. It is through their actions here in mortality, those mortals, alone, determine the level of glory; they will receive in Kingdom of Heaven. Brigham Young taught, even in mortality, "We are in eternity" (*JD 10:22*), and the object of this existence is "to learn to enjoy more, and to increase in knowledge and experience" (*JD 14:228*). "When we have learned to live according to the full value of the life we now possess, we are prepared for further advancement in the scale of eternal progression—for a more glorious and exalted sphere" (*JD 9:168*).

In one sense, eternal progression refers to everything God's spirit children learn and experience by their choices as they progress from the state of premortal life, to the state of mortality, to the state of post-mortal spirit life, to a resurrected state in the presence of God and it seems, this process continues into eternity. No official Church teaching attempts to specify all the ways in which God progresses in his exalted spheres, only to say: "there is no end to His works, neither to His words" (*Moses 1:38*). This is the gradually unfolding course of advancement and experience, which, began in our eternal past and will continue into age's future, referred to, as the law of eternal progression, which is the will of God. God's spirit children, accepted in the counsel in heaven whereby they expressed the desire to progress to the point where they become like Him. So, what is progression? The only definition of this law, mortals can understand comes from the Pearl of Great Price where the calling of God is given; "behold, this is my work and my glory, to bring to pass the immortality and eternal life of man" (*Moses 1: 39*). This statement leads people to believe, since immortality is given by the grace of God, only through the practice of helping ourselves and others obtain eternal life can one obtain glory and the achievement of glory is what the term progression means. During mortality, *work* is to live a righteous life, which helps mortals to progress and then missionary work, family research and all entailed in this will help others to progress, thus all may gain a small level of glory at some future date.

When examining progression from a mortal perspective, keep in mind these two schools of thought.

1. Progression changes form and substance depending on which sphere or state you are in.
2. Even a small amount of progression, as long as it's an increase in righteousness, complies with will of God, and that, of course is' for His children to become more like Him.

Personal progression is possible in each of these states, as mentioned above, but in each state, the purpose of being is different and so it follows, the results of achievement in each of these states would be different. Progression apparently started to occur in the preexistence where intelligences chose to obey the laws given to them by God. There was a time when those spirits were required to choose between Christ and Lucifer. Some chose to follow Christ and were deemed, noble and great and allowed to advance to the state, called mortality, while others chose to follow Lucifer and their advancement or progression was denied. Entering mortality afforded opportunities for further progression. Obtaining a physical body is a crucial step, enabling a person to experience physical sensations of all kinds and to progress in spiritual knowledge and understanding, all of which will rise with the person in the Resurrection (D&C 130:18). During the Resurrection and the Judgment, there is an assignment, for some people, to one of the three degrees of glory: telestial glory, terrestrial glory or celestial glory. Further progress is possible within each of these degrees. However, only while in the exalted state of Celestial Glory, marriage and family life continues, allowing eternal increase through the creation of spirit children. However, it is important to know two things about progressing up to and through these degrees of glory:

1. At any time during progression, from mortality and beyond, even while in any one of these degrees of glory, it is possible to stop all personal progression by choosing the path of Lucifer as the spirit children of God did in the preexistence when they chose to follow Lucifer instead of Christ. This reasoning is revealed to mortals who fully understanding of the Eternal Law of Agency and virtue.

2. That for the overwhelming majority of mankind, eternal progression has some very definite limitations. In the full sense, only those who receive exaltation enjoy eternal progression. All other persons who are assigned lesser rewards (telestial glory or terrestrial glory) and will find their progression is not unlimited but will have specific limitations placed on them as pertains to the specific sphere or glory where they reside. There will be truths such persons will never learn; powers they will never possess. Some are to become ministering servants, to minister to and for those who are worthy of receiving exaltation and those in this state of celestial glory will, "continue through all eternity, and ... forever and ever" (D & C. 132). Pres. Brigham Young says it this way, "all this and more. cannot enter into people's hearts to conceive, i.e. more than can even be imagined is promised to the faithful, and are but so many stages in the ceaseless progression of eternal lives" (D of BY).

Those who gain exaltation, having thus enjoyed the fullness of eternal progression, become like God. Exalted persons (those in the Celestial Kingdom) gain the fullness of the Father; they have all power, all knowledge, all wisdom; they gain a fullness of truth, comprehend all things, and become one with the Father.

Law of Free Grace

The law of free grace pertains to the current way Protestant Christian Churches, through their doctrine, explain, and teach the members about the fall of Adam and Eve, the reason the fall happened, and the effect transgression had upon all future generations as opposed to the doctrine of the Church of Jesus Christ of Latter Day Saints. The law of free grace, given to the Prophet Joseph Smith by revelation and is one of the pieces of doctrine setting this church apart from all other Christian denominations. This law set into place a more correct understanding of the events before, during, and after the fall of Adam and Eve.

To understand how Mormons view of the *Fall of Adam and Eve* requires a prior understanding of the Mormon concept of a pre-mortal existence, and the purpose of this earth life. Mormonism teaches, all mankind is of the same species as God. Mankind's origin is the product of procreation as children of God, born as spirits in some other realm. In this spirit world existence, those children progressed as far as was possible but, Heavenly Father wanted His children to continue to progress and became like Him. However, to become truly, like Heavenly Father there was a need to obtain physical bodies and go through a period of testing which would mean there would be the presence of sin and evil. Since Heavenly Father has progressed so far, and He cannot allow evil into His presence, it was necessary for His children to be removed from His presence and go to some other place where they could encounter and overcome evil themselves.

Therefore, this mortal world was prepared as a school, where God's children are sent to obtain physical bodies and to learn the lessons of mortality. They are expected to gain knowledge, educate, and train themselves. They were to control their urges and desires, master and control their passions, and overcome their weaknesses, small and large. They also needed to learn the difference between good and evil, truth and error, to love and exercise their agency by choosing between right and wrong, and to eliminate sins of omission and of sins of commission and to follow the laws and commandments given by Heavenly Father. In the Pearl of Great Price, while laying plans for earth life, the God said, "And we will prove them herewith, to see if they will do all things whatsoever the Lord their God shall command them" (*PGP, Abraham 3:25*). Therefore, earth was the place of mortal probation and the test was to obey all commandments given to by God for mortals to live by while on this earth. Adam and Eve were the first to obtain mortal bodies and the Lord taught them what was necessary for them to do to return to Heavenly Father. This curriculum is the Plan of Salvation.

Of course, for this whole plan to work, physical bodies had to be prepared in which Heavenly Father's spirit children could dwell. Thus, the first commandment on record is the commandment given to Adam and Eve to be fruitful and multiply (procreate), meaning fill the earth with Heavenly Father's spirit children but, in their condition of immortality in the Garden of Eden they could not procreate. If they remained in their present circumstance, they could not have children; wherefore they would have remained in a state of innocence, having no joy, knowing no misery; doing no good, for they knew no sin. Adam and Eve had to figure out how to become mortal in order to obey this first commandment. Additionally, while in the Garden of Eden there was a second commandment given which forbade Adam and Eve to eat from the tree of good and evil. Eve partook of the fruit and later, Adam chose to eat from this tree and thus the situation called the fall took place. It is not known exactly how the fall was accomplished but after Adam and Eve had thus complied with whatever the law was, mortality came into being and they then were in a position to procreate.

So, what does all this have to do with the law of free grace?
There are several issues surrounding events in the Garden of Eden that scholars interpret in different ways but it all comes down to sin v/s Transgression. These are the tainted birth of all mankind, the baptism of children in accordance with the concept of original sin and the belief that God was unfair when he gave Adam and Eve two conflicting commandments and then punished them when they broke one of them. Most Christian churches teach Adam and Eve's sin was the cause of their fall. The term, fall, actually is an abbreviation for the concept of, falling from grace, meaning, because of their doing something bad or something against the will of God, Adam and Eve no longer were entitled to receive the grace of God, this is spoken of as the original sin. This, fall from grace concept, the Catholic Church put forth as doctrine is still believed by Catholics, and some Protestant congregations, even until today. The reason this term is mentioned is it contributes to the mindset of Adam and Eve sinning when they ate from the tree of good and evil and were punished by being *kicked out* of the Garden of Eden. This view leads these churches to conclude, this original sin was inherited by all of Adam and Eve's children. Hence, the phrase; *all mankind is born in sin*. Because of this belief, the Catholic Church and some Protestant Churches baptize new borne children as soon as possible believing they have the power to wash away this inherited sin. The scriptures clearly say, no mortal can erase any sin since they themselves have sinned and are unclean in the eyes of God, only Christ is pure enough to wipe away sin and then, only under certain circumstances.

The Church of Jesus Christ of Latter Day Saints sees this entire doctrine of original sin and the belief and mindset of these Christian churches in a different way as the result of the teachings of the prophet Joseph Smith who gained his information by receiving revelation, called "the law of free grace". Each one of these issues can be taken separately and broken down in terms of LDS doctrine.

Sin v/s transgression;

The entire edict of sin, hinges on the idea, a mortal knows right from wrong but decides he will do the wrong thing. If a person acts without any knowledge of wrong doing, his actions are still wrong, but there is no sin. So it is with Adam and Eve in the garden, they were totally innocent and immortal; they did not know good from evil the knowledge of good and evil came after the first bite, so how could they have sinned prior to the knowledge? Although they did something, they were instructed not to do, it was done without malice, and in fact, it was done for good reason. This act can only be classified as a transgression.

The Mormon apostle and prophet Joseph Fielding Smith, Jr. wrote, "I never speak of the part Eve took in this fall as a sin, nor do I accuse Adam of a sin" (*DS, vol. 1, p. 114*). Again, this was a transgression of the law, but not a sin in the strict sense, for it was something Adam and Eve had to do. The fall of Adam and Eve was not a sin but an essential act upon which mortality depends" (*DS, vol. 1, p. 114*).

According to Mormon scripture, Eve is supposed to have exclaimed, "Were it not for our transgression we never should have had seed, and never should have known good and evil, and the joy of our redemption, and the eternal life which God giveth unto all the obedient" (*PGP, Moses 5:11*).

All mankind is borne into sin because of the sin of Adam; however, they are not sinners because of Adam.

Mormon doctrine says no other person is punished for Adam's transgression. Mankind will be redeemed from the effects of the fall. The consequences of Adam's action, physical, or temporal death, and spiritual death are overcome, by and through the Atonement of Christ. Temporal death is the natural death; it occurs when body and spirit separate, thus leaving the body to return to the dust whence it came. Spiritual death is being cast out of the presence of the Lord and to die as pertaining to the things of righteousness. Since it was not the fault of those living today that either of these deaths were introduced, the effect of these two deaths will both be removed by God's free grace. All mankind, will be resurrected with immortal physical bodies, and all will be brought back into the presence of God, for judgment, BoM, 2 Nephi 2:10. Those who are subsequently cast-out are rejected for their own unrepented sin. The second Article of Faith says; "We believe that men will be punished for their own sins and not for Adam's transgression". The Church of Jesus Christ of Latter Day Saints simply does not believe in inherited sin. Additionally, how can any sin be passed along from generation to generation when a sin was not actually committed.

Baptism of newborn children,

Mormons do not believe a child can be born into sin, nor is anyone else. The doctrine of the Church of Jesus Christ of Latter Day teaches, all children are in fact born in innocence and it is not until they reach the age of eight, they have sufficient knowledge of right and wrong to be responsible. In addition, the two paragraphs above pertain to children as well.

The two conflicting commandments;

Concerned members of other Christian faiths have weighed in on this issue and been asked this question. If the two commandments, given to Adam and Eve, one to multiply and fill the earth, and the other not to eat of the forbidden fruit, were in opposition, they could not both be obeyed at the same time. If the former was a greater commandment than the latter, then why were Adam and Eve not counted as transgressors before eating the forbidden fruit, for failing to multiply? Why did the fall not occur at that first transgression?
According to Mormon doctrine, the two commandments do seem to stand in opposition to each other until you put them into perspective.

The first, so called, conflicting commandment.

Why was Adam and Eve not counted as transgressors for not complying with the first commandment? Which was, to multiply and replenish the earth.

There are two answers to this question.

First answer, from the day of mortal birth, every child is under the same commandments and requirements as Adam and Eve and since all commandments have been given and recorded prior to the day of birth, there is not any excuse for any noncompliance. Can this be true in all cases? Obedience, as in all matters of obedience, hinges on ability and timing; no one is expected to be obedient to any commandment until they are ready, especially giving birth to newborn children. They have to wait until their bodies and emotions have sufficiently matured. Given that, a baby today, is born under the same commandment given to Adam and Eve while they were maturing and growing in the Garden of Eden. Mormons ask the Christian community this question; do non-Mormon Christians really believe a newborn baby of today will receive the wrath of God for not obeying the commandment to multiply and replenish the earth while still a child? On the other hand, do non Mormon Christians believe that children should have equally sufficient time in their lives to ready themselves for the event of bearing children as was given to Adam and Eve?

Second answer; where in the scriptures is there a time limit on obeying commandments? It seems that Adam and Eve were obedient to the commandment and did multiply and replenish the world or people simply would not be here.

Second question; why did Adam and Eve's noncompliance to the first commandment not incur the fall? Answer, because no sin or transgression occurred. There is not a single scripture, in any language that indicates that Adam and Eve were required to have children while in the Garden of Eden.

The Law if Health
(Often called the Word of wisdom)

In the LDS Church, compliance with the Word of Wisdom is currently a prerequisite for baptism, service in full-time missionary work, attendance at church schools, and entry into the church's temples; however, violation of the code is not considered grounds for excommunication or other disciplinary action. As practiced by the LDS Church, there is no firm restriction relating to meat consumption, but there are additional restrictions against narcotics, and all alcoholic beverages are forbidden, including mild drinks such as beer. The LDS Church interprets hot drinks to mean coffee and tea. The original revelation stated not by commandment or constraint, so when did the word of wisdom become a commandment and how did this happen and, how did soft drinks get involved?

According to Joseph Smith, Jr., the founder of the Latter Day Saint movement, the Word of Wisdom was received in 1833 as a revelation from God. After Smith's death, Brigham Young stated, the revelation was given in response to problems encountered while conducting meetings in the Smith family home:

"When they assembled together in this room after breakfast, the first they did was to light their pipes, and, while smoking, talk about the great things of the kingdom, and spit all over the room, and as soon as the pipe was out of their mouths a large chew of tobacco would then be taken. Often when the Prophet Joseph Smith entered the room to give the school instructions he would find himself in a cloud of tobacco smoke. This, and the complaints of his wife at having to clean so filthy a floor, made the Prophet think upon the matter, and he inquired of the Lord relating to the conduct of the Elders in using tobacco, and the revelation known as the Word of Wisdom was the result of his inquiry" (*Journal of Discourses, 12:158*). As Joseph Smith explained --- "A Word of Wisdom, for the benefit of the council of high priests, assembled in Kirtland, and the church, and also the saints in Zion— To be sent greeting; not by commandment or constraint, but by revelation and the word of wisdom, showing forth the order and will of God in the temporal salvation of all saints in the last days— Given for a principle with a promise, adapted to the capacity of the weak and the weakest of all saints, who are or can be called saints. Behold, verily, thus saith the Lord unto you: In consequence of evils and designs, which do and will exist in the hearts of conspiring men in the last days, I have warned you, and forewarn you, by giving unto you this word of wisdom by revelation" (*D&C 89*).

Originally, abiding by the recommendations and prohibitions of the Word of Wisdom was not considered mandatory: it explicitly declares itself to be not by commandment or constraint. In February 1834, however, Joseph Smith, Jr. proposed a resolution before the high council of the church stating, "No official member in this Church is worthy to hold an office after having the word of wisdom properly taught him; and he, the official member, neglecting to comply with and obey it" (*history of the Church*), this resolution was accepted unanimously by the council.

In 1842, Smith's brother Hyrum, who was the Assistant President of the Church and its presiding patriarch, provided an interpretation of the Word of Wisdom's proscription of hot drinks. "And again hot drinks are not for the body, or belly, there are many who wonder what this can mean; whether it refers to tea, or coffee, or not. I say it does refer to tea and coffee" (*Times and Seasons, 1 June 1842, p. 800*).

Adherence to the proscriptions of the Word of Wisdom was not made a requirement for entry into LDS Church temples until 1902. According to the 2006 Church Handbook of Instructions, for Stake Presidencies and Bishoprics, avoiding the prohibitions of the Word of Wisdom is a requirement for admission to LDS Church temples. Violation of the Word of Wisdom no longer results in church discipline, as it once did; concerning, church discipline, the church instructs its leaders "not to use discipline or threaten members who do not comply with the Word of Wisdom" (*handbook of instruction, bishops, stake presidencies*).

Although the Word of Wisdom was received on 27 February 1833, its acceptance by individual members of the Church was gradual. On 9 September 1851, some eighteen years after it was given, the Patriarch to the Church, John Smith, delivered a talk in general conference on the Word of Wisdom. During his address, President Brigham Young arose and proposed, "All Saints formally covenant to abstain from tea, coffee, tobacco, whiskey, and all things mentioned in the Word of Wisdom" (*Minutes of the General Conference, Millennial Star, 1 Feb. 1852, p. 35*). The motion was accepted unanimously and became binding as a commandment for all Church members thereafter.

In 1918, Frederick J. Pack, a Latter-day Saint professor at the University of Utah, published an article in an official church magazine in which he reasoned, because Coca-Cola contained caffeine, which is also present in tea and coffee, Latter-day Saints should abstain from Coca-Cola in the same way that they abstain from the Word of Wisdom "hot drinks". Since Pack's article, many Latter-day Saints have come to believe, the reason tea and coffee are proscribed is the presence of caffeine in the drinks. However, the church has never stated that this is the reason for the prohibition.

The church has no official stance on the consumption of caffeinated beverages and the consumption of such does not constitute a violation of the Word of Wisdom. However, a number of church leaders have discouraged the use of such products. For example, in 1922, Church President Heber J. Grant counseled the Latter-day Saints: "I am not going to give any command, but I will ask it as a personal, individual favor to me, to let Coca-Cola alone. There are plenty of other things you can get at the soda fountains without drinking that which is injurious. The Lord does not want you to use any drug that creates an appetite for itself".

Two years after making this statement, Grant met with a representative of the Coca-Cola Company to discuss the church's position on Coca-Cola. At the conclusion of their second meeting, Grant stated that he was sure I have not the slightest desire to recommend that the people leave Coca-Cola alone if the amount of caffeine in Coca-Cola is absolutely harmless, which they claim it is. Grant never again spoke out against the use of cola drinks.

This long period of patience on the part of the Lord was necessary for all, from the newest member to even the leaders. Joseph F. Smith observed: The early leaders of the Church thought, concerning the word of wisdom, why the Word of Wisdom was given, not by commandment or restraint, was at the time. At least, if it had been given as a commandment it would have brought every man, addicted to the use of these noxious things, under condemnation; so the Lord was merciful and gave them a chance to overcome, before He brought them under the law. Thus, early members were not expected to perfectly observance of the Word of Wisdom (especially in its modern application) from early leaders. The Lord and the Church did not expect it of them, though the principle was taught and emphasized. Therefore, it was not until 1902 it was used as a commandment and even afterwards, there were many who did not want to reconcile themselves to the idea, it was a commandment.

The Word of Wisdom as a commandment.

The Prophet Joseph Smith was ask how he received revelations. He answered thusly; first, God gives the Law, then the doctrine, then the commandment, and then the blessing.

One of the most interesting aspects of this law its ranking within the order of commandments. All commandments are headlined with an overarching headline, such as "Thou Shalt Not Kill", Thou Shalt Not Bear False Witness" and so on, as is the Law of Health. Surely, when these laws were given they were accompanied with a complete explanation of their meaning but over the years, we have lost all but the headline. Not so, with The Word of Wisdom, it is the most complete commandment in existence. There is very little doubt about where it came from and what it says. God designed and created the human body, it is logical to suppose He understands the foods and nutrients required to maintain the body in optimal condition. Thus, for the current dispensation, the Lord revealed his law regarding health and diet to Joseph Smith in section 89 of the Doctrine and Covenants, the Word of Wisdom. It is exciting to see how continuing scientific discoveries verify the wisdom in 1833, a revelation containing knowledge about health and nutrition far in advance of anything yet suggested by scientists.

Typically, the attention is placed on the restrictions in the Word of Wisdom, but focus should be placed on the positive points of the law. One general area foe positive action deals with herbs:

"And again I say unto you, all wholesome herbs God hath ordained for the constitution, nature, and use of man—every herb in the season thereof, and every fruit in the season thereof; all these to be used with prudence and thanksgiving" (D&C 89:10–11).

In a very general sense, herbs are simply edible plants, which produce seeds and die "back on the ground each year: and a fruit is the edible reproductive body of the seed plant. There are few vegetables and fruits that don't fit these categories" (Graves and Rogers 12). These foods provide vitamin C, vitamin A, iron, Calcium, trace minerals, and small amounts of other vitamins, and the Lord instructs mankind to use them "in the season thereof," when they are at their peak nutritionally.

The value of vitamins, minerals, and fiber found in fruits and vegetables for helping to maintain good health is strongly supported by medical evidence. "They are essential in protecting the body from diseases as diverse as hypertension, diverticulitis, viral infections, and even some forms of cancer" (*Graces and Rogers 12*). The daily diet should provide four or more servings of vegetables and fruits (*Swanson 110–23, 622–36*).

In addition to their nutritional value, the Lord emphasizes, fruits and vegetables are to be used with good judgment and thanksgiving. In Doctrine and Covenants 59, Joseph Smith recorded, "Yea, all things which come out of the earth, in the season thereof a, are made for the benefit and the use of man, both to please the eye and to gladden the heart; Yea, for food and raiment, for taste and for smell, to strengthen the body and to enliven the soul. And it pleaseth God that he hath given all these things unto man; for unto this end were they made to be used with judgment, not to excess" (D&C, 59 18–20).

From the Lord's view, while eating is a necessity, it is also an occasion for joy, thanksgiving, and prudence. "Flesh also of beasts and the fowls of the air" were "ordained for the use of man with thanksgiving" (D&C 89:12). Meat contains good quality protein and iron, as well as several vitamins and in the vitamin B group, such as thiamine, niacin, riboflavin, pantothenic acid, and pyridoxine (Swanson 119). Nevertheless, "they are to be used sparingly" (*D&C 89:12*), which seems to be confirmed through the years of observation and research (Sandsread 3). Meats (particularly red meats) contain saturated fats and cholesterol which are rink factors associated with cardiovascular disease, and too much meat in the diet may also be linked to colon cancer and diverticular disease (see Church and Church 22, 24, 30 34 51 55 123 186; Swanson 635–36; Updike 21–37, 60–74). The National Council Committee on Dietary Allowances estimates an individual needs, 0.8 grams of protein per kilogram of body weight daily (Recommended 46). In addition to meat, other products that will help provide the necessary protein intake are beans, nuts, cereal products, cheese, and milk.

In Doctrine and Covenants 89:13, the Prophet told, meats are be used "only in times of winter, or of cold, or famine." Perhaps this is because meats are so high in fat, and since fat contains more than twice the calories of an equivalent amount of either protein or carbohydrate, it may be of greatest value to the human body when needed to help stay warm, or for the extra calories in times of hunger (*Swanson 112*). Additional research is being done.

A third general area of positive recommendations deals with grains:

"All grain is ordained for the use of man and of beasts, to be the staff of life, not only for man but for the beasts of the field, and the fowls of the heaven, and all the wild animals that run or creep on the earth; And these hath God made for the use of man only in times of famine and excess hunger. All grain is good for the food of man; as also the fruit of the vine; that which yielded fruit, whether in the ground or above the ground— Nevertheless, wheat for the man, and corn for the ox, and oats for the horse, and rye for the fowls and for swine, and for all beasts of the field, and barley for all useful animals, and for mild drinks, as also other grain" (D&C 89:14– 17).

Throughout the history of mankind, grain has been "the staff of life," and the diverse species can be grown from within the Arctic Circle to the equator, ranging over all types of climates. Because the Lord has provided grains for the majority of populations may be one reason why he points out twice in these verses, "all grain" is for man's use. In addition, the complex carbohydrates (starches) in grains are probably the body's best and least expensive fuels (Swanson 110–11).

Whole grains contain fiber helps the gastrointestinal tract function normally, and some research indicates, fiber reduces the amount of cholesterol absorbed from food, is beneficial in treating constipation and diverticulitis, and reduces the risk of certain cancer and various other diseases, ranging from hemorrhoids, to appendicitis (Rosenfeld 132, 211– 12). he complex carbohydrates may also "reduce the risk of heart disease, be useful in the treatment of diabetes, and even aid in weight control by replacing fat and sugar in the diet" (*Graves and Rogers 13*). However, since grain has less protein, which is also of lower quality in meat, eggs, milk, cheese, peas, and beans, it should be consumed with other high-quality protein foods. This may be part of the reason for the Lord returning to the point of eating "fruit of the vine," wholesome herbs, and fruits (*D&C 89:16*). Apparently, a good variety in people's diet is important and is the Lord's counsel to the Prophet Joseph, as also confirmed in Doctrine and Covenants 59:18, "all things which come of the earth, in the season thereof are made for the benefit and the use of man."

Besides identifying and giving guidelines for kinds of foods, which contribute to health and vitality, the Word of Wisdom also identifies some substances, which are harmful. Joseph counseled, "Alcoholic drinks (strong drinks), tobacco, and hot drinks (identified as coffee and tea) are "not for the body, neither for the belly" (*D&C 89:5–9*). Massive studies done over the last two decades have generated volumes of medical evidence, which validates this part of the revelation given to Joseph Smith. Numerous reports issued by the Surgeon General, the American Heart Association, the National Cancer Institute, the American Cancer Society, the American Medical Association, and others have pointed out the detrimental effects of these substances to the body. Such as higher incidence of heart attacks, stroke, cancer, and other life-threatening diseases (Swanson 470–502, 632–36; LDS Church News [20 Feb 1983] 1–20 [The whole issue is on the Word of Wisdom]; Ensign 17:32–60 [There are several articles on the Word of wisdom in these pages]).

Recent reports from the National Cancer Institute show, Utah has the lowest rate or cancer in the United Sates, and researchers believe the lifestyle of the population, which is made up predominantly of members of the Church of Jesus Christ of Latter-day Saints, is a major factor. Brenda Edwards, associate director of the institute's surveillance program said, "It illustrates a group of individuals [that] have healthy practice in regard to diet because of the large Mormon population. There is an absence of smoking among most of the population [and] alcohol is not consumed. These factors are often related to cancer risk" (*Seamons 5*). Similarly, in 1982, " Professor Williams pointed out that in order to prevent cancer, people must be prepared to change their diets and alter lifestyle habits. It is completely established, smoking can cause lung cancer while excesses of alcohol, fat, coffee, smoked and pickled foods, cyclamates, saccharine and frugally contaminated carbohydrates are inadvisable. A diet rich in fiber, green vegetables, such as broccoli, Brussel sprouts, cabbage and cauliflower, with adequate vitamin C and A, fives protection'" (*The Scientist*). This sounds like the counsel given by Prophet Joseph Smith in the Word of Wisdom over 150 years ago.

Wisdom and good sense suggest there are also other substances not listed in D&C 89 that should not be used. President Spencer W. Kimball has said, "We hope our people will eliminate from their lives all kinds of drugs so far as possible. Too many depend upon drugs as tranquilizers and sleep helps, which is not always necessary. Certainly numerous young people have been damaged or destroyed by the use of marijuana and other deadly drugs. We deplore such" (*Spencer Kimball, Ensign 1974*).

The Word of Wisdom does endorse the use of alcohol, tobacco for some external medical purposes, the external use of alcohol is common for disinfecting the skin before operations, and needle punctures. Also, Tobacco "is an herb for bruises and all sick cattle, to be used with judgment and skill" (*D&C 89:8*). In 1982, Dr. Rulon S Fracis of the Human Performance Research Center at Brigham Young University said, his research indicated, and bruises treated with tobacco juice heat 20 percent faster than untreated bruises. He was prompted to investigate the healing effect of tobacco after BYU athletic trainer, Marvin Roberson, returned from 1971 Balkan games in Yugoslavia with stories of trainers spraying a commercially manufacture tobacco spray on basketball players' bruises. The healing may be produced by one of the alkaloids found in tobacco (*Francis*).

Faithful Saints who endeavor to live the Word of Wisdom are given promises, which are well worth the efforts required to learn obedience. In Doctrine and Covenants, Joseph recorded the following: "And all saints who remember and keep and do these sayings, walking in obedience to the commandments, shall receive health in their naval and marrow to their bones; And shall find wisdom and great treasures of knowledge, even hidden treasures; And shall run and not be weary and shall walk and not faint" (*D&C 89:18-20*).

"Thus, eat properly and walk in obedience to God's commandments, and receive the gifts of physical, mental, and spiritual health. Although it appears the Lord is primarily addressing spiritual blessings in verse 20, perhaps he is also indicating here, running and walking (exercise) are natural, positive activities should engaged in regularly, and by eating properly, individuals will be more successful in these activities" (*Updike 91*). "With regards to mental development, the higher-education quotient of the Latter-day Saints is the best in the United States. This is a very important feedback loop. Proper eating makes exercise easier and proper exercise and eating improve the mental attitude and the quality and longevity of life" (*Updike 97; Rosenfeld 224, 282, 307*).

The modern day Law of Health, called the Word of Wisdom, continues to be supported by modern scientific studies. Both the do and the do not guidelines are being proven in many laboratories throughout the world. As more and more Physicians and scientists note the correlation between the LDS lifestyle and health record, increasing numbers agree with the conclusion of Dr. James E. Enstrom, UCLA epidemiologist, "They must be doing something right" (Davidson 82; emphasis in original). It is remarkable; Joseph Smith taught these principles back in 1833.

The Law of Liberty

"But whoso looketh into the perfect law of liberty, and continueth therein, he being not a forgetful hearer, but a doer of the work, this man shall be blessed in his deed" (James, 1:25).

Grasping the width and depth of this law and the attached doctrine requires, "eyes of our understanding opened" (*D&C 138:11*) and our minds "enlightened" (*D&C 6:13*) by the Spirit of the Lord. Because "where the Spirit of the Lord is there is Liberty" (2 Corinthians 3:17). This article attempts to explain how the Law of Liberty and the Doctrine Freedom are each related to the Gospel of Jesus Christ and its liberating elements, such as repentance, forgiveness, love, resurrection and, of course, the atonement. More specifically, it shows how God's law, both revealed (Devine laws of God/ commandments) and natural (Eternal Laws of God), operate in concert to develop, promote, and protect freedom. Correct principles linked with true doctrine, once understood and fully comprehended, often have a quality of clear pure simplicity. Yet, sometimes, the more you comprehend, the more depth you perceive the doctrine to hold. Like gazing into a deep pool of crystal-clear water, you may be excited and astounded to learn the pool is many, many times deeper than at first perceived. This piece of doctrine contains all of those qualities if you are willing to look deep enough. While looking into this pool of Freedom you may discover depths "never attained to previously nor ever before had thought of" (*Joseph Smith History 1:74*). Such is the doctrine of freedom. This law is closely associated with the Law of Light and the Law of Agency. The Law of Light, as a vehicle, liberates the intelligences from outer darkness and the Law of Agency provides the only method of unshackling oneself from the grasp of the 'fall" (Mosiah, 16:3).

Freedom and liberty are the major themes throughout the scriptures. James said, the Gospel is the "perfect law of liberty" (*James 1:25*). Paul told the Corinthian Saints "where the Spirit of the Lord is there is Liberty" (*2 Corinthians 3:17*) and admonished Galatian Saints to continue to "stand fast therefore in the Liberty wherewith Christ hath made us free" (*Galatians 5:1*). Christ himself told his believers, if they continued in his word they would know the truth and the "truth would set them free" (*John 8:31–32*). There are numerous scriptures portraying the idea, the purpose of the Gospel is to free man from captivity, liberate him, and with the proper exercise of free agency, exalt him (Isaiah 58: 6; Exodus 21: 2).

Freedom, as understood by probably most Americans of the Eighteenth Century, consisted of the ability to exercise what they termed inherent and inalienable rights (Declaration of Independence). These "rights" when consolidated into their basic forms consist of at least three basic rights, basic elements of freedom: Life, Liberty, and Property. Truth or Knowledge, although not mentioned by the Founding Fathers as such, can be considered another essential element of freedom. After all, was it not Christ who said, knowing the truth can set you free? (*John 8:31–32*)

Because of man's propensity to sin, error, (*Mosiah, 16:3*) or ignorance man's ability to reason what is right and wrong intellectually, morally and intuitively becomes clouded. To prevent such clouding or bewilderment God reveals to his Prophets Commandments or laws to govern conduct. Revealed law, just as Natural law, was given to man by God to enhance, protect, and promote freedom. Two examples where Revealed law clearly promotes freedom are the commandments, "Thou shalt not kill" (*Exodus, 20:13*) or "Thou shalt not steal" (*Exodus, 20:15*) plainly in protection of Life and Property respectfully. God expects man to govern his conduct by using these two standards of law, the Revealed and the Natural. Under these standards, it is easy to see why the Founders could express their attitude toward government as such: "The sole object and only legitimate end of government is to protect the citizen in the enjoyment of life, liberty and property, and when government assumes other functions it is usurpation and oppression." (*Alabama State Constitution, Article 1 Section 35*).

The Gospel of Jesus Christ, operating under the Law of Liberty, affords the liberating elements, commented on above. When a person dies, the spirit leaves the bodies. Physical death is a separation of the body from the spirit. It is the spirit animating the body and gives it life. As James puts it, "The body without the Spirit is dead" (*James 2:26*). However, James's statement has a double meaning as well. Spiritual death is a separation from the "presence" or Spirit of God. Spiritual death involves "being cut off from the presence of the Lord" (*Helaman 14:16–17*) and to be "cast out" from the Lord's "presence" (*D&C 29:41*). The Fall of Adam introduced both types of death into the world. (*Moses 6:48*). Both types of death bring captivity or an impediment to progress (*two Nephi 9:8–12*). Both kinds of death are overcome by the Atonement. The atonement of Jesus Christ redeems man from the fall and restores the body to the spirit, thus overcoming physical death (*Alma 11: 41–44*) and making it possible to overcome spiritual death by enjoying the presence of God's Spirit and capable of enjoying "Spiritual Life" (*Articles of Faith 4*). Those who refuse to repent will not receive forgiveness and surely will continue as spiritually dead. As Paul stated, "The wages of sin is death" (*Romans 6:23)* and some are "dead while they liveth." (*1 Timothy 5:6*) Alma said, those who harden their hearts against the word will be condemned to this second death, "and now behold, I say unto you then cometh a death, even a second death, which is a spiritual death; this is the time, whosoever dieth in his sins, as to a temporal death, shall also die a spiritual death, yea he shall die as to things pertaining to righteousness" (*Alma 12:16*). If an individual can overcome the second death, he will be restored to the "presence" of God and receive a spiritual or Eternal Life. It is through the Divine birth process where beings are "born again" into a "newness of life" (*Romans 6:4*). Eternal life is the ultimate freedom possible, thus, the Doctrine and Covenants state, "Wherefore, it, the body shall be sanctified; yea, notwithstanding it shall die, it shall be quickened again, and shall abide the power by which it is quickened, and the righteous shall inherit it. For notwithstanding they die, they also shall rise again, a spiritual body. They who are of a celestial spirit shall receive the same body which was a natural body; even ye shall receive your bodies, and your glory shall be that glory by which your bodies are quickened." Each of the liberating elements of Law of Liberty, repentance, forgiveness, love, resurrection and the atonement, provides the opportunity to enjoy the fullness of the gospel, and only the love of Christ through the atonement that makes this all possible" (*D&C 88: 26–29*).

As stated above, the Law of Agency provides the only method of unshackling oneself from the grasp of the 'fall" (Mosiah, 16:3).

Agency, in terms of the Law of Liberty.

If the law, both Natural and Divine, is designed to promote, enhance and protect freedom, then men's actions in relation to freedom can be used as a standard to judge those actions. In fact, President David O. Mckay said, the freedom to use agency is a measuring rod to judge all the actions of men. Agency and freedom was two of the principal issues to arise in the pre-mortal Council in Heaven. They were the main causes of the conflict between the followers of Christ and the followers of Satan. Satan said, "Behold, here am I, send me, I will be thy son, and I will redeem all mankind, that one soul shall not be lost, and surely I will do it; wherefore give me thine honor" (*Moses 4:1*). In saying this, he "rebelled against God and sought to destroy the agency of man" (*Moses 4:3*) one wonders what Satan could have meant by "I will redeem all mankind, that one soul shall not be lost" (Moses 4; 1&2). It is usually assumed, Satan was going to force everyone back into the presence of God. This is the total loss of liberty and a complete violation of the Law of Liberty since all mortals would be in bondage to Satan. In 2 Nephi chapter 2, Nephi says, without agency nothing that is known to exist would have ever existed for there would not be any point. This sheds a much more serious light on Satan's plan, than just being argument over who gets God's honor. Jesus, on the other hand, obeyed the

Law of Liberty and agency and the same use of liberty and agency still exists.

"For the natural man is an enemy to God, and has been from the fall of Adam, and will be, forever and ever, unless he yields to the enticing's of the Holy Spirit, and putteth off the natural man and becometh a saint through the atonement of Christ the Lord, and becometh as a child, submissive, meek, humble, patient, full of love, willing to submit to all things which the Lord seeth fit to inflict upon him, even as a child doth submit to his father" (*Mosiah 3:19*).

THE LAW OF LIGHT
(Taken in part from an article by Rick Brunson & Argonne National Laboratory)

This law is extremely difficult to understand since the word "light" is used in so many circumstances, both secular and spiritual, and is so often used as an allegory to explain certain situations, but few of these discussions, either religious or secular really explain, or even try to explain, LIGHT as a Law of God and what it really is. In Genesis, God said, "Let there be light", and then there was light. As a novice in the church, this seemed to mean, the radiance shining down on us from the sun during the day was somehow, turned on. It was supposed, God was doing this in order to complete the creation. Then the scriptures revealed, Jesus is "light", "I am the light of the world" (*John 8:12*). Further, on in the scriptures it was revealed, God is "light. "That which is of God is light; and he that receiveth light, and continueth in God, receiveth more light; and that light groweth brighter and brighter until the perfect day" (*D&C 50:24*). Also found in the scriptures, intelligence and truth is light, "the glory of God is intelligence, or, in other words, light and truth. "Such light and truth forsake the evil one" (*D&C 93:36–37*). Light is also in us, "Then shall ye know that ye have seen me, that I am, and that I am the true light that is in you, and that you are in me; otherwise ye could not abound" (*D&C 88:49–50*). Somewhere along the way it starts to sink in, there is more to this light issue than originally thought. Now, after many years in the church, there is a clear distinction between physical light and spiritual light and it is now known, God did not pull some prototype machine out of His garage and flip it on so the sun would light up. But, it is obvious from this very small sampling of references (of which there are literally thousands) these lessons and talks are not dealing with any clear explanation or understanding of the Law of Light, they are correctly talk about light in terms of their specific subject matter but not about the essence of the law itself.

The scripture, known as "the olive leaf": "The Light of Christ "proceedeth forth from the presence of God to fill the immensity of space." It is "the light which is in all things, which giveth life to all things, which is the law by which all things are governed" (*D&C 88: 12&13*). Upon reading this, many have thought WHAT ON EARTH DOES THIS MEAN. This is not any light, or anything about light, commonly preached from the pulpit. In effort to start to get a grip on this, there is this very important scripture.

"Which glory is that of the church of the Firstborn, even of God, the holiest of all, through Jesus Christ his Son— He that ascended up on high, as also he descended below all things, in that he comprehended all things, that he might be in all and through all things, the light of truth; Which truth shineth. This is the light of Christ. As also, he is in the sun, and the light of the sun, and the power thereof by which it was made. As also, he is in the moon, and is the light of the moon, and the power thereof by which it was made. As also, the light of the stars, and the power thereof by which they were made. And the earth also, and the power thereof, even the earth upon which you stand. And the light which shineth, which giveth you light, is through him who enlighteneth your eyes, which is the same light that quickeneth your understandings; which light proceedeth forth from the presence of God to fill the immensity of space. The light which is in all things, which giveth life to all things, which is the law by which all things are governed, even the power of God who sitteth upon his throne, who is in the bosom of eternity, who is in the midst of all things. Now, verily I say unto you, that through the redemption which is made for you is brought to pass the resurrection from the dead" (*D&C88*).

People often say, "The Light of Christ" is synonymous with the Law of Light. While this is certainly true, the purpose in writing this section is to draw a distinction between the Light of Christ and the Law of Light, which is being done in this manner; Light of Christ is the thing, given or administered by Christ and the Law of Light is the overarching law governing the use of light. It is not possible to talk about the Law of Light without talking about the Light of Christ. Do not let this mixture create confusion as you read this section.

With this in mind endeavor to understand the scripture D&C 88: 5-14, Verse 6 of this scripture says, before Christ began the process of creating all things known, He, with the help of God, (verse 5) had to go through some sort of learning curve. (This is also stated in (D&C 93; 13), "And He received not of the fullness at first, but continued from grace to grace, until he received a fullness" in order to obtain the Light God possesses (verse 12), and have light proceed forth through Him and fill the immensity of space where the creation was to take place and, all the heavenly bodies were made employing the power of this light (verses8-11). Verse 13 explains why this light was necessary. It is the power of God and is the law governing all things, even God. Without Christ being in possession of this light and imparted it into all that was created, the planets would not stay in orbit, life would not exist, (D&C 88: 50) "Then shall ye know that ye have seen me, that I am, and that I am the true light that is in you, and that you are in me; otherwise ye could not abound", in other words we, nor anything else would have never existed. Then in verse 14, it is not just the creation, light governs. It is also the governing proviso which brings about atonement, justification, redemption, and resurrection. Then mortals are taught, this light from within can be enlarged, "That which is of God is light; and he that receiveth light, and continueth in God, receiveth more light; and that light groweth brighter and brighter until the perfect day" (D&C50:24). "and, if your eye be single to my glory, your whole bodies shall be filled with light, and there shall be no darkness in you; and that body which is filled with light comprehendeth all things" (*D&C 88: 67*).

OK, summarizing what was just learned: Light is an important attribute encompassing the power of creation for it is the law governing everything. This is the light, God possesses, and He passed this attribute along to Jehovah. With the ability to govern all things Christ now has the capacity to create this universe and all that is in it. In addition, Christ must impart some of this light into all living things, which includes everything He created. Without this light transfer, God to Christ and Christ onto His creations the process would never have happened since all of the newly created entities (which are made up of organized intelligences) would not be obedient to the governing power. Additionally, everything in the creation chain must participate in the experience since all are going to be judged in the end. After this small amount of light is instilled into all those receiving life and during their life, this portion of light can be expanded by edifying God until such time they comprehend all things. This Law of Light governs all progression of all things in all realms from beginning to end.

Now the scholarly still do not know exactly what this light really is and probably never know but many are closer to understanding the law of Light. It is normal think of a law as a set of rules but in this case, that sort of reasoning does not seem to be completely relevant since, clearly there is more to this law than just a set of rules. It seems the Law of Light is something of a coexistence or empowerment, in many ways it is similar to the Priesthood although, obviously, it is not the Priesthood but is similar in many ways, a few are listed below.

1. Priesthood has power---same with the light.

2. Priesthood has capacity---same with light.

3. The Priesthood is authority --- same with light.

4. Priesthood is ratified by God---same with light.

5. Priesthood is necessary for some things--- same with light.

6. Priesthood is passed along---same with light.

7. Priesthood is spiritual---same with light.

8. Priesthood is held by Deity--- same with light.

9. A Priesthood holder can advance toward God---same with light.

10. Priesthood has governance---same with light. Priesthood is eternal--- same   with light.

Having looked at, and discussed some relevant scriptures concerning the Law of Light and taking them on their face value and have summarized their meaning which presented a good foundation and understanding of this law. Now is a good time to take those same scripture and others and examine them from a more analytical viewpoint.

This subject, the law of Light, starts to unfold, with events taking place prior to creation. Any examination of the subject needs to start there. First, in God's realm, there are two kinds of space mentioned in the scriptures, unorganized space, and organized space. Within the organized space resides the universe, as currently known. As related in the scriptures, Jehovah, who now has "God status" (*D&C 88:5&6*) had some space available which needed to be organized and the material from which to build the universe. "We will go down, for there is space there ... and we will make an earth whereon these [the spirit children of Father in Heaven] may dwell" (*Abraham 3:24*). This never ending space existed forever with no bounds in any direction is referred to as unorganized space, conversely, what is call organized space exists within the confines of Jehovah's calling. This unorganized space is filled with what the Lord calls unorganized intelligences (*D&C 93:29*) and Christ needed to organize these intelligences so they could become the spirit children of God. There is not much known about intelligences; however, what is known is, they have agency and the ability to act, think, move, communicate, etc. Orson Pratt explained, "There is no substance in the universe which feels and thinks now, but what has eternally possessed that capacity" (*the Seer*).

The Lord also explains, these intelligences cannot be "created or made" (*D&C 93:29*). In other words, they have existed and will exist forever. Joseph Smith taught this principle when he said, "Element had an existence from the time [God] had. The pure principles of element are principles, which can never be destroyed; they may be organized and re-organized, but not destroyed. They had no beginning, and can have no end" (*Teachings of the Prophet Joseph Smith, p. 350*)

Therefore, the unorganized space is filled with these unorganized intelligences. The Lord goes into unorganized space, and gathers these intelligences. He then gives them laws (D&C 88:42) which they may choose to follow. If they are obedient to these laws, then they are brought into organized space along with other intelligences. This is really the beginning of the creation and this allows them, the intelligences who have received a portion of light from Christ, to progress in their existence. The Law of light is the law, which governs the process that is underway, therefore, the laws the intelligences need to obey is the same Eternal laws mortals have to obey, I.E. the law of gravity, the law of eternal progression, and so on. They can be organized into water particles, rocks, plant or animal life, human beings, in short everything existing in the known universe and presumable all the universes. They are first organized into spirit matter, (D&C 131:7-8) then, if they continue to be obedient to Gods laws, they are organized into some sort of physical matter based on their level of obedience. The intelligences outside of organized universe are constantly being brought into the organized universe, where they are organized and able to progress (God is eternal and this is part of the eternal process). Everything, within the organized universe, is constructed of individual intelligences, which have been organized together, "intelligence cleaveth unto intelligence" (D&C 88:40). It is in this way, God has organized everything in the universe.

As Brigham Young said, "There is not a particle of element, which is not filled with life, and all space is filled with element; there is no such thing as empty space, though some philosophers contend that there is" (*discourses of Brigham Young*).

Among these intelligences, some have progressed further than others have (Abraham. 3:10). Since each intelligence has, agency and can choose to obey or disobey Father in heaven. If it obeys, it will progress by becoming organized along with other intelligences; however, if these intelligences do not obey, they will not progress. This is the very reason why some intelligences have progressed, and will continue to progress further than others will. For instance, we, as mortals, are all intelligences who have progressed to this existing state (mortality). All mortals accomplished this by living a very high level of obedience to God and His laws. Some intelligences did not exercise the same level of obedience, and were therefore organized in other ways, for instance, as a plant, animal, or even a microorganism. In the pre-existence, the intelligences who were the most obedient were able to progress the furthest and were given spirit bodies in the image of Father in Heaven; this group includes all of us. After being organized as a spirit body, all found worthy were given the option of progressing even further by coming to earth and receiving a physical body, which if faithful, will be resurrected to a celestial body like Father in Heaven's. The Lord told Abraham, spirits were "added upon" again, when they came to earth and received physical bodies" (*Abraham. 3:26*). (At the end of the section there is an interesting article related to Abraham 3:26) In other words, during physical birth, the particles, having received the light, make up spirits, unite with the particles, which also have received light, and these two creations together make up physical or mortal bodies and they have to live in alliance with each other. If, while in this state of mortality this couplet can, through the correct use of agency, demonstrate obedience to God's laws (commandments) they can receive more light to the point of comprehending all things (Celestial status). In other words, obedience, the level of light obtained in the preexistence, determined the mortal's circumstances upon arrival in mortality and the level of obedience in mortality determines the situation in worlds to come. This is the great secret of progression within Gods kingdom. (D&C 93:28). Living the Devine Laws of God (commandments) generates progression and The Law of Light governs the cumulative reward. These two are inextricably connected in terms of eternal progression.

As Elder Orson Pratt said, "We cannot find a law throughout universal space, but what light has something to do with it" (*Journal of Discourses, 15:2310*).

As discussed in the scriptures, there is a place where there is no light and no law, that place is called outer darkness. Outer darkness and unorganized space are one and the same place. The intelligences outside the organized universe, have either not had the chance, or they have deliberately chosen not to obey Father in Heaven, thus restricting their progress. Outside the organized universe, there is no law, and therefore no light. Joseph Smith said, not even the Spirit of the Lord dwells there. (Journal of Discourses, 4:266). Also known, from the scriptures, it is possible to sin unto death while in mortality. Meaning, those who have committed such greaves sins due to their disobedience of God's laws will be returned to outer darkness. One last point, God is constant in His dealing with His children, so it logical to believe, when these intelligences agree to obey the law and receive the Light of Christ, this is done through covenant just as a covenant was also made by all who come into mortality. It is through these agreements and others, mortal's progress, either toward their final glory or to outer darkness, and their progression will be governed by the Law of Light, from then on.

On a side note about this *added upon concept of Abraham*, There is this article about a study conducted by Northwestern University and Argonne National Laboratory on the events that take place in the womb when the egg is fertilized by the sperm. This article can be compared to the scripture in (Abraham 3:26) where the Lord is talking about the connective bond that takes place when the spiritual and physical matter meets (presumable during conception) and the light that is involved in that connection. This *spark of light* at conception and the intensity of that light as it relates to the health of the embryo is very intriguing to say the least. This study does not add or subtract anything from the scriptural Law of Light, the doctrinal concept of light or even the religious belief in the creative process but further scientific studies may indeed give some secular credence to religious belief.

Wednesday, December 14th posted by Argonne National Laboratory, Evanston Ill,

Sparks latterly fly when an egg and a sperm hit it off. The fertilized mammalian egg releases from its surface billions of zinc atoms in "zinc sparks," one wave after another, a Northwestern University-led interdisciplinary research team has found. Using cutting-edge technology, they developed, the team is the first to capture images of these molecular fireworks, and pinpoint the origin of the zinc sparks tiny zinc-rich packages just below the egg's surface. Zinc fluctuations play a central role in regulating the biochemical processes that ensure a healthy egg-to-embryo transition, and this new unprecedented quantitative information should be useful in improving in vitro fertilization methods. "The amount of zinc released by an egg could be a great marker for identifying a high-quality fertilized egg, something we can't do now," said Teresa K. Woodruff, an expert in ovarian biology and one of two corresponding authors of the study. "If we can identify the best eggs, fewer embryos would need to be transferred during fertility treatments. Our findings will help move us toward this goal."

Woodruff is a Thomas J. Watkins Memorial Professor in Obstetrics and Gynecology and director of the Women's Health Research Institute at Northwestern University Feinberg School of Medicine.

The study is published today (Dec. 15) by the Journal Nature Chemistry, provides the first quantitative physical measurements of zinc localization in single cells in a mammal. The research team, including experts from the U.S. Department of Energy's Advanced Photon Source (APS), developed a suite of four physical methods to determine how much zinc there is in an egg and where it is located at the time of fertilization and in the two hours just after. Sensitive imaging methods allowed the researchers to see and count individual zinc atoms in egg cells and visualize zinc spark waves in three dimensions.

After inventing a novel vital fluorescent sensor for live-cell zinc tracking, scientists discovered close to 8,000 compartments in the egg, each containing approximately one million zinc atoms. These packages release their zinc cargo simultaneously in a concerted process, akin to neurotransmitter release in the brain or insulin release in the pancreas. These findings were further confirmed with chemical methods that trap cellular zinc stores and enable zinc mapping on the nanometer scale in a custom-designed electron microscope developed for this project with funding from the W.M. Keck Foundation. Additional high-energy X-ray imaging experiments at the APS synchrotron at Argonne National Laboratory enabled the scientists to precisely map the location of zinc atoms in two and three dimensions.

"On cue, at the time of fertilization, we see the egg release thousands of packages, each dumping a million zinc atoms, and then it's quiet," said Thomas V. O'Halloran, the other corresponding author. "Then there is another burst of zinc release. Each egg has four or five of these periodic sparks. It is beautiful to see, orchestrated much like a symphony. We knew zinc was released by the egg in huge amounts, but we had no idea how the egg did this."

O'Halloran is a Charles E. and Emma H. Morrison Professor in Chemistry in the Weinberg College of Arts and Sciences and director of Northwester's Chemistry of Life Processes Institute.

The study establishes how eggs compartmentalize and distribute zinc to control the developmental processes that allow the egg to become a healthy embryo. Zinc is part of a master switch that controls the decision to grow and change into a completely new genetic organism. The studies reported in Nature Chemistry are the culmination of six years of work and build on prior discoveries made by the Woodruff and O'Halloran labs using data from work performed at Northwestern and the APS. In previous studies in mouse eggs, this research team discovered the egg's tremendous zinc requirement for reaching maturity. In addition, the researchers determined that an egg loses 10 billion of its 60 billion zinc atoms upon fertilization in a series of four or five waves called "zinc sparks." Release of zinc sparks from the egg is essential for embryo formation in the two hours following fertilization.

"The egg first has to stockpile zinc and then must release some of the zinc to successfully navigate maturation, fertilization and the start of embryogenesis," O'Halloran said. "But exactly how much zinc is involved in this remarkable process and where is it in the cell? We needed data to better understand the molecular mechanisms at work as an egg becomes a new organism."

One major hurdle O'Halloran and Woodruff faced was the lack of sensitive methods for measuring zinc in single cells. To address this problem, they formed a collaborative team with other researchers in Northwester's Chemistry of Life Processes Institute to develop the tools they needed.

Key members of the team were Vinayak P. Dravid, the Abraham Harris Professor of Materials Science and Engineering at the McCormick School of Engineering and Applied Science, and Stefan Vogt, a physicist and group leader of microscopy at the Advanced Photon Source. Dravid and Vogt are co-authors of the paper.

"We had to develop a slew of methods to be convinced we were seeing the right thing," O'Halloran said. "Science is about testing and retesting ideas. All of our complementary results point to the same conclusion: the zinc originates in packages called vesicles near the cell's surface."

The researchers currently are working to see if they can correlate zinc sparks with egg quality, information that would be key to improving fertility treatments.

Not only are these new imaging techniques important for describing the zinc spark, they can be applied to other cells that likely use zinc in a similar way, but whose workings remain elusive due to the lack of sensitive and specific tools. This study lays the groundwork for understanding how zinc fluxes can regulate events in multiple biological systems beyond the egg, including neurotransmission from zinc-enriched neurons in the brain and insulin-release in the pancreas.

The National Institutes of Health, Eunice Kennedy Shriver National Institute of Child Health, and Human Development (grant U54HD076188) and the W.M. Keck Foundation supported the research.

The title of the paper is "Quantitative mapping of zinc fluxes in the mammalian egg reveals the origin of fertilization-induced zinc sparks."

In addition to O'Halloran, Woodruff, Dravid and Vogt, other authors of the paper are lead author Emily L. Que, Reiner Bleher, Francesca E. Duncan, Betty Y. Kong, Seth A. Garwin and Amanda R. Bayer, of Northwestern; and Sophie C. Gleber and Si Chen, of Argonne National Laboratory.

Law of Retribution

When all is said and done, People classify all the undesirable acts, which is possible for men to perform during their mortal probation, into two categories, one; undesirable acts, which one can be prevent or alter with some sort of force, and two, other acts which one can choose not to alter but to tolerate. It is in the drawing of this line between those acts and omissions, some are condemned and others are not, and it is, to some extent, that freedom in the hereafter is determined. God had instituted governments here on earth to execute His divine law of retribution by taking some element of freedom from those who destroy the freedom of others. Is there any personal role in the execution of the Law of Retribution? It is interesting to observe how this Law of Retribution was received and executed by those on earth when this law was introduced into their culture. Later in this article, an examination of how this law of retribution operates in the hereafter. The first written record of the Lord being involved with prosomal reprisals was in the Old Testament when the Law of Retribution was introduced to the Israelites by Moses (Ex.21: 23-25). (This is the Eye for an eye, tooth for tooth idea) This entire section deals with the proper way to deal justly with those people living and doing business around Israelites during and after the time of Moses, but, more specifically, verses 23 through 25 deals with those instances where violent damage was inflicted upon a person and what level of retribution was acceptable. What the scriptures do not reveal is who the Lord intended to be the righter of wrongs. During the time when this law was given there was a tremendous amount of aggression and war in the lives of these spiritually immature Israelites and, as the historical record reveals, the Israelites believed they were the ones appointed to carry out the punishment. In order for the Israelites to continue with this acts of retribution, as they did for almost a thousand years, they had to ignore the passage in (Deuteronomy 19:21) where the Lord says "To me belongeth vengeance and recompense". In some of these retribution cases the punishment was executed, oft times without a trial, by the damaged party or his family personally, and, as the historical record also reveals, this sometimes got out of hand and with deadly consequences. Of course, it should be understood, during this time in history, the Israelites lived in very rural environment and were pretty much on their own. They did not have the luxury of a strong justice system, nor the advancement of law enforcement, or a penal system like exists today. When the Savior came among the Jews, He challenged them for their behavior on this subject and gave a new law, instead of exacting eye-for-eye-tooth-for-tooth, the savior said, God's children were to turn the other cheek, give more than is required by law. Go the second mile willingly even after being compelled to go the first mile, and lend to those who ask with usury. Then He gave another law instructing mankind to love those who harm and hate you. In fact, the scriptures emphasize, repeatedly, mankind will be judged according to their treatment of their fellow men. "If we are charitable, we will be placed with the sheep in the Lord's kingdom rather than with the goats in outer darkness" (*Matt. 25:31-46*). "If we forgive, we may be forgiven" (*Matt. 6: 12*). Moreover, in Romans12, the Paul gave them a complete set of rules concerning the dealing of them with their fellow man. In short, people can expect to be treated in the next life as they treated others here. Thus, as stated above, the extent of personal freedom in the hereafter is somewhat determined by the line drawn when dealing with those who commit undesirable acts. If, in their lives, those who draw the line incorrectly will be found failing in their requirements of obedience by the Lord and will be dealt with in the hereafter. So, how and when does the Law of Retribution come in play and what does all this mean? Some say, the Lord found the law, as given to the Jews by Moses, unjust and revoked the law of retribution. Can this be true? The answer is no, He did not. The Law of Retribution is an eternal law of God which cannot be revoked or annulled and is still as fixed and eternal as are all of the other laws of the Almighty. There will be a day of retribution but certainly not by individuals taking it upon themselves to be the ministers of God's vengeance; for then they themselves would become the punishers and murderers and therefore subject to retribution themselves. "Dearly beloved, avenge not yourselves, but rather give place unto wrath: for it is written, Vengeance is mine; I will repay, saith the Lord" (*Rom.12:19*), and therefore this matter of retribution for offences committed must be left with God and those agencies He shall ordain to administer it. These, in part, are the secular governments who under law have provided severe punishments for crimes against people and for some of the more heinous crimes against society and government, such as murder in the first degree, etc. some have even instituted the death penalty. Therefore, the church is commanded to give up those who need to be dealt with according to the law of the land and in the 12th Article of Faith it says "We believe in being subject to kings, presidents, rulers, and magistrates, in obeying, honoring, and sustaining the law". From this, It is learned, the Church is not in the business of retribution at all, even when the matters are of the most serious nature. President Joseph Fielding Smith wrote, "The law of retribution is often slow, but it is sure. The Lord promised to punish his enemies and mete out to them suitable reward for all the evil they had heaped upon his servants. Punishment for sin does not always follow in this mortal life; the greater part of any reparation is generally held in reserve for a future day, therefore records must be kept on earth as well as in heaven as the Lord commanded". D&C Section 123 deals with this issue in detail. For those who still believe they have some roll to play in administrating retribution, and there are some, be warned. Take for instance those who seek a personal solution for crimes committed against them, sometimes it can be as simple as the occurrence of a situation they disagree with, they general do not publicly refer the Old Testament's, eye for an eye law as their motive to act. Nevertheless, they are participating in a misguided form of retribution which is rightfully called revenge. In fact, the Lord has explained, in seeking retribution, even in the smallest way, such as backbiting or gossiping about a disliked neighbor; this is a violation of His commandments. Personal behavior is spelled out in the following scripture.

"That the rights of the priesthood are inseparably connected with the powers of heaven, and that the powers of heaven cannot be controlled nor handled only upon the principles of righteousness. That they may be conferred upon us, it is true; but when we undertake to cover our sins, or to gratify our pride, our vain ambition, or to exercise control or dominion or compulsion upon the souls of the children of men, in any degree of unrighteousness, behold, the heavens withdraw themselves; the Spirit of the Lord is grieved; and when it is withdrawn, Amen to the priesthood or the authority of that man. No power or influence can or ought to be maintained by virtue of the priesthood, only by persuasion, by long-suffering, by gentleness and meekness, and by love unfeigned" (*D&C 121:36-37 &41*).

Mortals are to demonstrate all the virtues listed above but it is very difficult for men to be long-suffering, gentle, meek, forgiving and love mankind and demonstrate feelings of reprisals at the same time. In addition, people are also instructed in their behavior in terms of forgiveness in the following scripture. "Wherefore, I say unto you, that ye ought to forgive one another; for he that forgiveth not his brother his trespasses standeth condemned before the Lord; for there remaineth in him the greater sin. I, the Lord, will forgive whom I will forgive, but of you, it is required to forgive all men" (*D&C 64:9-11*).

What the Lord is saying, He will forgive or punish as He sees fit but mortals are commanded to only forgive, and not to attempt to get even, condemn or even find fault in any way. If a person does not forgive another person, they are committing a sin far greater than the sin the other person committed, no matter what the first sinner did.

There are others who believe that their earthly misfortunes are a result of God seeking retribution against them for some sin they have committed. These groups are thoroughly mistaken. Retribution is reserved by Deity for the purposes of the final judgment and, as far as it is known, is never dispensed during mortality even in the smallest way, for this would be a blatant violation of agency.

The Law of Sacrifice

In the secular world, the rational principle of conduct is, always act in accordance with the hierarchy of your values, and never sacrifice a greater value to a lesser one. Without such a hierarchy, neither rational conduct, considered value judgments nor moral choices are possible. This applies to all choices, including one's actions toward all others. However, in the kingdom of God, sacrifice is the exact opposite of this principle since it involves the surrendering of something of a greater value for the sake of a lesser one or of a nonvalue. Thus, unselfishness gauges a man's virtue by the degree to which he surrenders those things of value and the circumstances under which they are surrendered. As an example, helping a stranger or an enemy is regarded as more virtuous and less selfish than helping those one loves. For instance, in Luke 10:25-37, There is the story of the Good Samaritan. In this story, the Samaritan helps a man who has been robbed and beaten and who is of a different social class, and obviously, there is not any chance of repayment or reward. His deed would be regarded a most honorable act, Sacrifice does not mean the rejection of the evil for the sake of the good, but of the providing of good for the sake of the evil. Sacrifice does not mean the rejection of the worthless, but of the precious and is always the surrender of things, which is valued in favor of things, which are not. Here are some examples; if a person gives money to help a friend, this may not constitute a sacrifice; but, if given it to a worthless stranger, it is and this action makes the giver worthy of an increase in virtue. If a person gives a friend or a church a sum they can afford, it is not a sacrifice; if they give the money at the cost of their own discomfort, it is only beget partial virtue. According to this sort of moral standard, if valuables are given at the cost of disaster to oneself—that is true sacrifice, and worthy of virtue in full. This is exemplified in the New Testament. "Looking at him, Jesus felt a love for him and said to him, One thing you lack: go and sell all you possess and give to the poor, and you will have treasure in heaven; and come, follow Me" (*Mark 10:21*). If you renounce all personal desires and dedicate your life to those you love, you do not achieve full virtue: you retain a value of your own, which is your love. If you devote your life to random strangers, it is an act of greater virtue. If you devote your life to serving those, you hate—that is the greatest of the virtues you can practice. When the scriptures expresses that there must be opposition in all things, "For it must needs be, that there is an opposition in all things" --- (*2 Nephi 2:11*). The concept the text above has been talking about is the rational principle of conduct, and is the way of the natural man and the God's Law of Sacrifice is its opposite. It is living the Law of Sacrifice and the torment felt when being tested in these circumstances, people either rise or fall when faced with this opposition. While knowing, man cannot obtain perfect virtue while in this mortal world and a person can never be completely righteous, but they must try to be as successful as possible. The examples of great sacrifice given above are acts, considered most virtuous. Seldom, will a person find himself in a position, requiring a full level of philanthropy. Most personal sacrifices gain smaller amounts of virtue but never the less God requires sacrifice of all of his people both to make and renew covenants with him and to test their ultimate loyalties (D&C 98:12-15). When the Lord drove Adam and Eve from the Garden of Eden, he gave them the law of sacrifice, whereby they were to offer the firstlings of their flocks to him (Moses 5:5). From the beginning, offerings to the Lord involved the shedding of blood were in similitude of the future sacrifice of Jesus Christ, who would come to atone for the sins of mankind (Moses 5:6-8). The Book of Mormon includes accounts of Lehi's people making burnt offerings in compliance with the Law of Moses (1 Ne. 5:9; Mosiah 2:3).

With the sacrifice of Jesus, "the performances and ordinances of the Law of Moses" were fulfilled (*4 Ne. 1:12*), and his death ended the practice of sacrifices on an altar. To his disciples in the western continents, Jesus said he would no longer accept burnt offerings, but anyone who believes in him should offer a broken heart and a contrite spirit (3 Ne. 9:19-20; D&C 59:8).

For members of The Church of Jesus Christ of Latter-day Saints, sacrifice is required of those who wish to become the Lord's people (D&C 64:23). All are invited to come to Christ, rather than to a sacrificial altar-with humble, teachable spirits and repentant hearts, willing to sacrifice all things for the Lord and for one another (Mosiah 18:8-9). The Prophet Joseph Smith taught, only a religion that requires total sacrifice has power sufficient to produce the faith necessary for salvation (Lectures on Faith 6:5-7). To appreciate the need to sacrifice, one need only recall Jesus' words to the rich young ruler: "Sell all that thou hast, and distribute unto the poor…and come, follow me" (*Luke 18:22*).

Covenants made by Church members embrace the commitment to sacrifice all for the kingdom of God. Examples of willingness to sacrifice are legion among early Latter-day Saints who sacrificed homes, comforts, and even their lives for their beliefs. Prior to his martyrdom, Joseph Smith knew, he was going as "a lamb to the slaughter" (*D&C 135:4*). Sacrifices made by Mormon pioneers to establish the Church in the western United States have become legendary. In addition, sacrifices are still required of Latter-day Saints. For instance, contribute financially to mission funds, and give fast offerings for the poor. Missionaries spend one or two years preaching the gospel at their own or their families' expense while delaying education, employment, marriage, or retirement. Members serve their congregations without pay and they accept lay positions making it possible to operate all Church programs. It is service to others through formal callings and through personal concern for their welfare, which leads Church members to know, "sacrifice brings forth the blessings of heaven" (*Hymns, p. 27*).

The atonement of Jesus Christ is the central doctrine of Christianity, and all other Christian doctrines come out of and are appendages to it. Not only can these other doctrines be connected back to the Savior and His Atoning Sacrifice, but also if they are not, "there will be no life nor substance nor redemption in them," to use a phrase by (*President Boyd K. Packer*), an apostle of The Church of Jesus Christ of Latter-day Saints.

It is therefore not only important, but also necessary, when studying any doctrine, teaching, or appendage of the gospel of Jesus Christ, to connect it back to Jesus Christ and His eternal sacrifice.

When Adam and Eve were driven out of the Garden of Eden, they were commanded, "that they should worship the Lord their God, and should offer the firstlings of their crops and flocks, for an offering unto the Lord" (*Moses 5:5*). Yet M. Russell Ballard, another apostle of the Church, has said, some have wondered, "How could the slaughtering of an animal upon an altar have anything to do with the gospel of love" (*The Law of Sacrifice,*" *Ensign, Oct 1998, 7*)?

It can easier to understand the answer to this question when by understanding the two major purposes for the law of sacrifice. These purposes applied to Adam, Abraham, Moses, and the New Testament Apostles, and they apply to all today as the saints accept and live the law of sacrifice. The two major purposes of the law of sacrifice are to test and prove mortals and to assist them in coming unto Christ.

To Test and Prove;

"And we will prove them herewith, to see if they will do all the things whatsoever the Lord God shall command them" (Abraham 3:25). This is the test, mortals must obey all the commandments, which includes, obedience to the Law of Sacrifice.

"Adam was obedient unto the commandments of the Lord" (*Moses 5:5*). He offered up the firstlings of his flocks. This was not easy, especially in an era when one lived off their land and flocks. All of their harvests were very valuable possessions. It is important to realize, they, Adam and Eve, were to offer up a portion of their means, weather it was an animal or a portion of the crops they harvested. In addition, if they were not burdened enough, Adam and Eve did not even know why they were offering sacrifices. The record says, "after many days an angel of the Lord appeared unto Adam, saying: Why dost thou offer sacrifices unto the Lord? Adam said unto him, "I know not, save the Lord commanded me" (Moses 5:6). Sometimes it is necessary to start to obey a commandment in this same manner. Like Adam and Eve, members of the church are also asked to sacrifice. Most of people nowadays do not have any firstlings or first fruits to give up (though, the law was changed after Jesus Christ made the ultimate sacrifice anyway). Mortals are, however, being tried and proved, and sometimes a person "must learn to walk a few steps ahead into the darkness, and then the light will turn on and go before them," as Boyd K. Packer has written. Adam and Eve took a few steps into the darkness. They did not know why they were asked to give sacrifices, but they did it anyway. This is the process whereby God's children are tested and proved, where they are also asked to give up some of their means just as in the days of Adam and Eve.

To assist God's children in coming unto Christ

Now, notice, as the record continues, how Adam and Eve received a witness after the trial of their faith and were taught concerning the second of the two main purposes of the law of sacrifice, "to assist God's children in coming unto Christ" (*Ether 12:6*).

The record reads,

"Then the angel spake saying: This sacrifice is a similitude of the sacrifice of the Only Begotten of the Father, which is full of grace and truth" (*Moses 5:5*).

"Wherefore, thou shalt do all that thou doest in the name of the Son, and thou shalt repent and call upon God in the name of the Son forevermore" (*Moses 5:7-8*).

The righteous posterity of Adam continued to offer sacrifices, down to the children of Israel. Yet, one thing remained the same in all of these offerings: everything about Mosaic sacrifice focused on Christ. Like Christ, the priest acted as the mediator between the people and their God. Like Christ, the priest had to have the right parentage to officiate in his office. Like Christ, the offeror, through obedience, willingly sacrificed what was required by the law, meaning the Law of Moses.

Hence, the purpose of the Law of Moses was to persuade God's children "to look forward unto the Messiah, and believe in him to come as though he already was" (*Jerome 1:11*). In Old Testament times they conducted all ordinances in the similitude of Christ, since Christ was alive and after His death all ordinances are performed in the "name of Christ', but the ordinances remain the same.

About 74 years before Christ, Alma wrote, after the Saviors ultimate sacrifice the Law of Moses (not the law of sacrifice, for these two are not exactly the same thing) would be done away. He said,

"It is expedient that there should be a great and last sacrifice, and then shall there be, or it is expedient there should be, a stop to the shedding of blood; then shall the Law of Moses be fulfilled; yea, it shall be all fulfilled, every jot and title, and none shall have passed away. And, behold, this is the whole meaning of the law, every whit pointing to that great and last sacrifice; and that great and last sacrifice will be the Son of God, yea, infinite and eternal. And thus he shall bring salvation to all those who shall believe on his name; this being the intent of this last sacrifice, to bring about the bowels of mercy, which overpowereth justice, and bringeth about means unto men that they may have faith unto repentance" (Alma 34:13-15).

God loves us. He "doeth not do anything save it be for the benefit of the world" (*2 Nephi 26:24*). He gives His children laws and commandments pointing them to Christ. Giving up what a possession for the sake of something better is not easy. Sacrifice never was easy. It tries the faith, like all other doctrines of the Gospel of Jesus Christ, connects back, and brings people closer to the Savior.

While the Law of Moses was done away with, the law of sacrifice was not. Those who lived before Christ looked forward to Him as though He had already come. Today, it is looking back with a "broken heart and a contrite spirit" (*3 Nephi 9:20*).

Indeed, as Neal A. Maxwell, an apostle of the Church, has said, "Real, personal sacrifice never was placing an animal on the altar. Instead, it is a willingness to put the animal in us upon the altar and letting it be consumed!" (*Neal Maxwell, Gen conference 1995*).

Tithing, or tithe, means a tenth part of a person's increase. The paying of tithing to the Lord and His church has been a commandment for thousands of years. The first record of tithing is found in (Genesis 14:20), where Abraham paid tithing to Melchizedek. In the biblical days of the Lord's church, tithing was considered not only a commandment but also the law of the land. The question is, does the act of obeying any commandment represent sacrifice? Think of it this way, when living the commandment "thou shalt not kill", does that mean, refraining from killing people is a sacrifice?

So what are we ask, to sacrifice? A broken heart and a contrite spirit, nothing more.

The Law of Sufficient Reasoning
(Belief in God)

Scientific and religious theists use the law of sufficient reason as a litmus test for their theories. The law of sufficient reason simply says, as folks try to figure out this complex existence, all personal views postulated have to be, not only reasonable but also, sufficiently reasonable for others to believe in their theories. We, as religious people, postulate, there is a God and God created everything in the universe. The scientific community opposes this view and presents theories to persuade others, their beliefs are correct. In order for them to change other people's belief they must present, not just a reason but also, but a sufficient reason to do so, have they done this? So now, can anyone use the law of sufficient reason to confirm or refute, there is a God? There are five logical steps in this process.

The first logical step is through the argument of motion. Since all things in the universe are in motion and it follows, whatever is in the state of motion, must have been placed in motion by an act of some kind. Motion in and unto itself is nothing less than the transition of something from the state of potentiality to actuality. Because something cannot be in potentiality and actuality simultaneously, it follows; something cannot be a mover of itself. A simple example of this is a rubber ball lying motionless on a flat surface. It has the potential for motion, but is not currently in the state of actual motion. In order for the ball to move, something else must set the ball in motion, be it gravity, a collision with another moving object or the maybe the wind, and yet that something, other than the ball itself, must act upon the ball to set it in motion. All motion is classified as secondary movement and in order for secondary movement to occur there must be a primary mover. There is nothing in science explaining the first mover, thus, those of God claim the first and primary mover could only be God and there is not a sufficient reason for religious folks to change their minds.

The second logical step follows closely with the first and expounds the principle of causality. Both science and religion believe, in the world there is an order of causes and effects. There is a cause and effect for all things exist temporally (existing temporally is the effect) and nothing can cause itself into existence. An object cannot will itself into existence; it must be created and caused into existence by something else. Take a clock for example, the clockmaker creates a clock and causes its existence as a clock, and yet the material of the clock and the clockmaker did not cause themselves to exist. Something else must have caused their existence. All things must attribute their existence to a first cause that began all causes of all things. There is nothing in science explaining or identifying the first cause. Those who believe in God believe this first cause is an act by God. Again, the scientific community has not given sufficient reason for anyone to change their mind.

The third logical step, both scientific and religious theory conflict over the idea, all things of this universe have a transitory nature in which they are generated but will corrupt over time. The scientific community believes the things of nature can "possible to be and possible not to be". They say, since it is impossible for these things to have always existed and it reasonable to assume there was a time when they did not exist. The religious community has a slightly different view, i.e. temporal objects can fall into this transitory concept, but things of the spirit do not. The scientific community also says if there are things, which are transitory and are possible not to be, then at one time there could have been nothing in existence. Again, the religious community disagrees; they believed; there never has been a time when nothing existed since things of substance must be made from something. It defies the law of sufficient reason to say, anything can be generated or created from nothing. However, as was already explained in the second proof, there had to have been a first cause, not of a transitory nature that could have generated all things of this universe and the beginning of nature. This, in the view of many, defines God.

The fourth logical step notes, there is a certain gradation in all things. Hot things are grouped according to the varying degrees of heat perceptible in those objects deemed to be hot. In any classification of objects, there is always something, displaying the maximum fullness of the hot characteristic. The gradation of virtue in humankind can also be classified. While it impossible for any man to reach a fullness of virtue while in this temporal state, he can gain a certain amount of virtue, it is then reasonable to assume the initiator causing the existence of man had to possess a fullness of these characteristics in order to endow man with the awareness of virtue. Thus, the law of sufficient reason leads people to believe, it can only be God, who has reached the fullness of virtue, since this is the essence of Godhood. This concept is another place where religion disagrees with the scientific community and moves into to spiritual realm and it follows, from spiritual realm, God created all things known.

The fifth logical step, is, the order of nature presupposes a higher plan in creation. The laws' governing the universe presupposes a universal legislature who authored the order of the universe. Due to the law of sufficient reason, one cannot say, chance creates order in the universe since it would be an unreasonable statement. If you drop a cup on the floor, it shatters into bits and the random parts cannot reassemble themselves into a cup nor can the broken pieces generate any movement after the energy of the fall is depleted. This is an example of the inherent disorder prevalent in the universe when things are left to chance and for the scientific community to say, the order of the universe came into existence by chance defies the law sufficient reason. The existence of order and natural laws presupposes a divine intelligence authored the universe into being. It is reasonable to believe the divine intelligence is God.

The Law of the Harvest

A good number of talks have been given on the Law of Harvest quoting the Parable of the Sower for reference, making this the theme of their talk "you reap what you sow". One can make the case, the Parable of the Sower could support that premises but logically the meaning of both the Law of Harvest and the Parable of the Sower are far broader in scope and much deeper in doctrine than that. While everyone concedes that, the Law of the Harvest is closely associated with the Parable of the Sower, it takes more than one parable to flush out the doctrine contained in the Law of the Harvest. So, what dues the Parable of the Sower have to do with the Law of the Harvest. The Parable of the Sower is found in the gospel of Mark. "And he began again to teach by the sea side: and there was gathered unto him a great multitude, so that he entered into a ship, and sat in the sea; and the whole multitude was by the sea on the land. "And he taught them many things by parables, and said unto them in his doctrine, "Hearken; Behold, there went out a sower to sow: "And it came to pass, as he sowed, some fell by the way side, and the fowls of the air came and devoured it up. "And some fell on stony ground, where it had not much earth; and immediately it sprang up, because it had no depth of earth: "But when the sun was up, it was scorched; and because it had no root, it withered away. "And some fell among thorns, and the thorns grew up, and choked it, and it yielded no fruit. And others fell on good ground, and did yield fruit that sprang up and increased; and brought forth, some thirty, and some sixty, and some a hundred. And he said unto them, He that hath ears to hear, let him hear" (*Mark 4:1–9*). The above parable Jesus was teaching His disciples the reality of His doctrine concerning their coming missionary work; with the understanding, they would be carrying His message forward after He was gone.

This parable is reminiscent of the circumstances in the preexistence where Jesus (who was called Jehovah) said, some of God's children would be lost under the plan he proposed. The contention, in heaven, was Jesus said there were certain men who would not be saved and the devil said he could save them all. This parable is saying precisely the same thing Jesus said in the preexistence only it is saying it in parable format. Some of the seeds you plant (principles of the gospel taught) will, for various reasons, fail to yield fruit (bring souls to Jesus); while others, under better circumstances, they will bear fruit even multiple fruits. The last verse, "He that has ears, let him hear" (*Mark 4:23*), seems to be saying, some of the people that the disciples try to teach will not listen; this is a warning to them. All this is exactly the doctrine of Christ. If this was not the doctrine of Christ and none would fall by the wayside there would be no need for three separate kingdoms. Jesus did not teach His disciples everything at once, so there must be a continuation of the lessons of this parable where Jesus finalizes the doctrine, called the Law of Harvest. Another piece is found in the gospel of John. "And upon this came his disciples, and marveled that he talked with the woman: yet no man said, what seekest thou? Or, why talkest thou with her? The woman then left her water pot, went her way into the city, and saith to the men, Come, see a man, which told me all things that ever I did: is not this the Christ? Then they went out of the city, and came unto him. In the mean while his disciples prayed him, saying, Master, eat. But he said unto them, I have meat to eat that ye know not of. Therefore, said the disciples one to another, Hath any man brought him ought to eat? Jesus saith unto them, my meat is to do the will of him that sent me, and to finish his work. Say, not ye, there are yet four months, and then cometh harvest? Behold, I say unto you, lift up your eyes, and look on the fields; for they are white already to harvest. And he that reapeth receiveth wages, and gathereth fruit unto life eternal: that both he that soweth and he that reapeth may rejoice together" (*John 4:27-38*).

Combining the teachings of both of these scriptures, taking (John 4: 27-38) first, Jesus is teaching His disciples the Law of Harvest; when the disciples wanted Jesus to eat, He said "I have meat to eat that ye know not of... my meat is to do the will of him that sent me, and to finish his work". He meant, there were many things He knew about the will of His Father they did not know, but it had to do with the finishing if His work. He then told them, in four months the harvest would come, meaning, in four months, His father's work would be finished and He would be gone; the harvest (the converting of souls) would fall into their hands, in other words, Christ would return to His Heavenly father and the Disciples would go on their missions... Then He said, lift up their eyes (do not be sad or dismayed) and look on the fields (the people of the world); for they are white already to harvest (ready to be taught the gospel). Jesus then revealed the reward for the reaper and the sower, which is; both will rejoice in eternal life. Then add the Sower parable, where Jesus said, when they, the Disciples, took over the harvestings of souls some of those they would be teaching, for various reasons, would not listen, therefore they would not gain salvation, but there would be others who would listen and they would carry the message to others thereby expanding the gospel exponentially (Mark 4:1–9).

This is a good start in understanding the Law of the Harvest. What is now needed is the information about the will of His Father the disciples did not know. A small piece of information is recorded in (Acts 1:8), Jesus' last words on earth before He went to His heavenly home. This is where Jesus took his Twelve Disciples to the top of the Mount of Olives and said, "...And ye shall be witnesses unto me both in Jerusalem, and in all Judea, and in Samaria, and unto the uttermost part of the earth." The most significant part of this scripture is "the uttermost part of the earth". Where are the uttermost parts of the earth? Did this include only the known world at the time? Did it include the country, now called America and did the Disciples even know America was there? Maybe He was talking about something much broader, like, not only the people of His time but all of the people who have ever been born on this earth and all who will ever be born on this earth. I wonder if the Disciples understood the scope of His language or its meaning many today do not. And then, the final piece of the Law of the Harvest came after His crucifixion when the eleven disciples assembled on a mountain in Galilee and the Savior came to them and said, as recorded in (Mark 16:15). "...Go ye into all the world, and preach the gospel to every creature." And, in (Matt 28:18-20) "...All power is given unto me in heaven and in earth. Go ye therefore, and teach all nations, baptizing them in the name of the Father, and of the Son, and of the Holy Ghost. Teaching them to observe all things whatsoever I have commanded you: and, lo, I am with you always, even unto the end of the world. Amen."

Summing up the Law of the Harvest and combining the above text with the teachings Jesus gave to His Disciples on this subject, and indeed this has been given to us, since all are bound by covenant to obey all of His laws and commandments. The doctrine Jesus taught His Disciples concerning the Law of the Harvest is consistent with the doctrine of the church today. The world finds the world wide missionary effort ongoing and doing well while at the same time the church is actively petitioning other countries for the opportunity to place missionaries in their midst for purposes of teaching the gospel. As the membership grows in each of these countries, ward buildings, are erected and eventually temples are built, bringing with them all the eternal blessings for the ages of all time. While it is true, in some countries, the growth of the church is slow and many taught fall by the wayside as Jesus taught in the Parable of the Sower, the church has also found there are other countries that are, "white already to harvest" as John recorded. The church is persistent in following the admonition of the Savoir and is teaching the gospel in any nation where the people will take upon themselves His name, being baptized in the name of the Father, and of the Son, and of the Holy Ghost, and teaching them to observe all things whatsoever the Lord has commanded. Therefore, the Law of the Harvest and the associated teachings are considerably broader and deeper than "you reap what you sow". The Law of the Harvest is the complete missionary plan of the Savior to bring all those, in the entirety of the world, which will accept Him, into the fold.

Law of Unity

The best scripture that refers to this law is in John, "And the glory which thou gavest me I have given them; that they may be one, even as we are one. I in them and You in Me--that they may be perfectly united, so that the world may know that You sent Me and have loved them just as You have loved Me" (*John 17:22&23*). What Jesus is praying about is His desire for the application of the Law of Unity, being passed to the world through His disciples. What is the Law of Unity? To understand this law of Unity, first, some groundwork must be laid by talking about the purpose of life (mortality) and why all this came about. What caused God to set up this process called creation and include mortals in it? Well, God has the priesthood and a calling He must magnify and His calling is found in the book of Moses where God tells (Moses, 1:31), He made these things (all of creation) for His own purpose. Then in (Moses, 1: 39) He explains what His calling defines and the purpose, "For behold, this is my work and my glory---to bring to pass the immortality and eternal life of man". Now, it is understood, the creative process, which includes mortals, is God administering His calling and it is known He will always oversee things a unified way. His unified administration functions under what is called the Law of Unity and it manifests itself in mortal beings in two ways, externally and internally. So, how does this work? The external portion is the passing of God's calling onto His children, which are referred to, in the above scriptures, as *Man*. When Jehovah said, *thy will be done,* and thus became the savior, He took upon Himself the same calling of God. During His administration of His calling, which encompasses the entire universe, He, by the grace of God, gave all mankind immortality in the form of resurrection. "These the Lord taught, and gave them power to come forth, after his resurrection from the dead, to enter into his Father's kingdom, there to be crowned with immortality and eternal life" (*D&C 138:51*). In order to expedite God's calling He then passed the obligation for the rest of the calling onto His Apostles since He knew He was to leave them, and His passing is still relevant in Christian lives today. Jesus is God's administrator for the universe and holds the responsibility to pass this calling on. While Jesus administers the universe, the Prophet administers, as His subordinate, on earth. It is for this is the very reason His church was organized on earth, so when the president of the Church of Jesus Christ of Latter day Saints accepted his calling, he took upon himself the responsibility to administer God's calling to the entire world, bringing to pass the eternal life of everyone in the world. In order to accomplish this work, he then passes the calling on to his subordinates, the members of the church. Therefore, when called by the Prophet, all stake presidents take upon themselves the very same calling for all persons within the boundaries of their stakes. All bishops take upon themselves the same calling for everyone within their respective ward boundaries. Every calling issued in the church relates directly to the calling, God holds, right down to a primary worked or a Cub Scout leader. They are all helping to bring to pass the eternal life of man within the confines of their calling. When a person is baptized and *comes unto Christ,* the person is also taking on God's calling for themselves. This is where the external portion of the Law is working outside of oneself within the guidelines of a calling, stops and the internal portion of the Law of Unity begins, meaning, baptism brings about an internal responsibility, somewhat different from a called position within the church. It is clearly taught in Corinthians, baptism facilitates the union with Christ, "Therefore we are buried with him by baptism into death: that like as Christ was raised up from the dead by the glory of the Father, even so we also should walk in newness of life. For if we have been planted together in the likeness of his death, we shall be also in the likeness of his resurrection" (2 Corinthians, 4:4&5). Those baptized are responsible to live in a way where they become personably eligible for eternal life. President Brigham Young said it this way; people are responsible to gain enough righteousness and virtue in this life in order for Jesus to put His arms around them and call them His own. A father and mother, in unity, are to raise their children in the home with the same equivalence. This same homogeneity is also extended from the home to their neighbors in the community then onto the people of the city and onto the citizens of the nation and then to the entire population of the world. "And he commanded them that there should be no contention one with another, but that they should look forward with one eye, having one faith and one baptism, having their hearts knit together in unity and in love one towards another" (*Mosiah 18:21*). In other words, it is necessary to become a unified world under God, starting with each individual, therefore, each and every calling within the church have been placed there to help in

95

this endeavor, since God's calling is for all people, as God's children, to receive eternal life. This is the Law of Unity in operation throughout all of the Mormon religion. The scriptures explain, when any member of the Godhead speaks, they are speaking with the same voice as God, because they are the epitome of the Law of Unity. When the apostles and general authorities are traveling all around the world and are ask a question or giving a talk, even though they cannot immediately collaborate with those in Salt Lake, they are speaking with the same voice as the prophet and he speaks with the same voice as God. "Therefore, marvel not at these things, for ye are not yet pure; ye cannot yet bear my glory; but ye shall behold it if ye are faithful in keeping all my words that I have given you, from the days of Adam to Abraham, from Abraham to Moses, from Moses to Jesus and his apostles, and from Jesus and his apostles to Joseph Smith, whom I did call upon by mine angels, my ministering servants, and by mine own voice out of the heavens, to bring forth my work" (D&C, 136:37). This is because these righteous men hold the priesthood linked directly to the Prophet Joseph Smith and they live the Law of Unity. When a Sunday school teacher teaches a lesson in America and the same lesson is taught on the other side of the world, this is the Law of Unity in action due to the administration of the Prophet throughout the world.

For the purposes of this presentation, the external application of the Law of Unity was the first explored since the individual calling of God is the start of the progression, and it seemed to be the logical place to begin. The second exploration is extended it onto the internal element, but in reality, the unfolding of the Law of Unity is exactly the opposite of how it has been described in this discourse. People first arrive onto the path of unity through baptism and through their own internal efforts they experience an increase of their righteousness, and then start to participate (receiving callings) in the external functions designed to help increase the righteousness of others as cited above.

Law of witness

The scriptural law of witnesses requires, "from the mouth of two or three individuals shall every word be established" (Deut. 19:15; 2 Cor. 13:1; 1 Tim. 5:19). This law applies in divine as well as human relations, "for members of the Godhead bear witness of one another" (John 5:31-37; 3 Ne. 11:32), and books of holy writ "give multiple witness to the work of God in the earth" (2 Ne. 29:8-13). The law of witnesses is prominent in the history and practice of The Church of Jesus Christ of Latter-day Saints.

In mortal relationships, a witness gives personal verification of, or attests to the reality of, an event. To "witness" in the scriptural sense is much the same as in the legal sense: to give personal testimony based on firsthand evidence or experience. To bear "false witness" is a very serious offense (Deut. 5:20; 19:16-21). In mortal relationships as well as in legal affairs, testimony is usually related to what a person knows by the physical senses. When prophets have an experience with the Lord, often he commands them to bear record of him and of the truths, revealed, this suffices as the necessary witness. (1 Ne. 10:10, 11:7, D&C 58:59, 112:4, 138:60). In spiritual matters, there is additional knowledge or information received through the Holy Spirit.

The Apostle Paul wrote, "In the mouth of two or three witnesses shall every word be established" (*2 Corinthians 13:*1). Witnesses and witnessing are vital in God's plan for the salvation of His children. In the Godhead, the function of the Holy Ghost is to bear witness of the Father and the Son (2 Ne. 31:18). The Father has borne witness of the Son (Matt. 3:17; Matt. 17:5; John 5:31–39), and the Son has borne witness of the Father. (John 17). The Lord has commanded His servants to testify of Him (Isa. 43:10; Mosiah 18:9; D&C 84:62), and all of the prophets have borne witness of Jesus Christ (Acts 10:43; Rev. 19:10).

The scriptures state, "In the mouth of two or three witnesses shall every word be established" (*2 Cor. 13:1; D&C 6:28. Deut. 19:15*). The most important ordinances of salvation—baptism, marriage, and other ordinances of the temple—are required to have witnesses (D&C 127:6; D&C 128:3).

Witnessing or Testifying as mortals The Bible illustrates, God often works with mankind through two or more witnesses (Num. 35:30; Deut. 17,19:15; Matt. 18:15-16). Likewise, latter-day scripture teaches the need for witnesses (D&C 6:28, 42:80-81, 128:3). One person's word alone, even though it may be true, may not be sufficient to establish and bind the hearer to the truth. Witnesses provide the means of establishing faith in the minds of people, for faith come by hearing the word of God through the power of human testimony accompanied by the Holy Ghost (Rom. 10:17; TPJS, p. 148; Lectures on Faith, 2). In the Book of Mormon, the prophet Nephi 1 combined his brother Jacob's testimony with Isaiah's testimony to reinforce and verify his own witness of the divine Son ship of the Redeemer (2 Ne. 11:2-3). Likewise, Alma 2 called upon the words of Zenos, Zenock, and Moses to corroborate his own testimony of the Son of God (Alma 33:2-23).

When the keys of the priesthood were restored to the Prophet Joseph Smith and often when visions were received, a witness accompanied the Prophet. This is the case with the restoration of the Aaronic Priesthood, the

Melchizedek Priesthood, the keys given in the Kirtland Temple (Ohio), and the vision of the degrees of glory (D&C 13;76;110). Subsequent to the translation of the Book of Mormon and prior to its publication, three men on one occasion, and eight men on a separate occasion, in addition to Joseph Smith, became witnesses of the Book of Mormon plates (see Book of Mormon Witnesses). The Prophet Joseph was likewise accompanied in his martyr's death by his brother Hyrum, a second martyr or witness, making their testimony valid forever (D&C 135:3;136:39). The meaning of the Greek word martyr is witness. The scriptures also indicate other ways in which the law of witnesses applies:

The process for members to seek relief from issues with other members, by appealing to the Church Administration, is also found in the law of Witness. In the mouth of two or three witnesses, shall every word be established. The Lord gives witnesses establishing his words to us. This is a universal law. It is easy to comprehend, any person, desiring to do evil against his neighbor, might decide to accuse another falsely. Requiring at least one additional witness greatly decreases the ability for a person to testify falsely against another. Not only does it add the difficulty of convincing another person to participate in your lie, it also adds the burden of making sure two testimonies correspond. When at least two witnesses are required to establish every word, it adds a safeguard. It is not fool proof, but it is significantly stronger. The Lord wants people to understand and accept his word because it takes faith on their part for him to manifest his power in their lives. If His words are disbelieved, He cannot act in their lives. His desire is to lift His children up.

There are many people willing to teach lies in this world. Members must be like Adam and Eve, learn to recognize these people, and wait upon the Lord to send true messengers. It is necessary to possess the tokens and signs so when these messengers appear, they will be recognized and accepted. Satan wanted his words to be well received, but Adam would not receive them. He rejected the message of Satan and Satan himself and waited until the messengers from the Father appeared. When the messengers came, they cast out Satan and taught Adam and Eve pure truth. All righteous members ought to be concerned with exactness in their character. They must desire to live the word of God exactly as given to them. They should be careful in their speech and they need to speak only truth. They should strive to root out all untruth planted in their souls, rigorously seeking to replace lies with truth in their lives. When finding a member of this caliber, notice, their language is exact. They are unwilling to commit themselves to make statements that may not be correct.

The Bible witnesses of Jesus Christ by prophecies of His coming, by accounts of His ministry, and by the testimonies of those who carried His message to the world. The Book of Mormon has the same content: witnesses preceding, during, and following the ministry of the Messiah. The Book of Mormon is appropriately titled, *Another Testament of Jesus Christ*.

The Holy Ghost is the third member of the Godhead, sent forth by God to reveal all needful things. He teaches and testifies with divine power and clarity. His witness may go unheard or unheeded, forsaken or denied, but it is never misunderstood. "The Holy Ghost is a revelator", (*Joseph Smith, Teachings of the Prophet Joseph Smith, Joseph Fielding Smith [1976], 328*). Those things, which is received of Him has a more powerful effect upon the soul than anything else received in any other way. A millennium of experience through sight, sound, touch, taste, smell, and all the powers of the universe combined cannot approach the sublime and complete experience of one brief moment under the influence of the Holy Ghost.

The Divinity of Jesus Christ

John the Baptist testified of the divinity of Jesus (*John 1:15, 3:26, 5:32-39*), the Father testified of Christ (*Matt. 3:17, 17:5, John 8:18*), and Christ himself bore record of his own divinity as the Son of God (*Matt. 26:63-64; John 11:4, 13:31*). The theme of John 5- 8 illustrates the principle of witnesses. When Jesus spoke in his own behalf, some Jews, referring to the law of witnesses, said, "Thou bearest record of thyself; thy record is not true" (*John 8:13*). Jesus had earlier explained that both John the Baptist and the Father in Heaven had "borne record of him" (*John 5:31-39, 8:18*) and his testimony was therefore valid and binding. He declared that his works "testified that he was the Son of God" (*John 5:31-38*). Peter also bore testimony that "Jesus was the Son of God", a fact he had learned by revelation (*Matt. 16:16*).

Jesus's Resurrection from the Dead

Witnesses to the resurrection of Christ included groups of women, two disciples on the road to Emmaus, and the apostles (*Matt. 28; Luke 24; Acts 4:33, 5:32*). Paul records that there were in Galilee over 500 witnesses to Jesus' resurrected body (*1 Cor. 15:6*). The Book of Mormon reports that about 2,500 people in America witnessed the resurrected body of Jesus Christ by seeing and touching it, and did "bear record" of it (*3 Ne. 11:14-16, 17:25*).

In the Church, witnesses are officially present for all baptisms and marriages. Witnesses also confirm proxy baptisms, endowments, marriages, and sealing's in the temples on behalf of the dead (*D&C 127:6*). Missionaries travel in pairs as witnesses for one another (*Mark 6:7; Luke 10:1; D&C 42:6, 52:10, 61:35, 62:5*).

On Judgement Day, in the final judgment, God will render to all mankind, the fact of the gospel having been taught on the earth by multiple witnesses will be important. Nephi 1 has written, "Wherefore, by the words of three, God hath said, I will establish my word. Nevertheless, God sendeth more witnesses, and he proveth all his words" (*2 Ne. 11:3; cf. 27:14*).

In a very fundamental way, the Bible and the Book of Mormon are witnesses to each other. Each record establishes the truth found in the other, and the Doctrine and Covenants establishes the truth of them both (*1 Ne. 13:20-40; 2 Ne. 3:12, 29:8-14, Morm.7:8-9; D&C 17:6;2, 11-12, 42:12*). The written testimony of two nations, the Jews and the Nephites, is a witness to the world that there is a God (*2 Ne. 29:8*).

Testimony of the Three Witnesses

"Be it known unto all nations, kindred's, tongues, and people, unto whom this work shall come: That we, through the grace of God the Father, and our Lord Jesus Christ, have seen the plates which contain this record, which is a record of the people of Nephi, and also of the Lamanites, their brethren, and also of the people of Jared, who came from the tower of which hath been spoken. In addition, we also know that they have been translated by the gift and power of God, for his voice hath declared it unto us, wherefore we know of a surety that the work is true. In addition, we also testify that we have seen the engravings, which are upon the plates; and they have been shown unto us by the power of God, and not of man. And we declare with words of soberness, that an angel of God came down from heaven, and he brought and laid before our eyes, that we beheld and saw the plates, and the engravings thereon; and we know that it is by the grace of God the Father, and our Lord Jesus Christ, that we beheld and bear record that these things are true. And, it is marvelous in our eyes. Nevertheless, the voice of the Lord commanded us that we should bear record of it; wherefore, to be obedient unto the commandments of God, we bear testimony of these things. And, we know that if we are faithful in Christ, we shall rid our garments of the blood of all men, and be found spotless before the judgment-seat of Christ, and shall dwell with him eternally in the heavens.

And, the honor be to the Father, and to the Son, and to the Holy Ghost, which is one God. Amen" (*BoM Testimony of Three Witnesses*).

Testimony of the Eight Witnesses

"Be it known unto all nations, kindred's, tongues, and people, unto whom this work shall come: That Joseph Smith, Jun., the translator of this work, has shown unto us the plates of which hath been spoken, which have the appearance of gold; and as many of the leaves as the said Smith has translated we did handle with our hands; and we also saw the engravings thereon, all of which has the appearance of ancient work, and of curious workmanship. And, this we bear record with words of soberness, that the said Smith has shown unto us, for we have seen and hefted, and know of a surety that the said Smith has got the plates of which we have spoken. And, we give our names unto the world, to witness unto the world that which we have seen. And we lie not, God bearing witness of it" (*BoM Testimony of Eight Witnesses*).

All the world lies in sin. People have been taught lies for so long they have ceased to be able to discern truth. Courtrooms are a circus of evidence reflecting the love for a lie and the disdain for truth. They reflect a lack of trust in the Lord Jesus Christ. In the beginning of this country, the Forefathers were able to set up courtroom procedures reflecting their trust in the Lord. They believed, when setting a guilty person free, the guilty person still could not escape the justice of God. They were not afraid to allow a guilty person to get off if the burden of proof could not be met. Nowadays, the focus is on safety and on making sure no harm comes to others, all sorts of slip-shod witnesses are to be accepted and courts lean toward locking up a person if there is a shadow of doubt about his innocence instead of the other way around. The quality of witnesses in the world is not held to a higher standard, as were the witnesses of God.

Look at the language of these witnesses. It is exact. The eight witnesses do not testify the plates are made of gold; they testified they appear to be gold. Why, because it was the best and most precise way to explain their experience. They are only willing to correctly, report their experience with no elaboration. They are under duty to God to tell the exact truth.

Conclusion

The Book of Mormon requires a person to have actually seen or experienced an event in order for them to be a witness of it. Personal interpretation, personal philosophies even when mingled with scripture, are not sufficient as a witness. A true witness is someone who has experienced something and bears testimony in clear and unadulterated terms.

Just as a court of law (at least, one functioning under the laws of God) requires more than one witness in order to condemn a man, the Lord also offers more than one witness of his words. He does not expect acceptance of His word from one person alone. He allows dismissal of anything, not being established by at least two witnesses, but when it came to something as important as the coming forth of the Book of Mormon, He made sure there were three very firmly established witnesses, men who actually heard the voice of God and learned of the truthfulness of the Book of Mormon. God will call up two or three witnesses to the very words he expects to be kept.

"And in the mouth of three witnesses shall these things be established; and the testimony of three, and this work, in the which shall be shown forth the power of God and also his word, of which the Father, and the Son, and the Holy Ghost bear record—and all this shall stand as a testimony against the world at the last day" (*Ether 5:4*).

"Behold ye are worse than they; for as the Lord liveth, if a prophet come among you and declareth unto you the word of the Lord, which testifieth of your sins and iniquities, ye are angry with him, and cast him out and seek all manner of ways to destroy him; yea, you will say that he is a false prophet, and that he is a sinner, and of the devil, because he testifieth that your deeds are evil. But behold, if a man shall come among you and shall say: Do this, and there is no iniquity; do that and ye shall not suffer; yea, he will say: Walk after the pride of your own hearts; yea, walk after the pride of your eyes, and do whatsoever your heart desireth—and if a man shall come among you and say this, ye will receive him, and say that he is a prophet" (*Helaman 13; 26&27*).

While it ought to be simple to identify a true witness of God, it is not. It is easy to allow the inner self, natural man, to be guided astray, and thus, defeating ourselves.

Section 2
Subjects of interest

Acquiring the Holy Ghost

If anyone is seeking personal direction in life, the Lord has shown us the way through the Holy Ghost.

What Is the Holy Ghost?

The Holy Spirit (or Holy Ghost) is the third person of the Godhead whose special mission is to guide and teach, testify to God and comfort and sanctify human souls. Unlike God and Jesus, who have physical bodies, the Holy Spirit is pure spirit and has no body. Joseph Smith wrote, God revealed to him "the Holy Ghost has not a body of flesh and bones, but is a personage of Spirit. Were it not so, the Holy Ghost could not dwell in us. There is a difference between the Holy Ghost and the gift of the Holy Ghost. Cornelius received the Holy Ghost before he was baptized which was the convincing power of God unto him of the truth of the Gospel, but he could not receive the gift of the Holy Ghost until after he was baptized. Had he not taken this ... ordinance upon him, the Holy Ghost which convinced him of the truth of God, would have left him" (*History of the Church 4:555*).

What does the Holy Ghost do?

The Holy Ghost reveals that which is true. For example, in the Book of Mormon, there is a promise, anyone can know by the power of the Holy Ghost the truth of the words it contain. "And when ye shall receive these things, I would exhort you that ye would ask God, the Eternal Father, in the name of Christ, if these things are not true; and if ye shall ask with a sincere heart, with real intent, having faith in Christ, he will manifest the truth of it unto you, by the power of the Holy Ghost. And by the power of the Holy Ghost ye may know the truth of all things" (*Moroni 10:4-5*).

The Holy Ghost sanctifies, or cleanses, those who have repented of their sins through baptism. This is also called the baptism of fire or to be born of the spirit.

The Holy Ghost can also comfort and give peace when needed, "But the Comforter, which is the Holy Ghost, whom the Father will send in my name, he shall teach you all things, and bring all things to your remembrance, whatsoever I have said unto you. Peace I leave with you, my peace I give unto you: not as the world giveth, give I unto you. Let not your heart be troubled, neither let it be afraid" (*John 14:26-27*) The Prophet Joseph Smith goes on to say, "The Lord, through the Holy Ghost, can speak to your mind and heart" (*D&C, 8;2*). Sometimes the impressions are just general feelings. Sometimes the direction comes so clearly and so unmistakably, it can be written down like spiritual dictation. "I bear solemn witness that as you pray with all the fervor of the soul with humility and gratitude, you can learn to be consistently guided by the Holy Spirit in all aspects of your life" (*Richard Scott, Oct. Gen. Conf. 2009*).

The Lord can speak through the Holy Ghost as a "still small voice" just as he did with Elijah. "And, behold, the LORD passed by, and a great and strong wind rent the mountains, and brake in pieces the rocks before the LORD; but the LORD was not in the wind: and after the wind an earthquake; but the LORD was not in the earthquake: And after the earthquake a fire; but the LORD was not in the fire: and after the fire a still small voice" (*1 Kings 19:11-12*). The still small voice is when the Holy Ghost speaks to the spirit and because it is a spiritual sensation mortals have to listen more closely to recognize it.

Joseph Smith said, ". . . and if it is right I will cause that your bosom shall burn within you; therefore, you shall feel that it is right. But if it be not right you shall have no such feelings, but you shall have a stupor of thought that shall cause you to forget the thing which is wrong; therefore, you cannot write that which is sacred save it be given you from me" (*D&C 9:8-9*).

Often the whisperings from the Holy Ghost come into the mind and/or heart. This how people most often feel or sense the guiding influence of the Spirit. "Yea, behold, I will tell you in your mind and in your heart, by the Holy Ghost, which shall come upon you and which shall dwell in your heart. Now, behold, this is the spirit of revelation; behold, this is the spirit by which Moses brought the children of Israel through the Red Sea on dry ground" (D&C 8:2-3).

So, how does a person get the Spirit to approach us? This is through prayer, reverence, humility, sincerity, faith,

Elder Scott, in his talk, states, he felt spiritual revelation came to him, when he.

1. Sought a private location to receive it.
2. Wrote down the feelings of his heart and mind.
3. Pondered the feelings he had recorded to see if he had accurately expressed them in writing.
4. Made a few minor changes to what he had written as a result of his pondering.
5. Studied the meaning & application of what he had written in his own life.
6. Prayed, reviewing with the Lord what he thought he had been taught by the Spirit.

7. Felt peace and could then know he had correctly received the revelation.

8. Thanked Heavenly Father for the guidance given.

9. Asked, was there yet more to be given?

May the world strive to be guided by the Holy Ghost, who will disclose all the correct things man should do, what man is to do, where man is to go in life, these are the best guidelines anyone could ever hope for.

The Atonement of Christ

The Atonement of Christ is the doctrine concerning the reconciliation of God and humankind, especially as accomplished through the life, suffering, and death of Christ.

Did Jesus did not die on the cross to pay for sins? Did the death of Jesus itself contribute to the paying of sins? On the other hand, was His death only part of the resurrection process and his atoning act was the suffering and bleeding in the Garden?

The answers to these questions are found in scripture. "Wherefore, I, the Lord God, caused that he should be cast out from the Garden of Eden, from my presence, because of his transgression, wherein he became spiritually dead, which is the first death, even that same death which is the last death, which is spiritual, which shall be pronounced upon the wicked when I shall say: depart, ye cursed. But, behold, I say unto you that I, the Lord God, gave unto Adam and unto his seed, that they should not die as to the temporal death, until I, the Lord God, should send forth angels to declare unto them repentance and redemption, through faith on the name of mine Only Begotten Son. And thus did I, the Lord God, appoint unto man the days of his probation--that by his natural death he might be raised in immortality unto eternal life, even as many as would believe" (*D&C 29:41-43*).

Jesus Christ, as the Only Begotten Son of God and the only sinless person to live on this earth, was the only one capable of making atonement for mankind. By his selection and foreordination in the Grand Council before the world was formed, his divine Son ship, his sinless life, the shedding of his blood in the garden of Gethsemane, his death on the cross and subsequent bodily resurrection from the grave, he made a perfect atonement for all mankind. All are covered unconditionally as pertaining to the fall of Adam. Hence, all shall rise from the dead with immortal bodies, because of Jesus' atonement. "For as in Adam all die, even so in Christ shall all be made alive" (*1 Cor. 15: 22*),

Here is where the understanding of Resurrection, Redemption, and Atonement gets confusing. These three acts are generally discussed all together, as in the scriptures above, and they all happened about the same time, same place with all the same participants and many times the meaning of each gets cross-associated. As an example, some people think Atonement and Redemption are the same thing, are they? Think of these three in this way, Atonement cleanses the spirit, Resurrection restores the purity of the body, and Redemption, returns mankind to the innocent mindset needed to be in the presence of Heavenly Father.

In addition, there is the confusion between Grace and Works, which is inextricably associated with the subject at hand.

Redemption

The Mormon Church affirms *fall of man* unto mortal death, brought about by Adam's transgression, as seen in Mosiah. "For they are carnal and devilish, and the devil has power over them; yea, even that old serpent that did beguile our first parents, which was the cause of their fall; which was the cause of all mankind becoming carnal, sensual, devilish, knowing evil from good, subjecting themselves to the devil. Thus all mankind was lost; and behold, they would have been endlessly lost were it not that God redeemed his people from their lost and fallen state. But remember that he that persists in his own carnal nature, and goes on in the ways of sin and rebellion against God, remaineth in his fallen state and the devil hath all power over him. Therefore, he is as though there was no redemption made, being an enemy to God; and also is the devil an enemy to God. And now if Christ had not come into the world, speaking of things to come as though they had already come, there could have been no redemption" (*Mosiah 16: 3-4*). The process of gaining this redemption is explained in Mosiah. "For the natural man is an enemy to God, and has been from the fall of Adam, and will be, forever and ever, unless he yields to the enticing of the Holy Spirit, and putteth off the natural man and becometh a saint through the atonement of Christ the Lord, and becometh as a child, submissive, meek, humble, patient, full of love, willing to submit to all things which the Lord seeth fit to inflict upon him, even as a child doth submit to his father" (Mosiah 3;19). You may ask, w*hat is does it mean to be redeemed?* Redeemed means, *to get back or recovering something which was lost.* When Eve yielded to Satan's temptations, she lost her innocence and became a *Natural Man*. She passed the propensity to be a natural man on to her prosperity and it is still relevant today. Those entering the Celestial

Kingdom must follow the instructions in Mosiah 3:19 and exchange the natural man for the innocence which Adam and Eve had in the garden.

Resurrection

The Church teaches, the life of the Son produces resurrection for all earth-born humans (universal) with no regard for the individual's beliefs or conduct (unconditional) in the second estate. This unconditional gift for reversing human mortality is given to all mankind by the grace of God. The Son's death and resurrection served as something of a gateway for the resurrection of all mankind. While these two concepts, Resurrection and Redemption are theological entities they do not stand-alone but are in fact tied to the atonement, this will discuss later.

Atonement

The sacrificial atonement of the Son of God is not universal or unconditional but it does apply to all people and all sins, according to Mormonism. The Church of Jesus Christ of Latter Day Saints teaches, the sacrificial atonement of the Son occurred in Gethsemane and repeated on the cross before the Son's death. The death of the Son Himself was not the atoning act unto itself. The Son's death served as something of a gateway for the resurrection. The Church affirms the doctrine on the manner of the atonement of the Son in a way emphasizing the suffering and bleeding of the Son in Gethsemane. The Church does not reject, the atonement repeated on the cross. The sacrificial atonement of the Son is only operative method for reversing spiritual death due to sin. All earth-born humans, will be saved from the penalty of sin and will enjoy the state of Eternal Life because of their obedience to the laws of the Savior and their repentance for their sins due to the sacrificial atonement of the Son. Obedience and repentance (referred to as works) are the individuals conditions apply to the atonement. No action of repentance by any human would be satisfactory for salvation if it were not for the atonement of Jesus Christ (*Heb. 10: 1-9; 2nd Ne. 9: 5-24; Mosiah 13: 27-32*).
"Sin is lawlessness" (*1 Jn. 3: 4*), it is a refusal on men's part to "submit to the law of God" (*Rom. 8:7*). By transgression man loses control over his own will and becomes the "slave of sin" (*Rom. 7: 14*), and so incurs the penalty of spiritual death, which is "alienation from God" (*Rom. 6: 23*). The atonement of Jesus Christ redeems all mankind from the fall of Adam and causes all to be answerable for their own manner of life. This means of

"atonement is provided by the Father (*John 3: 16-17*), and is offered in the life and person of his Son, Jesus Christ" (*2nd Cor. 5: 19*).

The individual conditional aspect of the atonement relates to the degree of glory one may achieve on condition of repentance and obedience. The immortal body one receives at the resurrection is given to them unconditionally, and the eternal realm to which one is assigned, is conditionally granted based on the degree of one's repentance and obedience to the Laws of God. Were it not for the Atoning Sacrifice of Jesus Christ, Resurrection and Redemption would be of no value and there would be no salvation for mankind. Additionally, if mankind was not a recipient of Redemption, wherein he was returned to the innocence of Adam and Eve as they were in the garden and afforded immortality through the Resurrection, the Atonement would be for naught. Therefore, the three concepts are unique to themselves but tied together by the life and sacrifices of the Savior.

The atonement of the Son of God is also extended to all children who die before reaching eight years of age and the mentally impaired whose mental age is less than the mental age of a normal eight-year-old. In Mormon doctrine, these two kinds of earth-born humans are permitted to enjoy exaltation in the celestial realm without having proven themselves worthy prior to their mortal probation.

There are many Book of Mormon passages support this doctrine, consider the following selections from 2nd Nephi 9-10, Mosiah 3, Alma 42 and Mormon 9. A portion of 2nd Nephi 9-10 just about sums it up,

"For it behooveth the great Creator that he suffereth himself to become subject unto man in the flesh, and die for all men, that all men might become subject unto him. For as death hath passed upon all men, to fulfill the merciful plan of the great Creator, there must needs be a power of resurrection, and the resurrection must needs come unto man by reason of the fall; and the fall came by reason of transgression; and because man became fallen they were cut off from the presence of the Lord. Wherefore, it must needs be an infinite atonement--save it should be an infinite atonement this corruption could not put on incorruption. Wherefore, the first judgment, which came upon man, must needs have remained to an endless duration. And if so, this flesh must have laid down to rot and to crumble to its mother earth, to rise no more. The spirits of men will be restored one to the other; and it is by the power of the resurrection of the Holy One of Israel. And he suffereth this that the resurrection might pass upon all men, that all might stand before him at the great and judgment day. Wherefore, may God raise you from death by the power of the resurrection, and also from everlasting death by the power of the atonement, that ye may be received into the eternal kingdom of God, that ye may praise him through grace-divine" (*2 Nephi 9:21*).

LDS doctrines of the atonement of the Son are not only found in the Bible and the Book of Mormon. Joseph Smith's revelation inexplicitly taught a conditional aspect of the atonement of the Son. Speaking for God, The Prophet Joseph Smith said, "Endless punishment is God's punishment. Wherefore, I command you to repent, and keep the commandments which you have received by the hand of my servant Joseph Smith, Jun., in my name; And it is by my almighty power that you have received them; Therefore, I command you to repent--repent, lest I smite you by the rod of my mouth, and by my wrath, and by my anger, and your sufferings be sore--how sore you know not, how exquisite you know not, yea, how hard to bear you know not. For behold, I, God, have suffered these things for all, that they might not suffer if they would repent; but if they would not repent they must suffer even as I" (*D&C 19: 12-17*).

In addition to the Book of Mormon and the Doctrine and Covenants, LDS authorities also rely upon two selections from the Pearl of Great Price to support the Mormon doctrine of the atonement of the Son. Moses 1:39 is said to teach, the atonement of the Son has a twofold result. The atonement of the Son secures the universal and unconditional immortality of all men, and it makes eternal life (exaltation) possible on condition of repentance and obedience. The citation reads, "For behold, this is my work and my glory--to bring to pass the immortality and eternal life of man."

Apostle McConkie teaches the atonement of the Son produces complete salvation and conditioned upon faith together with a large number of actions. He wrote, "What is the true doctrine of the blood of Christ? Salvation comes because of the atonement, and the atonement was wrought out through the shedding of the blood of Christ. However, there are certain conditions attached to the attainment of salvation through his atoning blood. Salvation in the kingdom of God is available because of the atoning blood of Christ. Nevertheless, it is received only on condition of faith, repentance, baptism, and enduring to the end in keeping the commandments of God.

Thus the atonement of Christ is designed to ransom men from the effects of the fall of Adam in that both spiritual and temporal death are conquered; their lasting effect is nullified. The spiritual death of the fall was replaced by the spiritual life of the atonement, in that all who believes and obeys the gospel law gain spiritual or eternal life. Life, in the presence of God is where those who enjoy it are alive to things of righteousness or things of the Spirit. The temporal death of the fall is replaced by the state of immortality, which comes because of the atonement, and resurrection of the

Lord. Immortality comes as a gift, by the grace of God alone, without works of righteousness. Eternal life is the reward for "obedience to the laws and ordinances of the Gospel" (*McConkie, Mormon Doctrine*).

The understanding of Resurrection, Redemption, and Atonement is also complicated by the fact they are acts of a vicarious nature. (The Bible dictionary definition of vicarious; "an act exercised, received, performed, or suffered in the place of another"). These spiritual acts and indeed all spiritual acts are hard for a mortal to visualize. For instance, the judgment, which is totally a spiritual circumstance, is seen by some as a great courtroom in Heaven where they must stand to the bar, with shameful posture, and answer for their sins to an angry judge sitting above them. While others see it as a walk in the park, with the Savior's arm around them where He tells them their sins are forgiven. It seems humans need these visual images to facilitate understanding. It must be realized all spiritual things, which include prayers and the answering thereof, giving of blessings, all ordinances (the sacrament, baptism and temple and so on) are of a vicarious nature. Why is this so?

All the concepts mentioned in the text above are, not only of a vicarious nature, but for the most part pertain to the spiritual person living in side you. When prayer is answered, the answer is vicarious in nature (from God to the Holy Ghost from the Holy Ghost to your soul, wherein your mortal being benefits) (pay attention to the wording of the last sentence). If a person can grasp the concept of prayer and understand the vicariousness of it then it is a small step mentally to understand how blessings work. Blessings are obtained on the condition of obedience to the law that predicates the blessing. (D&C 130: 21) So, now the mortal is the one who is either obedient or disobedient and the blessing is given to the spirit how, does this work? The spirit receiving the blessing must be "clean" in the eyes of the Lord in order to receive. If the Mortal is disobedient, he is damaging his soul (making the soul unclean) and therefore, the soul cannot be attended by the blessing giver, thus no blessing. The mortal then repents which is the act of repairing the damaged soul, and then blessings can flow. Now move to the Atonement--- If the mortal is disobedient he is damaging his soul and therefore, the soul cannot be attended by the Atonement giver, thus no atonement. The mortal then repents which is the act of repairing the damaged soul, now the atonement can take place. Therefore, you see it is vicarious both ways. Remember ---all spiritual things have a vicarious essence---sin and all.

Calling and Election Made Sure

The experiences gained during mortality are necessary for mortals to continue their advancement toward eternal life, but not all things hinge exclusively on mortal endeavors. Keep in mind the concept of "calling and election made sure", is the commencement of the calling and the election process and is an occurrence mortals cannot remember since this starts prior to birth. The purpose of this section is to shed some light on these two events and their meaning to mortals. When studying the doctrine surrounding the concept of "Calling and Election made sure", the term "calling", and the term "election", used in this particular piece of doctrine which is not used in the same context as a calling one might receive from the Bishop, although there are similarities. When the Bishop calls a member to a certain position in the ward, this is a "calling". When the congregation sustains the member in the calling this is the "election". So when the calling is "made sure", much, much later. The scope of a ward calling is temporal and "Calling and Election Made Sure" is eternal in scope, this is the difference between the two events. When using the term, Calling and Election made Sure, as a point of doctrine, the scope of the term is expanded to cover the entire expanse of eternity and takes on an eternal meaning.

What is meant eternally by the word, calling? Moreover, who are the called of God?

This calling, as articulated in the phrase calling and election made sure, is the calling necessary for us, as spirit children, to receive in the preexistence, starting the march toward eternal life. The call originates with God, but only those, in mortality, who actually receive the gospel, who enter into the new and everlasting covenant, who cleave unto the truth and strive to live in harmony with the revealed word, only these are numbered among those whom the scriptures name as the "called of the Lord". The following scriptures speak of this calling and the contents thereof. Peter teaches, the saints are called to "eternal life" (*1 Tim 6:12*), called to "the promise of eternal inheritance", (*Heb 9:15*), and he also explains the Lord's callings are the result of "foreordination and grow out of faithfulness in pre-existence" (2 Tim 1:8-9). " hath from the beginning," from before the foundations of the world, "chose you , His saints, to salvation through sanctification of the Spirit and belief of the truth: Whereunto he called you by our gospel, to the obtaining of the glory of our Lord Jesus Christ." (*2 Thess 2:13-14*). In another glorious passage, Paul says, "We know that all things work together for good to them that love God, to them who are the called according to his purpose." The Lord's hand governs and controls in the lives of those whom He, in His infinite foreknowledge, hath called to be His people. And then:

"For whom He did foreknow, He also did predestinate (foreordained) to be conformed to the image of His Son, that He might be the firstborn among many brethren," which is to say that God in His infinite wisdom foreordained the noble and great spirits in pre-existence to become like Christ, to gain glory, power and might like unto the Son of God, so the Son becomes the firstborn, as it were, among many exalted sons. And then in glorious conclusion: "Moreover whom He did predestinate (foreordain), them He also called: and whom He called, them He also justified: and whom He justified, them He also glorified" (*Romans 8:28-30*).

That is, the saints were foreordained and called by God in the councils of eternity to believe the truth, to be sanctified, to save their souls, become like unto the Son of God; and then in this life it is necessary for them to achieve the dictates of that calling. Latter Day Saints believe that the Church of Jesus Christ of Latter Day Saints is the only place whereby these eternal promises can be fulfilled. In modern revelation given to this church the Lord confirms the doctrine of His ancient apostles, speaks of, "calling and election made in the church" (*D&C 53:1; 55:1*), of the fact "members are called to his everlasting gospel" (*D&C 101:39*), and names the elders of his Church as among those "whom he hath called and chosen in these last days" (*D&C 52:1:41:2*).

What is meant by making a calling sure?

All blessings promised in connection with the callings of God are conditional; offered to men provided they obey the "laws upon which their receipt is predicated" (*D&C 130:20-21*). "For all who will have a blessing at my hands," the Lord says, "shall abide the law which was appointed for that blessing, and the conditions thereof, as were instituted from before the foundation of the world" (*D&C 132:5*). It is clear, while calling are given in the preexistence, the requirements for fulfillment was also made known to all and children of God must have accepted those terms or they would not be allowed to come here.

It follows, then, when the law has been lived to the fullest, the promised blessing is guaranteed. "I, the Lord, am bound when ye do what I say; but when ye do not what I say, ye have no promise" (D&C 82:10). Accordingly, when a man lives the law to the extent that he qualifies for eternal life, the Lord is bound by his own law to confer the greatest of all gifts upon him. And if by a long course of trial and obedience, while yet in this life, a man proves to the Lord, he has and will abide in the truth, the Lord accepts the exhibited devotion and issues his decree, the promised blessings shall be received. The calling, which up to that time was provisional, is then ratified or made sure. The receipt of the promised blessings is no longer conditional; they are guaranteed.

What is meant by election? Who are the elect of God? To what, have they been elected? And why?

The term election primarily denoting God's choice of the house of Israel to be the covenant people with privileges and responsibilities, they might "become a means of blessing to the whole world" (*Rom. 9:11; 11:5, 7, 28*). Election is an opportunity for service and is on both a national and an individual basis. On a national basis, the seed of Abraham carry the gospel to the world. However, it is by individual faithfulness that all this is accomplished.

The elect has been chosen, even "before the foundation of the world," yet no one is unconditionally elected to eternal life. Each must, for himself, hearken to the gospel and receive its ordinances and covenants from the hands of the servants of the Lord in order to obtain salvation. If one is elected but does not serve, his election could be said to have been in vain, as Paul expressed in (*2 Cor. 6:1*).

Elections are not all of the same kind. Since election has to do with God's choice of persons or groups to accomplish his purposes, some may be elected by him to one thing and some to another. Although the Lord uses certain individuals to accomplish his purposes during mortality these activities are cannot always be classified as callings or elections, and it does not necessarily follow, these persons will automatically receive a fullness of salvation thereby. For instance, Nebuchadnezzar and Cyrus fulfilled certain purposes in the economy of God, but they apparently did it for their own reasons and not as conscious acts of faith and righteousness. On the other hand, salvation of one's soul comes only by personal integrity and willing obedience to the laws and ordinances of the gospel of Jesus Christ. Thus, there are some elections desired over others.

The term election of grace is a special term that has meaning other than the general usage of "election". An election of grace, spoken of in (*D&C 84:98–102*) and (*Rom. 11:1–5*) has reference to one's situation in mortality; being born at a time, at a place, and in circumstances where one will come in favorable contact with the gospel. This election took place in the premortal existence based on their valiant actions there. Those who are faithful and diligent in the gospel in mortality receive an even more desirable election in the life to come, and if they are valiant and faithful there "they can become the elect of God and receive the promise of a fullness of God's glory in eternity" (*D&C 84:33–41*). This scripture covers all earthly beings since the restoration of the gospel by Joseph Smith.

The concept held by many is, God unconditionally elected some to be saved and some to be damned without any effort, action, or choice on their part is not correct, for the scriptures teach, it is "only by faith and obedience that one's calling and election is made sure" (*2 Pet. 1; D&C 131:5*). By this, mortals, even those who are born as the elect, cannot become the elect until their calling and election becomes ratified. In fact, this birth into the elect is a detriment to them unless their calling and election is made sure.

The term, elect, in a general sense, is comprised of the whole "house of Israel" (Isa 45:4; 65:9). Jesus, Paul, and Peter speak of the elect as the saints, as the faithful believers, as those who love the Lord and are seeking righteousness. (*Mt 24:22; Mk 13:20; Luke18:7; Col 3:12; 2 Tim 2:10; Titus 1:1*). The Lord has promised to "gather and save his elect" (*D&C 29:7; 33:6; 35:20*). Paul speaks of the elect along with the called, setting forth; "they are foreordained to be like Christ, their conduct here is justified, and they shall be glorified hereafter" (*Rom 8:28-30*). Peter specifies, their high status is "according to the foreknowledge of God the Father" (*1 Pet 1:2*), and Isaiah assures, "great blessings shall flow to them during the Millennial Era" (Isa 65:22).
The scriptures above use the term "the elect" in a general way but in the Mormon Church today the usage of the term takes on a more specific meaning, "The elect of God comprise a very select group, an inner circle of faithful members of the Church.... They are the portion of church members who are striving with all their hearts to keep the fullness of the gospel law in this life so they can become inheritors of the fullness of the gospel rewards in the life to come. They are those men and women who have entered into and are striving to be obedient to the terms of the New and Everlasting Covenant.

"As far as the male sex is concerned, they are the ones, the Lord says, who have the Melchizedek Priesthood conferred upon them and who thereafter magnify their callings and are sanctified by the Spirit. In this way, 'They become the sons of Moses and of Aaron and the seed of Abraham, and the church and kingdom, and the elect of God' (*Mormon Doctrine, 2nd ed., 217*).

What is meant by making an election sure?

An election is a method of choosing and in this instance, the Lord chooses or elects one who is obedient and makes his conditional promises unconditional, thus, his election is sure. This process guarantees the obedient follower, it is sure t the Lord has chosen him for eternal life. It is with election as with calling: the chosen of the Lord are offered, all of the blessings of the gospel on condition of obedience to the Lord's laws; and they, having been tried, tested, and found worthy in all things, eventually

116

have a seal placed on their election, which guarantees the receipt of the promised blessing. Remember, this is a process not an event so it takes a while to develop.

What is meant by having a calling and election made sure?

A person having calling and election made sure is being sealed up unto eternal life. It is to have the unconditional guarantee of exaltation in the highest heaven of the celestial world. It is to receive the assurance of godhood. It is, in effect, to have the one's Day of Judgment advanced. The inheritance of all the glory and honor of the Father's kingdom is assured prior to the day when the faithful actually enter into the divine presence to sit with Christ in his throne, even as he is :set down" with his "Father in his throne" (*Rev 3:21*).

How is this calling and election done? And by whom?

In the Teachings of the Prophet Joseph Smith pages, 149-151, there are two Comforters discussed. One is the Holy Ghost; the same as given on the day of Pentecost, and the one all Saints receive after faith, repentance, and baptism. The impact of the Holy Spirit of Promise is so important and profound to the lives of mortals that the reader of this dissertation should read this section twice. This first Comforter or Holy Ghost influences only pure intelligence. One of the functions assigned and delegated to the Holy Spirit is to seal, and the following expressions are identical in thought and in content:

A. To be sealed by the Holy Spirit of Promise;
B. To be justified by the Spirit;
C. To be approved by the Lord; and
D. To be ratified by the Holy Ghost.

Accordingly, any act sealed by the Holy Spirit of Promise, is one, which is justified by the Spirit, approved by the Lord, ratified by the Holy Ghost. As revealed to Joseph Smith, the Lord's law in this respect is: "All covenants, contracts, bonds, obligations, oaths, vows, performances, connections, associations, or expectations, that are not made and entered into and sealed by the Holy Spirit of promise, of him who is anointed, both as well for time and for all eternity, and that too most holy, by revelation and commandment through the medium of mine anointed, whom I have appointed on the earth to hold this power (and I have appointed unto my servant Joseph to hold this power in the last days, and there is never but one on the earth at a time on whom this power and the keys of this priesthood are conferred), are of no efficacy, virtue, or force in and after the resurrection from the dead; for all contracts that are not made unto this end have an end when men are dead" (D&C 132:7).

By way of illustration, this means, baptism, partaking of the sacrament, administering to the sick, marriage, every covenant man ever makes with the Lord, plus all other contracts, bonds, obligations, oaths, vows, performances, associations, or those who are called and set apart by one who holds the proper keys, must perform expectations in righteousness. And is received by people who are worthy to receive whatever blessing is involved, otherwise whatever is done has no binding and sealing effect in eternity.

Since "the Comforter knoweth all things" (*D&C 42:17*), it follows, it is not possible to lie to the Holy Ghost and thereby gain an unearned or undeserved blessing. So by this provision all things must be sealed by the Holy Spirit of Promise, if they are to have "efficacy, virtue, or force in and after the resurrection from the dead" (*D&C 132:7*). This is the Lord's system for dealing with absolute impartiality with all men, and for giving all men exactly what they merit, neither adding to nor diminishing from them.

When the Holy Spirit of Promise places his ratifying seal upon a baptism, or a marriage, or any covenant, except one's calling and election made sure, the seal is a conditional approval or ratified; it is sealed in eternity only in the event of subsequent obedience to the terms and conditions of whatever covenant is involved.

The Second Comforter

The other Comforter spoken of is a subject of great interest when it comes to the subject of Calling and Election made sure and the events that follow. After a person has faith in Christ, repents of his sins, and is baptized for the remission of his sins and receives the Holy Ghost, (by the laying on of hands), which is the first Comforter. Then let him continue to humble himself before God, hungering and thirsting after righteousness, and living by every word of God, and the Lord will soon say unto him, Son, thou shalt be exalted.

When the Lord has thoroughly proved him, and finds the man is determined to serve Him at all hazards, then the man will find his calling and his election made sure, then it will be his privilege to receive the other Comforter, which the Lord hath promised the Saints, as is recorded in the testimony of (*St. John, 14: 12-27*). Note the 16, 17, 18, 21, 23 verses are also quoted.

Now what is this other Comforter? It is no more nor less than the Lord Jesus Christ Himself; this is the sum and substance of the whole matter. When any person obtains this last Comforter, they will have the personage of Jesus Christ to attend them, or appear unto them from time to time, even He will manifest the Father unto them, they will take up their abode with them, and the visions of the heavens will be opened unto them. The Lord will teach them face to face, and they may have a perfect knowledge of the mysteries of the Kingdom of God. This is the state and place the ancient Saints arrived at when they had such glorious visions, Isaiah, Ezekiel, John upon the Isle of Patmos, and St. Paul in the three heavens. Including all the Saints who held communion with the general assembly and Church of the Firstborn

What is the relationship between celestial marriage, having one's calling, and election made sure?

In the same sense, baptism opens the door and starts repentant persons traveling on the path leading to eternal life, so also does celestial marriage enable the couple to continue on the same path. This holy order of matrimony also opens a door leading to celestial exaltation. "In the celestial glory there are three heavens or degrees; and in order to obtain the highest, a man must enter into this order of the priesthood [meaning the new and everlasting covenant of marriage]; and if he does not, he cannot obtain it. He may enter into the other, but that is the end of his kingdom; he cannot have an increase" (*D&C 131:1-4*).

As everyone who has been married in the temple knows, those so united by the power and authority of the holy priesthood and by virtue of the sealing power restored by Elijah--are promised an inheritance of glory, honor, power, and dominion in the kingdom of God. However, as with baptism, all the promises are conditional, they are specifically and pointedly stated as being contingent upon the subsequent faithfulness of the participating parties. If they keep the commandments after celestial marriage, their union continues in the life to come; if they do not conform to the standards of personal righteousness involved, their marriage is not of force when they die and they revert to their separate and single status.

No person can gain exaltation or eternal life alone; because exaltation includes the continuation of the family unit in eternity; because the whole thrust, of revealed religion is to perfect and center everything in the family; and because having one's calling and election made sure is the receipt of a guarantee of eternal life. It was the most natural thing in the world for the Lord to reveal both the doctrine of eternal marriage and the doctrine of being sealed up unto eternal life (meaning having one's calling and election made sure) in one and the same revelation. In effect, one grows out of the other. The one is a conditional promise of eternal life; the other is an unconditional promise but one must fulfill the first in order to receive the second.

The Doctrine and Covenants begin by talking of celestial marriage in these words: "If a man marry a wife by my word, which is my law, and by the new and everlasting covenant, and it is sealed unto them by the Holy Spirit of Promise, by him who is anointed, unto whom I have appointed this power and the keys of this priesthood," but then proceeds to consider the matter of having their callings and elections made sure by saying: "and it shall be said unto them, meaning, that in addition to the marriage sealing, it shall be said unto them--Ye shall come forth in the first resurrection; ... and shall inherit thrones, kingdoms, principalities, and powers, dominions, all heights and depths--then ... they shall pass by the angels, and the gods, which are set there, to their exaltation and glory in all things, as hath been sealed upon their heads, which glory shall be a fullness and a continuation of the seeds forever and ever" (D&C,132:19).

Those who desire to marry in the temple must understand, after celestial marriage, after entering into sacred covenants in the house of the Lord, after receiving the conditional promise of the continuation of the family unit in eternity and after receiving power to gain kingdoms and throne, those involved must so live as to receive the guarantees to which they have thus been called, and the assurances that appertain to their election. Which were given on a conditional basis only in celestial marriage. As with baptism, so it is with celestial marriage, after the glorious promise of eternal life that is part of each of these covenants, the covenant makers must press forward in righteousness until the calling and election is made sure; and this high achievement grows out of and is the crowning reward of celestial marriage.

What is the relationship between holding the holy Melchizedek Priesthood, and having one's calling and election made sure?

The Melchizedek Priesthood is conferred with an oath and a covenant--a covenant on the man's part where he will receive the priesthood and magnify his calling therein, and an oath on God's part the man shall, consequently, be "made like unto the Son of God, abiding a priest continually." (*Inspired Version [JST], Heb 7:3; D&C 84:33-44*). Also, see (*Heb 7:1-3, 18-22*). In other words, those who magnify their callings shall gain eternal life. However, one cannot keep a covenant before it is made; a calling in the priesthood cannot be magnified until it is received. The covenant is the contract, which sets forth the terms and conditions by obedience to which eternal life may be won; the obedience comes after the call; and when it is whole and complete, the worthy son, has his calling and election made sure, and he inherits the promised reward.

Is having one's calling and election made sure the same as being sealed by the Holy Spirit of Promise?

The Holy Ghost is the Holy Spirit; he is the Holy Spirit promised the saints at baptism, or in other words the Holy Spirit of Promise, this exalted name-title signifying, the promised receipt of the Holy Spirit, as on the day of Pentecost, is the greatest gift man can receive in mortality.

The gift of the Holy Ghost is the right to the constant companionship of the member of the Godhead based on faithfulness. It is bestowed with a promise, the member shall receive revelation and be sanctified if he or she is true and faithful and so live as to qualify for the companionship of the Holy Spirit who will not dwell in an unclean temple. (1 Cor. 3:16-17; 6:19; Mosiah 2:37; Hela 4:24) The receipt of the promise is conditional! If after receiving the promise, and the commandments are thereby kept, the member gains the companionship of the Godhead, and not otherwise.

When the Holy Spirit of Promise places his ratifying seal upon a baptism, or a marriage, or any covenant, except one's calling and election made sure, the seal is a conditional approval or ratification; it is sealed in eternity only in the event of subsequent obedience to the terms and conditions of whatever covenant is involved. But when the ratifying seal of approval is placed upon someone whose calling and election is thereby made sure--because there are no more conditions to be met by the obedient person--this act of being sealed up unto eternal life is called being sealed by the Holy Spirit of Promise. Having one's calling and election made sure is the ratification process ending the conditional part of the covenant and bestows upon the recipient prior promises made and sets the stage for recipient of the other or second Comforter and this is no less than companionship of the Lord Jesus Christ Himself. Thus, sealed by the Holy Ghost is sealed up unto eternal life; and sealed up unto eternal life is thus, being sealed by the Holy Spirit of Promise. Having only partial knowledge of this concept, one will find this doctrine to be misunderstood, difficult, or confusing and unless the whole concept of the sealing power of the Spirit is understood, it is difficult to sort out the true meaning of the scriptures and other prophetic utterances that repeatedly bear witness to this part of the plan of salvation.

121

Celestial Marriage

Celestial marriage refers to a type of marriage, which Mormons believe is intended to last beyond the grave and through eternity. Celestial means heavenly, and indeed, a celestial marriage is a heavenly marriage. This does not indicate a marriage that takes place in heaven, but rather a kind of marriage that is heavenly in function; it is divine in its origin and potential.

Mormons assert, for a celestial marriage to occur, several key steps must be followed.

First, the man and woman must be sealed, or bound, by one holding the authority of God to perform such sealing, which can only take place in Mormon temples.

Second, the couple must seek, with all their hearts, to individually and jointly follow Jesus Christ, and live their marriage in a celestial manner. Third, God through His Spirit must confirm the sealing. All Celestial marriages start as Temple marriages and only become Celestial marriages when ratified by the Holy Spirit of Promise.

Eternal marriages do not just happen; faithful Mormons do not consider them a checklist item that can be performed at a specific place and time and then be forever done. Rather, eternal marriages are a constant work in progress. Although the start of the eternal marriage starts from the point at which the sealing was done with proper authority, the couple must live their lives in a way worthy of the blessing of eternal marriage.

A couple shows their continued desire for their marriage to be eternal by following Christ in their daily life. Faithful Mormons who have been sealed together strive to understand and keep God's commandments. They continually try to be like Christ, seeking to be humble, patient, honest, obedient, loving, forgiving, and kind. These are but a few of the godly attributes, which they try to instill in their lives and in their relationship.

After a couple has been sealed together by the proper authority, and after they have proven their commitment to an eternal marriage through persistent actions, they have the opportunity to have their sealing confirmed by God's Holy Spirit. This is not an earthly ordinance; it only comes through revelation from God directly to the individuals in the marriage. Such a divine confirmation may occur in this life, or but most, if not all, are confirmed in the next life.

In many ways, the confirmation of a couple's sealing is a stamp of approval given by God, a divine recognition their union will be eternal. This is the true definition of a celestial marriage, one that has been ratified by God as being in full force for the eternities.

To build an eternal family is not an easy task. It requires faith, commitment, and a lot of hard work. Not everyone is successful. Faithful Mormons live with the God-given hope that through the three elements previously discussed they can live the first two elements, sealing, living in such a way, the third, ratification will occur.

Born in the Covenant/Sealing of Children

Sealing power is integral to creating a celestial marriage and has a role to play in the rest of the family. Children sealed to their parents by the same priesthood authority, with certain expectation, can endure through this life, and extend into the hereafter. If a couple was sealed together prior to the birth of their children, then those children are, in Mormon terminology, born in/under the covenant, and are partakers of the divine promise possible through the sealing of their parents. If a couple becomes, sealed after their children are born, then the children can be sealed to the parents in a special ceremony in a holy temple.

Charity in Mormonism

The world understands charity to be the act of giving donations to the poor and needy, of offering contributions to various organizations striving to do good things in the world. However, this is not the actual meaning Mormonism gives to the word charity. Just giving donations to the poor and needy may be a product of charity but not always. For example, some people enter into charitable situations and give money, food, and services for so-called charities, without feeling any true charity in their hearts. Rather, their motivation might stem from a desire for glory and praise, for tax write-offs, or for a good name in the public's mind.

Mormons believe charity is much more than this. In fact, charity is the pure love of Christ. The meaning behind the phrase "love of Christ" can be threefold.

First, it represents the reason Jesus underwent so many trials and suffering for us: He loved all mankind and continues to love them with the utmost mercy, hoping, all people will accept His sacrifice and follow Him to perfect joy—in this sense, charity could be rephrased as love from Christ.

Second, charity can be described in terms of love for Christ—if one truly loves Jesus, why not be willing to indeed follow Him and do all He asks? It is the mortal's duty to foster a deep affection for Jesus and let His love guide them in all their decisions and actions.

Third, charity is a Christ like love, or a love like that of Christ. Those who wish to follow His example in all things would definitely notice and appreciate how much He loves us, then turning around, and loving each other in a similar manner. In the midst of agony, Jesus uttered, "Father, forgive them; for they know not what they do." These few words speak volumes about what it means to love. Christ's perfect example of forgiveness, and anxiety for the welfare of others over self, is an example, all should aspire to emulate, in every contact with each other as brothers and sisters under God. Mormons have both the Bible and the Book of Mormon to teach them the importance of charity. First Corinthians chapter 13 emphasizes, if a person has no charity, then his case is hopeless and vain even if he has all knowledge, or has faith enough to move mountains, or gives all his possessions for the poor, or suffers a martyr's death. The prophet Mormon teaches, charity is the greatest of all spiritual gifts—greater than faith, hope, and meekness—and "whoso is found possessed of it at the last day, it shall be well with him. The Bible and the Book of Mormon use similar language in describing a person who has charity: "And charity suffereth long, and is kind, and envieth not, and is not puffed up, seeketh not her own, is not easily provoked, thinketh no evil, and rejoiceth not in iniquity but rejoiceth in the truth, beareth all things, believeth all things, hopeth all things, endureth all things" (1 Corinthians 13:4, Mor. 7:45).

The pure love of Christ causes a person to want to serve others. This might include giving monetary donations to any effort supporting the health or education of less fortunate individuals. More often, a charity-filled person actually gets involved in the lives of other people and seeks for ways to effectively touch them for good.

There are a lot of problems and suffering in the world. Some of these sufferings are part of the mortal probation and cannot be completely avoided. However, Mormonism also teaches, many problems and suffering are a consequence of transgressions (whether ignorant or deliberate) of God's commandments. Unfortunately, many people do not realize the importance of, or even scoff at, God's commandments and they underestimate the importance of such things as prayer to a loving Heavenly Father, study of His word in the scriptures, wholesome family activities, chastity, forgiveness, selfless kindness, and purity of mind, body, and spirit.

After the death of Christ and His apostles, the true doctrines of Christ's gospel were changed or lost because of neglect and even wickedness. Mormonism is the Restoration of the true Christ's gospel, and because of feeling of charity, Mormons wish to share their knowledge with the rest of humanity. This is why Mormonism stresses the value of missionary work, and each year tens of thousands of members of the Mormon Church leave their homelands to share the restored gospel of Jesus Christ with others. Charity causes many of these Mormons to feel as did missionaries of old who are described in the Book of Mormon: "Now they were desirous that salvation should be declared to every creature, for they could not bear that any human soul should perish; yea, even the very thoughts that any soul should endure endless torment did cause them to quake and tremble" (*Mosiah 28:1*).

Since charity is so crucial in motivating a person to do good things and in helping him gain salvation, how it is obtained? The Book of Mormon teaches us: "Wherefore, my beloved brethren, pray unto the Father with all the energy of heart, that ye may be filled with this love, which he hath bestowed upon all who are true followers of his Son, Jesus Christ; that ye may become the sons of God; that when he shall appear we shall be like him, for we shall see him as he is; that we may have this hope; that we may be purified even as he is pure. Amen" (Moroni 7:41).

There are many scriptures that define charity, here are a few. The pure love of Christ (Moro. 7: 47); the love that Christ has for the children of men and that the children of men should have for one another (2 Ne. 26: 30; 33: 7-9; Ether 12: 33-34); the highest, noblest, strongest kind of love, not merely affection.

Knowledge puffs up, but charity edifies, (1st Cor. 8: 1). Charity, a pure love, excels and exceeds almost all else, (1st Cor. 13). The end of the commandment is charity out of a pure heart, (1st Tim. 1: 5). Add to brotherly kindness charity, (2 Pet. 1: 7). The Lord has commanded that all men should have charity, (2 Ne. 26: 30 (Moro. 7: 44-47). See that ye have faith, hope, and charity, (Alma 7: 24). The love that the Lord has for men is charity, (Ether 12: 33-34). Without charity men cannot inherit that place prepared in the Father's mansions, (Ether 12: 34 (Moro. 10: 20-21). Moroni wrote Mormon's words on faith, hope, and charity, (Moro. 7). Charity qualifies men for the Lord's work, (D&C 4: 5-6 (D&C 12: 8). Clothe yourselves with the bond of charity, (D&C 88: 125). Let thy bowels be full of charity, (D&C 121: 45).

Often, there are talks/lessons about developing charity, claiming it is good works that constitute the act of charity. The scriptures seem to clearly refute this idea as read in 1st Cor. 13. "Even though one sells all their belongings, feed the poor, and have not charity, they are nothing." Even though one brings cookies to the neighbors and have not charity, they are tinkling cymbals. Even though some have the gift of prophecy or can teach by the power of the Holy Ghost, and have not charity they are nothing, and as Joseph Smith said, all are liable to fall until filled with charity, or something to that effect. Everything else fails because having charity means being like Christ not acting like Christ. Having charity goes hand in hand with having a knowledge of God. As Peter stated in 2nd Peter 1, if they (meaning, God's children) have Charity (the last on a laundry list of necessary characteristics) they will not be barren nor unfruitful in the knowledge of the Lord Jesus Christ. Paul also commented, "For now (not having a fullness of charity) we see through a glass, darkly; but then (when we are endowed with a fullness of charity, like a mantle to wear) face to face: now I know in part; but then shall I know even as also I am known" (*1st Cor. 13*).

The knowledge gained with Charity is the knowledge of Christ. Thus, it is intimately linked to Eternal Life, which is to know Christ. Christ longs after the souls of his children or God's children. A 3rd century bishop said, Charity is something, when held, causes those around him to love God. Robert Millet once said, Charity is an intense and painful desire to share the gospel. One must develop a working definition of charity they must have in their heart, mind, and soul the fullness of the desires of Christ. Therein striving to become the sons of God, become like him and sees him as he is. Saints are told to pray with all the energy of heart for this gift. To know Christ then, can come only thru revelation. It comes from obedience to the Word of Christ. Mortals receive the companionship of the Holy Ghost. Therefore, one cannot" develop" charity for themselves, at all, no more than they can get eternal life by themselves. It is something entirely bestowed upon people by Christ by his will and of course, in response to the law that the bestowal of charity is predicated upon.

Chastity

(The greatest gift given to mortals is the one most often and blatantly abused)

Physical intimacy between husband and wife is beautiful and sacred. It is ordained of God for the creation of children and for the expression of love within marriage. In the world today, Satan has led many people to believe, sexual intimacy outside of marriage is acceptable, ever desirable. However, in God's sight, it is a serious sin; it is an abuse of the power He has given mortals to create life. The prophet Alma taught, sexual sins are more serious than any other sins except murder and denying the Holy Ghost (Alma 39:3–5). Sometimes people try to convince themselves sexual relations outside of marriage are acceptable if the participants love one another. This is not true. Breaking the law of chastity and encouraging someone else to do so is not an expression of love. People who love each other will never endanger one another's happiness and safety in exchange for temporary personal pleasure. When people care for one another enough to keep the law of chastity, their love, trust, and commitment increase, resulting in greater happiness and unity. In contrast, relationships built on sexual immorality sour quickly. Those who engage in sexual immorality often feel fear, guilt, and shame. Bitterness, jealousy, and hatred soon replace the positive feelings; they once felt in their relationship.

Our Heavenly Father has given the law of chastity for personal protection. Obedience to this law is essential to personal peace and strength of character and to happiness in the home. Those who keep themselves sexually pure will avoid the spiritual and emotional damage, which always comes from sharing physical intimacies with someone outside of marriage. Those who keep themselves sexually pure will be sensitive to the Holy Ghost's guidance, strength, comfort, and protection and will fulfill an important requirement for receiving a temple recommend and participating in temple ordinances.

Sexual Sins

The Lord and His Prophets condemn sexual immorality. The prophet Alma taught, sexual sins are more serious than any other sins except murder and denying the Holy Ghost (Alma 39:3–5). All sexual relations outside of marriage violate the law of chastity and are physically and spiritually dangerous for those who engage in them.

The Ten Commandments include the command where in God's children are forbidden to commit adultery, which is sexual intercourse between a married man and someone other than his wife or between a married woman and someone other than her husband (Exodus 20:14). The Apostle Paul said, it is the will of God, all must abstain from fornication, which is sexual intercourse between an unmarried person and anyone else (*1st Thessalonians 4:3*). Latter-day prophets repeatedly speak out against these sins and against the evil practice of sexual abuse.

Like other violations of the law of chastity, homosexual activity is a serious sin. It is contrary to the purposes of human sexuality (*Romans 1:24–32*). It distorts loving relationships and prevents people from receiving the blessings found in family life and the saving ordinances of the gospel.

Merely refraining from sexual intercourse outside of marriage is not sufficient in the Lord's standard of personal purity. The Lord requires a high moral standard of His disciples, including complete fidelity to one's spouse in thought and conduct. In the Sermon on the Mount, He said, "Ye have heard that it was said by them of old time, Thou shalt not commit adultery: But I say unto you, that whosoever looketh on a woman to lust after her hath committed adultery with her already in his heart" (*Matthew 5:27–28*). In the latter days He has said, "Thou shalt not . . . commit adultery, nor do anything like unto it" (*D&C 59:6*). In addition, He has reemphasized the principle He taught in the Sermon on the Mount: "He that looketh on a woman to lust after her, or if any shall commit adultery in their hearts, they shall not have the Spirit, but shall deny the faith and shall fear" (*D&C 63:16*). These warnings apply to all people, whether they are married or single.

Church members who have committed sexual sin should speak with their bishop or branch president, who can help them through the process of repentance. Those who find themselves struggling with sexual temptations, including feelings of same-gender attraction, should not give in to those temptations. People can choose to avoid such behavior and receive the Lord's help as they pray for strength and work to overcome the problem.

Keeping the Law of Chastity

No matter how strong temptations seem, the Lord will help people withstand them if they choose to follow Him. The Apostle Paul declared, "There hath no temptation taken you but such as is common to man: but God is faithful, who will not suffer you to be tempted above that ye are able; but will with the temptation also make a way to escape, that ye may be able to bear it" (*1st Corinthians 10:13*). The following counsel can help people overcome the frequent and blatant temptations in the world today:

Decide now to be chaste. One needs to make this decision only once. Make the decision now; before the temptation comes, and let the decision be so firm and with such deep commitment, the decision can never be shaken. Determine never to do anything outside of marriage to arouse the powerful emotions expressed, only in marriage. Determine now to be completely true to your spouse.

Control all thoughts. No one commits sexual sin in an instant. Immoral acts always begin with impure thoughts. If one allows their thoughts to linger on obscene or immoral things, they have already taken the first step toward immorality and they must flee immediately from situations and may lead to sin and pray for constant strength to resist temptation and control all thoughts. Make this a part of daily prayers.

Stay away from pornography. Never view, read, or listen to anything depicting or describing the human body or sexual conduct in a way that can arouse sexual feelings. Pornographic materials are addictive and destructive. They can rob people of their self-respect and of a sense of the beauties of life. They can tear resistance down and lead to evil thoughts and abusive conduct.

Any single person dating must always treat dates with respect. Those who are dating must never treat their date as an object of lustful desires. They should carefully plan positive and constructive activities so

128

they are not alone without anything to do. They should stay in areas of safety where they can easily control themselves. They should not participate in conversations or activities where sexual feelings are aroused, such as passionate kissing, lying with or on top of another person, or touching the private, sacred parts of another person's body, with or without clothing.

If married, be faithful to spouses in thoughts, words, and actions. The Lord has said, "Thou shalt love thy wife with all thy heart, and shalt cleave unto her and none else. And he that looketh upon a woman to lust after her shall deny the faith, and shall not have the Spirit; and if he repents not he shall be cast out" (*D&C 42:22–23*). Never flirt in any way. As much as possible, avoid being alone with anyone of the opposite sex and ask ourselves if a spouse would be pleased if he or she knew of your words or actions.

Remember the Apostle Paul's counsel: " abstain from all appearance of evil " (*1 Thessalonians 5:22*). When one stays away from such circumstances, temptation gets no chance to develop.

Forgiveness for the Repentant

The best course is complete moral cleanliness. It is wrong to commit sexual sins with the thinking it will be easy to repent later. This attitude is a sin itself, showing irreverence for the Lord and the covenants made with Him. However, the Lord can forgive those who have committed sexual sins if they repent.

Repentance is difficult, but it is possible (*see Isaiah 1:18*). Always remember, the despair of sin replaced with the sweet peace of forgiveness.

Chiasmus

It was recently discovered, writers of ancient Middle Eastern poetry, including the Bible, often used a poetical form called chiasmus, a form of parallelism in which key ideas are structured in a mirror image reflective form such as A,B,C,C',B',A'. Some of the most powerful and beautiful examples of this ancient form are found in the Book of Mormon (first discovered in 1967 by John Welch). The importance of chiasmus in ancient Semitic writings has only been recognized in this century, and still today very few educated people have ever heard of it. Its strong presence in the Book of Mormon is evidence, its writers possessed an ancient Semitic literary tradition, as the Book of Mormon claims, and single-handedly refutes the claim, the Book of Mormon is the product of a 19th century writer (though there are numerous other factors refuting such a claim). This is fascinating evidence proves the Book of Mormon is an authentic ancient document.

Chiasmus is a form of parallelism used as a poetical structure in some ancient writings from the Middle East and Greece. The word chiasmus derives from the Greek letter chi (X) which symbolizes the top-to-bottom mirror image reflection achieved by elements of text. Here are two examples from Isaiah,

(a) "Make the heart of this people fat,

(b) And make their ears heavy,

(c) and shut their eyes;

(c') lest they see with their eyes,

(b') and hear with their ears,

(a') and understand with their heart,

And convert [return], and be healed" (*Is. 6:10*).

(a)" Come ... to the house of the God of Jacob; and ...

(b) and we will walk in his paths...

(c) And he shall judge among the nations...

(d) they shall beat their swords into plowshares

(d') and their spears into pruning hooks

(c') nation shall not lift up sword against nation...

(b') O house of Jacob, come ye,

(a') and let us walk in the light of the LORD" (*Isaiah 2:3-5*).

The example from Isaiah 2 shows the pattern can be complicated with groups of parallel elements (a-b-c) treated as a single element. The conjugate elements in a chiasmus (e.g., b and b') can be related in several ways - direct repetition (synonymous parallelism), contrasting ideas or terms (antithetic parallelism), complimentary concepts (synthetic parallelism) in which one item completes or compliments the other, and more. "Through such techniques, very sophisticated structures can be created" (*Ludlow, op. cit., pp. 31-39*). In major passages of chiasmus, the most important regions tend to be the central or pivotal point (the focal point) in the middle of the chiasmus, and then the ends (top and bottom).

Chiasmus was a common form of presenting ideas among those with literary skills in the ancient world and was used to create powerful poetry. This form, however, was not widely appreciated as a hallmark of ancient writing in the Middle East until this century.

Chiasmus appears to have begun as a structural form, which then developed into an intriguing rhetorical device, which has been used sporadically in prose and poetry by many authors for nearly three thousand years. Nevertheless, the awareness of such a form, except in isolated cases, remained a part of the intellectual sub consciousness of modern Western Europe until frequent chiasma passages were discovered in the Bible. Since the mid-nineteenth century, there have been several reputed scholars, mostly theologians, who have published on the subject. Their works indicate that, although some chiasms appear in Greek, Latin, and English, the form was originally Hebrews and dates at least to the eighth and tenth centuries B. C. in Isaiah and in the Psalms....

Interestingly, the Book of Mormon, which claims to have its literary roots in the ancient Middle East, shows many excellent examples of what appear to be deliberate, crafted chiasmus. The examples are strong enough and they are difficult to explain if the assumption is Joseph Smith, (or any other person in the 1820s) wrote the book himself. In most people's opinion, there is simply no way a poorly schooled farm boy could have constructed sophisticated examples of an ancient writing form, completely unknown to him. Moreover, even if chiasmus was understood and even if Joseph had been able to craft examples of it in his text, he and his followers would surely have pointed out its existence as evidence of authenticity. In fact, chiasmus was not searched for or discovered in the Book of Mormon until the late 1960s, when LDS scholar John Welch learned of scholarly work on chiasmus in antiquity and hypothesized, the Book of Mormon might contain examples as well. His findings were truly surprising; revealing clear, distinct, and elegant passages of chiasmus existed in the Book of Mormon. Since then, many chiasmic structures have been found. See, for example, Donald W. Parry's The Book of Mormon Text Reformatted According to Parallelistic Patterns, FARMS, Provo, Utah, 1992 (order as PAR-92 for $18.50 from FARMS), which also includes an excellent essay on Semitic poetry in general and the role of chiasmus.

Several brief examples of chiasmus in the Book of Mormon.

" (Men will drink damnation to their souls unless)

(a) They HUMBLE themselves

(b) and become as little CHILDREN

(c) believing that salvation is in the ATONING BLOOD OF CHRIST;

(d) for the NATURAL MAN

(e) is an enemy of GOD

(f) and HAS BEEN from the fall of Adam

(f') and WILL BE forever and ever

(e') unless he yieldeth to the HOLY SPIRIT

(d') and putteth off the NATURAL MAN

(c') and becometh a saint through the ATONEMENT OF CHRIST

(b') and becometh as a CHILD

(a') submissive, meek and HUMBLE" (*Mosiah 3:18,19*).

(a) And now it shall come to pass, that whosoever shall not take upon him the NAME of Christ

(b) must be CALLED by some other name;

(c) therefore, he findeth himself on the LEFT HAND of God.

(d) And I would that ye should REMEMBER also, that this is the NAME

(e) that I said I should give unto you that never should be BLOTTED out,

(f) except it be through TRANSGRESSION;

(f') therefore, take heed that ye do not TRANSGRESS,

(e') that the name be not BLOTTED OUT of your hearts,

(d') I say unto you, I would that ye should REMEMBER to retain the NAME   (c') written always in your hearts, that ye are not found on the LEFT HAND of God,

(b') but that ye hear and know the voice by which ye shall be CALLED,

(a') and also, the NAME by which he shall call you" (*Mosiah 5:10-12*).

The early writings of Nephi contain multiple examples of chiasmus; in fact, the entire first two books of Nephi appear to have organized in an overarching chiasmus. Perhaps even more interesting is the structure of the Book of Mosiah, which is organized into a complex chiasmus, which focuses on the Messianic teachings of Abinadi, and puts emphasis on the powerful teachings of Benjamin and Mosiah (see Welch, BYU Studies, Vol. 10, No. 1, p.82):

A King Benjamin exhorts his sons (1:1-8)
 B Mosiah chosen to succeed his father (1:10)
  C Mosiah receives the records (1:16)
   D Benjamin's speech and the words of the angel (2:9-5:15)
    E People enter into a covenant (6:1)
     F Priests consecrated (6:13)
      G Ammon leaves Zarahemla for the land of Lehi-Nephi (7:1-6)
      H People in bondage, Ammon put in prison (7:15)
       I The 24 gold plates (8:9)
        J The record of Zeniff begins as he leaves Zarahemla (9:1)
         K Defense against the Lamanites (9:14-10:20)
          L Noah and his priests (11:1-15)
           M Abinadi persecuted and thrown in prison (11-12)
            N Abinadi reads the old law and old Messianic prophecies to the priests (13-14)
            N' Abinadi makes new prophecies about Jesus Christ (15-16)
           M' Abinadi persecuted and killed (17:5-20)
          L' Noah and his priests (18:32-20:5)
         K' Lamanites threaten the people of Limhi (20:6-6-26)
        J' Record of Zeniff ends as he leaves the land of Lehi-Nephi
       I' The 24 gold plates (21:27, 22:14)
      H' People of Alma in bondage (23)
     G' Alma leaves the land of Lehi-Nephi for Zarahemla (24)
    F' The Church organized by Alma (25:14-24)
   E' Unbelievers refuse to enter covenant (26: 1-4)
   D' The words of Alma and the words of the angel of the Lord (26-27)
  C' Alma the Younger receives the records (28:20)
 B' Judges chosen instead of a king (29:5-32)
A' Mosiah exhorts his people (29:5-32)

The most powerful and beautiful example of chiasmus in the Book of Mormon, and perhaps anywhere is in Alma section 36. The structure is obviously chiastic, but there are some very sophisticated and elegant perturbations, which have been the subject of careful and lengthy analysis. Welch (1989, 1991) presents several levels of chiasmic structure. Here I reproduce the overall structure, which is Level 1. In addition, he analyzes the complete text to show the extensive chiasmic detail, including fascinating relationships between larger paired sections and the subtle use of weaving factors (transitions) providing remarkable unity and a smooth flow of thought throughout the chapter. Welch also assesses the degree of causticity, showing this is not a contrived example or chance occurrence but fits objective criteria for intentional and deliberately crafted chiasmic structures. Finally, a comparison of other accounts of Alma's conversion story in the Book of Mormon show only this one is presented in chiasmic form, indicating this passage was crafted about 20 years after the initial experience he describes, had been carefully reorganized to yield a masterful and poetical statement of his conversion. So here, it is Welch's outline of the overall structure of Alma 36:1-30. (Again, this is only scratching the surface of the rich structure in this chapter, but what a scratch!) Only the key phrases and concepts shown, with the verse number indicated on the right in parentheses.

(a) My son, give ear to my WORDS (1)

(b) KEEP THE COMMANDMENTS of God and ye shall PROSPER IN THE LAND (2)

(c) DO AS I HAVE DONE (2)

(d) in REMEMBERING THE CAPTIVITY of our fathers (2);

(e) for they were in BONDAGE (2)

(f) he surely did DELIVER them (2)

(g) TRUST in God (3)

(h) supported in their TRIALS, and TROUBLES, and AFFLICTIONS (3)

(i) shall be lifted up at the LAST DAY (3)

(j) I KNOW this not of myself but of GOD (4)

(k) BORN OF GOD (5)

(l) I sought to destroy the church of God (6-9)

(m) MY LIMBS were paralyzed (10)

(n) Fear of being in the PRESENCE OF GOD (14-15)

(o) PAINS of a damned soul (16)

(p) HARROWED UP BY THE MEMORY OF SINS (17)

(q) I remembered JESUS CHRIST, SON OF GOD (17)

(q') I cried, JESUS, SON OF GOD (18)

(p') HARROWED UP BY THE MEMORY OF SINS no more (19)

(o') Joy as exceeding as was the PAIN (20)

(n') Long to be in the PRESENCE OF GOD (22)

(m') My LIMBS received their strength again (23)

(l') I labored to bring souls to repentance (24)

(k') BORN OF GOD (26)

(j') Therefore MY KNOWLEDGE IS OF GOD (26)

(h') Supported under TRIALS, TROUBLES, and AFFLICTIONS (27)

(g') TRUST in him (27)

(f') He will deliver me (27)

(i') and RAISE ME UP AT THE LAST DAY (28)

(e') As God brought our fathers out of BONDAGE and captivity (28-29)

(d') Retain in REMEMBRANCE THEIR CAPTIVITY (28-29)

(c') KNOW AS I DO KNOW (30)

(b') KEEP THE COMMANDMENTS and ye shall PROSPER IN THE LAND (30) This is according to his WORD.

Note the focal point of this story, the key element in his conversion story: Jesus Christ, the Son of God. As Welch notes, "Alma shows it was not the angel or his suffering or the prayers of others that caused his conversion. It was not until he remembered his 's teaching of the atonement of Christ and then exercised faith to call upon Christ, his conversion occurred, bringing a rapid change in which guilt and the pains of hell were replaced with joy and a taste of heaven. I find this story to be powerful and moving, and knowing the underlying chiasmic structure greatly enhances my appreciation of this marvelous text" (*Welch*).

Commandments

Commandments (the correct name for commandments is "the Devine Laws of God"). There are several questions about commandments that have perplexed folks in the past.

1. Why are there commandments?
2. What are commandments?
3. How many commandments are there?
4. Is there a special way we are supposed to deal with commandments?

Why do we have commandments?

There are four reasons, each very different from the other.

The first reason, there are commandments revolving around the question of virtue. In Matthew "Be ye therefore perfect, even as your Father which is in heaven is perfect" (*Matthew 5:48*). In this set of scriptures, verses 1 through 48, they are talking about living the commandments. The Disciples are being directed to be perfect, but perfect in what, Virtue. When investigating further, "Be more like our Heavenly Father" (*D&C 76: 5*). In another scripture, one learns if they are successful in their efforts to live the commandments during mortality they will inherit the Celestial kingdom and be Gods. This hypothesis is explained in the Doctrine and Covenants, "Then shall they be gods, because they have no end; therefore, shall they be from everlasting to everlasting, because they continue; then shall they be above all, because all things are subject unto them. Then shall they be gods, because they have all power, and the angels are subject unto them. Verily, verily, I say unto you, except ye abide my law ye cannot attain to this glory" (*D&C 132: 20 & 21*).

Here it is understood, during mortality the ability to live the law, (meaning commandments), is the means to the end most desired, to be living as Gods with God, in the Celestial Kingdom sometime in the future. Conversely if it is demonstrated, during mortality, one is unable to live the Devine Laws of God, he will have to accept a reward lesser than the Celestial kingdom. What does being more like Heavenly Father during mortality, mean? In other words, what does God have that mortals can attain by living the commandments during this life? The answer is "virtue", God is completely virtuous, if He was not He would cease to be God, as was explained in the 40th section of Alma, in the Book of Mormon. Now, if God can cease to be God by losing virtue it is reasonable to assume, mortals cannot become gods with the small amount of virtue they may now possess, in their fallen state. People must understood to become, as God, they need to obtain the same virtues God possesses. So where does a person start? Here on earth is where everyone starts learning how to handle themselves in virtuous situations. In this respect, commandments serve as a guide for virtuous efforts. Mortals are kind of, practicing, to handle things in a small way, as God handles things in a big way. So how does living commandments help in the effort to gain a small amount of virtue? For instance, the commandment "love you neighbor as you love yourself", (*Matthew 22:39*), this helps people learn, in a small way, the virtue necessary to develop a greater love similar to the love God has for all his children. When living the commandment "thou shall not steal", there is an increase virtue by not forsaking others and by being honest, as God said, He would never forsake people by taking anything from them, but rather He offers all He has to His children, which is the virtue of charity, also needed to progress to a Celestial state. It is the same with all Commandments or Devine Laws, given by God, which are designed to help start the process of attaining all the virtues God has. "His lord said unto him, well done, thou good and faithful servant: thou hast been faithful over a few things, I will make thee ruler over many things: enter thou into the joy of thy lord" (*Mathew 25:21*). Adding this to Joseph Smith's statement, "As man is, God once was; and as God is, man may become" (*Teachings of Presidents of the Church: Lorenzo Snow Chapter 5*). What was just learn? Life in mortality is a condensed version of celestial life and during this mortal state God's children must learn, how to be "as Gods" by living the laws and commandments given to us, by God. In other words, all mortals, acquainted with a small amount of knowledge and power now, to practice with, to see if they can handle the glory and power inherited later. This part of the test comes with mortal life. Mortals must live the commandments and develop the virtues necessary to be next to God or as God. The scriptures stated above are just a sampling of scriptures discussing the relationship of being obedient to the commandments and inheriting a place next to God or being disobedient or even somewhat disobedient, and finding ourselves receiving a lesser reward.

The second reason there are commandments is that, eventually, a person must come to realize, they simply cannot be perfect when it comes to living all of the commandments. The fact is. all mortals are commanded to live to a strict level of inward righteousness, coupled with the fact, they are almost certain to fail, creates within them an ongoing need to repent and call upon the Holy Ghost for help and the Lord for forgiveness. Therefore, because of this second reason, the Lord has provided a pathway for mortals to improve their dependency on, and improve their relationship with, Him. Thus, through living the commandments, one must humbly learn to rely on the Atoning sacrifice of the Savior.

Understanding the third reason requires some perspective about ourselves. All mortals are a couplet, meaning they are of two parts, each part depending on the other. One part is the temporal person (root word, temporary). This is the mortal body as seen in the mirror and spoken of in the scriptures as the *vessel*. The other part is the spirit person, housed inside the vessel, often referred to in the scriptures as the *soul*. It is important to thoroughly understand, this spirit person is the real us, having lived with Heavenly Father before mortality and going on to eternal life while the mortal remains decay in the dust for a while. The point of all this, and the third reason mortals have commandments is, all mortals have a personal responsibility to return their spirit to Heavenly Father in a good and untarnished condition "no unclean thing can dwell with God" (*1st Nephi 10:21*). All have heard or read the scripture "the Lord is no respecter of persons" (*Romans 2:11*), which, in part, means, no matter who you are -- rich, poor, -- young, old, -- healthy, sick, no matter what the earthly situation is, the first responsibility of all mortals is to their counterpart, the spirit person residing within them. The concept of living the commandments is the only way a mortal can fulfill this responsibility given to him by God.

The fourth reason there are commandments, they are one of the ways of judging mortals. Think about it, someone arriving at some point in their progression, standing at the judgment bar before God, and finding themselves sorely lacking in virtue, a heavily damaged spirit, and a supporting variety of unrepented sins because of disobedient to some or all of the commandments, what is going to be their reward?

What are commandments?

Some religions say all commandments are temporal. To justify this belief, they use the commandments "thou shalt not steal", "Thou shalt not commit adultery", and "honor your father and mother" (*Old Testament*). Their rational is, these things are purely things of this earth and in the afterlife you cannot steal anything since you cannot take anything with you and sex, is also only of this earth and so on. This notion is false. Commandments were ordained in the preexistence and were given spiritually before the earth was formed and carry on into the eternities. From the mortal perspective, it may be difficult to understand the concept of stealing or sex or parenthood in the eternal realm. The reason a temporal commandment has never been given is all commandments are always based on God's law and all of God's laws are spiritual even though they are in full force here in mortality. Commandments are those things, mortals do or do not do, that causes the soul to be kept clean and strengthened, or oft times damaged, in some cases irreparably damaged. God has set these rules out for his children to live by, "And there stood one among them that was like unto God, and he said unto those who were with him: We will go down, for there is space there, and we will take of these materials, and we will make an earth whereon these (meaning His spirit children housed in a mortal body) may dwell; (*Abraham 3:24-26*).

"And we will prove them (meaning us) herewith, to see if they will do all things whatsoever the Lord their God shall command them; and they who keep their first estate shall be added upon; and they who keep not their first estate shall not have glory in the same kingdom with those who keep their first estate; and they who keep their second estate shall have glory added upon their heads for ever and ever" (*Abraham 3:25*).

It is the ability to do the things, when commanded, (keeping the second estate) that have a direct connection to salvation. You might say the commandants are the owner's, manual for mortals to live by. If living commandments is the reason this earth was formed and the reason mortals were placed here and living the commandments is the only way they can get back to Heavenly Father, attention must be paid to these commandments. Can anyone answer this question?

How many commandments are there?

Now, one would think, considering all the importance placed on the commandments, at a minimum, one should know how many commandments there are. Some of you will say 10 maybe more; here is a hint--- in the New Testament there are 38 commandments or 42 depending on how you read them. Then there is the D&C, Pearl of Great Price and Book of Mormon and latter day revelations concerning Priesthood, Temples and so on. Some might think, with all this emphasis on commandments, the Mormon Church should just print a book listing all the commandments and then two or three pages of explanation on how to live each individual law. If a person were to go to Deseret Book, looking for a book of that nature they would not find one published by the Church. The General Authorities are smart enough not to fall into that trap. To understand the reason the church opts out on this is a matter of understanding history. During the time of Jesus, He was upset with the Jewish leaders and called them hypocrites. What were they doing, he did not like? Well, they were doing many things He did not like, but one of the main things was the way they taught religion. The Jewish people were taught to comply with the laws of Moses, written down about 400 years before Christ, and in these texts was written instructions on all the rituals associated with each commandment. These rituals became the law. The Jews did not obey the commandments by faith but were taught, by the Sadducees and Pharisees (the general authorities of the day) to read the scriptures and to comply with the letter of the law. So all the Jews thought, by living by the law for the sake of the law, they did not need to obey the law by faith, they did not even need faith and they certainly did not need a Savior. Because of these written instructions, it was almost as if the Jewish population was worshiping the written Law of Moses and God was just directing traffic. This false teaching upset the Lord and his teachings clearly illustrated this point.

Is there a special way to deal with commandments?

The answer is yes, there is a special way to deal with commandments, and to understand this one needs to look in the book of Moses, "For behold this is my work and my glory -- to bring to pass the immortality and eternal life of man" (*Moses 1; 39*). In all the text above, the dialogue is about the works part of this scripture, doing God's work (living the commandments). The other part, not talked about is the glory part of this scripture. The question is, since God, in His Celestial realm, has no need for any temporal substance, how is He glorified? Additionally, if mortals are responsible for the glorification of God, how are they to accomplish this? Lo' the many times members of the church have heard, study the scriptures, do not just read the scriptures, but study the scriptures? What are members supposed to achieve while studying the scriptures? People are to search the scriptures to learn the will of God, or in other words, learn Gods Laws (commandments). Once found, study them out, ask questions of the church leaders, learn the doctrine associated with each commandment, pray about it, receiving a testimony of that principle of the gospel from the Holy Ghost, and incorporate the principle or law into their lives through faith. Now this is true obedience, not compliance as the Jews were taught for centuries.

Members of the church often hear someone asking the question "why do people do such and such". Often the answer is "because it's a commandment". This thinking is incorrect and dangerous. Members should never to do anything, pertaining to the Lord, just because it is, commanded. To repeat, live the law, not because it is a commandment, but live the law because of the love for and of the Lord and want to be obedient to all his wishes through faith. It is living the commandments through faith, mortals can personally glorify God, and this is the only way anyone can hope to gain salvation.

Coming of Elijah

The coming of Elijah is somewhat difficult to understand. Personal study, Priesthood and Sunday School Lessons provided only pieces and parts of the concept, but when reading this chapter in Truman's book, the concept became clear, there was not anymore to say, he had really nailed it.

Quoting from chapter 7, from Truman Madsen's book, "The Temple, Where Heaven Meets Earth"

"Elijah did come. He came to the Kirtland Temple on April 3, 1836. Jewish literature is replete with the promise and expectation of Elijah's coming, right up to the last promise of the Old Testament, in the last verses of

Malachi. Moreover, it is Jewish tradition; on the second night of Passover they must leave the door open and a place at the table head an empty chair and a goblet full of wine in the expectation of the coming of Elijah. It is interesting, especially in light of Jewish tradition, April 3, 1836, was the second day of Passover. The symbolism is beautiful, Elijah did come, not as they expect, but to a home, the Lord's home. He came to turn hearts, which is more than just changing minds He turns hearts to hearts. He somehow bridges some gap, some alienation, and some separation occurring in the human family.

Ordinarily, it has often been said, Elijah did something pertaining to the dead or work for those who are dead and gone, a half-truth. In the first place, no one is, actually, dead. Of course, the temporal body is in the grave but the spirit, which is the real and everlasting person, is alive and in the spirit or eternal world. Those who are in the spirit world are in some ways more alive than some people are here on earth. For instance, Elder Melvin J. Ballard said, they have every feeling intensified spiritually. As for them being gone, no, they are not gone either. The prophets teach, the spirit world is not in some remote galaxy, it is here, it is near. As the Prophet put it, speaking of their feelings for us -- those righteous souls who are bound to us somehow by the anxieties of their forbearing – "their bowels yearn over us". He said they "are not idle spectators in the last days" (*Truman Madsen chapter 7*).

Therefore, Elijah does have something to do with them. However, the Prophet taught, Elijah also has something to do with the living. Had he not come, the whole earth would be cursed; or, in another version, the earth would be utterly wasted at Christ's coming. Wasted, in this context, means at least two things.

First, it would be in a sense a waste, if this earth created by our Father and Son as the dwelling place of their family, turned out to be a house barren,not a home, nor a place of genuine familial love. In this sense, it would have been a waste to create it.

Second, were there not a family welded and united and full of love for Christ, it would be the case, all mankind, unable to endure His presence would be laid waste at His coming. I thank God for the restoration of the power to prepare such a family. The conferral came through Elijah.

Then, there is forgiveness. "I suggest that it may be difficult to forgive your enemies, but it is even more difficult to forgive your loved ones who have sometimes manifested hate--and you have to forgive them in response. It is harder to forgive your loved ones, because you care about them and you have to go on living with them, or struggling to, and they can go on hurting you over the years and the decades. But our hearts will never

141

turn to our fathers in the way this spirit of which we have been testifying motivates us to do unless we forgive" (*Truman Madsen chapter 7*).

"...But you and I are all involved...and therefore, as you look back at your seventy or so forbears -- that is what it would take, at fifty years each, only seventy generations to get you back to Abraham--you might recognize that you have inherited the blood of many generations. ...which means hereditary, the inheritance of tendencies, and all of us have them... So perhaps you do have problems that you can blame on your ancestors, and if you forgive that and choose to stand close to the Lord in the process of purifying your life, that will affect your whole family in both directions. You are not alone. There is no way you can gain solitary and neutral ground. You are in it -- you are involved. And this, I believe, is one of the profound meanings of that long, laborious allegory in the book of Jacob, the allegory of the tame and wild olive trees. If you take a wild branch and graft it into a tame one, if the branch is strong, enough it will eventually corrupt and spoil the tree all the way to the roots. But, if you take a tame branch and graft it in to a wild tree, in due time if that branch is strong enough, it will heal and regenerate to the very roots. You will then have been an instrument in the sanctification even of your forbears" (*Truman Madsen chapter 7*).

"Do these considerations ever sober us in moments when we suppose either that no one cares for us or that whether they care or not, our life makes no difference? To be that kind of branch and achieve that kind of transformation backward and forward is perhaps the greatest achievement of this world. But to do it one must great; one must be linked, bound to the Lord Jesus Christ. One must be mighty. One must be something of a savior. And that is exactly what the Prophet Joseph Smith said we are: "saviors on Mount Zion. Thus is it our privilege and calling to become in our own limited way redemptors of the human family, His, and ours. It is impossible to love Him truly and not love what is His; and God assigned Him to all of us. And it is not possible for us to really love ourselves unless we love what is truly us, and that is the whole house of Israel to which we belong" (*Truman Madsen chapter 7*).

Commitment

What if someone was to ask this question; what would be considered an adequate heavenly reward for your gospel performance thus far? What would be the answer from any member of the church? This is a difficult question; right? The problem is there never seems to be an adequate method to measure their performance level in terms of people's everyday lives.

Folks assume when they are converted to the Gospel of Jesus Christ, that single testimony will automatically and outwardly manifest itself into actions acceptable by the Lord. They presume they are doing whatever is necessary to magnify their callings and be faithful in all the worthy acts that constitute a good and faithful member of the church. Members seek this high performance level, which is frequently arbitrary, without understanding the enormous scope of behavior necessary to achieve the highest kingdom. The Lord explains, "He who is not able to abide the law of a celestial kingdom cannot abide a celestial glory" (*D& C 88: 22*). Of course, everyone desires to live the gospel principles to the fullest so they can successfully experience the greatest amount of glory, but it seems, by their own nature, they only can manage to advance in their worthiness one small step at a time and even these small steps, oft times require a great amount of discipline and effort. All members must understand their initial conversion to the gospel, their first spiritual witness, although important, is really just a first preparatory step in a long process of growth and change occurring over a lifetime of commitment. The level of commitment needed for people who desire to be counted as "people on Zion" will not happen overnight and most certainly does not happen with one single act or event. In order to advance the discussion and yet keep it on a personal level, here is a question to start with; what areas of gospel principles and religious activity is needed in order to have a good understanding of the decisions a person will have to be make in order to move forward in this quest for salvation?

To find the answer to this question there are seven matters of concern to be discussed and they are classified into three categories, "Giving", "Having" and "Doing". In the "Having" category there are two separate topics involved (Knowledge and Virtue), and in the "Doing" category there are also two separate topics involved (Obedience and Sacrifice).

So, it looks like this"

1- Giving
2- Having
    A- Knowledge
    B- Virtue
3- Doing
    A- Obedience
    b- Sacrifice

These seven matters blended together with your level of commitment will reveal the degree of success one might experience if they make the appropriate decisions. In discussing these matters, keep in mind, one's ultimate successful participation in God's eternal cause, is always predicated on their level of commitment during mortality. In other words, the degree of glory you might receive, or any lack thereof, is a direct result of your level of commitment and your successful fulfillment of these three categories. It is important to take an in-depth look at these three categories and four matters.

First is Giving

In order to start, in a small way, to measure performance level people must be familiar with this growth process. It comes in four basic steps of giving, and they are,

1- Giving a small portion of their time and effort. Sometimes this is nothing more than reading the scriptures or going to church.

2- Starting to pay tithes and offerings, becoming more obedient, accepting callings, and helping advance the cause of the church in temporal matters.

3- Becoming worthy enough to go to the temple, taking out their endowments, and if your circumstances are right, participate in an eternal marriage.

4- Consecrating all property, time, talent, and effort to all sacred uses may be required. This means a person needs to maintain a consistent attitude of meek willingness to offer all they are capable of giving at any time while helping those about them do the same.

As you can see from these four steps, the level of commitment grows with each step. The average person may never be asked to give all, but their willingness to put everything upon His holy alter is a sign between them and God; they are willing to fully commit to His cause during mortal probation. The greatest example of this willingness to put everything upon His holy alter is the biblical story of Abraham and Isaac.
To illustrate this point following there is a story about a chicken and a pig who found themselves discussing the contributions they were required to give to the farmer's breakfast table. The hen bemoaned having to donate her

eggs for breakfast. The pig replied, yes, but for you, it is just a small sacrifice. For me, it is total commitment!

This anecdote contains some obvious lessons for members of the church. The question is:

1- Are you the kind of member who feels giving an occasional egg or two toward the building up of the kingdom is sufficient?

2- Do you truly want to be categorized among those who consecrate their all to God's cause and wish to receive all God has to offer?

Second is Having. (A + B)

It is evident, while in the preexistence, circumstances were such those residing there could only progress so far and Heavenly Father wanted them to progress much farther, indeed, He wanted all of them to be like him and thus, He developed the plan of salvation so they could have the opportunity to become like Him. Two of the things those spirit children did not have and could not get while in the preexistence were certain kinds of knowledge and certain levels of virtue. It is certain that God's children needed to "Have" certain "knowledge" and "Have" certain "virtues" to successfully progress through the eternities even unto life eternal.

(A) *Knowledge*, in order to obtain the required knowledge each church member needs to make a strong commitment to live as righteously as possible to enjoy the companionship of the Holy Ghost. Commit to studying the scriptures and learning the gospel and then, through prayer, receive the witness from the Holy Ghost, whereby each person can have knowledge of the eternal truths of God. This eternal knowledge is discussed in the Doctrine and Covenants, "Whatever principle of intelligence we attain unto in this life, it will rise with us in the resurrection" (*D& C 130:18*). It is commonly believed, it is necessary for a person to acquire most of their eternal knowledge during mortality. "And if a person gains more knowledge and intelligence in this life through his diligence and obedience than another, he will have so much the advantage in the world to come" (*D&C 130:19*). Do not be confused here; this scripture is not talking about temporal learning such as high school diplomas or college degrees. It is about spiritual knowledge and intelligence, not about a person's I.Q. It is about using the knowledge acquired from the Holy Ghost to make correct intelligent decisions and advancing the plan of God. The receiving of this spiritual knowledge is discussed in the Doctrine and Covenants, "If thou shalt ask, thou shalt receive revelation upon revelation, knowledge upon knowledge, that thou mayest know the mysteries and peaceable things—that which bringeth joy, that which bringeth life eternal" (*D&C 42:61*).

(B) *Virtue*, to be like God requires attaining as much virtue as possible during this probationary period and it seems obvious, while in the preexistence, spirit children had advanced as far as possible. Further advancement can only be accomplished in mortality by a strong commitment to live the commandments. Commandments are designed to introduce and teach how to live in such a way virtue is acquired and as members continue to be more obedient and submissive to God's plan their virtue grows. The scriptures clearly instruct mortals on the necessity of exercising virtue. (*D& C 38:24*) "And let every man esteem his brother as himself, and practice virtue and holiness before me." (D&C25:2) "A revelation I give unto you concerning my will; and if thou art faithful and walk in the paths of virtue before me, I will preserve thy life, and thou shalt receive an inheritance in Zion".

Third is Doing. (A + B)

(A) *Obedience,* certain things must be done during this mortal probation that cannot done anywhere else and these things must accomplished here, in order to prepare for the next step taken in the march forward toward eternal life. The reason mortals must be involved in this "doing" is because only during mortality can anyone physically demonstrate their love for Heavenly Father. This can only be done by performing certain acts of obedience or certain sacrifices while going through this very difficult test.

"And there stood one among them that was like unto God, and he said unto those who were with him: We will go down, for there is space there, and we will take of these materials, and we will make an earth whereon these may dwell. And we will prove them herewith, to see if they will do all things whatsoever the Lord their God shall command them" (*Abraham3: 24 &25*). Also "Behold, verily I say unto you, for this cause I have sent you—that you might be obedient, and that your hearts might be prepared to bear testimony of the things which are to come" (*D&C 58:6*). Here a person learns from reading the scriptures the very reason everyone was sent to earth is to be obedient. Of course the "cause" is for God's children to prove they truly want to be like be like Him and the part about preparing their hearts to bear testimony is referring to the "knowledge", as previously discussed, obedience will facilitate the Holy Ghost in people's lives so those worthy saints can bear testimony of God's mysteries. The way to show love for God is spell out in (Deuteronomy 11:1), "Therefore thou shalt love the Lord thy God, and keep his charge, and his statutes, and his judgments, and his commandments, always". "Thou shalt" means, mortals are commanded to demonstrate love of God and this requires a certain level of commitment to the law of obedience. In the very first paragraph of this article talked about the desire to reach the Celestial Kingdom. Entry into this kingdom can only happen if and when a particular blessing is obtained from God. How is this blessing obtained? The answer is given, "There is a law, irrevocably decreed in heaven before the foundations of this world, upon which all blessings are predicated— And when we obtain any blessing from God, it is by obedience to that law upon which it is predicated" (*D&C 130:20&21*). Therefore, during mortal probation, there must be physical demonstration of love for God through obedience because, this blessing is so desired, and which God also desires to give to us, is the blessing of Eternal life.

(B) *Sacrifice*, rather than give a brief account of the Law of Sacrifice here, go to the first section of this publication and read the entire law there.

Confession

Confession and repentance are inextricably linked. Talking to the elders of the church the Lord said, "Behold, he who has repented of his sins, the same is forgiven, and I, the Lord, remember them no more" (*D&C 58: 1*). "By this ye may know if a man repenteth of his sins—behold, he will confess them and forsake them" (*D&C 58: 42-43*). This means, unless a man confesses his sin, he has not truly repented of it, even if he forsook (stopped doing) the sin. The sin must be confessed before repentance is complete and before it is blotted out and forgotten by the Lord. Now, the all-important question:

To whom are members to confess?

There are three classes of people to whom members are to confess depending on the circumstances of the confession. There is the Offended Party, the offended party and the non-offended party.

Confession to the Offended Party (God).

The first class is God himself. "If any shall offend in secret, he or she shall be rebuked in secret, that he or she may have opportunity to confess in secret to him or her whom he or she has offended, and to God, that the church may not speak reproachfully of him or her" (*D&C 42: 92*).

"But remember that on this, the Lord's Day, thou shalt offer thine oblations and thy sacraments unto the Most-High, confessing thy sins unto thy brethren and before the Lord" (*D&C 59: 12*). "Nevertheless, he has sinned; but verily I say unto you, I, the Lord, forgive sins unto those who confess their sins before me and ask forgiveness, who have not sinned unto death" (*D&C 64: 7*). All sins offend God and thus members are required to confess all sins to him in prayer. Sometimes, only God is the Offended Party, no other person being involved in the sin. Such "private sins" require only confession to God in order to obtain forgiveness.

Confession to the offended party (man).

Other sins, however, offend, hurt, or cause damage to other people and members must confess these sins to these people in order to obtain forgiveness from the Lord. "But remember that on this, the Lord's Day, thou shalt offer thine oblations and thy sacraments unto the Most-High, confessing thy sins unto thy brethren and before the Lord" (*D&C 59: 12*). "If any shall offend in secret, he or she shall be rebuked in secret, that he or she may have opportunity to confess in secret to him or her whom he or she has offended, and to God, that the church may not speak reproachfully of him or her" (*D&C 42: 92*).

Those seeking reconciliation.

If a person has sinned only against God and repents (confesses to God and forsakes the sin) God usually forgives him. "There are those among you who have sinned; but verily I say, for this once, for mine own glory, and for the salvation of souls, I have forgiven you your sins. I will be merciful unto you, for I have given unto you the kingdom. And the keys of the mysteries of the kingdom shall not be taken from my servant Joseph Smith, Jun., through the means I have appointed, while he lived, inasmuch as he obeyeth mine ordinances. There are those who have sought occasion against him without cause; nevertheless, he has sinned; but verily I say unto you, I, the Lord, forgive sins unto those who confess their sins before me and ask forgiveness, who have not sinned unto death" (*D&C 64: 3-7*).

If a man has sinned against another man and repents (confesses to God and to the offended man and forsakes the sin), God usually forgives him but the offended man is required to always forgive him. "I, the Lord, will forgive whom I will forgive, but of you it is required to forgive all men" (*D&C 64: 10*). "And if thy brother or sister offend thee, thou shalt take him or her between him or her and thee alone; and if he or she confess thou shalt be reconciled" (*D&C 42: 88*).

For all the non-death sins, see D&C 64: 7, the sinner becomes reconciled to God and to the offended party when confession to both parties takes place.

Whether confessing to God in private, personal prayer or confessing to an offended mortal party, all confessions are to be done in secret (privately.) Only the repentant sinner and the offended parties are to hear the confession. "And if thy brother or sister offend thee, thou shalt take him or her between him or her and thee alone; and if he or she confess thou shalt be reconciled" (*D&C 42: 88*). "If any shall offend in secret, he or she shall be rebuked in secret, that he or she may have opportunity to confess in secret to him or her whom he or she has offended, and to God, that the church may not speak reproachfully of him or her" (*D&C 42: 92*).

Even when confession takes place among un-offended parties (ecclesiastical authorities), which will be addressed in a moment, it is to be done privately, not publicly. "And if he or she confesses not thou shalt deliver him or her up unto the church, not to the members, but to the elders. And it shall be done in a meeting, and that not before the world" (*D&C 42: 89*).

Not forgiving confessed sin brings condemnation.

The offended party is required to forgive the sinner who confesses his sin and asks forgiveness, no matter how many times this occurs. "And if thy brother or sister offend thee, thou shalt take him or her between him or her and thee alone; and if he or she confess thou shalt be reconciled" (*D&C 42: 88*).

If reconciliation does not occur after a genuine confession, the offending party commits sin and requires repentance (confessing the sin to the unforgiven sinner.) This law applies equally whether the unforgiven sinner is LDS or whether he is non-LDS. "My disciples, in days of old, sought occasion against one another and forgave not one another in their hearts; and for this evil they were afflicted and sorely chastened. Wherefore, I say unto you, that ye ought to forgive one another; for he that forgiveth not his brother his trespasses standeth condemned before the Lord; for there remaineth in him the greater sin. I, the Lord, will forgive whom I will forgive, but of you, it is required to forgive all men. And ye ought to say in your hearts—let God judge between me and thee, and reward thee according to thy deeds" (*D&C 64: 8-11*). "And again, verily I say unto you, if after thine enemy has come upon thee the first time, he repent and come unto thee praying thy forgiveness, thou shalt forgive him, and shalt hold it no more as a testimony against thine enemy—and so on unto the second and third time; and as oft as thine enemy repenteth of the trespass wherewith he has trespassed against thee, thou shalt forgive him, until seventy times seven" (*D&C 98: 39-40*).

As long as an offended party remains unrepentant of his unwillingness to forgive the repentant offender, his sins remain unforgiven by the Lord. "Verily, verily, I say unto you, my servants, that inasmuch as you have forgiven one another your trespasses, even so I, the Lord, forgive you" (*D&C 82: 1*).

Confession to un-offended parties (ecclesiastical authorities)

Only when a sinner refuses to repent, offering no confession of guilt to the party offended, are the ecclesiastical authorities, informed of the sin. "And him that repenteth not of his sins, and confesseth them not, ye shall bring before the church, and do with him as the scripture saith unto you, either by commandment or by revelation. And this ye shall do that God may be glorified—not because ye forgive not, having not compassion, but that ye may be justified in the eyes of the law, that ye may not offend him who is your lawgiver—verily I say, for this cause ye shall do these things" (*D&C 64: 12-14*). "And if thy brother or sister offends thee, thou shalt take him or her between him or her and thee alone; and if he or she confesses thou shalt be reconciled. And if he or she confess not thou shalt deliver him or her up unto the church, not to the members, but to the elders. And it shall be done in a meeting, and that not before the world" (*D&C 42: 88-89*).

The purpose of reporting is two-fold:

1.   To help the sinner repent of the sin by confessing to the offended parties (D&C 42: 92).

2.   To keep the church free from unrepentant sinners.
      "And him that repenteth not of his sins, and confesseth them not, ye shall bring before the church, and do with him as the scripture saith unto you, either by commandment or by revelation. And this ye shall do that God may be glorified—not because ye forgive not, having not compassion, but that ye may be justified in the eyes of the law, that ye may not offend him who is your lawgiver—verily I say, for this cause ye shall do these things" (*D&C 64: 12-14*).

The Church is justified members who sin, repent and in order for the Church to remain justified the members must remain repentant. If the church ever becomes composed of unrepentant sinners (unjustified people), the church itself becomes unjustified.

The Lord has set up a process of cleaning house. The unrepentant sinners are brought to the ecclesiastical authorities and if they repent by confessing and forsaking their sins, no judgment is pronounced upon them. If, however, they refuse to repent, they are cast out of the church (excommunicated), thereby keeping the church justified.

The law of witnesses.

Although, a person may be accused by someone of committing an unrepentant sin and the accused may be reported to his ecclesiastical authority, he is always innocent until proven guilty. He need not respond to the accusations. Even if a Bishop or Stake President asks him directly, did you or did you not commit such and such a sin? If the accusation is only reported to the authorities by one person, they cannot even ask about his guilt in any official capacity. He is under no obligation to respond to such questioning, whether he is innocent or guilty. The onus is on the testimonies of the two or more witnesses. In addition, these must be bona fide witnesses, having personal knowledge that (a) he committed the sin and (b) he did not repent of it by appropriate confession to the offended parties and by forsaking it. Hearsay testimony does not constitute a witness. The ecclesiastical authority obtains jurisdiction as a judge only when there are two or more witnesses. Since the ecclesiastical authority is not an offended party and does not have personal knowledge of the unrepentant sins in question, he must rely upon at least two LDS witnesses who are shown to be trustworthy, otherwise no judgment can happen. "And it came to pass that Alma did not know concerning them; but there were many witnesses against them; yea, the people stood and testified of their iniquity in abundance" (*Mosiah 26: 9*).

The only reason members should be reported to the ecclesiastical authority is that they did not repent. Merely having knowledge of a sin is not enough. A witness must have knowledge the sin has not been confessed to the offending parties and the sin has not been forsaken. "And he said unto the king: Behold, here are many whom we have brought before thee, who are accused of their brethren; yea, and they have been taken in diver's iniquities. And they do not repent of their iniquities; therefore we have brought them before thee, that thou mayest judge them according to their crimes" (*Mosiah 26: 11*). One witness is insufficient to convict (or condemn) because it is merely one man's word against another's. However, two or more LDS witnesses empower a bishop or other ecclesiastical authority to pass judgment.

Confession to a bishop without witnesses or inquiry is non-scriptural.

There is not a single passage of scripture stating or even hinting, to receive forgiveness a member must seek out his bishop and confess to him a sin he has committed if there are no witnesses testifying of his impenitence or if there are no inquiries regarding his spiritual state. No church official has any part in forgiving any sin because forgiveness of sin is granted by the Lord and the Lord alone. All forgiveness hinges upon a person's repentance (confession to the offended parties and forsaking of the sin) and whether the sin is a *sin unto death*. Stake Presidents and Bishops should always remember this scripture, "I, the Lord, will forgive whom I will forgive, but of you it is required to forgive all men" (*D&C 64:10*). If a person has sinned, and all have, and after having confessed to the Lord and forsaken the sin, all ecclesiastical authorities are required to forgive you without precondition of any penitence or even a lecture. This scripture leaves no room for punishment of any kind!

Confession during trials.

After a trial is set up and two witnesses testify against the accused man, if he confesses and has duly repented, the judgment must be stayed. He is to be forgiven and all parties reconciled. This is the law. "Therefore I say unto you, go; and whosoever transgresseth against me, him shall ye judge according to the sins which he has committed; and if he confesses his sins before thee and me, and repenteth in the sincerity of his heart, him shall ye forgive, and I will forgive him also. Yea, and as often as my people repent will I forgive them their trespasses against me? And ye shall also forgive one another your trespasses; for verily I say unto you, he that forgiveth not his neighbor's trespasses when he says that he repents, the same hath brought himself under condemnation. And whosoever repented of their sins and did confess them, them he did number among the people of the church" (*Mosiah 26: 29-31, 35*). Only when the sinner still refuses to confess, even in the face of witnesses, is his name to be blotted out. "Now I say unto you, go; and whosoever will not repent of his sins the same shall not be numbered among my people; and this shall be observed from this time forward. And those that would not confess their sins and repent of their iniquity, the same were not numbered among the people of the church, and their names were blotted out" (*Mosiah 26: 32, 36*).

The special sin of adultery.

(This is the first time this issue is spoken of in the scriptures).

Adultery, like other sins, requires confession to God and to the offended parties, in order to be forgiven. It does not require automatic confession to the ecclesiastical authority. Only in cases of unrepentant adultery, where witnesses give irrefutable evidence of both the sin and the unrepentant state of the sinner, is the case to be brought to the ecclesiastical authority for judgment. However, if the adulterer or adulteress confesses, he or she is to be forgiven. "Therefore I say unto you, go; and whosoever transgresseth against me, him shall ye judge according to the sins which he has committed; and if he confesses his sins before thee and me, and repenteth in the sincerity of his heart, him shall ye forgive, and I will forgive him also. Yea, and as often as my people repent will I forgive them their trespasses against me. And ye shall also forgive one another your trespasses; for verily I say unto you, he that forgiveth not his neighbor's trespasses when he says that he repents, the same hath brought himself under condemnation, And whosoever repented of their sins and did confess them, them he did number among the people of the church" (*Mosiah 26: 29-31, 35*).

"But he that has committed adultery and repents with all his heart, and forsaketh it, and doeth it no more, thou shalt forgive" (*D&C 42: 25*). However, if the man or woman is again taken in adultery, with witnesses testifying of both the sin and the unrepentant nature (lack of confession) and is brought to his or her ecclesiastical authority for judgment a second time, regardless of the second time confession, he or she is to be cast out. "But he that has committed adultery and repents with all his heart, and forsaketh it, and doeth it no more, thou shalt forgive; but if he doeth it again, he shall not be forgiven, but shall be cast out" (*D&C 42: 25-26*).

This is the two strikes rule of adultery. It does not apply to those who commit adultery and then confess to the offended parties, never being brought by witnesses to trial. The rule applies only to adulterers and adulteresses who are dragged by witnesses to the ecclesiastical authority to be judged for their unrepentant nature and lack of confession TWICE. The first time, if they then confess, they are forgiven, but the second time, even if they confess; they are to be cast out.

When inquiries are made.

Inquiries are made when people are desirous to be baptized, as to whether they have committed and repented of their sins. This is entirely scriptural. "Behold, verily I say unto you, that whatever persons among you, having put away their companions for the cause of fornication, or in other words, if they shall testify before you in all lowliness of heart that this is the case, ye shall not cast them out from among you; but if ye shall find that any persons have left their companions for the sake of adultery, and they themselves are the offenders, and their companions are living, they shall be cast out from among you. And again, I say unto you, that ye shall be watchful and careful, with all inquiry, that ye receive none such among you if they are married; and if they are not married, they shall repent of all their sins or ye shall not receive them" (*D&C 42: 74-77*).

Inquiries are also made for temple recommends and priesthood ordination. A simple "yes" or "no" to each question is a sufficient response. No elaboration is required.

Silence is also your right, should you decide to use it. Silence does not indicate guilt, only of your unwillingness to answer the question. Both Alma and Amulek employed such a tactic, see Alma 14: 17, Matthew 26: 62-63, Mark 15: 3 etc., as well as the Lord himself, when he was questioned by the ecclesiastical authorities of the church of his time. As all accused are innocent until proven guilty and the burden of proof is upon the witnesses and judge, no one in the church has to prove his or her innocence. Therefore, when faced with false accusations, it is within the right of every accused member to shut their mouths and remain silent.

Witch-hunts: the danger of non-scriptural confessions

Witch hunts can and do happen currently, even in the church. People in authority are naturally disposed to abuse it. "We have learned by sad experience it is the nature and disposition of almost all men, as soon as they get a little authority, as they suppose, they will immediately begin to exercise unrighteous dominion" (*D&C 121: 39*). Because of this, the jurisdiction of ecclesiastical authorities was designed by the Lord to be established by two or more witnesses. If a bishop, a police officer, or a Child Protection Services agent is anonymously tipped off that some person are doing something sinful or illegal, the natural tendency is to view them with suspicion and to engage in a witch-hunt and inquiry, to reveal some dirt that can and will be used against you. Such people will use the garb of authority to intrude on people's lives and invade their privacy. This particular brand of tyranny is especially bad when ecclesiastical authorities engage in this practice because they are using their priesthood illegitimately.

The modern trend of ecclesiastical authorities is to obtain jurisdiction over members through voluntary confession of sins. These leaders falsely teach the members, certain sins are bad enough to warrant a talk and perhaps discipline from church leaders and cannot be forgiven by the Lord unless the sins are first voluntarily confessed to the appropriate ecclesiastical authority. It is understandable why leaders follow this practice. Obtaining witness is a hard, often futile process. Sometimes, dishonestly circumventing the Law of Witness is the only way to obtain the jurisdiction to judge a member's spiritual standing in the church. When the law of witness is circumvented in this manner, the ecclesiastical authorities set themselves up as both witness, judge, jury and executioner, as the sinner's confession to them is thought to both establish jurisdiction and to convict (condemn.) This sets up a conflict of interest (the loss of impartiality) and puts an enormous amount of power in the hands of one man, power that was never meant to be there. It also conflicts with established scriptural order, as once someone confesses to a sin and shows remorse, they are to be forgiven, and thus no discipline could or should ever take place.

By obeying the proper protocols of repentance and confession and exercising one's right to silence, as explained in the Lord's scripture, such tyranny is nipped in the bud and all attempts at usurpation of priesthood authority will be quashed.

Covenant of Law & Grace

This is written for the purpose of enlarging the conversation on the Biblical meaning of the words "work" and "grace". These two words have caused considerable confusion among God-fearing people for hundreds of years. Some say obedience to the Law (meaning works) is the correct avenue to Heaven; others say Christ has forgiven all sins and thereby all are saved by His grace alone, this debate will be addressed. Also examined will be the genesis of this work v/s grace debate that has been brewing and some modern revelations given to resolve the issue. The scriptures currently used are called the New Testament and the Old Testament. This is the name given to them around the 5th century by the Greeks, what were they call before then? This issue will be addressed because it is germane to the discussion of work and grace.

To preface any remarks on work and grace, the reader needs to realize God wants His children to be successful in their quest to become like Him and return to Him and He has left the scriptures to guide them down the correct path. However, over time, mortals have been able to confuse, corrupt, and confound the scriptures to the point they cannot seem to recognize the truth when presented. However, in spite of this tremendous failing on people's part all mortals are still required to obey God's will. This is not an easy thing to do, recognizing there is a great void between the characteristics of God and mortals. There are two components to the explanation of this void,

First, God is perfectly just and eternally just, perfectly holy and eternally holy, perfectly faithful and eternally faithful. God is without any variableness or shadow in His virtue, but perfectly continuing the same, and therefore He cannot and will not cease to be God as to alter or change the nature of His Godhead. As He is thus the perfection of all perfections, He gave out His Law to be obeyed; but if any offend it, then they fall into the hands of this His eternal justice, and so must suffer under His irrevocable wrath, which is the execution of perfect justice. Therefore, now the law has been broken, all mortals have experienced spiritual death, and justice must take place, and thereupon each mortal soul will see and understand the execution of justice levied against him has been justly done with all mercy.

Second, humans, in their mortal state, are not as infinite as God, they are likened to a weed, here today and gone tomorrow, and since all are in mortality for such a short period, they have not and cannot acquire sufficient virtuous qualities which would enable them have equivalence with God in His essence. Because of their mortal being, and attributes; all are bound to offend His law, and individuals, in their finite state can do nothing infinite in such a way as to acquit themselves from the offences committed against God, which is an infinite God in all His attributes. Therefore, everyone finds themselves fully dependent on His eternal mercy.

Members of the church must, as best as they can, turn to the scriptures to advance their understanding and to draw parallels between them in order to gain as much knowledge, wisdom and virtue as possible while here on this earth.

There are three great covenants have brought about three great sets of scriptures; the covenants are, "The Old Testament," which, prior to the 5th century, was called "the Covenant of Works and Law," is the Jewish scriptures discussed in 2nd Cor.3:6-18; Heb. 9:1-4. "The New Testament" which, prior to the 5th century, was called "the Covenant of Faith and Grace" mentioned in Jer. 31:31-34, and many other places. "The New and Everlasting Covenant" pertaining to modern day prophesy. Starting with the Covenant of Works and Law this commentary will examine each covenant. Throughout the scriptures, this ancient covenant, the Covenant of Works and Law is commonly referred to as the Law, Law of Moses, work, and old Covenant, was given to the Hebrews by Moses during and after their exodus from Egypt. The Covenant of Faith and Grace is mentioned in Jer. 31:31-34, and many other places. Jesus' followers believed Jesus as the Christ delivered this covenant to them during His ministry. The people of the Book of Mormon lived under the Covenant of works and Law at the outset of their journey and after Christ visited them, they lived under the Covenant of faith and Grace. How they made the change will be understood later. The covenant made with Joseph Smith is called The New and Everlasting Covenant. This covenant is the gospel of Jesus Christ and is the sum of all gospel covenants God has ever made with mankind encompassing all covenants contained in the Covenant of Faith and Grace and the Covenant of Works and Law. The new and everlasting covenant includes all the covenants, from God, necessary for salvation and are "new" in the since, they are renewed with each dispensation and are "everlasting" in the sense, once these covenants are entered into they are forever binding and valid only if they are not broken by transgression or sin.

All covenants and promises instituted by God are governed by certain stipulations and conditions and his children must comply with these stipulations and conditions to make any covenant or promise valid. This pertains to the Covenant of Works and Law, the Covenant of Faith and Grace and New and Everlasting Covenant, since all were instituted for the fullness of God's glory…. "And verily I say unto you, that the conditions of this law are these: All covenants, contracts, bonds, obligations, oaths, vows, performances, connections, associations, or expectations, that are not made and entered into and sealed by the Holy Spirit of promise, of him who is anointed, both as well for time and for all eternity,…by revelation and commandment through the medium of mine anointed,…are of no efficacy, virtue, or force in and after the resurrection from the dead; for all contracts that are not made unto this end have an end when men are dead" (*D&C 132:5-7*).

The Lord has said, "I, the Lord, am bound when ye do what I say; but when ye do not what I say, ye have no promise" (*D&C 82:10*).

Now the groundwork has been laid, and starting with--- the Covenant of Works and Law and the Covenant of Faith and Grace, these are two distinct covenants, they were made in diver's ways, in different times, and under very dissimilar conditions. As God-fearing people turn to the scriptures they have difficulty reconciling the two books, as saith the Apostle, "the righteousness of the law saith one thing, and the righteousness of faith saith another" (*Rom 10:4-6*).

The Covenant of Works and law, here spoken of, is the law delivered upon Mount Sinai to Moses, in two tables of stone, which are the "first 5 books of the Old Testament; Genesis, Exodus, Leviticus, Numbers, Deuteronomy" (Galatians 4). The great condition in the Covenant of the law is that; If, you do these things, which are the 644 commandments given to the Israelites, you shall live by them, therefore salvation is to be gained by obedience to the letter of the law. Do this, and then thou shalt live; otherwise, "cursed is every one that continueth not in all," in every particular thing or "things which are written in the book for the law to do

157

them" (*Gal 3:10*). Those under the first covenant stand thus, and only thus, as they are under the covenant, or law. Even though they may be ignorant of the nature of the Covenant of Works and Law they are under, they may think their state is not half bad; when, alas, there is none in the world in such a sad condition; for, indeed, they do not understand these things, therefore they cannot in any wise gain salvation.

The Apostle Paul, speaking of the Covenant of Faith and Grace, tells the Apostles, the Lord Himself called them to this covenant, and the condition of this covenant is to have faith your sins will be forgiven by the Grace of Jesus Christ, out of the Covenant of law, but faith on your part will move you forward. "To him that worketh not, saith the Apostle [that is] for salvation, "but believeth on Him that justifieth the ungodly, his faith is counted for righteousness" (*Rom 4:5*). So that we, saith he, "conclude that a man is justified by faith without the deeds of the law" (*Rom 3:28*). "In the Covenant of Grace; the word "grace," therefore, in this Scripture Romans 6:14 is to be understood of the free love of God in Christ to sinners, by virtue of the new covenant, in delivering them from the power of sin, from the curse and condemning power of the old covenant, from the destroying nature of sin, by its continual workings; as is all evident if you read with understanding these words–"For," saith he, "sin shall not have dominion over you," or, it shall not domineer, reign, or destroy you, though you have transgressed against the Covenant of Works and Law; and the reason is rendered in these words, "For ye are not under the law"–that is, under that which accuseth, chargeth, condemneth and brings execution on the soul for sin,–"but under grace"; that is, under that which frees you, forgives you, keeps you, and justifies you from all your sins, adversaries, or whatever may come in to lay anything to your charge to damn you. For that is truly called grace in this sense that doth set a man free from all his sins, deliver him from all the curses of the law, and what else can be laid to His charge, freely, without any foresight in God to look at what good will be done by the party that hath offended; and also that doth keep the soul by the same power through faith–which also is his own proper gift–unto eternal glory"(*John Bunyan, Law and Grace, 1669*).

Therefore, this is the genesis of the confusion and debate going on for some time. The people who site (*Galatians 3-10*), believing if they do this and then they shall live (meaning they will live in the presents of God forever) simply do not understand they, by themselves, cannot live the commandments to such a degree they can be as infinite as God can. If they could, then they would become "as God" while in mortality and this is not possible. Therefore, there has to be more to the process of salvation than they have knowledge of and mortals have to do the *work* (live the

158

commandments) but they need the help of Christ (grace) when if they fail. Conversely, those who read Romans 3:28 "So that we conclude that a man is justified by faith, without the deeds of the law", and this is interrupted to mean, with complete absence of obedience to the commandments, their faith and their faith alone will bring them to Heavens door are equally mistaken. Seekers of the truth only have to read, 1 John 3:22, 23, "And whatsoever we ask we receive of Him, because we keep His commandments, and do those things that are pleasing in His sight", to know they have to keep the commandments to "receive" from Christ. These mistakes are made when people take the words of Paul out of context. When Paul uses the word work and the word law, together or separately, he is referring only to the Covenant of Work and Law, not your personal work nor your personal obedience to the law. When He uses the word faith and the word grace, together or separately, he is referring only to the Covenant of Faith and Grace not your personal faith nor of you receiving grace from Christ personally. The confusing, corruption and confounding of the scriptures and the truth is such, most people simply do not understand what all this means so they busy themselves with petty arguments like the one about work v/s grace. Nor do they understand, both of these covenants are still, to this very day, in full force and have a profound effect on their lives and their salvation and there is not any argument about it.

It is necessary examination the condition of man as he lives in mortality with both of these covenants in force.

First, as a man stands before God, how does he know whether he is living under the Covenant of Works and Law or the Covenant of Faith and Grace? Consider this proposition. Namely, all men naturally come into the world and live their lives as they wish, for they have agency. If they live as natural men then they fall under the Covenant of Works and Law. If they shake off the natural man and pattern their lives after Jesus then they fall under The Covenant of Faith and Grace. Paul explains, "examine thyself whether thou art in the faith, and to prove thy own self whether thou hast received the Spirit of Christ into thy soul, whether thou hast been converted, whether thou hast been born again, and made a new creature, whether thou hast had thy sins washed away in the blood of Christ, whether thou hast been brought from under the old covenant into the new" (*2 Corinthians 13:5*). Here, again, Paul is referring to the Covenant of works and the Law and the Covenant of Faith and Grace. So what is a *natural man*? The Book of Mormon, explains this; "For the natural man is an enemy to God, and has been from the fall of Adam, and will be, forever and ever, unless he yields to the enticing of the Holy Spirit, and putteth off the natural man and becometh a saint through the atonement of Christ the Lord, and becometh

159

as a child, submissive, meek, humble, patient, full of love, willing to submit to all things which the Lord seeth fit to inflict upon him, even as a child doth submit to his father" (*Mosiah 3:19*). As you can see, if you are living under the Covenant of Works you are living as a natural man and you certainly will not be behaving as prescribed above.

Some people will say, things are going well, and folks are living well, and striving to serve God as well as they can. Everyone must labor to do what he or she can do and what he or she cannot do, and Christ will do the rest for them.

Ah, this is to make Christ but a piece of a Savior, people will do something, and Christ shall do the rest; they will set their own things in the first place, and when they are done at last, then, they will just borrow of Christ; these are the folks which causes Christ the greatest injury of all. First, they undervalue His merits by preferring of their own works before His, they are making Christ's atonement nothing more than an afterthought; and, secondly, by intentionally mingling their dirty works and ragged righteousness with His. Go back and read where Paul says "are you in the faith, and to prove thy own self whether thou hast received the Spirit of Christ into thy soul, whether thou hast been converted, whether thou hast been born again, and made a new creature" (*2 Corinthians 13:5*), this is where you are doing your best after your conversion and in conjunction with Christ, not just having Christ do the rest.

Then one would say, what would people do, nothing? Would people make Christ such a drudge as to do all, while sitting idly by?

Ah, the mistake is saying, people, are making Him a drudge in letting Him do all; Be assured, He counts it as His great honor and glory to do all for everyone, and it is a great dishonor unto Him for you to think otherwise. Look at these scriptures and deeply contemplate their meaning "Saying, Thou art worthy to take the book and to open the seals thereof" (*Rev 5:9*). "Worthy is the Lamb that was slain, to receive power, and riches, and wisdom, and strength, and honor, and glory, and blessing" (*Rev 5:12*). And why so? Read (*Rev. 9*) again, "For Thou wast slain, and hast redeemed us to God by thy own "blood".

Again, some folks say: Is not coming to Christ as a sinner the way to make Christ loath us. You know when children fall down in the dirt, usually, before they go home, make their clothes as clean as they can, for fear their parents should chide them; and so they think everyone should do the same when dealing with the Lord.

Ah, this comparison is wrongly applied, if a person can, in any way, can make himself clean (that is, attempting to atone for his own sin) before God he has no need of Christ; for the whole, the clean, and righteous have no need of Christ, but those who are foul and sick most certainly do. Physicians, do not bid the patients first make themselves whole or clean, and then come to them, but bid them come with their sores all running on them, as the woman with her issue.

"But, do not expect you shall have any part or share in the large promises and mercy of God, for the benefit and comfort of your soul, while you are under the old covenant. Because, in the end, if you are out of Christ you shall find God a just God, a sin-avenging God, a God that will by no means spare the guilty. Therefore, be sure that everyone that is found out of Jesus Christ will be found guilty in the judgment day, upon whom the wrath of God shall smoke to their eternal ruin" (*John Bunyan, Law and Grace, 1669*). Now, therefore, consider of it, and take the counsel of the Apostle Paul, which is, to "examine thyself whether thou art "in the faith," and to prove thy own self whether thou hast received the Spirit of Christ into thy soul, whether thou hast been converted, whether thou hast been born again, and made a new creature, whether thou hast had thy sins washed away in the blood of Christ, whether thou hast been brought from under the old covenant into the new; and do not make a slight examination, for thou hast a precious soul either to be saved or damned" (2 Corinthians 13:5).

Now comes the New and Ever Lasting Covenant that was made with Joseph Smith at the beginning of this dispensation. This covenant is the gospel of Jesus Christ and is the sum of all gospel covenants God has ever made with mankind encompassing all contained within the Covenant of Faith and Grace and the Covenant of Works and Law. This is the process of unlocking the door, which leads one to move out of the Covenant of Works and Law into Covenant of Faith and Grace wherein the natural man can be put off and the saintly life of a disciple of Christ can begin. This process starts with Faith, though faith may be small it is enough to lead one to a small amount of repentance, just enough to be baptized in the name of Jesus Christ and be confirmed with the Holy Ghost. From there this new follower of Christ can receive, through a lifetime of obedience and service, all Heavenly Father has to offer.

Conclusion; A person's first course of business is to seriously inquire whether they are under the second covenant and are in a position to involve themselves in the New and Everlasting Covenant, for unless they are, "I regard them not Saith the Lord, forasmuch as you are a sinner" (*He 8:9*). In addition, if God should be so good as to give anyone a share in the second covenant, they shall have all your sins pardoned, and will certainly have eternal life, eventhough they have been a great sinner. Jesus Christ, through whom God conveyeth His mercy, grace, and love to sinners. "For all the promises of God in Him are yea, and in Him amen" (*2 Corinthians 1:20*).

Indeed, His mercy, grace, and love are very great, but they are treasured up in Him, given forth in Him, through Him. "But God, who is rich in mercy, for His great love wherewith He loved us, that He might show the exceeding riches of His grace and His kindness towards us through Jesus Christ" (*Ephesians 2:4*).

THE DAY OF PENTECOST

In the first chapter of Acts, it states, just before Jesus ascended to heaven, He told His disciples they should remain in Jerusalem and wait for the promised gift of the Holy Ghost. In the second chapter there was a group of Christians, amongst them His disciples, who were gathered together in a room on the day of Pentecost when all of a sudden. "There came a sound from heaven as of a rushing mighty wind...and there appeared unto them cloven tongues like as fire, and it sat upon each of them and they were all filled with the Holy Ghost and began to speak with other tongues as the Spirit gave them utterance" (*Acts 2:2-4*).

To many who read the Bible, this is the explanation of how the Holy Ghost comes upon someone once they accept Christ.

To further bolster, this idea, in the tenth chapter of Acts, is the story of a Gentile named Cornelius who had sent for Peter to teach him and others about the gospel. While Peter was speaking to them "the Holy Ghost fell on all of them that heard the word" (*Acts 10:44-46*), and the Gentiles suddenly began to speak in tongues, just as the Disciples of Christ did on the day of Pentecost.

Then Peter said to the Christian Jews with him, "Can any man forbid water that these Gentiles should not be baptized which have received the Holy Ghost as well as we" (*Acts 10:47*)? Since these Gentiles had received the Holy Ghost apparently the same way and to the same extent, the apostles had on the day of Pentecost, many reason, this is the way the Holy Ghost comes to everyone.

On the other hand, Latter-day Saints believe the gift of the Holy Ghost is given by the laying on of hands by someone who has the authority to confer this gift upon others. But the scripture just quoted clearly show, at least some of the early Gentile Christians received the Holy Ghost, not by the laying on of hands or even after they had been baptized, but had it come upon them from heaven simply because they expressed their faith in Christ.

If this is true, then why did the apostles go about, laying their hands on other believers, to give them this gift, (*Acts 8:17-19*)? Can the Holy Ghost be bestowed in many different ways or is there just one way it can be received?

To confuse this issue even more, in the 20th chapter of the gospel of John it says, on the evening of the day Jesus rose from the grave, He appeared to His disciples in a locked room where He showed them His hands and side to prove He was alive. "And when he had said this he breathed on them and saith unto them, Receive ye the Holy Ghost" (*John 20:22*).

Did they received this gift of the Holy Ghost at that time, if so, what happened on the day of Pentecost?

Although the early Christians clearly understood this principle, the Bible does not clearly explain the doctrine of how to receive the Holy Ghost; therefore, members must search the scriptures to find clues to will help them solve this perplexing question.

To clarify what happened on the day of Pentecost and beyond. The search begins in an upper room during the feast of the Passover. Jesus had just eaten His last supper while in mortality and Judas Iscariot had already left the building, leaving only eleven apostles in the room with the Savior. Jesus knew in a matter of a few hours He was to be taken from His disciples by force and in less than twenty-four hours, He would be dead.

At this moment in the life of Christ He had tremendous compassion for His beloved apostles, whom He knew, did not fully realize what was about to happen to both Him and them. Therefore, in what little time He had left He sought to give His faithful followers some degree of comfort to help them endure what they were about to experience. It was during this time, Jesus told them, "But the Comforter, which is the Holy Ghost, whom the Father will send in my name, he shall teach you all things and bring all things to your remembrance" (*John 14:26*). "But when the Comforter is come, whom I will send unto you from the Father...he shall testify of me" (*John 15:26*).

It is said, people remember only ten percent of what they hear and, since Jesus had much to say in a short period of time, how could these eleven men be expected to remember everything He was about to tell them? Worse yet, they understood so little of what He was trying to tell them. In fact, the scriptures indicate they did not believe He would actually be killed. However, Jesus knew when it happened they would be fearful for their own lives and become confused and demoralized.

Realizing this, Jesus tried to assure them by saying, after He had left, He would send someone to comfort them, someone to help them remember everything He had told them, someone who would help them remain strong in the faith and show them what to do. That someone was the Holy Ghost.

Nevertheless, when Jesus gave them the Holy Ghost? He explained, "It is expedient for you that I go away: for if I go not away, the comforter will not come unto you; but if I depart, I will send him unto you" (*John 16:7*). Jesus would send them the Holy Ghost only after He had departed from them. Where was He going? He told them, "I go unto the Father" (*John 14:28*).

What Jesus told them was the Holy Ghost would be sent to them only after He had returned to His Father in heaven.

When Jesus told His disciples these things, it was Thursday evening. Shortly thereafter, the Roman soldiers took him captive, and by Friday evening, He was dead. By then the apostles were in a state of shock and they began to question among themselves how this could be if He was truly the Son of God. When Sunday morning came, Mary Magdalene went to the sepulcher where Jesus was buried, and, after seeing the empty tomb, ran to the apostles and told them what she had seen. At first, none of them believed her but then two of the apostles raced to the gravesite and found it was indeed empty. That night, when the apostles assembled behind locked doors, Jesus suddenly appeared before them. At first, they were frightened, thinking they had seen a ghost, but Jesus comforted them and invited them to touch and feel him. Now they knew He was not dead but very much alive! It was during this visit Jesus breathed on them and said, "Receive ye the Holy Ghost." Why did He do that? The Holy Ghost was to be a comforter only when Jesus was not there, but He was there and was comforting them. Then why did He tell them to receive the Holy Ghost at that time?

Before this question is answered, it is necessary to understand where the Holy Ghost comes from. In Acts 10:38, "God anointed Jesus of Nazareth with the Holy Ghost." What this reveals is the Father gave the Holy Ghost to His Son Jesus who then was able to give it to His apostles, which He did after His resurrection. Even though Jesus had given it to them then they did not actually receive it at that time. The reason is Jesus had not yet gone to His Father in heaven (resurrected). Furthermore, as long as He was still personally with them, they had no need for the Holy Ghost. Then why did Jesus tell them to receive the Holy Ghost? Our understanding is, it was necessary for Him to be there, in their presence to transfer the Holy Ghost from Himself to them. To further gain understanding of what happened at this time, look back into the Old Testament for similar examples. Moses was the supreme leader of the Israelite nation, yet eventually he would pass away and someone needed to take his place. The person chosen for this position was Joshua. However, long before his death, the Lord commanded Moses to set Joshua apart as the next leader of Israel (*Numbers 27:18*). "And Moses did as the Lord commanded and he took Joshua and set him before Eleazar the priest and before the congregation and he laid his hands upon him and gave him a charge as the Lord commanded by the hand of Moses" (*Numbers 27:22,23*).

Joshua was given the authority to rule over Israel but he could not exercise his authority while Moses was still alive. When the Israelites came to the Promised Land, Moses was not permitted to go with them, so he stayed behind, and Joshua was ready to exercise the charge the Lord had given him "by the hand of Moses". It was only then could Joshua assume full command of his people.

Another example is how David was chosen to be the King of Israel. A prophet named Samuel went to the house of Jesse to find the person God had chosen to be made king, and although David was but a young boy, "Samuel took the horn of oil and anointed him in the midst of his brethren and the Spirit of the Lord came upon David from that time forward" (*1 Samuel 16:13*).

David was anointed to be the king of Israel when he was but a teenager, even though Saul was already the ruler over Israel. Does this mean Israel now had two kings? Not at all, although David was anointed to be a king, he could not exercise any authority while Saul held the position. Although years passed between the time of David's anointing and the time he finally became king, Samuel's ceremony was valid and necessary at the time he performed it.

Therefore, it was same with the apostles. Jesus could only perform the ceremony of giving them the Holy Ghost, while He was in their presence but they did not actually receive it until the day of Pentecost. The feast of Pentecost comes fifty days after the Passover so the apostles just had to wait.

However, the account in Acts also makes known, on the day of Pentecost, there were more than just eleven apostles who suddenly received the Holy Ghost. In fact, the number was a hundred and twenty people. What about them? Had Jesus given them the Holy Ghost prior to Pentecost as well? The Bible does not say, but it is possible the apostles had performed a ceremony giving all these people, already baptized believers, the Holy Ghost by the laying on of hands before they actually received it.

What is known, is once the apostles were in possession of this gift they ceremoniously gave it to others by the laying on of hands. As stated above, God, the Father gave the Holy Ghost to His Son, and Jesus gave it to His apostles who then gave it to those who believed on Jesus.

This was the pattern for everything in the Mormon Church. God the Father ordained His Son (Hebrews 5:4, 5), the Son ordained twelve apostles (Mark 3:14, 15), and the apostles ordained other apostles (Acts 1:22), deacons (Acts 6:6), elders (Acts 14:23) and bishops.

The Bible does not clearly explain how these ordinations was always performed, however, from the few places where they have been recorded;

the indications are, the blessing was always given by the laying on of hands. This is the way Paul and Barnabas were set apart to be missionaries (Acts 13:3), and people were healed (Acts 9:12, 28:8). The laying on of hands set Joshua apart, and it is known, that the apostles gave the Holy Ghost by the laying on of their hands.

Then what about Cornelius and his friends? How did these people get the Holy Ghost to the same degree as the apostles without receiving it by the laying on of hands?

To find the answer to this question we need to put this incident in its proper setting. Peter was a Jew, and as such, Jewish law forbid him to associate with the Gentiles who were considered unclean (Acts 10:28). One day, while Peter was praying, he fell into a trance and saw a vision of unclean meat, and heard the voice of the Lord telling him to eat, but Peter refused saying, he intended to be faithful to the Jewish law forbidding him to eat such things. Three time the Lord said to Peter, "What God hath cleansed call not thou unclean" (*Acts 10:15*), and almost immediately afterwards, a group of Gentiles came to his house and the Spirit told Peter, God wanted him to go with them.

Peter took six Christian Jews with him when he went to see Cornelius (*Acts 11:12*). When they arrived, Cornelius then told the apostle how an angel had appeared unto him and instructed him to send for Peter. Peter then began teaching Cornelius and his household about Jesus Christ, and "While Peter yet spake these words, the Holy Ghost fell on all of them, which heard the word and they began speaking in tongues" (*Acts 10:44-48*).

Also in this account is expressed, when this happened, the Christian Jews there with Peter were astonished. Remember, the Jews felt they alone were the chosen people of God, and that salvation was only for their race. To them it was unthinkable that a Gentile would find favor in God's eyes, yet now they were witnessing for themselves a very convincing sign that God had indeed accepted these men.

"Can any man forbid water, that these should not be baptized, which have received the Holy Ghost as well as we"? (*Acts 10:47&48*). Apparently, none of the Jews present objected to this, but how could they? It was clear to them that God was extending salvation unto these Gentiles.

Why did these Gentiles seem to have the Holy Ghost without receiving it through the laying on of the apostles' hands? Because it was a sign to those who were with Peter, what God was calling the gentiles clean, they, the Jews, were not to call the gentiles unclean, and it was a sign these Christian Jews could understand and accept. Without this sign, it is extremely doubtful they would have allowed Peter to baptize Cornelius and his Gentile household.

Consider what happened after this incident. Here was Peter, the chief spokesmen for the apostles, a man who had been very close to Jesus, a man who was held in very high esteem by the early Christians, but when he got back to Jerusalem and word got out, he had baptized some Gentiles; he was in instant hot water. The Christian Jews in Jerusalem contended with him (*Acts 11:1-3*). Imagine contending with Peter about a point of Christian doctrine! Yet, it happened and only after Peter explained everything and how the Gentiles received the Holy Ghost in such a miraculous manner the Jews finally "held their peace" (*Acts 11:18*).

Consider the case of Paul when he baptized some Gentiles while on his first missionary journey with Barnabas. When he came home, the Christian Jews in his hometown were quite upset when they learned about this, and it was the cause of a tremendous amount of arguing among the believers in Christ. Feelings ran deep on this subject, and eventually, the matter was taken before the apostles and elders in Jerusalem to be resolved.

Once there, from the account in Acts, the Christian Jews immediately started condemning this practice. After a period of debate, Peter stood up and retold the story of how he had baptized Cornelius and how God had made it clear through a sign, this should be so. "Then all the multitude kept silence and gave audience to Barnabas and Paul declaring what miracles and wonders God had wrought among the Gentiles by them" (*Acts 15:12*). After Peter spoke, everyone held their peace and agreed, Barnabas and Paul had done no wrong. However, notice, there were *miracles and wonders*, not only surrounding Paul and Barnabas' experienced, but also the episode of Peter. Without witnessing these miracles, it is extremely doubtful the Jews would have accepted this doctrine.

Apparently, in the case of Cornelius, instead of this being the common way of receiving the Holy Ghost, it seems this was a special occurrence designed to convince the Christian Jews, salvation was also for the Gentiles. In addition, after this incident, the apostles continued to give the gift of the Holy ghost by the laying on of hands (*Acts 19:6*).

Rather than receiving the Holy Ghost automatically by simply believing in Jesus, this gift was routinely given by the laying on of the apostle's hands, and only under special and unusual circumstances did this event happen differently. In fact, the clear implication throughout Biblical history is, all Godly gifts, blessings, and authority were imparted to others by the laying on of hands of someone authorized by God to perform such acts of service. It is therefore inconsistent with the way God has always behaved to think the Holy Ghost be given in any other manner.

On Pentecost, a large group shared a common experience, saw certain sights, and heard certain sounds; so it was at the baptism of Christ, events at the Mount of Transfiguration, at the Ascension. There always was a *plurality* of witnesses; always they are astonished by what happens; always definite things are seen and heard, and definite knowledge is imparted to the human race. There was nothing self-induced and nothing expected in these experiences. The Way of Light, in the ancient Christian Doctrine of the Two Ways, is not the Mystic Way of Illumination: It always explicitly explained as the keeping of the Lord's commandments, and the reward was not the sudden flash of mystic illumination nor involvement in the Cloud of Unknowing, but a strong and steady testimony of the gospel.

Sidney B. Sperry added, "In the mind of the writer no doubt remains that Joel foresaw the dispensation in which we live and God's judgments upon the world. This he expressed in figures would be easily understood by his people. So acutely and painfully were the judgments that Joel saw impressed upon his mind that he cried out in anguish—as if he were present—to the people of today to repent and escape God's wrath." (*The Voice of Israel's Prophets, p. 297*) The last days can be characterized as the pouring out of the Spirit upon all flesh. Peter, experiencing a rich and wonderful outpouring of the Spirit on the day of Pentecost, quoted Joel (see Acts 2:17–21), who spoke of the latter days, the time just before the Lord's Second Coming when He would pour out His Spirit upon all flesh. This Spirit is not only the Holy Ghost but also the Spirit of Christ, the Spirit which enlightens everyone (see Moroni 7:16; D&C 93:2). Sons and daughters will prophesy—preach, exhort, pray, and instruct to benefit the Church. Direct revelation will be given. Young men and women who are representatives of the Lord will be inspired. The gifts of teaching and inspiration will be given to all classes and levels of people. The Lord will call and qualify those He chooses. He will pour out His Spirit upon them, and they will be endowed with the gifts necessary to convert sinners and to build up the Church. Certainly, this prophecy is now beginning to be fulfilled. The message of this passage is fourfold:

1. There will be a rich outpouring of the Spirit of the Lord in the latter days.
2. Certain signs will be fulfilled before Christ's Second Coming in the clouds of heaven.
3. His coming will be great for the righteous and terrible for the wicked; and
4. The remnant of Israel in the latter days, will be those who are left after the period of tribulation and scattering is over.

Small Matter of Death

All live today know, eventually this tremendously important experience of the mortal estate will come to its deadly end. Even though all are promised resurrection, some still have a tremendous amount of trepidation about this journey into the unknown called death. It is important to know, mortals are actually two people or personages, one is the mortal or temporal person (flesh and blood), and the other is the spirit personage (the soul) which is housed inside the mortal body. Even though during this mortal probation the mortal side is dominant, make no mistake, the spirit person is actually the real us, and death is the nothing more than the separation of the temporal body from the spiritual entity. The temporal (meaning temporary) body is not the real us, it is just temporary. The soul or the spirit is the eternal being that lived with our Heavenly Father before earth life and it is only in this mortal sphere to obtain a body and be tested. When this mortal probation is finished and the temporal body is laid aside and the spirit person will continue its journey on into eternity. In the following quote from the Prophet Brigham Young, he starts to deal with the important rational all must have about death as they learn about the principle of eternal life. He explains when people finally and fully understand the design of their probation here on earth and the true principle of eternal life, death becomes a small matter. The following text, will attempt to explain how and why death can become a "small matter". "The Body Must Return to Mother Earth. Every person possessing the principle of eternal life should look upon his body as a product of the earth. The body must return to mother earth. True, to most people it is a wretched thought that their spirits must, for a longer or shorter period, be separated from the body, and thousands and millions have been subject to this affliction throughout their lives. If they understood the design of this probation and the true principles of eternal life, it is but a small matter for the body to suffer and die". (*Disc. B. Young 7-240*).

To start, everyone needs to understand what death is. The following quote explains, death is nothing more than the spirit moving from one sphere of existence to another sphere of existence. "Death is merely a change from one status or sphere of existence to another" (*Revelation 20:13; 2 Nephi 9:10–15*)" (*Bruce R. McConkie, MD, pg. 184-185*). So how many spheres of existence have people's spirits been through and now many does it have to go? Well, it can be speculated, when spirits left the sphere or existence where is called "intelligences" and was born into the existence called the preexistence as a spirit child of Heavenly Father, according to Brigham Young, the spirit experienced some form of death and rebirth. It is known; when spirits left the sphere of the preexistence, they had to experience death in order to be born as a child in the sphere of mortality. It also known, when any spirit leaves the sphere of mortality it will experience death and move onward, by rebirth, into the sphere called the Spirit or Eternal World, (also known as Paradise or Hell). When leaving the Spirit or Eternal World, and moving into the millennial sphere, will there be an experience another death and rebirth? How about when, during the Millennium or thereafter, when the body and spirit become a resurrected being, do they experience death and rebirth yet again? Then, when moving on to one of the "three degrees of glory" and become a glorified being, sometime after resurrection, is there a death and rebirth involved in this sphere change? Maybe so the reader must decide. What is illustrated here is, people, as spirits, are old hands at this death business and there is not anything to be frightened about. They are simply moving through the stages of the Plan of Salvation as Heavenly Father set out in order for His children can return to Him and be assured, He is not in the business of doing anything to would hurt them.

Here is a good question, what is the purpose of burial and why does the body have to decompose? Most people have heard the question ask by those secular intellectuals, how long does it take the spirit to leave the body after the body dies? President Young says this is thinking in reverse, the facts are, the body instantly dies when the spirit leaves the body and not before and President Joseph Fielding Smith says, when the spirit enters the fetus sometime prior to birth, is when life begins. Additionally, Brigham Young states, death does not destroy the body but death is only the cause and effect of the spirit leaving the mortal body. So, why is decomposition necessary? It is well known, the spirit is purified by the atonement of Christ. It is also known, "no unclean thing can enter into the kingdom of Heaven" (3 Nephi 27:19), and when entering the Kingdom of Heaven as a resurrected being, the spirit and bodies are back together as one. So when and how is the body purified and what is it purified of? It is purified through the process of decomposition where all the "stains" of mortality are erased. These stains were identified by President Young as illnesses lingering in the body and the clinging accumulation of sins that contaminated the body during mortality. These things need to be removed from the body and so the body must be reduced to its elemental state to accomplish this purification, thus the body will be "pure" after resurrection. "What is commonly called death does not destroy the body, it only causes a separation of spirit and body, but the principle of life, inherent in the native elements, of which the body is composed, still continues with the particles of that body and causes it to decay, to dissolve itself into the elements of which it was composed, and all

170

of which continues to have life. When the spirit given to man leaves the body, the tabernacle begins to decompose is that death? No, death only separates the spirit and body, a principle of life still operates in the untenanted tabernacle, but in a different way, and producing different effects from those observed while it was tenanted by the spirit. By and by, sooner or later, the body, this that is tangible to you, that you can feel, see, handle, etc., returns to its mother dust. Is the spirit dead? No. You believe the spirit still exists, when this body has crumbled to the earth again, and the spirit that God puts into the tabernacle goes into the world of spirits. What is their situation? Is there any 'opportunity for them whatever? Yes, there is" (*Disc. B. Young 2:138*).

"Our bodies are composed of visible, tangible matter, as you all understand; you also know that they are born into this world. They then begin to partake of the elements adapted to their organization and growth, increase to manhood, become old, decay, and pass again into the dust. Now in the first place, though I have explained this many times, what we call death is the operation of life, inherent in the matter of which the body is composed, and which causes the decomposition after the spirit has left the body were that not the fact, the body, from which has fled the spirit, would remain to all eternity, just as it was when the spirit left it, and would not decay. Yes, we will lay down these bodies in the grave. What for? That the dust, mother earth, that composes the house of the spirit, may be purified by passing through this ordeal, and be prepared to be called up and united with the intelligent heavenly body that God has prepared. This is nothing but a change, it is not the dissolution of the creature; it is merely putting off the flesh that pertains to this world. The particles of this earth that now compose this body will be rearranged, and the spirit will be clothed with an immortal tabernacle Let the spirit reign predominant over the flesh, and bring into subjection the whole man, every feeling and every desire of his heart, and let him be devoted wholly, body and spirit, to the end for which he has been created. When the flesh is brought into subjection, it is made worthy through that means" (*Disc. B. Young 8:43*).

It is common knowledge, the spirit goes to heaven or the spirit world after death, where is this place? What is it like when the spirit arrives there? Is it possible to know or recognize other people there? President Young says the spirit does not go anywhere, the spirit world is right here on earth; it is incorporated within this celestial system. He said all things were brought forth upon this earth for the express purpose of inhabiting it to all eternity. At the time of death, it is just a change or move to another dimension and every person, who ever lived and died on earth, is in that dimension. He goes on to say, movement from the mortal sphere into the spiritual sphere is so comfortable and natural, the spirit hardly notices. Spirit persons look very much like their mortal counterpart and will be able to recognize others and they will, in turn, recognize others in the spirit world. In this existence, the spirit will not be hindered by any illnesses and will spend time learning the gospel or teaching others who have not heard the gospel. Will there be bad people there? Yes, they will, and they will have the same bad attitude and will be doing many of the bad things they were doing while alive on earth.

In the last part of this quote, President Young talks about traveling around after while in the spirit world. Some may find this interesting. "When you lay down this tabernacle, where are you going, into the spirit world. Are you going into Abraham's bosom? No, not anywhere nigh there but into the spirit world. Where is the spirit world? It is right here. Do the good and evil spirits go together? Yes, they do. Do they both inhabit one kingdom? Yes, they do. Do they go to the sun? No. Do they go beyond the boundaries of the organized earth? No, they do not. They are brought forth upon this earth, for the express purpose of inhabiting it to all eternity. Where else are you going? Nowhere else, only as you may be permitted" (*Disc. B. Young 3:69*).

"The spirits that dwell in these tabernacles on this earth, when they leave them go directly into this world of spirits. What a congregated mass of inhabitants there in spirit, mingling with each other, as they do here? Yes, brethren, they are there together, and if they associate together, and collect together, in clans and in societies as they do here, it is their privilege No doubt they yet, more or less, see, hear, converse and have to do with each other, both good and bad. If the Elders of Israel in these latter times go and preach to the spirits in prison, they associate with them, precisely as our Elders associate with the wicked in the flesh, when they go to preach to them" (*Disc. B. Young 2:137*).

"When the breath leaves the body, your life has not become extinct; your life is still in existence. And when you are in the spirit world, everything there will appear as natural as things now do Spirits will be familiar with spirits in the spirit world will converse, behold, and exercise every variety of communication with one another as familiarly and naturally as while here in tabernacles. There, as here, all things will be natural, and you will understand them as you now understand natural things. You will there see that those spirits we are speaking of are active; they sleep not and you will learn that some are striving with all their might laboring and toiling diligently as any individual would to accomplish an act in this world to destroy the children of men" (*Disc. B. Young 7-239*).

"Here, we are continually troubled with ills and ailments of various kinds in the spirit world we are free from all this and enjoy life, glory, and intelligence. When we advance in years, we have to be stubbing along and be careful lest we fall down. We see our youth, even, frequently stubbing their toes and falling down. But yonder, how different! They move with ease and like lightning If we want to visit Jerusalem, or this, that, or the other place and I presume we will be permitted if we desire. There we are, looking at its streets If we want to behold Jerusalem as it was in the days of the Savior; or if we want to see the Garden of Eden as it was when created, there we are, and we see it as it existed spiritually, for it was created first spiritually and then temporally, and spiritually it still remains" (*Disc. B. Young 14.231*).

So, as stated, is death is a "small matter"? Think of it like this way, people certainly have died before, and will certainly die again, and all of this is simply changing existences and progressing along the path set out by God. When arriving at the "other side" the spirit will feel great and look the same or better, they will associate with people they know, their families, and friends, and will be busy learning and teaching the gospel and will have total memory of the past (that will be a relief). There will not be a feeling of discomfort in any way.

Elijah and the Temple
(The Temple, Where Heaven Meets Earth)

Elijah did come. He came to the Kirtland Temple on April 3, 1836. Jewish literature is replete with the promise and expectation of Elijah's coming right up to the last promise of the Old Testament, in the last verses of Malachi. Moreover, it is Jewish tradition, on the second night of Passover, they must leave open the door, a place at the tables head, an empty chair, and a goblet full of wine in the expectation, Elijah may come. It is interesting, especially in light of Jewish tradition, April 3, 1836, was the second day of Passover. The symbolism is beautiful...Elijah came, as was expected, to a home -- the Lord's home...He came to turn hearts, which is more than changing minds -- he turns hearts to hearts. He somehow bridges some gap, some alienation, and some separation occurring in the human family.

Ordinarily it is said, Elijah did something pertaining to the dead or work for the dead --a half-truth. In the first place, no one is dead. Those who are in the spirit world are in some ways more alive than some here on earth. For instance, Elder Melvin J. Ballard said they have every feeling "intensified" spiritually. Moreover, as for their being dead and gone, no,

173

they are not gone either. The prophets teach, the spirit world is not in some remote galaxy, it is here, it is near. As the Prophet put it, speaking of their feelings for us, those righteous souls who are bound to mortals somehow by the anxieties of their forbearing, their bowels yearn over us. He said they are not idle spectators in the last days. Therefore, Elijah does have something to do with them (the spirit children). However, the Prophet taught, Elijah, also has something to do with the living. Had he not come, the whole earth would be cursed; or, in another version, the earth would be utterly wasted at Christ's coming. Wasted, means at least two things. It would be in a sense a waste if this earth, created by the Father and Son as the dwelling place of their family, turned out to be a house barren--not a home, not a place of genuine familial love. In this sense, it would have been a waste to create it. Second, were there not a family welded and united and full of love for Christ, it would be the case, mankind would be unable to endure His presence and all would be laid waste at His coming. Mortals should thank God for the restoration of the power to prepare such a family, which, conferral came through Elijah."

"First, there is forgiveness. Accept this suggestion, while, it may be difficult to forgive your enemies, but it is even more difficult to forgive your loved ones who have sometimes manifested hate--and you have to forgive them in response. It is harder to forgive your loved ones, because you care about them and you have to go on living with them, or struggling to, and they can go on hurting you over the years and the decades. But our hearts will never turn to our fathers in the way Elijah prescribes and which has been testified to above in order to motivate us, unless we forgive."

"...But you and I are all involved...and therefore, as you look back at your seventy or so forbears -- that is what it would take, at fifty years each, only seventy generations to get you back to Abraham--you might recognize that you have inherited the blood of many generations. ...which means hereditary, the inheritance of tendencies, and all of us have them... So perhaps you do have problems that you can blame on your ancestors, and if you forgive that and choose to stand close to the Lord in the process of purifying your life, that will affect your whole family in both directions. You are not alone. There is no way you can gain solitary and neutral ground. You are in it -- you are involved. Moreover, I believe this is one of the profound meanings of that long, laborious allegory in the book of Jacob, the allegory of the tame and wild olive trees. If you take a wild branch and graft it into a tame one, if the branch is strong, enough it will eventually corrupt and spoil the tree all the way to the roots. However, if you take a tame branch and graft it in to a wild tree, in due time if that branch is strong enough, it will heal and regenerate to the very roots. You will then have been an instrument in the sanctification even of your forbears."

"Do these considerations ever sober us in moments when we suppose either that no one cares for us or that whether they care or not, our life makes no difference? To be that kind of branch and achieve that kind of transformation backward and forward is perhaps the greatest achievement of this world. However, to do it one must great; one must be linked or bound to the Lord Jesus Christ. One must be mighty. One must be something of a savior. This is exactly what the Prophet Joseph Smith said we are "saviors on Mount Zion."

"Thus is it our privilege and calling to become in our own limited way redeemers of the human family, ours, and His. It is impossible to love Him truly and not love what is His; and God assigned Him to all of us. And it is not possible for us to really love ourselves unless we love what is truly us, and that is the whole house of Israel to which we belong" (*taken from 1977 talk by Truman Madsen Elijah's mission*)

ELITISM V/S POPULISM

There are two different and distinctive schools of thought within the LDS community on church callings and the fulfilment of those callings. This subject is seldom if ever discussed and they are--- elitism and populism.

The elitist view is Church callings should always promote maximum efficiency within a program by calling only those with specific skills, talents, or knowledge to function in programs requiring those skills, specific talents or some greater knowledge. Oft times, members who harbor these elitist feelings think, certain callings in some way validates the righteousness or worthiness of the person who has been called, or themselves when they are called to a, so called, advanced calling and thus, they are constantly seeking out or hoping for any advanced calling to enhance their personal validation and bolsters their ego. This can lead to such members coveting certain callings and then feeling disgruntled when called to a lesser calling. Those who have this elitist attitude, view callings as some in the business world view climbing the corporate ladder. Where a member starts out with a calling of little significance and as they go along, they receive more advanced callings, until such time they reach the top, each defining *the top* in their own way. In each of these callings, the performance of the elitist member, providing their performance is satisfactory, entitles them to a greater calling. This sense of entitlement is where the elitist view starts to fall apart in terms of humility and service. Unfortunately, those with an elitist mentality will not ask for help when the calling starts to go south and since their performance is ego driven rather than faith driven and Holy Ghost assisted they have very little to fall back on. The elitist who is functioning in a calling and trying to advance the cause based on ego has little chance to resolve any problems as they arise or experience any measure of growth since they cannot recognize or accept any culpability on their part, therefore they must resort to blaming others and finger pointing because they simply cannot be wrong. When a person loses sight of his responsibility for his own transgressions or failings, no matter how small, he simultaneously also loses sight of the need for repentance, thus he is less likely to notice, regret, and repent of his sins and transgressions. Therefore, an enlarged ego can have damning consequences. But to be fair, those have recently receiving callings such as Bishop or Stake President almost always have some level of ego boost. Maybe a tingling of validation mixed with honor, and some amount of fear and trepidation at the start, but this is just human nature and not to be confused with a true elitist who revels, full out, in a so-called advanced calling. Of course, if the Bishop or Stake President allows himself to play into this validation and let their enlarged ego go unchecked, then there is an elitist issuing callings based on some level of ego, and, from sad experience, it is known, ego chases away humility, one can only guess where it all would lead. This attitude is in part mentioned in Doctrine and Covenants, "We have learned by sad experience that it is the nature and disposition of almost all men, as soon as they get a little authority, as they suppose, they will immediately begin to exercise unrighteous dominion" (*D&C 121:39*). The insertion of as-they-suppose is the pivotal part of this scripture. This is where the elitist lets his ego cloud his judgment since he now is special, and it is in this context that, unrighteous dominion could be defined as functioning in a calling for purposes other than the purposes of the Lord.

The populist view is Church callings should be extended to provide maximum opportunity to the greatest number of worthy members, and trust in the member's faith and in the Holy Ghost to help maximize the efficiency of the calling. A few callings, such as ward organist, may require specialized talent, but, in the populist's mind, most callings do not, as opposed to the elitist mind, where most callings do require a level of expertise. Those leaders with the populist view often times find themselves calling members to and having them accept positions where the member can easily be overwhelmed since they don't have the necessary skills to advance the calling and the person extending the calling has no way to assess their relationship with the Holy Ghost or their level of faith. This is especially true when issuing callings to new members but is equally important with members who recently move into a ward or a new Stake President or new Bishop who does not know his flock well. This is where this populist view starts to fall apart and those who extend callings need to be alerted to this dilemma and proceed with caution if they expect those who are called to

176

have any measure of success. In the atmosphere of lay ministry, the premise of church callings is they be geared primarily to help people grow spiritually, increases their talents, and help develop gifts of the spirit as they pursue and grow in their callings, it is necessary for the leadership to establish a network of members as support for the newly called member. Since all callings involve ministration to and interaction with others, these others (meaning church members) can have a positive effect on the success of the calling. Without these other ward members having some grasp of the situation at hand they will not always know when or how to proceed for fear of offending the newly called member or they may be taken aback by the ineptness of the newly called member and refuse to participate. The person issuing callings must anticipate this and arrange for some kind of support so the newly called member will not feel abandoned. The most vulnerable callings are "President "positions, since the membership have greater expectations from these leaders. These callings are the most sought after by the elitist and the most troubling to the populist, but the dilemma is present in all callings. As an example, if the calling involves teaching adults, the class members, on their own, can,

1   Choose to complain and hold back their support,

2   Participate constructively in the class to help the teacher overcome any deficiencies.

In turn, they grow spiritually by learning greater tolerance, and may even uncover hidden talents of their own, but when teaching young adults or children the second choice probably will not be the case. All too often the arranging of any kind support group is neglected, resulting in the called member being handed a manual of some kind, maybe receiving a smattering of "training" then left to his or her own devices. If those members, who will be interacting with the newly called, chose not to participate, for whatever reason, this is surely a prescription for failure.

There is a third line of thought concerning this calling issue, in light of elitism or populism. Is a calling from the bishop or Stake President a calling from the Lord? Latter-day Saints are taught to believe this is so. They are also are taught these leaders are entitled to the power of discernment and put their trust in them. Most callings extended to the members by Bishops or Stake Presidents are probably inspired but, in reality, a small number probable are not inspired but based strictly on necessity.

This being said, consider the two schools of thought outlined above in terms of a Bishop or Stake President administering in their calling.

One- Should leaders, when, extending a calling, even consider either of these two schools of thought, or not?

Two- If any leader refuses to consider either one of these views and says they just put their trust in the Lord, then, why are they given the power of discernment, and is it really any use to them?

Three-Additionally if any Bishop or Stake President would subscribe to and administer from one or the other of these two schools of thought mentioned above, how would this affect the quality of their callings and the spiritual health of their congregations?

Most of the time when extending callings leaders has a direct and positive effect of the subject at hand. They ask members, not to immediately accept a calling but to take time to pray about it personally, and if married, communicate with their spouses before accepting or rejecting a calling, because the support of spouses is part of the necessary support system that needs to be set up. Now, leaders do not always do this in connection with elitism or populism but it is related. The member who actually prays for an answer to a calling is likely to have the Holy Ghost usurp any feelings of despair or entitlement and level the playing field. The spouse can also have the same effect if the marriage is healthy. Members, can choose not to accept a calling without jeopardizing their membership in any way, but how can the leader, who extends the calling, (based on his power of discernment) going to know if the member is acting from either one of the two schools of thought? Example, on one hand the elitist would refuse the calling because it is beneath him in his progression to the "top". Or the elitist could accept the calling and then when his entitlement attitude and ego surfaces he would run the chance of offending everyone he has been working with, leaving the program in a mess and the Bishop to clean it up. On the other hand, the populist would refuse the calling because he cannot see the necessary support system, which would garner him, success. Alternatively, the populist could also accept the calling and possibly, through his naiveté and lack of support, cause the program to fail, only to be released and someone else called to pick up the pieces.

It seems, any insight on this would be a great help to any leader. An insightful leader could also place some carefully worded questions during the second interview giving him some further knowledge into the nature of the one called if he is concerned about either of these two issues.

Conclusion;

The leadership of the church, weather they personally subscribe to either one of these schools of thought or simply ignore both of them and forge on ahead, must find an avenue of thought, communication, consideration and inspiration whereby their administrative term will be successful and the membership will grow in the Lord. It is evident the issues described above have a direct effect on the health of a ward and the enthusiasm or complacency, activity or inactivity of the members. These issues are brought to light, purposefully for stimulating thought about this process called religion and people's involvement in it.

ENDURE TO THE END

In Job38:7 while in the first estate the spirit children of God were so overjoyed at the prospect of coming here they shouted for joy. Now amidst all the trials and tribulations of this second estate one might wonder what the shouting was all about. A person can surely look back on the early membership of this church with all the special stresses and strains they carried and marvel at the cheerful and patient attitude they displayed while enduring these unusual burdens. Members of the church can only follow their lead if they fully understand this concept of enduring.

When this concept of enduring is mentioned in a sacrament talk or in some other meeting, most of the congregation, but especially the young folks, quickly lose interest since they associate this challenge with those in the congregation of advanced age. This question must be answered. Is the commandment, to endure, a commandment for some of the members which comes into play at a certain time of their lives or does it apply to all members all the time?

To answer this question, one needs to examine the concept in steps. Looking at this concept in full, there are three applications of enduring, which, mortals are to endure, they are ask to patiently endure, they are ask to endure well, and they are ask to endure to the end. Now for some scriptures. "And so, after he had patiently endured, he obtained the promise" (*Hebrews, 6:15*). "Endure well and God will exalt the on high; thou shalt triumph over all thy foes" (*Doctrine and Covenants, 121:8*). "If you keep my commandments and endure to the end you shall have eternal life, which gift is the greatest of all the gifts of God" (*Doctrine and Covenants, 14:7*

There are five areas to be considered where the concept on enduring

takes place,

1- As a requirement

2- In terms of Timing

3- In terms of Faith

4- In terms of Agency

5- In terms of Repentance

Requirement

The "if you keep my commandants" stated in D&C 14:7 is not something one can fail to do and still find the grace and mercy to be forgiven, through repentance and the atonement of Christ. To be clear, the atonement does not create any alternate route to the blessing promised here in mortality or in eternal life. To the contrary, this revelation was given long after the atonement had been made, and represents the duty of man even giving consideration to the atonement. It is what one must do in order to obtain grace and mercy, and have the atonement applied to oneself for the forgiveness of sins. This concept is not an option as the Prophet explained; it is the duty of man.

Timing

Faith in God includes faith in his timing. For instance, God did not rush the restoration, which required adequate religious freedom among other things, even though He surly knew about all of the calamities facing those who lived in the pre-restoration ages. If he had rushed the restoration, the lack of sufficient free agency and political freedom the restoration would have run the risk of failure.

Likewise, things cannot be rushed in people's lives and the instructions are clear. People learn, line on line, precept upon percept. They only grow, in terms of obedience, as fast as they can assimilate spiritual knowledge into their lives. For example, if a couple, rushes into baptism before they have fully repented there surly will be problems later. For this reason, the mission requires an interview prior to the baptism. People cannot rush the answers to their prayers no matter how desperate they may seem to be, they must be patient with themselves and allow time for the Lord to work. In the scriptures it is learned, God is waiting for spiritual readiness to continue the mortal progression. "The Lord is not slack concerning his promise, as some men count slackness: but is long suffering to us-ward, not willing that any should perish, but that all should come to repentance" (*2 Peter 3:9*).

Faith

There will be times in each person's life when their faith cannot and must not, be conditional upon God's rescuing or relieving them, because He may not respond in the manner or speed of their choosing. Whether the test is illness, pain, deprivation, just being passed over, or working one's way through doubt, what has to be sustained is trust and faith in God and His plan. While living God's plan, life may seem ordinary and somewhat plain wrapped but it behooves mortals to realize life is a cluster of soul-searching experiences. People need to live in deeds, not years, in thoughts, not breaths, in feelings, not in apathy and in this way to build faith as we endure.

Agency

People interacting in this mortal world with so many others, on a daily basis, means enduring each other's immaturity and to a large part, each other's misuse of free agency. With a gift such as agency given to mankind, life cannot possibly present a perfect tidy picture. The lifelong circumstances of having to endure are partly, if not largely, the cumulative result of the varied use of moral agency, and the structure of life itself.

Repentance

Taken the scripture in D&C, 14:7 at face value, this is saying, to receive eternal life one must not sin in any way. The statement says, one must "keep the commandments," which, being unqualified, must be understood as all, not some, of the commandments must be obeyed.

Of course, everyone has already sinned, and Heavenly Father knows that. It does not mean one must never have sinned in all one's life. It does mean one must stop sinning and "endure to the end of your repentance," - stop sinning everlastingly.

To keep Christ's commandments and endure to the end as required, here is simply a description of repentance. It is what repentance looks like. "Behold, he who has repented of his sins, the same is forgiven, and I, the Lord, remember them no more. By this ye may know if a man repenteth of his sins - behold, he will confess them and forsake them" (D&C 58:42-43). The Prophet Spencer Kimball explained the last verse this way, the forsaking of sin must be a permanent one. True repentance does not permit making the same mistake again.

So what is the answer to the question asked above? --- Is this a commandment for some of the members, which comes into play at a certain time of their lives or does it, apply to all members all the time?

To "endure", "endure well" and "endure to the end" is actually enduring from the very beginning and continue to endure through the repentance process throughout your life unto death. This endurance quest starts in the preexistence and lasts throughout the plan of salvation.

Faith and Belief

Faith and belief are not the same thing but oft times, and with some regularity, the words faith and belief are used interchangeably. Speaking of those who profess a certain faith some often call such people believers, making it appear, professing faith and having belief are the same. If those folks are not mindful, the false imprecision they are giving can mislead others and those around them. Faith rather than belief is central to Christianity. However, if the two are not properly equated, then the difficulties in understanding belief can become an obstruction in the development of faith. While belief is an element of faith, not seeing the difference between the two can have deadly spiritual consequences.

It is appropriate to look at the relationship of belief being an element of faith. The New Testament uses the Greek word *pastis* which when translated into the English word *faith*, and it means trust or fidelity. A person of faith is a person who trusts and who can be trusted. If one trusts in Jesus Christ to redeem him from the fallen state of a human being, then he is a person of faith. If one trusts in Him, then he is obliged to be trustworthy. Can a person be trusted to work at living the life to which, he is called? In the relationship of trust, one will certainly have certain beliefs. Some do not know what it would mean to trust in Jesus if they do not believe He exists and is divine, then, there will be no faith. Nevertheless, while trust and belief are not the same thing, one cannot be faithful to the message of the gospel, without also having beliefs. Logic predicts, if ones beliefs are not the same as ones trust, then it follows, one's beliefs are not the same as their faith. Moreover, many beliefs, perhaps even most of them, can waver or even fail without having any measurable effect on the level of one's faith. As a person grows in the gospel his beliefs, can and certainly will change. Some beliefs can wane or even disappear while others can develop in unexpected directions. People can hold certain beliefs that are somewhat different from others in their Church and can be equally faithful. None of these belief changes will not or should not necessarily dictate a change in faithfulness because faith is eternal and resides in the spiritual and belief is secular and resides in the temporal. Therefore, a person's level of faithfulness is his demonstration of his love for the Savior; while his beliefs, no matter how strong, cannot do anything of the sort.

Looking at this faith/belief issue from a more serious angle, which is not seeing the difference between faith and belief, can have deadly spiritual consequences. Members of the Mormon Church claim the Church continues to be led by a living prophet, who guides the Church by revelation. Less well known, but equally important is each level of leadership and each member of the Church is explicitly expected also to lead by revelation: seeking divine guidance in all decisions. Though there are handbooks giving the broad guidelines for what different leaders are to do, the details of the work is supposed to be decided by inspiration, and when prompted by the Spirit a leader can even do what is not in line with those guidelines. The principle goes even further, to individuals: as individuals, as family members, as members of congregations, they are supposed to live their lives under the direction of the Holy Ghost. Being confirmed a member of the LDS Church is to be commanded, in a spiritual blessing, to do that very thing: Receive the Holy Ghost, this is at the heart of the confirmation rite. This is undoubtedly the spiritual side of religion. In light of this, can anyone say their belief system is sufficient to beckon the Holy Ghost to his or her side? Of course, not, having the constant companion of the Holy Ghost requires some degree of faith, but therein lies the problem. Any member who is confused on this issue cannot know whether they are being led by the Spirit or by their own desires. They can easily believe their desires and those of God are so in line their belief and their faith is the same. If a member is confused and cannot see the difference between faith and belief they may think their beliefs are sufficient to get them through the ordnances of the New and Everlasting Covenant. This is certainly not the case since all these ordnances and their relationship with the Holy Ghost is spiritual, their secular beliefs simply will not suffice and most assuredly will lead to their spiritual downfall.

Families can be together forever

What does this "Families can be together forever" statement mean? If a people go the Mormon Church web site and research this subject, there are many statements and articles concerning this often-repeated declaration but very little information advancing their understanding of its meaning. Mostly the theme given in the Church web site is about situations and events surrounding family relations during mortality. There is almost nothing said concerning the impending life, which the statement seems to be representing. Although the web site does say, under certain circumstances, mortals can participate in a family in eternity but there is not an explanation of how this eternal family structured or the terms of eligibility.

While teaching a priesthood class, the priesthood holders were asked for their take on this, families can be together forever, issue. Almost all agreed the word, forever, meant the Celestial Kingdom. Most thought that the word, family, meant their extended mortal family. The word, can, really threw them, they could not decide what it meant, did it mean, be capable of, or did it mean, be able to, or did it mean, be eligible for? There was some question about the meaning of the word, together, did it mean, communally, or did it mean, in concert with? Since all had agreed the word, forever, meant the Celestial kingdom, the doctrine of the three degrees of glory threw a wrench in understanding the word, together. Before the class, discussion started all those priesthood brothers thought they fully comprehended this, families can be together forever, statement, and after this meeting, some left with a fair amount of reservation.

Father   Mother

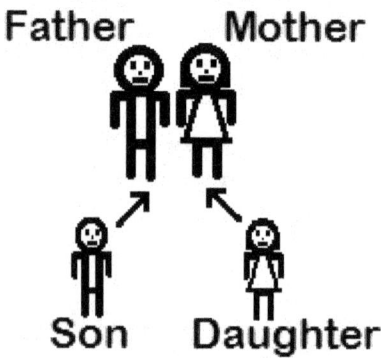

Son   Daughter

Here is what caused all of the confusion with these priesthood holders. First is option #1 **The immediate earthly family,** as shown in this illustration.

When ask if children would be with their parents in the Celestial Kingdom? The universal answer was yes. In addition, everyone thought his or her grandchildren would also be there. When ask, if they were sure, their daughter and their wife would be together with them? Again, the answer was yes! (No question). The pointed was then made; if their daughter joins them in their Celestial family then the wife would have to be with her father in his Celestial Family. In addition, her mother would have to be with her father and their son, as shown in this illustration, would only have his daughter with him and so on. It is not possible for a priesthood holder to have his wife, son, and daughter with him and leave his father in law and his father without any children since God guarantees everyone the same family opportunity. Under this first option, a Celestial Family would only consist of only fathers and daughters. Therefore, logically, this scenario does not nor cannot represent the true meaning of the "Families can be together forever" declaration.

After mulling this over for a while, the common consensus was, it must be all one big family, which would include every family member

This brings about Option#2. **The entire earthly family as one unit** as shown in this illustration.

They were then ask if their, all on one, Celestial Family would include Uncle Tom, who was a violent, unrepentant pedophile and Great Aunt Sally, an unrepentant "black Widow" who had killed her four husbands for the insurance money and any other unworthy family members? (This is the togetherness problem) If these relatives have presence in the Celestial Family, there would not be any need for the three degrees of glory since everyone, no matter their worthiness, would be in the same kingdom. Again, this surely does not nor cannot represent the true meaning of the "Families can be together forever" declaration. This is where the discussion ended because class time ended, there was not any subsequent follow-up, and they never mentioned the subject again.

If these two options do not represent the meaning of the declaration "Families can be together forever", this can only mean there is another, completely different meaning than the two discussed above. One only eluded to in the church web site and in talks from the podium. Nevertheless, to be sure, this declaration is absolutely true and accurate. The problem, for most people, starts when they attempt interpret or visualize these spiritual statements or events from a mortal perspective. They take their mortal experience and trying to apply it to something in the eternal existence, which is of a purely spiritual nature and in doing so their scope of thinking is far too limiting. This is why the two options, discussed above, exist, which some truly believe, but they will never not pass the logic test. Think of it this way; if your viewpoint or visualization of any eternal situation does not cover all of mankind or all of mankind's issues equally then something is amiss, since God is the God of all.

To explain further, take the first word, forever. If all agree this word in the declaration is referring to the Celestial kingdom then the, family is a Celestial Family, which has very little to do with the mortal family since some, if not most, of the extended mortal family may not qualify for the Celestial Kingdom. The truth is, mortals know very little about the structure of a Celestial Family but since it is spiritual, it has to be very different from a mortal family; therefore, the mortal family experience may not be the best model when trying to grasp this spiritual situation. The second word, can. This word implies certain conditions or requirements need to be met before

185

qualification, and just being in a mortal family, or even sealed therein, is no guarantee. Now, the words, be together. This implies, members of this family, however it is structured and wherever it is located, are united in cause and spirit. "Forever" of course means eternity and in the scriptures, the Celestial Kingdom is the only eternal place known where there is an identifiable family.

Actually, there is not much known about this spiritual transformation but within the limited mortal capacity, people do know certain things. There is scriptural evidence the Prophet Abraham received a promise called "the Abrahamic covenant". People also know, from the Doctrine and Covenants, members of the Mormon Church have adoption rights to Abraham's covenant. It is for sure, participation in the New and everlasting Covenant is the required process through which members gain adoption and thus, they join the seed of Abraham. It is clear the promise to Abraham was only his seed would inherit the Celestial kingdom and all those in the Celestial Kingdom are automatically in the Family of Christ.
So, what does the phrase "Families can be together forever" mean? The best way to answer this question is the rephrasing of the declaration. Here goes! "Those individual members of earthly **families** which **can** meet the righteous requirements for adoption into the Abrahamic Covenant will **be together** in the Family of Christ in the Celestial Kingdom **Forever**".

FINAL JUDGEMENT
(The purpose of the final judgment)

The pre-mortal, mortal and spirit world labors of every man will culminate when they are reviewed or examined during the experience called "the final judgment". This is the point in time where a line of demarcation is drawn between man's time of preparation for reception of the blessing promised by God and the actual receiving of them. Life, which is made up of the pre-mortal, mortal and spirit world is not made up of one single event nor is our judgment but rather, all lives are made up of a series of events and a series of judgments and the final judgment is the process finalizing or concluding of all these judgments. Mortals are being continually judged in everything they do and these judgments started in the pre-existence when a judgment was made wherein some would continue into mortality and others would not and these judgments will surely continue right up until the time of the final judgment. The purpose of the final judgment is to determine the extent and quality of all man's labor whereby they will be sent to the appropriate kingdom of glory they have earned during the three periods mentioned above. The final judgment process is one of the more important components of the plan of salvation. It operates under the law of eternal progression and will accomplish at least eight objectives which are necessary in the plan of salvation. These objectives are:

1   Cause man to see his own actions determined his fate.
The judgment is not designed for God's benefit He already knows the outcome for each individual and has known from the beginning. The judgment is intended to benefit the man who is under examination. When the man being examined realizes he and he alone has sealed his fate by his actions he will not be able to claim God's foreknowledge controlled his actions and predestined him to his fate. While it is true, he was tested and challenged during his probation he was given his agency to choose liberty and eternal life or to choose captivity and death, nor was he challenged beyond his capacity to choose wisely. At the time of his judgment, no man will be able to assert, he was denied his agency and will be compelled to admit he chose the very actions governing his eternal fate.

2   Cause man to review his actions during his mortal life and perhaps all of his actions during the entire time of his probation. During this judgment, each man will review his entire mortal probation and will have a perfect knowledge of all his deeds both good and bad. This review will enable man to fully understand the reason for the reward he earns.

3   Cause man to acknowledge the justice of God's judgment.
A third responsibility man must fulfill at the final judgment is to acknowledge the Lord's determination of his final reward is just and true.

4   Cause man to acknowledge Jesus as the Christ.
Although many will come before the bar at judgment day have already, during their lives, acknowledged Jesus as the Christ and have changed their lives as the Savior has asked. There will also be many that will come who have refused to accept the gospel in their lives, never the less, all will be compelled to acknowledge His divinity and proclaim that He is the Supreme King and lawgiver.
The four purposes of the judgment listed above are all to be fulfilled by the person under examination and judgment. The Lord or His representatives will accomplish purposes five through eight.

5   Grant forgiveness of sin.
God has revealed, no unclean thing can enter His kingdom, and, ye cannot be saved in your sins. However, all have sinned and come short of the glory

of God. Unless there is a way in which man could repent and be forgiven of his sins, no man would be able to enter any kingdom of God. Christ provided the way through his atonement. Christ is able to either allow man to suffer for his sins or to excuse him from suffering through the process of forgiveness. This decision is based on a person's readiness to live a life in the manner prescribed by the Lord. The laws of God and the commandments, which are embodied in the teachings of Christ, will provide the standard of conduct by which all men will be judged. This lifestyle (following the teachings of Christ) consists of a person's attitude, works, degree of repentance and willingness to confess his sins at the Day of Judgment. If they do this, they will find the Lord's promise fulfilled at judgment day and their sins and iniquities will be remembered no more.

6   Make intercession to God in behalf of man.
Christ is managing the affairs of earth on behalf of God and is to deliver up the kingdom and present it unto His Father, spotless. God has committed all judgment into the hands of Christ and will accept His witness concerning the worthiness of those who come into the kingdom. Man receives Christ's witness of approval before the Father by striving to keep the Lord's commandments and seeking to be a recipient of His Atoning Sacrifice. A portion of the judgment process, then, is Christ will advocate man's cause before the Father and certify of the correctness of the judgment, witnessing, all men have merited the reward they receive.

7   Restore men to good or evil.
This function is to restore men to the reward, which is compatible to their mortal works and desires. Thus, man's final reward is regarded as being a continuation of his mortal course, and the judgment serves to restore him to the conditions he truly sought and relished while in mortality.

8   Assign man to the place of his final inheritance. The final judgment will serve as the time when man will be assigned to his personal inheritance in one of the many mansions of the Father. It should be noted, man will already be resurrected, having complete remembrance of his actions, at the Day of Judgment and will probably be aware of which kingdom of glory he will inherit. Yet it would appear the Day of Judgment will be the time of further summation and delineation of man's status and reward. Man's celestial inheritance, however, cannot be occupied until the earth is reformed as a celestial sphere following Christ's reign, the second resurrection, and the completion of the judgment process.

How are mortals judged?

The final judgment process will rely on several kinds of records in order for the outcome to contain the elements of justice and mercy.

The first record brought forth will be the memory of the person being judged. Remember, at the time of the final judgment everyone will be a resurrected being and will possess a clear and complete memory of all the things, which have transpired from the pre-existence up until then. Man himself will bear testimony at the final judgment day, which will either exalt him or condemn him. It is because of the self-judgment, which man will render, Jesus said "I can do mine own self nothing: as I hear, I judge: and my judgment is just" (*John 5:30*). This self-judgement will deal especially with the stewardships the man was called to fulfill during mortality. How equitable this method of judgment is, for every man will testify concerning his deeds knowing the degree of understanding of good and evil, which he had when the deeds were committed. Each man will know if his mortal misdeeds were intentional or accidental, deliberate sin or happenstance, and will testify accordingly. He will judge himself according to the knowledge or judgment he had and used during mortality. Man's judgment will cover every aspect of his life his actions and works, his sins of both commission and omission. It appears, in addition to the personal account each man must give during the Day of Judgment, men will also by confronted by witnesses and a history kept by the church and heavenly records. Moroni warns the readers of the Book of Mormon, he would confront them at the judgment bar of God. Indeed, angels will act as witnesses proclaiming the thoughts, intents, and secret acts of men at the Day of Judgment.

John the Revelator proclaimed, "The dead were judged out of those things which were written in the books, according to their deeds" (*Rev. 20:12*). Seven types of books are mentioned in the scriptures as playing a role in the judgment process.

All will be judged by these records

1- The scriptures, as seen above, contain the criteria for judgment. The words written in the scriptures prescribe the way of life acceptable to the Lord and the prescribed way of life will surely be juxtaposed against the lifestyle lived.

2- Church minutes and statistical records---These records will show membership in the Church, the ordinances fulfilled by each member, the degree of activity and attendance, their financial contributions, and the

Church assignments and callings they have fulfilled. These records are kept in local wards and stake centers.

3-   Books of the Laws of God--- In the general history and records of the Church there are indications of the valor or lack of diligence of various Church members, together with comment as to their degree of consecration, their faith, their works, their genealogies, etc. These Materials are also to be considered in the great judgment day.

4-   Miscellaneous records and histories --- Various secular records such as court records, school records, histories, personal journals, etc., will also contain commentary on man's deeds during mortality and if necessary and pertinent, may be scrutinized during judgment as all the evidence is considered.

5-   Books of Remembrance --- A true book of remembrance is a personal accounting of one's deeds and thoughts. Failure to have one's name and vital information recorded in a valid book of remembrance is a serious offence in the sight of the Lord.

6-   Records of family and family relationships --- Man must be able to properly establish his rightful place in the patriarchal order by having an acceptable record of his ancestors and descendants. Failure to keep this type of record, kept individually and compiled collectively by the Church, may have serious consequences.

All of the above records are temporal in nature and written on perishable material that will eventually decay or return to dust. They will not be lost to God, however, for "all things are written by the Father; therefore, out of the books which shall be written shall the world be judged" (*3 Nephi 27:7*).

There is a seventh type of record influencing man in the great day of judgment. This record is not a mortal record, but is an important record maintained in heaven.

7-   The Lambs Book of Life --- This is the most important of the judgment records and is the record most frequently mentioned in the scriptures. It appears this is "the book of the names of the sanctified, even them of the celestial world" (*D&C 88:19-24*), who have joined "the general assembly and church of the firstborn" (*D&C 76:54*), and who will enter into God's holy city. They are those who have labored in the gospel and overcame all things in their effort to follow the Lord. This record will aid in the selection of those who are to come forth in the first resurrection. This book of life represents the binding force of the gospel ordinances.

What was outlined above is the judgment process but it is important to note, not all men will be judged by this process. There are those who have fully rejected the Lord, are judged in another way. During His mortal ministry, Christ taught concerning those who chose not to believe in His words, saying, He would not personally judge such an individual, but His word (scriptures) would still serve as the judgment norm:

"If any man hear my word and believe not, I judge him not: for I came not to judge the world, but to save the world. He that rejecteth me, and receiveth not my words, hath one that judgeth him: the word that I have spoken, the same shall judge him in the last day" (*Jn. 12:47-48*).

Summery

When thinking about advancing to the Celestial kingdom, take into consideration, each kingdom is governed by the laws specific to that kingdom. Mortals now live in a similitude of the telestial kingdom; if they follow and live the lifestyle prescribed by this kingdom, the best they can inherit will be the telestial kingdom. If they truly want to inherit the Celestial kingdom, they have to demonstrate their ability to live above the lifestyle offered by the telestial kingdom, not living to the next level, but to the level above that. This is the quality of living prescribed by the Savior and is clearly found in the tenets of the Mormon Church.

Formation of the Articles of Faith

Oliver Cowdery, Joseph Young, Orsen Pratt, Orsen Hyde, and Joseph Smith were all involved in the formulation of the Articles of Faith at different times and in different places.

Probably, the earliest formulation of the beliefs of the Church was published by Oliver Cowdery in the first issue of the Latter-day Saints' Messenger and Advocate in October 1834. This summary, as Elder Cowdery explained was published to give the Saints an assurance of the correctness of their own system, so none would engage in any religious controversy without knowledge. These specific points are well worth church member's reflection today: (The numbers in brackets and words in italics indicate wording closely resembles wording in the present Article of Faith with that number.)

[1] "We believe in God, and his Son Jesus Christ. We believe that God, from the beginning, revealed himself to man; and that whenever he has had a people on earth, he always has revealed himself to them by the Holy Ghost, the ministering of angels, or his own voice. [6] We do not

believe that he ever had a church on earth without revealing himself to that church; consequently, there were apostles, prophets, evangelists, pastors, and teachers, in the same.

"We believe that God is the same in all ages; ... and that, as He is no respecter of persons, [9] always has, and always will reveal himself to men when they call upon him.

[10] "We believe that God has revealed himself to men in this age, and commenced to raise up a church preparatory to his second advent, when he will come in the clouds of heaven with power and great glory.

"We believe that the popular religious theories of the day are incorrect. ...

[11] "We believe that all men are born free and equal; that no man, combination of men, or government of men, have power or authority to compel or force others to embrace any system of religion, ... so long as they do not molest or disturb others in theirs, in a manner to deprive them of their privilege as free citizens—or of worshiping God as they choose. ...

[10] "We believe that God has set his hand the second time to recover the remnant of his people, Israel. ...

[13] "And further: We believe in embracing good wherever it may be found; of proving all things, and holding fast that which is righteous".
"This, in short, is our belief, and we stand ready to defend it upon its own foundation whenever it is assailed by men of character and respectability. —And while we act upon these broad principles, we trust in God that we shall never be confounded" (*Cowdery 1834*).

Several of the Articles of Faith begin to take shape here. Although not fully developed and not divided into individual sections, Oliver Cowdery's enumeration of "our principles" bears important similarities to the statements of Joseph Smith eight years later. Like the Articles of Faith, Oliver Cowdery's list begins with the basic principle of belief in God and in his son Jesus Christ. The Holy Ghost is also mentioned here, but only in his role as the revelator of God. Elder Cowdery also affirms the true church contains apostles, prophets, evangelists, pastors, and teachers, and asserts the Church's belief in the restoration of Israel, Christ's second coming, and each man's right to worship God as he chooses.

There are, however, also important differences between Oliver Cowdery's statement and the Articles of Faith. Oliver Cowdery does not touch on such important subjects as the atonement of Christ, the ordinances of the gospel, the gifts of the spirit, the Bible, or the Book of Mormon. He does mention the general gathering of Israel, but gives few specifics. On the other hand, Oliver Cowdery fervently declares the error of the religions of his day and affirms the constancy of God in dealing with mankind—ideas which do not appear in the Articles of Faith.

The most fundamental difference between Oliver Cowdery's statement and the Articles of Faith, however, lies in their basic characters. Oliver Cowdery simply asserts certain abstract principles, whereas the Articles of Faith simultaneously set standards for conduct and declare principles of faith. For example, where Elder Cowdery says, "We believe that God has revealed himself to man," Joseph Smith will say, "We believe all that God has revealed" (italics added). The difference is apparent: it is one thing to believe God has revealed himself; it is another to believe that which has been revealed. Where Oliver states a belief in certain civil liberties, Joseph Smith will go on to impose a duty upon all who believe in such liberties to "obey, honor, and sustain the law." This difference in approach is significant, for what religious value do statements of belief have if they do not lead directly to righteous conduct?

Joseph Young

Joseph Young, a brother of Brigham Young, penned a second early statement of the beliefs of the restored Church. While proselyting in Boston in 1836, Joseph Young was approached by John Hayward, a local editor, who asked for a written statement of the "creed, doctrines, sentiments, or religious notions" of the Church. Within three days, Elder Young delivered the following statement:

"This Church was organized on the 6th of April, 1830, in the State of New York, and its principal articles of faith are,

1. [1] "A belief in one true and living God, the creator of the heavens and the earth, and in his Son Jesus Christ, who came into this world 1800 years since, at Jerusalem; was slain, rose from the dead, ascended on high, and now sits on the right hand of the Majesty in the heavens; [3] that through the atonement thus wrought out, all men may come to God and find acceptance; all of which they believe is revealed in the holy Scripture".

2. [4] "That God requires all men, wherever his gospel is proclaimed, or his law known, to repent of all sins, forsake evil, and follow righteousness; that his word also requires men to be baptized, as well as to repent; and that the direct way pointed out by the Scriptures for baptism, is immersion. After which, the individual has the promise of the gift of the Holy Spirit. ... This gift of the Holy Spirit was anciently bestowed by the laying on of the apostles' hands: [5] so this church believes that those who

193

have authority to administer in the ordinances of the gospel have this right and authority. ...."

3. [10] "That God will, in the last days, gather the literal descendants of Jacob to the lands anciently possessed by their fathers; that he will lead them as at the first, and build them as at the beginning. ... [7] And that, as men anciently saw visions, dreamed dreams, held communion with angels, and conversed with the heavens, so it will be in the last days, to prepare the way for all nations, languages, and tongues, to serve him in truth".

4. "That the time will come when the Lord Jesus will descend from heaven, accompanied with ten thousand of his saints; that a mighty angel will lay hold on the dragon, bind him, cast him into the pit. ...."

5. "They believe in the resurrection of the body; that all men will stand in the presence of God, and be judged according to the deeds, or works, done in this life" (*Joseph Young 1836*).

Elder Young's statement reflects the keen awareness in the restored Church of Christ's atonement and of man's need to repent, be baptized, and receive the Holy Ghost. Thus, in the first three of Joseph Young's "articles of faith," There are many parallels to the present Articles of Faith. It is interesting, most of the points which Oliver Cowdery's statement lacked are present here, while many of the points included by Oliver Cowdery are omitted by Joseph Young.
All of the ideas in Joseph Young's statement are not clearly refined, and there are some significant differences between his statement and the present Articles of Faith. In Joseph Young's statement, God is still not referred to, as the Father, and the Holy Ghost is not yet named as a member of the Godhead. Elder Young speaks of the gathering of the literal descendants of Israel; Joseph Smith declares the literal gathering of Israel. Moreover, the approach taken by Joseph Young is fundamentally different from which would be employed by Joseph Smith. Joseph Young's style is somewhat expository and detached, unless this characteristic was contributed by Hayward's editing.

In 1840, yet another statement of the "faith and doctrine of the Church" appeared. This was authored by Orson Pratt, an apostle of the Church, and was written while he was a missionary in Scotland. It was over seven pages long as it originally appeared in Pratt's tract *Interesting Account of Several Remarkable Visions and of the Late Discovery of Ancient American Records*. It is an intricate statement, which soon came to be used as a standard explanation of the teachings of the Church. As is readily apparent, it seems to have had many definite influences on Joseph Smith's ultimate formulation of the Articles of Faith. Due to its length, only a small part of it will be quoted here:

"We now proceed to give a sketch of the faith and doctrine of this Church.

[1] "First, we believe in God the Eternal Father, and in his Son Jesus Christ, and in the Holy Ghost, who bears record of them, the same throughout all ages and forever".

[2] "We believe that all mankind, by the transgression of their first parents, and not by their own sins, were brought under the curse and penalty of that transgression, which consigned them to an eternal banishment from the presence of God, and their bodies to an endless sleep in the dust, never more to rise. ..."

[3] "We believe, that through the sufferings, death, and atonement of Jesus Christ, all mankind, without one exception, are to be completely, and fully redeemed, both body and spirit from the endless banishment and curse, to which they were consigned, by Adam's transgression. ... After this full, complete, and universal redemption, restoration, and salvation of the whole of Adam's race, through the atonement of Jesus Christ, without faith, repentance, baptism, or any other works, then, all and every one of them, will enjoy eternal life and happiness, never more to be banished from the presence of God, if they themselves have committed no sin. ..."

[4] "We believe that the first condition to be complied with on the part of sinners is, to believe in God, and in the sufferings and death of his Son Jesus Christ. ... That the second condition is, to repent. ...

"That the third condition is, to be baptized by immersion in water, in the name of the Father, Son, and Holy Ghost, for remission of sins; and that this ordinance is to be administered by one who is called and authorized of Jesus Christ to baptize, otherwise it is illegal, and of no advantage, and not accepted by him. ..."

"And that the fourth condition is, to receive the laying on of hands, in the name of Jesus Christ, for the gift of the Holy Ghost; and that this ordinance is to be administered by the apostles or elders, whom the Lord

Jesus hath called and authorized to lay on hands. ... These are the first conditions of the gospel. ...

"They are then required to be humble, to be meek and lowly in heart, to watch and pray, to deal justly, and inasmuch as they have the riches of this world, to feed the hungry and clothe the naked. ...

[6] "It is the duty and privilege of the saints thus organized upon the everlasting gospel, to believe in and enjoy all the gifts, powers, and blessings which flow from the Holy Spirit. Such, for instance, as the gifts of revelation, prophecy, visions, the ministry of angels, healing the sick by the laying on hands in the name of Jesus, the working of miracles, and, in short all the gifts as mentioned in Scripture, or as enjoyed by the ancient saints".

[7] "We believe that inspired apostles and prophets, together with all the officers as mentioned in the New Testament, are necessary to be in the Church in these days.
"We believe that there has been a general and awful apostasy from the religion of the New Testament. ..."

[8] "The gospel in the 'Book of Mormon', is the same as that in the New Testament, and is revealed in great plainness, so that no one that reads it can misunderstand its principles. ..."

[9] "Many revelations and prophecies have been given to this church since its rise, which have been printed and sent forth to the world. These also contain the gospel in great plainness, and instructions of infinite importance to the saints. ... We believe that God will continue to give revelations by visions, by the ministry of angels, and by the inspiration of the Holy Ghost, until the saints are guided unto all truth. ..."

"We believe that God has raised up this church, in order to prepare a people for his second coming. ...And we now bear testimony to all, both small and great, that the Lord of Hosts hath sent us with a message of glad tidings—the everlasting gospel, to cry repentance to the nations, and prepare the way of his second coming. ... Therefore, remember, O reader, and perish not" (*Orsen Pratt 1840*).

This statement of the truths of the gospel is full and eloquent. Only occasional wordiness detracts from its effectiveness. In most respects, the teachings of the Church are accurately and powerfully restated here by Orson Pratt.
Orson Pratt's inclination toward logic and thoroughness permeates this 1840 exposition. For example, there is a systematic explanation both of the human condition and the steps, which must be taken to improve it. Here also there is an explanation of what one might term the "second principles of the gospel"—humility, prayerfulness, fairness, generosity, sympathy,

196

endurance, and observance of the sacrament. However, while thoroughness is often a strength, it may also hinder a writer's effectiveness. Here Elder Pratt requires three full pages to state the truth, men will be punished for their own sins and not for Adam's transgression, and they can be saved through Christ's atonement by obedience to the laws and ordinances of the gospel—truths which Joseph Smith would encapsulate into two short sentences. Although his account is technically correct and extremely interesting, Orson Pratt produced a statement so detailed that is difficult to use, much less to memorize.

Orson Hyde

Even more cumbersome is the next set of articles of faith, which appeared in a treatise, published by Orson Hyde in Frankfurt, Germany, in 1842, entitled A Cry from the Wilderness. The fourth chapter of this tract consists of sixteen articles, called "Articles of Faith and Points of Doctrine." Elder Hyde prefaces this chapter by explaining, he compiled these points of doctrine himself while serving in responsible positions within the Church. Each article is, in and of itself, a seasoned essay, containing very valuable information. The approach to specific issues, however, is rather disjointed at times. The titles of these articles reflect their content.

The first article is entitled "About the Godhead," and the second "About the Use and the Validity of the Scriptures of the Old and New Testament in Our Church." Noticeably, neither the Book of Mormon nor the need for a correct translation of the Bible is mentioned here. Examples of other titles are "Faith," "Repentance," "Baptism," "Confirmation by the Laying on of Hands After Baptism," "The Sacrament of the Bread and Wine," "The Confession of Sins and the Method of Dealing with Members Who Act Contrary to The Laws of the Church," "Baptism for the Dead," "Prayer and the Manner of Prayer," and "Patriarchal Blessings and A Word About Marriage" (*Orsen Hyde 1842*).

It is apparent from the titles, Elder Hyde focuses his attention on are the ordinances of the priesthood. Furthermore, where he is not discussing these ordinances themselves, Elder Hyde considers items closely related to them, such as the absence of paid ministry in the Church, the proper age at which to baptize children, prayer, and the Sabbath day.

The importance of priesthood ordinances in the Church cannot be overstated; still, Orson Hyde's statement is more an explanation than a succinct declaration of belief—that task fell to the Prophet Joseph Smith.
Joseph Smith's Final Version

In light of the varied approaches taken by Oliver Cowdery, Joseph Young, Orson Pratt, and Orson Hyde, the need for an official statement of the Church's beliefs is clearly visible. With many writers and Church leaders stressing different aspects of the gospel, confusion over the fundamental teachings of the Church could easily have resulted.

In 1842, at the invitation of John Wentworth, the editor of the Chicago Democrat, Joseph Smith wrote a letter designed for publication in which he sketched the history and faith of the Latter-day Saints. Joseph Smith's response to Wentworth is now known as the Wentworth letter. It appeared in many publications both within and outside the Church for many years after it was written. The letter, signed by Joseph Smith, closed by stating thirteen points of faith. These have come to be known as the Articles of Faith. Except for certain minor changes, particularly in the fourth, fifth, sixth, and tenth articles, these statements are still used today as they were originally appeared on 1 March 1842.

Several things need to be said about the Articles of Faith. First, they are brief and succinct. Joseph Smith states each proposition with unusual clarity and economy. This is particularly noticeable when one compares Joseph Smith's Articles of Faith with those of Orson Pratt or Orson Hyde.

In addition, despite their brevity, Joseph Smith's statements are remarkably complete. The Prophet selects his language with great precision. Further, the scope of his statements is broad, encompassing a full range of gospel principles. He covers more main points of the gospel than most of the other authors combined. In addition, the Prophet is not limited by attentiveness to any single aspect of the gospel, as was Orson Hyde, nor by any theoretical constraints, as was Oliver Cowdery.

Joseph Smith's approach is declarative and affirmative. He makes no effort to justify these principles—they are firm statements, which stand on their own merit. Each epitomizes a fundamental point of doctrine. Each is directed toward actively influencing the lives of the Saints.

Some have suggested, Joseph Smith wrote the Articles of Faith in response to the religious controversies of his time. This is doubtful, however, because Joseph Smith's Articles lack the argumentative language commonly found in the earlier articles of faith. Apparently, he did not feel this was either the time or the place for pointing out the errors of other denominations.

In light of the obvious similarities between certain of the Articles drafted by Joseph Smith and statements made earlier by Oliver Cowdery and Orson Pratt, it is natural to wonder how heavily Joseph Smith relied on those earlier articles of faith. At the same time, due to the many common threads, which consistently run throughout all of these early statements, it is equally necessary to recognize the Prophet himself probably already stood closely behind those earlier formulations. Although the elements of dependency and contribution cannot be traced here, it can reasonably assume Joseph Smith's words and thoughts contributed, either directly or indirectly, to the articles of faith written by Oliver Cowdery, Joseph Young, Orson Pratt, and Orson Hyde. The fact all of these early statements are quite similar to each other shows the same gospel principles were consistently taught under Joseph's leadership.

It also follows, of course, Joseph Smith's composition of the Articles of Faith was not a matter of spontaneity. There had probably been considerable discussion among Church leaders on points of faith prior to the Wentworth letter. But whether Joseph Smith was following the language of Orson Pratt or Oliver Cowdery, or excerpting Pauline passages from the New Testament 3 (compare A of F 1:4 with Heb. 6:1–4, A of F 1:6 with Eph. 4:11, A of F 1:7 with 1 Cor. 12:22, and A of F 1:13 with 1 Cor. 13:7 and Philip. 4:8), the vision of Joseph Smith was to see clearly the best of what had been said.

Joseph Smith's Articles of Faith quickly received wide recognition throughout the Church and abroad. John Hayward, who had previously published Joseph Young's statement of the beliefs of the Church, immediately included Joseph Smith's Articles of Faith in his Book of Religions, printed in 1842.

Although the Prophet's Articles of Faith were widely acknowledged, the spirit of personal pamphleteering also remained strong and active within the Church for several decades. This spirit manifested itself in many ways, one of which was the practice of embellishing Joseph Smith's Articles of Faith. For example, in 1850 the Frontier Guardian, edited by Orson Hyde, carried a statement of Joseph Smith's Articles of Faith with certain additions. To the fourth article of faith was added "the Lord's Supper" as the fifth ordinance of the gospel. To the seventh article of faith was added "the gift of faith, discerning of spirits, wisdom, charity, and brotherly love" as further powers and gifts of the spirit. The eighth article of faith was restated to read, "We believe the word of God recorded in the Bible, we also believe the word of God recorded in the Book of Mormon, and in all other good books." A fourteenth article was added to read, "We believe in the literal resurrection of the body, and that the rest of the dead live not again until the thousand years are expired." Finally, the last article ends with the resounding utterance:

"Everything virtuous, lovely, praiseworthy, and of good report we seek after, looking forward to the recompense of reward; but an idle or lazy person cannot be a Christian, neither have salvation. He is a drone, and destined to be stung to death and tumbled out of the hive." Other even more extensive elaborations on Joseph Smith's Articles of Faith also appeared in the 1850s and 1860s. 4

Thus, several years had to elapse before Joseph Smith's Articles of Faith became solidified in the minds and experiences of the members. In 1880, the membership of the Church voted at general conference to accept and use only the Articles of Faith as prepared and distributed by Joseph Smith. Understanding and further appreciation of these Articles grew with the publication of The Articles of Faith by James E. Talmage.

Ever since the Articles of Faith were written, they have taught, inspired, and directed the members of the Church in the basic principles of the gospel. At the same time, they have also gone forth among the peoples of the world to proclaim and explain the gospel to many who hear it for the first time. Yet it is one and the same set that serves all these functions. This versatility reflects the fact that the Articles of Faith emerged as the best of many similar statements produced during a fluid, formative period in Church history.

However, more than versatility, the Articles of Faith are a precious reflection of truth expressed with precision and purpose. Unlike creeds, which are delimiting and dogmatic, the Articles of Faith are living and open. They invite further thought. They influence people in numerous ways, as they give lives both clarity and breadth. They enhance understanding of certain principles and give simultaneously to all, a commitment toward living the same. They belong in the scriptures perhaps more than anyone can fully comprehend.

God So Loved the World

What are the most important five words you have ever heard? Many times when someone is giving a talk, reading the scriptures or explaining the doctrine of the church, this phrase is heard, God so loved the world ---- then the speaker goes on to make his point. This phrase God so loved the world leads people to know, God's Love for them is what inspired Heavenly Father to create spirits and everything else known and it is the same love that led the Savior to the Garden of Gethsemane to make Himself a ransom for sins. Love is the grand motive of the plan of salvation; love is the foremost source of happiness, in mortally and eternity, it is the ever-renewing spring of healing, and it offers people an unending fountain of hope. Therefore, as a congregation of Christians, there is a clear external view of the love of God and what He has done for us. However, looking further into this subject, from the internal perspective of mortality, there are some things about this concept of love, not so cut and dried. For example, in the book of Matthew in New Testament, the commanded to "love the Lord thy God with all thy heart, and with all thy soul, and with all thy mind" (this being the first and greatest commandment). For the most part, it is accepted as a wonderful commandment, but there are times when it is difficult to know if and when this task is being accomplished. In addition to people loving God, they are commanded to love all fellow men, which is the second greatest commandment: "Love your neighbor as yourself". This commandment is a little harder to accept in many cases and it is substantially more difficult to incorporate this into a person's life.

So there are two questions, first, why are mortals commanded to love? One would think with any understanding of God's love, it could be easy to relate to all love and there would be no need for these commandments. Second, is there anything, anywhere out there, showing how to accomplish all this? The answer to these two questions encompasses two unique pieces of Mormon Church doctrine, which, among other things, makes Mormonism different from all other religions. They are;

1- The doctrine, mortals are able to become as God and like God, and

2- The doctrine explaining the reason mortals have been given commandments to live by. Now there are four different reasons for commandments but for the purposes of this talk, only one will be explored.

These two pieces of doctrine need to be examined within the context of love. In June of 1840, the Lorenzo Snow made this doctrinal statement, "As man is, God once was; as God is, man may become". And in Aug of 1844 this was recorded at the funeral of King Follet, Joseph Smith, during the course of the sermon, said the following, "Here, then, is eternal life--to know the only wise and true God. And you have got to learn how to be Gods yourselves--to be kings and priests to God, the same as all Gods have done--by going from a small degree to another, from grace to grace, from exaltation to exaltation, until you are able to sit in glory as do those who sit enthroned in everlasting power" (*General Conference 7 April 1844*). Additionally, in the book "Teachings of the Prophet Joseph Smith, the Prophet declares that mortals can become "as Gods and like Gods". Section 132:20 of the Doctrine and Covenants also tells that mortals can become Gods and then goes on to explain what that means.

So, what does as God mean, and what does like God mean? As God means having all of the power, knowledge, dominion, wisdom and so on, which God possesses. On the other hand, being "Like God" is more closely associated with the nature or goodness of God. Being like God, will be people's focus since their love for God and His love for His children is where most people find the doctrinal answers to their questions.

What can mortals do to be like Heavenly Father during mortality? In other words, what does God have that can attain during this life? Answer is the nature and goodness of God, which, in the vernacular of the day, translates to "virtue". When reading the B. of M., 40th section of Alma, Alma is telling his son about the virtues of God. In these pages, he says that, "if God was not--- just or --- merciful, He (God) would cease to be God". It follows then, if God is not honest, trustworthy, consistent, and charitable or for that matter, if He were lacking in any amount of virtue, He would cease to be God.

God is totally virtuous and this has been explained in (*Doctrines of Salvation, vol. 1, pp. 5-10*) where Joseph Fielding Smith says, "It should be realized that God is not progressing in knowledge, truth, virtue, wisdom, or any of the attributes of godliness. He has already gained these things in their fullness".

Now, if God can cease to be God by losing virtue it is reasonable to assume, mortals cannot become gods with the small amount of virtue they might possess, in their fallen state as mortals, without some effort on their part. So if people are to become like God during this mortal probation, they need to obtain the same virtues, in a small way, God possesses, in their fullness. Likewise if mortals are in the currently in possession of anything of a virtuous nature, they need to advance this quality as far as possible, of course, everyone realizes they cannot rise to God's level of virtue during their lifetime.

So where does this, virtue advancement, start? It starts here, in this church, now. This is where mortals start learning how to handle ourselves in situations, which challenge all morals, ethics, beliefs, sense of fairness and by maintaining the values and principles of religion, expressed through the commandments. This mortality is the place where God's children start to build virtue.

Do the scriptures teach anything about some process or methodology, if employed, will help achieve success? The answer is YES, the methodology, is called, simple enough, living the commandments. This is clearly illustrated in the 132 section of the doctrine and covenants that were talked about, where God explained to Joseph Smith that mortals can become Gods and so on, the very next verse (verse 21), says "Verily, verily, I say unto you, except ye abide my law ye cannot attain to this glory" (*D&C 132:21*).

Section 132 verses 20&21 clearly show, during mortality the ability to live the "law", meaning commandments, is the means to the end which is most desire, to be like God, living as Gods, with God, in the Celestial Kingdom sometime in the future. Conversely --- if people can demonstrate, during mortality, their inability to live God's Laws, they will have to accept a reward lesser than the Celestial kingdom.

So how does living commandments help in the effort to gain a small amount of virtue? Take the commandment "love your neighbor as you love yourself" as an example. What this commandment does, if lived correctly, will help people start to learn how to extend their love to those outside of their homes. People get to "practice" on their neighbors. If they are successful, they find, within ourselves, an increase in the virtue of love, which moves us, closer to God. As this methodology is extended beyond one's immediate neighbors and their love is offered to more of their fellow man, their virtue will continue to expand and their relationship with God will increase.

It is necessary to begin this process while here in mortality and later in the eternal realm, exercising the ability to build upon this small start and eventually to develop a greater love similar to the love God has for all his children.

All commandments work this way. Take, for instance, the commandment "thou shall not steal", by living this law people increase, within themselves, the virtue of honesty, by not forsaking others and by being honest, as God has said, He would never forsake anyone by taking anything from them, but rather He offers them, all He has, and thus He starts teaching about the virtue, charity. This wonderful virtue also needs to developed to it is fullness in order to progress to a Celestial state.

However, the process is to start small and learn as you go. It is the same with all the commandments or laws given by God, all of which are designed to help start the process of attaining the virtues of God, and it is through obedience to these laws, God's blessings are received.

This growth process is corroborated in New Testament scriptures; (*Mathew 25:21*) "His lord said unto him, well done, thou good and faithful servant: thou hast been faithful over a few things, I will make thee ruler over many things: enter thou into the joy of thy lord".

Moreover, corroboration of blessings for obedience in the *(Doctrine and covenants, section 130:20&21)*, "There is a law, irrevocably decreed in heaven before the foundations of this world, upon which all blessings are predicated—And when we obtain any blessing from God, it is by obedience to that law upon which it is predicated".

In doctrine and covenants section 46, where the Lord is instructing the members about church meetings, gifts of the spirit and other things, right at the end of the section, in verse 33 it say "practice virtue and holiness continually" (*D&C 46:33*). Can mortals actually "practice" virtue? Yes, they can, repeatedly obeying any commandment causes any mortal to get better and better at the virtue the commandment is trying to teach. By using the Savior's teachings model and His life as the archetype, members of the church can move forward, "by going from a small degree to another", in obtaining eternal life.

If anyone is having difficulty knowing if their love for God is adequate, they must increase their obedience to the commandments. This will increase their level of virtue, their faith will increase, they will feel closer to God, and He will bless them.

If there, is any hesitation in approaching your neighbors and extend love to them, just go on over there, knock on their door, and ask them how they are doing. There will be an increase a person's level of virtue, they will feel closer to God, He will bless them, and they may make a new friend.

Remember the commandment, love your neighbor as you love yourself, has two parts, the first part, love your neighbor, is what was being talking about above and the second part is, love yourself,--- don't forget to love yourself. The old adage "My cup runneth over with love" (*Ed Ames*) is good council for one's life but you must first fill your cup to capacity before it can run over.

Brothers and sisters it is clear, mortals are designed to be a loving group of people. In addition, it should be a testimony, when a person lives the commandments and extend their hands and hearts toward others in Christ like love, something wonderful happens. Our spirits will become healed, more refined, stronger, happier, more peaceful, and more receptive to the whisperings of the Holy Spirit.

Happiness and Joy
(Is happiness and joy the same thing?)

Is a feeling of merriment, a time when someone is pleased, joy, or happiness? Are people happy or joyful when they are obedient? True joy (as opposed to happiness) is arrived at through righteous living. True joy leaves no bad after- taste, it is not followed by any depressing reaction, and it calls for no repentance, brings no regret, and entails no remorse.
Alma 40: 12 "The righteous are received into a state of happiness"
John: 13; 17 "If ye know these things, happy are ye if you do them".
Joy is a state of being. Joy is gained by obedience.

Abr. 3: 25 "And we will prove them here-with, to see if they will do all the things whatsoever the Lord their God shall command them".

D&C 42: 61 "If thou shalt ask, thou shalt receive revelation upon revelation, knowledge upon knowledge, that thou may know the mysteries and peaceable things- that which bringeth joy, that which bringeth life eternal".

If living the commandments and having the Holy Ghost for a companion brings happiness and joy, why are so many people, in the church, unhappy and not joyful?

Think about this--- Members get many promissory notes in church i.e. teachers or speakers disseminating advise on what must or must not be done. If you have family Home Evening, your children will get along with each other and they will turn out ok; if you are obedient, you will be happy; if you work harder, longer, better or do more things, you will be blessed. Mothers will find joy and fulfillment in bearing and raising children, single women will find joy in preparing to marry and raise children; if single women, who are faithful in the gospel, they will find a good husband; widows and widowers are supposed to find joy in enduring to the end. In addition, when all is coming apart, marriage failing, no job, kids in trouble, what advice is given? --- PRAY. If all this could surly come true everyone would know how to act and live, then it would easy to be joyful and happy. It must not be working, 1 out of 10 Mormons suffer from depression (much higher than the national average), and in a recent survey in Utah depression and guilt are the leading causes of unhappiness. The list of, *supposed*, solutions given above and the universal *prayer* answer are cookie cutter solutions, where one cookie cutter fits all.

Look at D&C 42: 61 and the variety of solutions offered.
1. Ask and receive revelation.
2. Receive knowledge.
3. Know the mysteries.
4. Know peaceable things.
   Notice this scripture does not even mention any of those things that are supposed to be done and these are not cookie cutter solutions.

Why do mortals have to ask of God? Two reasons;

1. The Lord will not violate your agency even to give good things.
2. He is never going to lure anyone into a conversation with Him against his or her will.

Why is a relationship with the Savoir through the Holy Ghost so important? Because the information received is tailored to the individual and not the "one cookie cutter fits all approach" The revelations received always comes in two parts,

1. Revelation about God and the nature of life. (testimony)

2. Revelations concerning specific information regarding your daily life (personal)
   Happiness and joy versus depression and guilt

Depression:

If a person is truly suffering from clinical depression, the causes have become so intense they probable cannot reason themselves out of it and need help beyond what they could get in church, but there are some things they can do, which may help.

Forgiveness:

For some reason people find it difficult to forgive them self. These feelings of condemnation and self-incrimination sometimes can contribute to depression. If this is the case, it is important for you to find help in forgiving yourself.

Service to others

The most recommended way of bringing yourself out of feelings of depression is to get involved in serving others.

There is an old Chinese tale about a woman whose only son died. In her grief, she went to the holy man and asked, what prayers, what magical incantations do you have to bring my son back to life? Instead of sending her away or reasoning with her, he said to her, fetch me a mustard seed from a home that has never known sorrow. We will use it to drive the sorrow out of your life. The woman went off at once in search of that magical mustard seed. She came first to a splendid mansion, knocked at the door, and said, I am looking for a home that has never known sorrow. Is this such a place? It is very important to me. They told her, you have certainly come to the wrong place, and began to describe all the tragic things that recently had befallen them. The woman said to herself, who is better able to help these poor, unfortunate people than I, who have had misfortune of my own? She stayed to comfort them, and then went on in search of a home that had never known sorrow. However, wherever she turned, in hotels and in other places, she found one tale after another of sadness and misfortune. The woman became so involved in helping others cope with their sorrows that she eventually let go of her own. She would later come to understand that it was the quest to find the magical mustard seed that drove away her suffering.

Guilt is a very selfish endeavor and guilt will burn anyone out. If a person is feeling guilty about something, they have done, rectify it, and repent. If they are feeling guilty about all the things they should be doing, change your lifestyle. Guilt is paying the same bill over and over.

In other words, shed the guilt. "And again I say unto the poor, ye who have not and yet had sufficient, that ye remain from day to day; I mean all you who deny the beggar, because ye have not; I would that ye say in your hearts that: I gave not because I have not, but if I had I would give. And now, if ye say this in your hearts ye remain guiltless, otherwise ye are condemned: and your condemnation is just for ye covet that which ye have not received" (Mosiah 4:24-25).

The Joy of the Atonement:

The atonement is the single and greatest source of relief ever given to humankind. A real understanding of the atonement can go a long way to relieving concerns about missteps in life and provide a source of joy.

True Happiness and Joy comes through a first-hand, personal, intimate daily relationship with Jesus Christ. This is the only must that the scriptures mention in developing that relationship with Christ where people can find happiness and gain joy in their lives. After all, God lives in a complete fullness of joy and placed mortals here to practice for the event of celestial glory.

INTELLIGENCE

1- Intelligence, or, in other words, light and truth.
2- Intelligent beings-called intelligences-existed in the premortal existence.
3- Intelligence, knowledge of the things of God, received by revelation.
Light and truth
According to latter-day scripture, "The glory of God is intelligence, or, in other words, light and truth, mankind, too, may be glorified by gaining intelligence" (D&C 93:36). Note, D&C 93:28-30 does not say knowledge. As Christ did not receive a fullness of intelligence at first but continued from "grace to grace until He received fullness" (D&C 93:11-13, 27-28),

so it is with all persons. "Whatever principles of intelligence they gain in mortality will rise with them in the Resurrection" (*D&C 130:18-19*). Intelligences-existed in the premortal existence.

"Intelligences, however defined, is not created, or made" (*D&C 93:29*); "it is co-eternal with God" (*TPJS, pp. 353-54*). Some LDS leaders have interpreted this to mean, intelligent beings-called "intelligences-existed before and after they were given spirit bodies in the premortal existence" (*Abr. 3:22; JD 7:57; 2:124*). Others have interpreted it to mean intelligent beings were organized as spirits out of eternal intelligent matter and they did not exist as individuals before they were organized as spirit beings in the premortal existence. The Church has taken no official position on this issue.

Learning is defined as receiving instructions and becoming informed.

Knowledge is defined as the fact or state of knowing through experience, study, or investigation.

Intelligence is defined as the capacity to reach conclusions through reasoning and comprehension.

(Make sure you do not confuse the learning of information with knowledge or confuse the learning of information and knowledge with intelligence)

In all cases, when the prophets have used the words knowledge or intelligence they are not referring to any secular or temporal information a person may have learned. Is our earthly knowledge remembered after death? Yes, but remembrance of all the things while in this mortal state, earthly experiences and learning are not the saving knowledge or intelligence needed to gain salvation. If earthly experiences and learning was the saving knowledge needed for salvation, then only the people with advanced degrees would be the ones inheriting the Celestial Kingdom and all the rest of the people would have to settle for something less.

Knowledge of the things of God

Latter-day Saints believe certain forms of "knowledge is essential for salvation and eternal life" (*John 17:3*). The Prophet Joseph Smith taught "a man is saved no faster than he gets knowledge, for if he does not get knowledge, he will be brought into captivity," and thus human beings have a need for "revelation to assist us, and give them knowledge of the things of God" (*TPJS, p. 217*). One of the purposes of the priesthood, which is the authority to administer the gospel, is to make this saving "knowledge of God" available to all (*D&C 84:19*). "Those who die without a chance to obtain a knowledge of the gospel of Jesus Christ will be given opportunity to receive and accept the gospel in the life after death to become "heirs of the Celestial Kingdom" (*D&C 128:5; 137:7-9; 138:28-34; see Salvation of the Dead*). 'Knowledge makes possible moral agency and freedom of choice" (*John 8:32; 2 Ne. 2:26-27; Hel. 14:30-31; Moro. 7:15-17*). Those who receive knowledge are responsible to live in accordance with it. "Those who sin after having received knowledge of the truth by revelation bear greater condemnation than those who sin in ignorance" (*Heb. 10:26-27; two Pet. 2:20-21; Mosiah 2:36-39; Alma 24:30*), while "mercy is extended to those who sin in ignorance or without knowledge of the truth" (*Mosiah 3:11; Alma 9:14-17; Hel. 7:23-24*).

"Knowledge is one of the gifts of the spirit that all people are commanded to seek" (*1 Cor. 12:8; Moro. 10:9-10; D&C 46:17-18*). "Knowledge of the truth of the gospel of Christ is conveyed as well as received by the power of the Holy Ghost" (*Moro. 10:5; 1 Cor. 2:9-16; D&C 50:19-21*). Similarly, knowledge of the mysteries of God also comes through personal revelation. Shared knowledge of the things of God is available in the scriptures and other teachings of his prophets.

Knowledge is closely associated in scripture with other virtues such as "meekness, long suffering, temperance, patience, godliness, kindness, and charity" (*2 Pet. 1:5-7; D&C 4:6; 107, 30-31; 121:41-42*). It is intimately related to truth; "genuine knowledge is truth" (*D&C 93:24*). Knowledge is understood to be an active, motivating force rather than simply a passive awareness, or collection of facts. This force is seen, for example, "in acts of faith" (*Alma 32:21-43*) and "obedience" (*1 Jn. 2:4*). The word "knowledge" is also used to refer to vain or false knowledge, "and to the pride that often comes with knowledge based on human learning unaccompanied by righteousness and the spirit and knowledge of God" (*1 Cor. 8:1-2; 2 Tim. 3:7; 2 Ne. 9:28-29*).

All people are encouraged to seek deeply and broadly "to gain knowledge of both heavenly and earthly things" (*D&C 88:77-80*). "Such knowledge comes by study of the works of others, and by faith" (*D&C 88:118*). The LDS Church has traditionally encouraged and supported the pursuit of knowledge and education by its members. Knowledge gained through study and by faith is obtained "line upon line and precept upon precept" (*D&C 98:11-12; 128:21*). "All principles of intelligence gained in this life stays with those who attain it and rises with them in the resurrection, bringing some advantage in the life to come" (*D&C 130:18-19*). Bruce R. McConkie, in his Mormon Doctrine Page 427, states, the knowledge spoken of in (*D&C 130:18-19*) can only be obtained by revelation from the Holy Ghost and is referred to as "saving knowledge". On page 426, he states, "all types of knowledge however are not of equal worth, all do not reward the acquirer with equal progress toward exaltation. Knowledge of arts and sciences-- of mathematics, chemistry, history, medicine and the like have no direct and immediate bearing on the attainment of salvation". The next life holds the promise of "perfect knowledge" or understanding *(2nd Ne. 9:13-14)*.

Intelligence,

To gain increased intelligence, "individuals must be agents to act for themselves" *(D&C 93:30)*, which means they must be "tried and tempted" *(D&C 29:39)*, and at the same time, the "works of the Lord must be plainly manifest to them" *(D&C 93:31)* so they will have choice. In premortal life, men and women were "intelligent beings" *(Abr. 3:21-22)* who were "given agency by God" *(Moses 4:3; D&C 29:36)*. In mortality, they are also "given agency by God" *(D&C 101:78)*, to gain knowledge of good and evil *(Moses 5:11)*. Intelligence increases as individuals "forsake evil and come to the Lord, calling on his name, obeying his voice, and keeping his commandments" *(D&C 93:1-2, 28, 37)*. Intelligence is lost through "disobedience, hardening of hearts, and clinging to false traditions" *(Mark 8:21; D&C 93:39)*.

A later revelation adds, "Whatever principle of intelligence we attain unto in this life, it will rise with us in the resurrection. And if a person gains more knowledge and intelligence in this life through his diligence and obedience than another, he will have so much the advantage in the world to come" *(D&C 130:18-19)*. The word "knowledge," in this scripture, is not to be confused with secular information, which anyone can accumulate but cannot act upon. Rather, it refers to the knowledge of God, without which we cannot relate to or comprehend Him *(Ether 3:20; D&C 84:19; 121:26; Abraham 1:2)*. In the Doctrine and Covenants it says all commandments are spiritual, "nor at any time have I given unto you a law which was temporal" *(D&C 29:30-35)*. Therefore, it can be postulated, the intelligence and knowledge referred to in the scriptures is spiritual in nature and was in force before any earthly knowledge was available is not referring to any secular knowledge.

Lehi's Dream of the Tree of Life
(Sometimes called the Vision of the Iron Rod)

The purpose of this section is to examine the tree of life vision received by the Prophet Lehi around 600 BC, and the subsequent tree of life vision received by Nephi concerning the fate of God's children. Lehi's entire vision was recorded in highly symbolic terms, the people of Lehi's time found it very hard to understand, and still, even today, this vision is not fully understood. This section also examines the proposition; Nephi's vision was an expansive, prophetic interpretation of Lehi's dream of the tree of life. There were four occasions where this vision was recounted or an interpretation given and they can be found in 1st Nephi chapter 8, chapter 11, chapter 12, and chapter 15. A close examination reveals each time an interpretation was given the scenario was completely different. These interpretations have generally been seen by some church historians as unrelated to the interpretation of Lehi's dream of the tree of life, these "other visions" are often considered just a bonus given to Nephi in addition to the dream's interpretation. It is the view of this writer and the thesis of this section, such is not the case, but rather the entire panoramic vision of the future received by Nephi from chapter 8 through chapter 15 is unto itself a complete and diverse interpretation of Lehi's dream of the tree of life. In chapter 8 the scenario seems to take place during mortality and the teachings of the church seem to center on this singular view, however, to conclude this is the sole interpretation of the tree of life dream would be missing the richness, diversity and some very important messages derived from this section of the Book of Mormon. This writer also believes that this particular chapter 8 interpretation may be only one of several levels of meaning received by Nephi from the symbols of Lehi's dream. For instance, in chapter1, 1st Nephi receives a great tree of life panoramic vision of the future, beginning with the birth of the Savior in mortality and culminating with the final destruction of the wicked at his second coming. In addition, in chapter12 the tree of life vision shifts its focus from the Savoir and events on the Eastern Hemisphere to events on the Western Hemisphere. This entire chapter 12 deals exclusively with the fate of Nephi's descendants. Then in chapter 15 Nephi proceeds to embark on a new interpretation of the symbols of the tree of life dream, and in so doing teaches his older brothers concerning the state of the souls of humanity in the afterlife. Therefore, you can see. Lehi's dream of the tree of life rightfully takes its place as one of the most divine, richest, flexible, expansive, and far-reaching pieces of symbolic prophecy contained in the all of the standard works.

I will deal with each of these scenarios in the order given above. Let's now have a quick review of Lehi's dream as recorded by Nephi starting with verse 9, the entire text can be found in the Book of Mormon, 1st Nephi 8: 9-35.

9 And it came to pass after I had prayed unto the Lord I beheld a large and spacious field.

10 And it came to pass that I beheld a tree, whose fruit was desirable to make one happy.

11 And it came to pass that I did go forth and partake of the fruit thereof; and I beheld that it was most sweet, above all that I ever before tasted. Yea, and I beheld that the fruit thereof was white, to exceed all the whiteness that I had ever seen.

12 And as I partook of the fruit thereof it filled my soul with exceedingly great joy; wherefore, I began to be desirous that my family should partake of it also; for I knew that it was desirable above all other fruit.

13 And as I cast my eyes round about, that perhaps I might discover my family also, I beheld a river of water; and it ran along, and it was near the tree of which I was partaking the fruit.

14 And I looked to behold from whence it came; and I saw the head thereof a little way off; and at the head thereof I beheld your mother Sariah, and Sam, and Nephi; and they stood as if they knew not whither they should go.

15 And it came to pass that I beckoned unto them; and I also did say unto them with a loud voice that they should come unto me, and partake of the fruit, which was desirable above all other fruit.

16 And it came to pass that they did come unto me and partake of the fruit also.

17 And it came to pass that I was desirous that Laman and Lemuel should come and partake of the fruit also; wherefore, I cast mine eyes towards the head of the river, that perhaps I might see them.

18 And it came to pass that I saw them, but they would not come unto me and partake of the fruit.

19 And I beheld a rod of iron, and it extended along the bank of the river, and led to the tree by which I stood.

20 And I also beheld a strait and narrow path, which came along by the rod of iron, even to the tree by which I stood; and it also led by the head of the fountain, unto a large and spacious field, as if it had been a world.

21 And I saw numberless concourses of people, many of whom were pressing forward, that they might obtain the path which led unto the tree by which I stood.

22 And it came to pass that they did come forth, and commence in the path which led to the tree.

23 And it came to pass that there arose a mist of darkness; yea, even an exceedingly great mist of darkness, insomuch that they who had commenced in the path did lose their way, that they wandered off and were lost.

24 And it came to pass that I beheld others pressing forward, and they came forth and caught hold of the end of the rod of iron; and they did press forward through the mist of darkness, clinging to the rod of iron, even until they did come forth and partake of the fruit of the tree.

25 And after they had partaken of the fruit of the tree they did cast their eyes about as if they were ashamed.

26 And I also cast my eyes round about, and beheld, on the other side of the river of water, a great and spacious building; and it stood as it were in the air, high above the earth.

27 And it was filled with people, both old and young, both male and female; and their manner of dress was exceedingly fine; and they were in the attitude of mocking and pointing their fingers towards those who had come at and were partaking of the fruit.

28 And after they had tasted of the fruit they were ashamed, because of those that were scoffing at them; and they fell away into forbidden paths and were lost.

29 And now I, Nephi, do not speak all the words of my father.

30 But, to be short in writing, behold, he saw other multitudes pressing forward; and they came and caught hold of the end of the rod of iron; and they did press their way forward, continually holding fast to the rod of iron, until they came forth and fell down and partook of the fruit of the tree.

31 And he also saw other multitudes feeling their way towards that great and spacious building.

32 And it came to pass that many were drowned in the depths of the fountain; and many were lost from his view, wandering in strange roads.

33 And great was the multitude that did enter into that strange building. And after they did enter into that building they did point the finger of scorn at me and those that were partaking of the fruit also; but we heeded them not.

34 These are the words of my father: For as many as heeded them, had fallen away.

35 And Laman and Lemuel partook not of the fruit, said my father.

Chapter 8, the interpretation in terms of mortality;

This vision brings to mind a picture of a place where God's children (Lehi's family included) are participating in a journey and came to a straight and narrow path leading toward a space where there is a tree offering a delicious fruit and from the base of the tree flows a fountain of pure water. The path leads dangerously close to the edge of a large gorge and at the bottom of the gorge flows a river of filthy water. Parallel to the path there is a rail or rod extending alongside the edge of the gorge for safety purposes. There seems to be some sort of a dark vapor or mist rising up over part of the path blocking the view of those trying to traverse the path to get to the tree. On the other side of the gorge there is a large building situated alongside the gorge and a multitude of God's children can be seen in the building, which incidentally is suspended in the air. The vision also shows a group of God's children approaching the path, following others who are holding onto the safety rail and making their way toward the tree. Some of the travelers refuse to attempt whatsoever to follow the path and the ones in the building are using various means to try to dissuade anyone from trying. Some of the travelers seem to get distracted and lose their way and they are seen meandering around. There are others who make it onto the path and hold onto the rod, but while trying to make their way to the tree, they for various reasons, fall into the gorge and drown in the river of filthy water. "many were drowned in the depths of the fountain" (*1 Nephi 8:32*), this means they drowned in the filthy water of the river not the fountain of pure water by the tree). There are some, who make it through the mist and congregate around the tree. Some of those congregated at the tree feel ashamed, leave the area of the tree, and are lost while the rest stay at the tree and partake of the fruit.

This scenario of the tree of life dream is familiar to most Latter-day Saints and the basic interpretation of the symbols of the dream is as follows:
1. The tree of life represents "the love of God" (*1st Nephi 11:22, 25*) as does also "the fountain of living waters" (*1st Nephi 11:25*).
2. The rod of iron represents "the word of God" (*1st Nephi 11:25; 15:24*).
3. The people on the path are members of the church, trying to return to Heavenly Father while the people in the building represent the secular people of the world. (*1st Nephi 11:21&27*)
4. The great and spacious building represents "the pride of the world" (*1st Nephi 11:26; 12:18*).
5. The river of filthy water represents "the depths of hell" (*1st Nephi 12:16; 15:29*).
6. The mists of darkness or vapor represent "the temptations of the devil" (*1st Nephi 12:17*).
When all these symbols and their interpretations are put together, the message commonly taught by the Mormon Church is, the rod of iron is the word of God; and whosoever would faithfully follow the rod of iron (by reading the scriptures, and obey the word of God) will ultimately partake of the fruit of the tree of life (i.e., the love of God). They would never perish; neither will they either fall into the temptations and the ridicule of the

adversary [i.e., the mists of darkness and the people in the great and spacious building] or be overpower by them unto blindness, to lead them away to destruction or hell [i.e., falling into the river of filthy water].

While this version of the dream is certainly of great importance in the personal quest to return to the presence of Heavenly Father, this particular interpretation may be only one of several levels of meaning derived by Nephi from the symbols of Lehi's dream.

Chapter 11, the interpretation in terms of the Savior;

1st Nephi 11 is records Nephi's great panoramic vision of the future, beginning with the birth of the Savior in mortality and culminating with the final destruction of the wicked at his second coming. This is one of the interpretations; some say stands alone and is not part of Nephi's interpretation of his father's dream. However, in verse 1 of chapter 11, Nephi desired to see the things his father had seen in his dream. In verse 4 the tree of life is identified as the thing Nephi is asking about, then, in verse 1, Nephi ask if he could know the interpretation thereof, (meaning Lehi's tree of life vision). Then in verse 12 the angel commences to give Nephi the interpretation of the tree of life dream in terms of the Savior's birth. It is also clear all through the eleventh chapter there are references to all of the symbols found in chapter eight and an enlargement on some of them.

Let's now have a quick review the full Nephi's vision as recorded in the Book of Mormon, 1st Nephi 11: 13- 36.

1 "For it came to pass after I had desired to know the things that my father had seen, and believing that the Lord was able to make them known unto me, as I sat pondering in mine heart I was caught away in the Spirit of the Lord, yea, into an exceedingly high mountain, which I never had before seen, and upon which I never had before set my foot.

2 And the Spirit said unto me: Behold, what desirest thou?

3 And I said: I desire to behold the things which my father saw.

4 And the Spirit said unto me: Believest thou that thy father saw the tree of which he hath spoken?

5 And I said: Yea, thou knowest that I believe all the words of my father.

6 And when I had spoken these words, the Spirit cried with a loud voice, saying: Hosanna to the Lord, the most high God; for he is God over all the earth, yea, even above all. And blessed art thou, Nephi, because thou believest in the Son of the most high God; wherefore, thou shalt behold the things which thou hast desired.

7 And behold this thing shall be given unto thee for a sign, that after thou hast beheld the tree which bore the fruit which thy father tasted, thou shalt also behold a man descending out of heaven, and him shall ye witness; and after ye have witnessed him ye shall bear record that it is the Son of God.

8 And it came to pass that the Spirit said unto me: Look! And I looked and beheld a tree; and it was like unto the tree which my father had seen; and the beauty thereof was far beyond, yea, exceeding of all beauty; and the whiteness thereof did exceed the whiteness of the driven snow.

9 And it came to pass after I had seen the tree, I said unto the Spirit: I behold thou hast shown unto me the tree which is precious above all.

10 And he said unto me: What desirest thou?

11 And I said unto him: To know the interpretation thereof—for I spake unto him as a man speaketh; for I beheld that he was in the form of a man; yet nevertheless, I knew that it was the Spirit of the Lord; and he spake unto me as a man speaketh with another.

12 And it came to pass that he said unto me: Look! And I looked as if to look upon him, and I saw him not; for he had gone from before my presence.

13 And it came to pass that I looked and beheld the great city of Jerusalem, and also other cities. And I beheld the city of Nazareth; and in the city of Nazareth I beheld a virgin, and she was exceedingly fair and white.

14 And it came to pass that I saw the heavens open; and an angel came down and stood before me; and he said unto me: Nephi, what beholdest thou?

15 And I said unto him: A virgin, most beautiful and fair above all other virgins.

16 And he said unto me: Knowest thou the condescension of God?

17 And I said unto him: I know that he loveth his children; nevertheless, I do not know the meaning of all things.

18 And he said unto me: Behold, the virgin whom thou seest is the mother of the Son of God, after the manner of the flesh.

19 And it came to pass that I beheld that she was carried away in the Spirit; and after she had been carried away in the Spirit for the space of a time the angel spake unto me, saying: Look!

20 And I looked and beheld the virgin again, bearing a child in her arms.

21 And the angel said unto me: Behold the Lamb of God, yea, even the Son of the Eternal Father! Knowest thou the meaning of the tree which thy father saw?

22 And I answered him, saying: Yea, it is the love of God, which sheddeth itself abroad in the hearts of the children of men; wherefore, it is the most desirable above all things.

23 And he spake unto me, saying: Yea, and the most joyous to the soul.

24 And after he had said these words, he said unto me: Look! And I looked, and I beheld the Son of God going forth among the children of men; and I saw many fall down at his feet and worship him.

25 And it came to pass that I beheld that the rod of iron, which my father had seen, was the word of God, which led to the fountain of living waters,

or to the tree of life; which waters are a representation of the love of God; and I also beheld that the tree of life was a representation of the love of God.

26 And the angel said unto me again: Look and behold the condescension of God!

27 And I looked and beheld the Redeemer of the world, of whom my father had spoken; and I also beheld the prophet who should prepare the way before him. And the Lamb of God went forth and was baptized of him; and after he was baptized, I beheld the heavens open, and the Holy Ghost come down out of heaven and abide upon him in the form of a dove.

28 And I beheld that he went forth ministering unto the people, in power and great glory; and the multitudes were gathered together to hear him; and I beheld that they cast him out from among them.

29 And I also beheld twelve others following him. And it came to pass that they were carried away in the Spirit from before my face, and I saw them not.

30 And it came to pass that the angel spake unto me again, saying: Look! And I looked, and I beheld the heavens open again, and I saw angels descending upon the children of men; and they did minister unto them.

31 And he spake unto me again, saying: Look! And I looked, and I beheld the Lamb of God going forth among the children of men. And I beheld multitudes of people who were sick, and who were afflicted with all manner of diseases, and with devils and unclean spirits; and the angel spake and showed all these things unto me. And they were healed by the power of the Lamb of God; and the devils and the unclean spirits were cast out.

32 And it came to pass that the angel spake unto me again, saying: Look! And I looked and beheld the Lamb of God that he was taken by the people; yea, the Son of the everlasting God was judged of the world; and I saw and bear record.

33 And I, Nephi, saw that he was lifted up upon the cross and slain for the sins of the world.

34 And after he was slain I saw the multitudes of the earth, that they were gathered together to fight against the apostles of the Lamb; for thus were the twelve called by the angel of the Lord.

35 And the multitude of the earth was gathered together; and I beheld that they were in a large and spacious building, like unto the building which my father saw. And the angel of the Lord spake unto me again, saying: Behold the world and the wisdom thereof; yea, behold the house of Israel hath gathered together to fight against the twelve apostles of the Lamb. 36 And it came to pass that I saw and bear record, that the great and spacious building was the pride of the world; and it fell, and the fall thereof was exceedingly great. And the angel of the Lord Spake unto me again, saying:

Thus shall be the destruction of all nations, kindreds, tongues, and people that shall fight against the twelve apostles of the Lamb" (*1st Nephi 11: 13-36*).

There are several parts to this interpretive scenario, so I will take each one in turn, discuss the scripture and the symbol as they relate to the tree of life vision given to Lehi. Note, while some of the symbols found in chapter 8, still retain the original meaning, the interpretation of the symbols here is expanded somewhat.

The Birth of Jesus Christ; as an interpretation of the tree of life symbol, Nephi was given a vision of the birth of Jesus Christ. Nephi was shown the tree of life in vision by "the Spirit of the Lord" (*1st Nephi 11:1, 8*). Nephi then requested to know "the interpretation thereof" (*1st Nephi 11:11*). In direct response to his request, Nephi was shown a "beautiful and fair" virgin in "the city of Nazareth" (*1st Nephi 11:13–15*). At this juncture, the Spirit of the Lord, who had taken Nephi up to the mountain top and had introduced him to the vision, disappears, and an angel takes his place as Nephi's escort (*1st Nephi 11:12–14*). In continuing the demonstration of the interpretation of the tree of life, the angel now shows Nephi the condescension of God.

The word condescend means to waive dignity or superiority voluntarily and assume equality with an inferior." This is precisely what Nephi's guide proceeds to show him. Nephi sees the virgin being "carried away in the Spirit" and subsequently giving birth to a child who is identified by the angel as "the Lamb of God, yea, even the Son of the Eternal Father!" (*1st Nephi 11:18–21*). Thus is depicted the "condescension of God", God the Son, the Creator of all things under the direction of his Father, would of his own volition descend from the celestial courts of glory to take upon himself a mortal tabernacle of flesh and blood and become equal with members of the human race. Such is the interpretation of the tree of life given by the angel to Nephi.

The interpretation having been given, the angel next quizzes Nephi as to whether he understands the meaning of the tree of life (*1st Nephi 11:21*). Nephi replies, "Yea, it is the love of God, which sheddeth itself abroad in the hearts of the children of men" (*1st Nephi 11:22*).

The Baptism of Jesus Christ; Next, Nephi beholds the rod of iron which his father had seen, "which led to the fountain of living waters, or to the tree of life" (*1st Nephi 11:25*). The living waters flow from the base of the tree of life as interpreted in chapter 8 as the Love of God but now the living waters interpretation is expanded to be the divine drink going along with the divine food (i.e., the fruit of the tree of life). To be given to those who reach the end of the straight and narrow path. Here, though, the angel gives to Nephi another, prophetic, interpretation. The symbol of the living represents the waters of the Jordan River in which John the Baptist baptized Christ. Indeed, this is exactly what is shown Nephi in vision immediately after he beholds the living waters (*1st Nephi 11:26–27*).

The Ministry and Atonement of Jesus Christ; In conjunction with the symbol of the living waters discussed above, Nephi also saw the rod of iron which his father had seen, which "led to . . . the tree of life," and which Nephi was given to know represented "the word of God" (*1st Nephi 11:25*).

In his vision, Nephi then received a prophetic interpretation of the symbol of the rod of iron, which included an account of Christ's mortal ministry (*1st Nephi 11:28*), his choosing of the twelve apostles (*1st Nephi 11:29*), and his healing of the sick (*1st Nephi 11:31*), culminating with the Savior's being "lifted up upon the cross and slain for the sins of the world" (*1st Nephi 11:33*).

As stated above, Nephi was informed, the rod of iron was "the word of God" (*1st Nephi 11:25*). It is significant in this context, one of the name-titles for Jesus Christ is "the Word of God" (*John 1:1, 14*). This fits with the interpretation given Nephi of "the rod of iron," or "word of God," as representing the ministry and death of Christ, for Christ was the Word of God incarnate. Christ, as the Word of God, came to earth not to do his own will, but the will of his father (*John 6:38*), up to and including enduring the agony of the atonement and crucifixion (*Matthew 26:39*).

The Apostasy from the Church Christ Established, after beholding the "Son of the everlasting God" being "slain for the sins of the world," Nephi was shown in vision "the multitudes of the earth . . . gathered together to fight against the apostles of the Lamb" (*1st Nephi 11:34*). Nephi further beheld this "multitude . . . was gathered together . . . in a large and spacious building" (*1st Nephi 11:35*). Because they were gathered together in a "large and spacious building," it is logical, this multitude was an interpretation of the great and spacious building symbol of Lehi's dream.

The angel of the Lord then gives Nephi two interpretations of the great and spacious building, one specific and one general. The specific interpretation of the great and spacious building is "the house of Israel [who] hath gathered together to fight against the twelve apostles of the Lamb" (*1st Nephi 11:35*). The general interpretation of the great and spacious building, on the other hand, is given when Nephi identifies it as "the pride of the world" (*1st Nephi 11:36*).

In the first session of the April 1989 General Conference, President Ezra Taft Benson stated: It was through pride, Christ was crucified. The Pharisees were wroth because Jesus claimed to be the Son of God, which was a threat to their position, and so they plotted his death. (*See John 11:53*) everyone can well imagine the same pride that motivated the wicked members of the house of Israel to crucify the Lamb would also motivate them to fight against his twelve apostles.

Next, Nephi sees the great and spacious building fall, "and the fall thereof was exceedingly great" (*1st Nephi 11:36*). In a revelation with this, much symbolism this would likely be a figurative manner of expressing the destruction and scattering of the house of Israel, which began in A.D. 70 when the Romans demolished Jerusalem.

The Final Destruction of the Wicked; Nephi then receives a prophetic warning from the angel: Thus shall be the destruction of all nations, kindred's, tongues, and people, not just the house of Israel but all those who shall fight against the twelve apostles of the Lamb. (*1st Nephi 11:36*)

Chapter 12, is another interpretation in terms of the Nephi's Decedents.

As 1st Nephi 12 begins, the focus shifts from events concerning the mission of Christ to events concerning the descendants of Nephi. When beginning to read the twelfth chapter of Nephi it may seem there is not any connection to the Lehi's vision of the tree of life but in verses 16, 17 and 18 the same angel who was in chapter 11 is still talking to Nephi about Lehi's vision but coming at it from a different premise or prospective. In Lehi's dream, there are three separate multitudes or groups of people attempting to make their way along the strait and narrow path to the tree of life, each multitude achieving a different degree of success. It is important to note, while spoken of in previous chapters; the multitudes have not been identified or referred to in this manner. These three multitudes of Lehi's dream symbolize the prophetic destiny of Nephi's seed. The first and second multitudes are identified in chapter 12 but the third is identified in chapter 14, so do not let this be confusing. As these scriptures are analyzed, some of the symbols found in chapter 8 and in chapter 11 are given a different or expanded interpretation in chapter12.

The full text as recorded in 1st Nephi, 12: 1-23

1 And it came to pass that the angel said unto me: Look, and behold thy seed, and also the seed of thy brethren. And I looked and beheld the land of promise; and I beheld multitudes of people, yea, even as it were in number as many as the sand of the sea.

2 And it came to pass that I beheld multitudes gathered together to battle, described one against the other; and I beheld wars, and rumors of wars, and great slaughters with the sword among my people.

3 And it came to pass that I beheld many generations pass away, after the manner of wars and contentions in the land; and I beheld many cities, yea, even that I did not number them.

4 And it came to pass that I saw a mist of darkness on the face of the land of promise; and I saw lightnings, and I heard thunderings, and earthquakes, and all manner of tumultuous noises; and I saw the earth and the rocks, that they rent; and I saw mountains tumbling into pieces; and I saw the plains of the earth, that they were broken up; and I saw many cities that they were sunk; and I saw many that they were burned with fire; and I saw many that did tumble to the earth, because of the quaking thereof.

5 And it came to pass after I saw these things, I saw the vapor of darkness that it passed from off the face of the earth; and behold, I saw multitudes who had not fallen because of the great and terrible judgments of the Lord.

6 And I saw the heavens open, and the Lamb of God descending out of heaven; and he came down and showed himself unto them.

7 And I also saw and bear record that the Holy Ghost fell upon twelve others; and they were ordained of God, and chosen.

8 And the angel spake unto me, saying: Behold the twelve disciples of the Lamb, who are chosen to minister unto thy seed.

9 And he said unto me: Thou rememberest the twelve apostles of the Lamb? Behold they are they who shall judge the twelve tribes of Israel; wherefore, the twelve ministers of thy seed shall be judged of them; for ye are of the house of Israel.

10 And these twelve ministers whom thou beholdest shall judge thy seed. And, behold, they are righteous forever; for because of their faith in the Lamb of God their garments are made white in his blood.

11 And the angel said unto me: Look! And I looked, and beheld three generations pass away in righteousness; and their garments were white even like unto the Lamb of God. And the angel said unto me: These are made white in the blood of the Lamb, because of their faith in him.

12 And I, Nephi, also saw many of the fourth generation who passed away in righteousness.

13 And it came to pass that I saw the multitudes of the earth gathered together.

14 And the angel said unto me: Behold thy seed, and also the seed of thy brethren.

15 And it came to pass that I looked and beheld the people of my seed gathered together in multitudes against the seed of my brethren; and they were gathered together to battle.

16 And the angel spake unto me, saying: Behold the fountain of filthy water which thy father saw; yea, even the river of which he spake; and the depths thereof are the depths of hell.

17 And the mists of darkness are the temptations of the devil, which blindeth the eyes, and hardeneth the hearts of the children of men, and leadeth them away into broad roads that they perish and are lost.

18 And the large and spacious building, which thy father saw, is vain imaginations and the pride of the children of men. And a great and a terrible gulf divideth them; yea, even the word of the justice of the Eternal God, and the Messiah who is the Lamb of God, of whom the Holy Ghost beareth record, from the beginning of the world until this time, and from this time henceforth and forever.

19 And while the angel spake these words, I beheld and saw that the seed of my brethren did contend against my seed, according to the word of the angel; and because of the pride of my seed, and the temptations of the devil, I beheld that the seed of my brethren did overpower the people of my seed.

20 And it came to pass that I beheld, and saw the people of the seed of my brethren that they had overcome my seed; and they went forth in multitudes upon the face of the land.

21 And I saw them gathered together in multitudes; and I saw wars and rumors of wars among them; and in wars and rumors of wars I saw many generations pass away.

22 And the angel said unto me: Behold these shall dwindle in unbelief.

23 And it came to pass that I beheld, after they had dwindled in unbelief they became a dark, and loathsome, and a filthy people, full of idleness and all manner of abominations.

The First Multitude; the first multitude is described in the dream of Lehi as follows:

"And I [Lehi] saw numberless concourses of people, many of whom were pressing forward, that they might obtain the path which led unto the tree by which I stood. And it came to pass that they did come forth, and commence in the path which led to the tree. And it came to pass that there arose a mist of darkness; yea, even an exceedingly great mist of darkness, insomuch that they who had commenced in the path did lose their way, that they wandered off and were lost". (*1st Nephi 8:21–23*).

As related above, Lehi saw "numberless concourses of people," many of whom were pressing forward. As an interpretation thereof, Nephi sees in vision "multitudes of people" upon the "land of promise," and these multitudes are his seed and the seed of his brethren (1st Nephi 12:1). (Here the "spacious field symbol becomes the "promise land") and it is reasonable to assume "his seed and the seed of his brethren" is referring to the Nephites and the Laminates.

Next, Nephi is shown great battles and wars among his seed and the seed of his brethren, which last for the space of many generations (*1st Nephi 12:2–3*). Then Nephi sees a "mist of darkness" on the face of the land of promise. This "mist of darkness" beheld by Nephi is an interpretation and elaboration of the "mist of darkness" Lehi saw cause the destruction of the first multitude in his dream, causing them to "lose their way, they wandered off and were lost" (*1st Nephi 8:23*).

As a prophetic interpretation of this symbolic destruction of Lehi's first multitude, Nephi beheld in vision the destruction of his people attending the vapor of darkness:

"I saw lightning's, and I heard thundering, and earthquakes, and all manner of tumultuous noises; and I saw the earth and the rocks, that they rent; and I saw mountains tumbling into pieces; and I saw the plains of the earth, that they were broken up; and I saw many cities that they were sunk; and I saw many that they were burned with fire; and I saw many that did tumble to the earth because of the quaking thereof" (*1st Nephi 12:4*).

The Second Multitude; the second multitude is described in the dream of Lehi as follows:
"And it came to pass that I [Lehi] beheld others pressing forward, and they came forth and caught hold of the end of the rod of iron; and they did press

forward through the mist of darkness, clinging to the rod of iron, even until they did come forth and partake of the fruit of the tree" (*1st Nephi 8:24*).

This second multitude surely represents the righteous part of the people of Nephi who were not slain by the great destructions attending the mists of darkness at the crucifixion of Christ. (Note, Lehi saw them press forward through the mists of darkness. They were not killed, as was the first multitude, their more wicked brethren, but were spared, and Lehi saw them come forth and partake of the fruit of the tree.

This "partaking" of the fruit of the tree" is a representation of the second multitude's obtaining the "love of God" (*1st Nephi 11:22,25*) and their incorporation of His love into their society, enabled them to live for approximately two hundred years in the glorious and blessed state described at length in the book of 4 Nephi:

"And it came to pass that there was no contention in the land, because of the love of God which did dwell in the hearts of the people" (*4th Nephi 1:15*).

This interpretation of the second multitude was given to Nephi in his vision when he saw the vapor of darkness passing from off the face of the earth; and behold; I saw multitudes that had not fallen because of the great and terrible judgments of the Lord. (*1st Nephi 12:5*)

Unfortunately, however, in Lehi's dream the second multitude was not to remain forever at the tree of life. As Lehi records "and after they [the second multitude] had partaken of the fruit of the tree they did cast their eyes about as if they were ashamed. And I also cast my eyes round about; and beheld, on the other side of the river of water, a great and spacious building; and it stood as it were in the air, high above the earth. And it was filled with people, both old and young, both male and female; and their manner of dress was exceedingly fine; and they were in the attitude of mocking and pointing their fingers towards those who had come at and were partaking of the fruit. And after they had tasted of the fruit, they were ashamed, because of those scoffing at them; and they fell away into forbidden paths, and were lost "(1st Nephi 8:25–28).

In Nephi's vision, he is shown the prophetic meaning behind the symbolic imagery of Lehi's dream: "And it came to pass that I saw the multitudes of the earth gathered together" (*1st Nephi 12:13*). Whereas the first gathering together of multitudes (chapter 11) was a representation of the house of Israel assembling in order to fight against the twelve apostles of the Lamb, this second gathering of multitudes (chapter 12) represents the seed of Nephi and his brethren who gather together for their final great battle against the Laminates, which would result in the virtual annihilation of the Nephite society (*1st Nephi 12:14–15*). Once again, the phrase, a multitude gathering together, is being used to interpret the symbol of the great and spacious building of Lehi's dream. In chapter 8 the great and spacious building represented the pride of the world, so there is a slight twist in the meaning of this symbol.

The Third Multitude; In Lehi's dream, which is divided into two groups, is described as follows:

"Lehi saw other multitudes pressing forward; and they came and caught hold of the end of the rod of iron; and they did press their way forward, continually holding fast to the rod of iron, until they came forth and fell down and partook of the fruit of the tree" (*1st Nephi 8:30*).

Lehi saw a great polarization or division occurring among the inhabitants of the earth, for not only did he see multitudes pressing toward the tree of life, but He saw also multitudes feeling their way towards that great and spacious building. . . "And great was the multitude that did enter into that strange building" (*1st Nephi 8:31, 33*).

Lehi saw in his dream the fate of the third multitude that had pressed forward and obtained the tree of life was happier than the former two multitudes:

"And after [the wicked] did enter into that building they did point the finger of scorn at me and those that were partaking of the fruit also; but we heeded them not" (*1st Nephi 8:33*).

The lack of heed given by those at the tree of life to the scorn of the wicked leads to the conclusion they did not fall away from the tree as did their predecessors, but remained there permanently. Thus concludes the dream of Lehi.

In Nephi's vision, the interpretation of the third multitude from Lehi's dream is recorded in (*1st Nephi 14:7*): "For the time cometh, saith the Lamb of God, that I will work a great and a marvelous work among the children of men; a work which shall be everlasting, either on the one hand or on the other? either unto the convincing them unto peace and life eternal, or unto the deliverance of them to the hardness of their hearts and the blindness of their minds unto their being brought down into captivity, and also unto destruction, both temporally and spiritually, according to the captivity of the devil, of which I have spoken".

From this verse, it is clear the prophetic interpretation of the third multitude of Lehi's dream consists of those persons in the last days who are committed unto peace and life eternal. They make it to the tree of life, partake of the fruit, and fall not away. And the rest of the people in Lehi's dream who do not come to the tree of life but gathered themselves around the great and spacious building. This is interpreted by Nephi as their being "brought down into captivity and destruction both temporally and spiritually" (*1st Nephi 14:7*). As Lehi's dream appears to depict a polarization between the wicked and the righteous in the days of the third multitude, there are similarly depictions in Nephi's vision a great polarization among the peoples of the earth, "a work which shall be everlasting either on the one hand or the other" (*1st Nephi 14:7*). In subsequent verses, Nephi further describes the polarity that will occur in the last days. "And he [the angel] said unto me: Behold there are save two churches only; the one is the church of the Lamb of God, and the other is the church of the devil; wherefore, whoso belongeth not to the church of the Lamb of God belongeth to that great church, which is the mother of abominations; and she is the whore of all the earth" (*1st Nephi 14:10*).

Nephi is then shown that the numbers of the church of the devil will far exceed the numbers of the church of the Lamb of God (*1st Nephi 14:11–12*), even as the same situation had been typified in Lehi's dream (*1st Nephi 8:33*).

Next, Nephi beholds "that the great mother of abominations did gather together multitudes upon the face of all the earth, among all the nations of the Gentiles, to fight against the Lamb of God" (*1st Nephi 14:13*). As the vision of Nephi concludes, he describes the "power of the Lamb of God descending upon the church of the Lamb" (*1st Nephi 14:14*) and the "wrath of God being "poured out upon that great and abominable church, insomuch that there were wars and rumors of wars among all the nations and kindred's of the earth" (*1st Nephi 14:15*).

The angel next exhibits to Nephi three symbols from Lehi's dream which, when combined, contributed to the destruction of the people of Nephi:

1. The "fountain [river] of filthy water," the interpretation of which the angel gives as "the depths of hell" (*1st Nephi 12:16*). This is the destination of the descendants of Nephi, who died in their wicked and rebellious state.

2. The "mists of darkness," the interpretation of which the angel gives as "the temptations of the devil, which blindeth the eyes, and hardeneth the hearts of the children of men, and leadeth them away into broad roads, that they perish and are lost" (*1st Nephi 12:17*). These temptations are the outer force eventually leading to the destruction of the Nephites.

3. The "great and spacious building," the interpretation of which the angel gives as "the vain imaginations and the pride of the children of men" (*1st Nephi 12:18*). This pride is the inner force causing the Nephites' overthrow.

In vision, Nephi then beholds the interpretation of the above three symbols as applied to the destruction of his people:

"I beheld and saw that the seed of my brethren did contend against my seed, according to the word of the angel; and because of the pride of my seed [the great and spacious building], and the temptations of the devil [the mists of darkness], I beheld that the seed of my brethren did overpower the people of my seed" (*1st Nephi 12:19*).

However, what of the remnant of the people who survived the cataclysmic battle? The dream of Lehi gives a symbolic answer to the question and the vision of Nephi offers a corresponding interpretation.

In Lehi's dream, "They [the second multitude] fell away into forbidden paths and were lost" (*1st Nephi 8:28*). In the vision Nephi beheld, the angel said unto him: "Behold, these [survivors of the last great battle of the Nephites] shall dwindle in unbelief. And it came to pass that I beheld, after they had dwindled in unbelief they became a dark, and loathsome, and a filthy people, full of idleness and all manner of abominations" (*1st Nephi 12:22–23*).

Thus is symbolized and interpreted the complete apostasy, which was to occur among the descendants of Nephi and his brothers. Spiritually speaking, "they did fall away into forbidden paths and were lost" (*1st Nephi 8:28*).

Chapter 15, the interpretation in terms of the Afterlife

It is nothing short of amazing, the varied and complex list of events described in Nephi's vision were derived from the few, simple symbols used in Lehi's dream of the tree of life. However, this is not the end of it, for Lehi's dream does not symbolize things related to this world alone. In this section, the discussion will cover how the tree of life scenario lends itself to an interpretation of the events that will occur to the wicked and the righteous in the afterlife. Also considered there is evidence of another alternate interpretation of the tree of life dream included a description of the afterlife and the ultimate destinies of the wicked and the righteous.

Nephi's vision of the tree of life is recorded in chapter 15 starting with verse 21, the entire text can be found in the Book of Mormon, 1st Nephi 1: 1-36.

21 "And it came to pass that they did speak unto me again, saying: What meaneth this thing, which our father saw in a dream? What meaneth the tree that he saw?

22 And I said unto them: It was a representation of the tree of life.

23 And they said unto me: What meaneth the rod of iron that our father saw, that led to the tree?

24 And I said unto them that it was the word of God; and whoso would hearken unto the word of God, and would hold fast unto it, they would never perish; neither could the temptations and the fiery darts of the adversary overpower them unto blindness, to lead them away to destruction.

25 Wherefore, I, Nephi, did exhort them to give heed unto the word of the Lord; yea, I did exhort them with all the energies of my soul, and with all the faculty, which I possessed, that they would give heed to the word of God and remember to keep his commandments always in all things.

26 And they said unto me: What meaneth the river of water which our father saw?

27 And I said unto them that the water which my father saw was filthiness; and so much was his mind swallowed up in other things that he beheld not the filthiness of the water.

28 And I said unto them that it was an awful gulf, which separated the wicked from the tree of life, and also from the saints of God.

29 And I said unto them that it was a representation of that awful hell which the angel said unto me was prepared for the wicked.

30 And I said unto them that our father also saw that the justice of God did also divide the wicked from the righteous; and the brightness thereof was like unto the brightness of a flaming fire, which ascendeth up unto God forever and ever, and hath no end.

31 And they said unto me: Doth this thing mean the torment of the body in the days of probation, or doth it mean the final state of the soul after the death of the temporal body, or doth it speak of the things, which are temporal?

32 And it came to pass that I said unto them that it was a representation of things both temporal and spiritual; for the day should come that they must be judged of their works, yea, even the works which were done by the temporal body in their days of probation.

33 Wherefore, if they should die in their wickedness they must be cast off also, as to the things which are spiritual, which are pertaining to righteousness; wherefore, they must be brought to stand before God, to be judged of their works; and if their works have been filthiness they must needs be filthy; and if they be filthy it must needs be that they cannot dwell in the kingdom of God; if so, the kingdom of God must be filthy also.

34 But behold, I say unto you, the kingdom of God is not filthy, and there cannot any unclean thing enter into the kingdom of God; wherefore there must needs be a place of filthiness prepared for that which is filthy.

35 And there is a place prepared, yea, even that awful hell of which I have spoken, and the devil is the perpetrator of it; wherefore the final state of the souls of men is to dwell in the kingdom of God, or to be cast out because of that justice of which I have spoken.

36 Wherefore, the wicked are rejected from the righteous, and also from that tree of life, whose fruit is most precious and most desirable above all

other fruits; yea and it is the greatest of all the gifts of God. And thus I spake unto my brethren. Amen".

Shortly after Nephi received his great vision, Laman and Lemuel inquiring of him as to the meaning of such things as, "what meaneth this thing, which our father saw in a dream? What meaneth the tree, which he saw? What meaneth the rod of iron, which our father saw, that led to the tree? What meaneth the river of water which our father saw? Nephi proceeds to embark on a new interpretation of the symbols of the tree of life dream, and in so doing teaches his older brothers concerning the state of the souls of mankind in the afterlife. Nephi says of the river, And I said unto them that the water which my father saw was filthiness; and so much was his mind swallowed up in other things that he beheld not the filthiness of the water. And I said unto them that it was an awful gulf, which separated the wicked from the tree of life, and also from the saints of God. . . . And I said unto them that our father also saw that the justice of God did also divide the wicked from the righteous; and the brightness thereof was like unto the brightness of a flaming fire, which ascendeth up unto God forever and ever, and hath no end"(*1st Nephi 15:27, 29–30*).

This scene of a yawning gulf separating the wicked from the righteous is likely a representation of the spirit world prior to the atonement and resurrection of Jesus Christ. Up until that time, there was no intercourse between the two hemispheres of the spirit world and no preaching of the gospel to the wicked and ignorant by the righteous (*D&C 138; Luke 16:19–31*). Therefore, in terms of the period of time in which Nephi spoke (between 600 and 592 B.C.), his description of the spirit world was correct.

It is a simple matter to see how this situation in the spirit world was interpreted from Lehi's dream of the tree of life. The righteous part of the people, are on one side of the river and the wicked on the other. Presumably, the righteous are on the side of the tree of life, and the wicked are on the side of the great and spacious building. Indeed, there is just such a tableau in Lehi's dream. Enlarging and amplifying upon the symbols of Lehi's dream, however, the river here seems not to be a mere stream of water running level with the ground. Instead like the Colorado River, cutting through the chasms and gorges of the Grand Canyon, so as to create a great gulf of division between the righteous and the wicked, over which neither group may pass.

Next, Nephi describes to his brothers the scene on the judgment day: "The day should come that they must be judged of their works, yea, even the works which were done by the temporal body in their days of probation. Wherefore, if they should die in their wickedness they must be cast off also, as to the things which are spiritual, which are pertaining to righteousness;

wherefore, they must be brought to stand before God, to be judged of their works" (*1st Nephi 15:32–33*).

Though not mentioned in this text, several other scriptural passages referring to the judgment day speak of a "bar." Both Jacob and Moroni speak of the pleasing bar of God, before which all mankind shall be judged (Jacob 6:13; Moroni 10:34). Though the word, bar as used in this context obviously has legalistic implications. It is interesting, the foremost definition of the word bar is a straight piece of wood or metal, longer than it is wide, and has various uses. This definition of a bar as a long-shaped piece of metal fits the description of the iron rod leading to the tree of life. It is therefore possible this judgment scene described by Nephi was typified in Lehi's dream by the transportation of the wicked multitude by some means across the gulf to stand before the rod of iron (judgment bar) along with the righteous in order to be judged of their works.

The bar, or the rod of iron, is the place where the people are judged. It will be remembered, the fundamental interpretation of the rod of iron is "the word of God" (*1st Nephi 11:25*). As pointed out above, one of the most common scriptural uses of the phrase the word of God is as a name for Jesus Christ. Therefore, the bringing of all people before the rod of iron (judgment bar or word of God) to be judged of their works may symbolize the scriptural verity. Christ will be the judge of all mankind (*John 5:22*), and all will be brought to stand before him in that great judgment day to be judged of their works, whether they be good or whether they be evil (*Revelation 20:12–13*).

Nephi then describes for his brothers the fate of the wicked and the righteous subsequent to the final judgment, all in terms of symbolism derived from his father's dream:

If their works have been filthiness, they must needs be filthy; and if they were filthy, it must needs by they cannot dwell in the kingdom of God; if so, the kingdom of God must be filthy also. But behold, I say unto you, the kingdom of God is not filthy, and there cannot any unclean thing enter into the kingdom of God; wherefore there must needs be a place of filthiness prepared for those which are filthy.

"And there is a place prepared, yea, even that awful hell of which I have spoken, and the devil is the perpetrator of it; wherefore the final state of the souls of men is to dwell in the kingdom of God, or to be cast out because of that justice of which I have spoken. Wherefore, the wicked are rejected from the righteous, and also from that tree of life, whose fruit is most precious and most desirable above all other fruits; yea, and it is the greatest of all the gifts of God" (*1st Nephi 15:33–36*).

From Nephi's interpretation, it can be concluded that, in terms of Lehi's dream, once the wicked are brought across the gulf to be judged of their works before the judgment bar of God, they are not simply put back where they once were on the opposite side of the gulf. They are cast into the gulf itself and the river which winds its way through it, while the righteous remain at the tree of life, to partake of its fruit forever.

As will be recalled, Nephi further interpreted the river of filthy water as, "A representation of that awful hell, which the angel said unto me, was prepared for the wicked, and the brightness thereof was like unto the brightness of a flaming fire, which ascendeth up unto God forever and ever, and hath no end" (*1st Nephi 15:29–30*).
It is feasible to interpret this passage as describing the river of water as burning or glowing in some manner, as "a flaming fire." The use of a "burning" body of water to represent hell is not without precedent in the scriptures, being the equivalent of the familiar "lake of fire and brimstone."

(*1st Nephi 15:30*) states, "the justice of God did also divide the wicked from the righteous." It is the justice of God that keeps the wicked from returning to his presence along with the righteous. Adam sinned and was cast out of God's presence in the beginning. All have sinned personally and thereby come short of the glory of God. In the terms used in Lehi's dream, all have become filthy through the commission of sin and are therefore bound for the river of filthy, burning water as their eternal resting place. There is only one other alternative, God has provided, and it is the tree of life, which now comes to represent the presence of God himself. In addition, the only way by which anyone may reach the tree of life is the straight and narrow path, along which stretches the rod of iron. There is no other way provided by which access may be gained to the tree of life.

Early on in Nephi's vision (1st Nephi 11:26–33), the interpretation of the rod of iron was given as the ministry and atonement of Jesus Christ. It is easier now to more fully appreciate the symbolism involved in that interpretation. Even as the rod of iron is the only manner by which the multitudes can approach and obtain the fruit of the tree of life, so is the atonement of Jesus Christ the only way by which mortals can overcome the effects of the fall, be forgiven of sins, and return to the presence of God (see Mosiah 3:17).

(*1st Nephi 15:36*) states, "the fruit of the tree of life is the greatest of all the gifts of God". Similarly, (*Doctrine and Covenants 14:7*), declares, "And, if you keep my commandments, and endure to the end, you shall have eternal life, which gift is the greatest of all the gifts of God." Thus, the act of partaking of the fruit of the tree of life is likely symbolic of partaking of eternal life, both gifts being described as the greatest of the gifts of God.

Just as the dream of Lehi left the reader hanging, so does the vision of Nephi. The similarity in abrupt endings of Nephi's vision and Lehi's dream tends to confirm the hypothesis, the vision of Nephi is an interpretation of Lehi's dream, up to and including the cliffhanger ending. However, at the conclusion of Nephi's vision, the reason behind the premature finale is given.

Nephi was forbidden by God to record the conclusion of the vision. He saw more than he was allowed to write down. Nephi was shown the apostle John would be ordained to write the rest of the things Nephi was shown but forbidden to include in his record (1st Nephi 14:18–28). This accounts not only for the abrupt ending to Nephi's vision, but also for the similarly abrupt ending to the dream of Lehi. It is likely that, even as the record of Nephi's vision was curtailed due to the anticipated account of John, so was the record of Lehi's dream cut short for the same reason.

Long-Suffering

Almost everyone has heard, be patient and suffer long, or something similar as the pat-answer. when parents or members of the Church seek help with the problems they face at home or in a church calling. Honestly, these kinds of abbreviated answer leave a lot to be desired. Without a full explanation of how patients and long-suffering can be exactly implemented in any predicament, these kinds of, pat answers, providing the asker tries to follow this abbreviated advice without any further help, can eventually lead to frustration and personal burn out. Unfortunately, most of those in administrative positions in the Church really do not have a complete answer and often do not even have a good knowledge of the biblical meaning of patients and long-suffering. As people, who are struggling with the problem, find the lack of results becoming harder and harder to manage, they often start wondering if they should find a new situation where they don't have to be exposed to this constant trying and rarely achieving circumstance. This change of venue is difficult to do at home but is often the avenue of choice when dealing with ones calling. It is incumbent on advice givers, to realize when invoking a biblical solution to a temporal problem there is a spiritual element involved. Oft times this is where the problem solving effort goes off the rails.

There are eighteen scriptures combined in the Old Testament, New Testament, Book of Mormon and Doctrine and Covenants talking about long-suffering. There is a list of them at the end of this section. The most recited one and the most complete is; "No power or influence can or ought to be maintained by virtue of the priesthood, only by persuasion, by long-suffering, by gentleness and meekness, and by love unfeigned"; "By kindness, and pure knowledge, which shall greatly enlarge the soul without hypocrisy, and without guile". "Reproving betimes with sharpness, when moved upon by the Holy Ghost; and then showing forth afterwards an increase of love toward him whom thou hast reproved, lest he esteem thee to be his enemy" (*D&C121:41–43*).

The power and influence of the Priesthood extends into three different areas of life where one might find the need to be long-suffering,

1- Personal lives combined with the lives of the family,

2- Obligations to the Church through callings, membership and assignments,

3- Periods of probation called mortality and the efforts therein.

Personal lives and the family

Sometimes life stinks and some people seem to be handed a bad deal all around, even so, Heavenly Father knows what His children are about, what they are dealing with, and yes, He knows the outcome beforehand. However, the important part is, individuals are free to choose how they deal with their problems. They are free to handle the situation or not. If they choose to handle the situation then they must decide what to do. There is scriptural guidance in these matters but one must be willing to study and learn the doctrine in order to understand how righteous behavior affects the outcome. Heavenly Father only intervenes when there is a cry for help. People must do the knee work required and then they must take what which is presented before them, knowing the solution may take years of effort on their part to come to a full resolution. It will not work if people pray only and do nothing to improve their condition. In situations where nothing can be done to change the outcome, those who are suffering must continue to reach out to Heavenly Father. Some people will only pray to Heavenly Father during the good times and forget Him during the bad times. When bad things happen, often people turn to or away from Heavenly Father.

Some feel it is by His hand they did not receive the outcome when and how they desired and turn away from His guidance and His loving embrace. This is the time for them to examine their understanding of "long-suffering". Long-suffering says, OK you are in this, now what? What can a person do to make things better while they endure for this season, be it a long one, or short one? The text above has been looking at long-suffering as it pertains to the Lord but the situation is the same when discussing people's long-suffering and dealing with their fellow man. President Uchtdorf said this;

"As the Lord is patient with us, let us be patient with those we serve. Understand that they, like us, are imperfect. They, like us, make mistakes. They, like us, want others to give them the benefit of the doubt. Never give up on anyone. And that includes not giving up on yourself." (Continue in Patience," Ensign, May 2010).

Obligations to the Church

As a priesthood leader, but the same is true for most callings, there is an accountability for a lot of results, or helping others improve and repent, but often, when advice is given and it gets ignored – repeatedly, this becomes discouraging. One Bishop mentioned leadership is "a lot of work that doesn't pan out to anything, with flashes of success". In spite of this bishop's assertion, to a priesthood leader, there is always an expectation, things will improve and the number of endowed members with temple recommends, number of people who join the church etcetera, and if your numbers are unusually, low, there is going to be a conversation about it -- in varying degrees of nice-etude. So, if members think life is like this and particularly, service in the Church, how does one maintain enthusiasm and positivity when they feel like they are ever trying but rarely achieving the results they are seeking? What doctrine, scriptures, or other solid philosophies apply to help them persist in these kinds of activities for long periods, without getting discouraged? A perspective is needed on this subject, so try this; as the leaders in the Church, it is expected, they put their hands into and on the stuff, which is not theirs, and often due to dire circumstances. They are helping Heavenly Father "bring to pass the immortality and eternal life of man", and therefore they are encouraging and hoping others will change their habits and serve the Lord more intensely. However, during these cut and dried afflictions, those whom those leaders are trying to help can always choose how they conduct themselves in relation to their testimonies and faith. This perspective helps to recognize there are things these leaders do or do not have control over but one thing is for sure; no leader can exercise control over another due to the doctrine of agency. Thus, long-suffering comes in when there is a problem in need of fixing and it is not getting fixed. So, when faced with such a problem, think about it like this,

1- Is said problem something anyone can control, change, or fixed? If so, then, with the help of the Lord, solutions can be found! No long-suffering necessary.

2- If said problem can be controlled, are extenuating circumstances are getting in the way? Then, with the help of the Lord and all parties involved formulate a plan, which, will see either the problem fixed despite the circumstances or once those circumstances are no longer hindering, the ability to find a remedy will happen. You might have to be patient with the extenuating circumstances, but you now have a plan.

3- Is said problem something over which there is no control? Then, leave it up to the Lord, and do not worry about it.

This last bit, for many, is the hardest, but it is really their choice whether or not to worry about something. They do not need to waste their time and energy worrying over something unfixable. When it comes to spiritual matters no mortal is the fixer, the Lord is, and people are just the messengers. In spite of the demands made through any calling a person can do no more than the Lord deems fit at the time and they cannot know what or how much or even why. The old adage states, "Worrying is like paying a debt now for a problem you do not have yet"

The period of probation called mortality.

During this time of probation, difficult situations are part of everyday life and are the essence of this temporal state. What comes out of those situations is spiritual education and eternal blessings. When accepting the will of the Father, a person has to say, OK, obviously, Heavenly Father has a reason for this, and all things will always work together for good and according to His will. Therefore, if any trial is supposed to be endured (long-suffering) then it is necessary to pay attention and seek help from Heavenly Father. If something new is learned which, was not known before or a mountain thought impossibly to climb suddenly becomes a stepping stone, it makes the acceptance of Heavenly Father's Will and the long-suffering involved in waiting for the blessings, much sweeter. However, for many people, life will continue to be difficult because they cannot humble themselves and accept, they cannot live a secular life and never have a serious problem, thus, they will continue to suffer and fall. Failing to see the blessings Heavenly Father can give us, the inability to humble ourselves, and accepting God's presentation can be the source of much suffering and it can last for a long time. It is not to say, people should not try to improve their situation, far from it, only their life-style needs to be change. Heavenly Father wants people to change and become the perfected souls His guidance will cause them to become. Changing one's behavior is the part of the test, which one must endure, while in this mortal state. Compared to eternity, everything here is short term but, while living here in the temporal existence, things can seem like an eternity, which is where long-suffering, comes in.

There is another similitude to long-suffering, which offers a completely different point of view. There are those who have a certain way about them, which is difficult to live with. They are not long-suffering; in fact, they are just the opposite. They consider any inconvenience, no matter how small, as unacceptable and suffering in any way is deplorable. If the least little thing bothers them they immediately get outraged and let the person considered at fault know, they, the guilty party, need to change their ways. Of course, there are many degrees of this conduct, this example is being use in the extreme, but everyone knows the type spoken of here. The overall perspective on this kind of behavior starts with the founding of this country. The founding fathers believed that, God granted people certain freedoms and they were free to anything they wanted as long as their actions did not impede or diminish the freedom of others. With this in mind, consider those who are hard to live with. They, those who are hard to live with, feel they should be free to live without having any inconveniences imposed upon them and they are correct up to a point, but just because they are perturbed, this does not necessarily mean, the other party needs to change their behavior. What is being dealt with here, is these intolerant individuals, who are hard to live with, and who so vehemently protect their personnel freedom are more than willing to deny freedom to those who irritates them, deigning them freedom of action, freedom of personal expression, or even freedom of their own natural deportment. Therefore, there is tremendous injustice in this behavior. These intolerant people are demonstrating the lack of patience or long-suffering and they need to change their behavior. When looking at the scriptures below it will become clear, the Lord expects people to be civil, courteous, patient, understanding and long-suffering, indeed He has commanded them to love one another.

a. Lord God, merciful and gracious, longsuffering: (Ex. 34:6)
b. Endured with much longsuffering the vessels of wrath: (Rom. 9:22)
c. Charity suffereth long: 1st. Cor. 13:4. (Moro. 7:45)
d. By pureness, by knowledge, by longsuffering: (2nd. Cor. 6:6)
e. The fruit of the Spirit is love, joy, peace, longsuffering: (Gal. 5:22)
f. With longsuffering, forbearing one another: (Eph. 4:2)
g. Put on therefore, as the elect of God, meekness, longsuffering: (Col. 3:12)
h. In me, Christ might shew forth all longsuffering: (1st. Tim. 1:16)
i. Exhort with all longsuffering and doctrine: (2nd. Tim. 4:2)
j. Long-suffering of God waited in the days of Noah: (1st Pet. 3:20)
k. Lord … is longsuffering to us-ward: (2nd. Pet. 3:9)

l. Long-suffering of our Lord is salvation: (2nd. Pet. 3:15)

m. Come to a knowledge of the goodness of God, and his long-suffering: (Mosiah 4:6)

n. Ye should be ... long-suffering: (Alma 7:23, Alma 13:28)

o. May his ... long-suffering ... rest in your mind forever: (Moro. 9:25)

p. Decisions ... to be made in ... long-suffering: (D&C 107:30)

q. Do this in all lowliness ... and long-suffering: (D&C 118:3)

The Millennium
Clearing the Ground

First things first, it is worth noting, when the subject of the Millennium is discussed, copious amounts of speculation and mythology abound about ideas are not found in the scriptures or the teachings of latter-day prophets. In addition, when the Saints have a discussion on the Millennium it eventually leads to wild speculation about what it will be like to live with Christ on the earth, what it will be like to live without the wicked around, what it will be like to live with resurrected folks, etc. The scriptures and, for the most part, the modern day Prophets, are entirely uninterested in such details. These speculative opinions border on false doctrine so it is incumbent on all to be carefully, study, know what is being talking about, and avoid such conjecture.

To find few examples of this speculation, one needs to look no farther than a simple comparison of the gospel essentials lesson books published by the church in the last few years. In the first book, a certain line of thought is printed and in the next publication, it is changed or left out.

(1) The first major deletion is this line: "It [the Millennium] will be the final thousand years of the earth's temporal existence", this statement was removed from the next publication.

(2) A little further along, this statement: "Jesus and the resurrected saints will probably not live on the earth all the time but will visit whenever they please or when necessary to help in the governing of the earth." This statement was also removed from the next publication.

(3) Later still, this too-widely accepted idea has been nixed: "There will not be different continents as we have now, but the land will be gathered in one place as it was in the beginning."

(4) From the earlier book an entire paragraph was removed, and replaced in the second edition, with a section headed, "Righteous Government," which included the following speculative interpretation of

scripture: "At this time there will be two capitals in the world, one in Jerusalem, the other in America."

(5) What is now the section on "No Death" was before "No Disease or Death," and the following statement has, accordingly been entirely removed: "Even though mortals will live on the earth during the Millennium, they will not have diseases as we do now."

(6) An entire subsection on "Changes in the Animal Kingdom" has been removed, including the following common but wildly speculative interpretation of Isaiah: "Animals, now eating flesh will eat grass and grain." So, when members are faced with these inconsistencies, they must go to the scriptures and start to study and sort it all out for themselves.

The Millennium in the Ancient Scriptures

This part of the discussion begins with the following question: What volumes of scripture, actually leads anyone to believing, at all, in the Millennium? Is there anything in the Old Testament, nope? How about, the New Testament, only a very small part in the Book of Revelation? Does the Book of Mormon have this story, significantly, nothing? Anything in the Doctrine and Covenants, unquestionably, yes. The Pearl of Great Price, yes, but only in the Book of Moses. In spite of the lack of scriptural documentation, there is an interesting kind of trajectory here. The oldest scriptural source on the Millennium is the Book of Moses, where the Millennium is introduced in the record of Enoch. Next comes, many years later, the Book of Revelation, which gives some further reflection on the Millennium and it seems clear, Revelation and Moses are connected. Finally, there is a scattering of revelations in the Doctrine and Covenants. The rest of the scriptures seems not only uninterested in the Millennium, but, frankly, unaware of it.

These are the three basic scriptural sources:
(1) the Pearl of Great Prices' vision of Enoch found in the Book of Moses;
(2) the New Testament's Book of Revelation;
(3) only two relevant revelations in the Doctrine and Covenants out of the five.

Enoch

It is quite significant; the only non-Mormon scriptural source on the Millennium which is the less than interpretively secure of the three, the Book of Revelation. However, it is recommend to look at scholarly commentaries on Revelation, specifically as regards its presentation of a thousand-year period to follow the final conflagration. The commentators universally point out; the idea of such a period was in circulation before it appeared in Revelation. These early circulations are confined to the apocalyptic literature of Second Temple Judaism. More information on the Millennium can be found in the more apocalyptic texts among what is now call the apocrypha and pseudepigraphal. In those sources, that period is not always one of a thousand years, interestingly, but often of another number (four hundred, for example). What is particularly interesting, though, is that the commentaries systematically point out, the idea of a millennium in one form or another seems to have originated in, of all things, the Enoch literature. There are, as many may be aware, at least three distinct books of Enoch that have been unearthed dating back to Second Temple Judaism, none of which has been canonized. Why is this interesting? Because the earliest source in Mormon scripture, on the idea of a millennium, is precisely, the Book of Moses account of Enoch's vision. Therefore, in or out of canonized scripture the idea of a millennium seems to go back to Enoch, although most of these accounts are united in concept but they are not unified nor replete in detail.

Here is the passage from Moses 7 where the Millennium is introduced and it is definitely worth mentioning, there are no significant textual variants in the JST manuscripts here; that is unique and a bit shocking.

"And the Lord said unto Enoch: As I live, even so will I come in the last days, in the days of wickedness and vengeance, to fulfill the oath which I have made unto you concerning the children of Noah; and the day shall come that the earth shall rest, but before that day [there will be destruction coupled with a preservation of the Lord's people or the elect, who will then be gathered into what] shall be called Zion, a New Jerusalem. And the Lord said unto Enoch: Then shalt thou and all thy city meet them there, and we will receive them into our bosom, and they shall see us; and we will fall upon their necks, and they shall fall upon our necks, and we will kiss each other; and there shall be mine abode, and it shall be Zion, which shall come forth out of all the creations which I have made; and for the space of a thousand years the earth shall rest. And it came to pass that Enoch saw the day of the coming of the Son of Man, in the last days, to dwell on the earth in righteousness for the space of a thousand years" (*Moses 7:60-65*). (Note, this is all Moses had to say about it!)

What information can be gathered concerning the Millennium from this passage?

First, it should be said, the Millennium is His coming to fulfill His oath concerning the seed of Noah and is associated directly with the meeting up of the two Zions, the one from heaven, Enoch's city (which was translated and is often referred to as Zion) and the one on earth (the New Jerusalem). This is where the thousand years seem here to begin when the two Zions meet up and Christ takes up His abode in the jointure between the two.

Second, it should be said, the thousand years is a period for the earth to rest, something closely tied to other parts of Enoch's vision. Remember, Enoch has heard "a voice from the bowels" of the earth expressing its pain at the wickedness of its inhabitants, something which led Enoch to weep and cry out, "O Lord, wilt thou not have compassion upon the earth? Wilt thou not bless the children of Noah" (*Verses 48-49*)? Remember, further, after the Lord established a covenant with Enoch concerning Noah's children concerning the remnant of Noah's seed. Enoch pressed the Lord still with this first agonized question: "When the Son of Man cometh in the flesh, shall the earth rest" (*Verse 54*). Because he was then shown the earth suffering, further during Christ's mortal advent, "the earth groaned," (*verse 56*). He cried a third time: "When shall the earth rest" (*Verse 58*)? It is only in response to this, finally, the assurance concerning the meeting up of the Zions and the establishment of a thousand years of rest for the earth, is described. In all this, it must not be missed, the Millennium is, in Enoch's vision, a period of rest for the suffering earth, is first and, apparently, foremost.

Third, it should be said, the thousand years is a period of Christ's presence. Though the Lord Himself emphasizes the earth resting (and from which one can conclude, given the rest of the vision, the thousand years are characterized by a general righteousness, or at least a rest from wickedness), the report of Enoch's vision of the thousand years describes it as the time during which, the Son of Man . . . dwells on the earth. There is no specific talk of government of Christ reigning, or any such thing. Only of dwelling or taking up an abode.

Revelation

The Book of Revelation, chapter 20 mentions the idea of a millennium in only a single passage. Here it is in its entirety:
"And I saw an angel come down from heaven, having the key of the bottomless pit and a great chain in his hand. And he laid hold on the dragon, that old serpent, which is the Devil, and Satan, and bound him a thousand years, and cast him into the bottomless pit, and shut him up, and set a seal upon him, that he should deceive the nations no more, till the thousand years should be fulfilled: and after that he must be loosed a little season. And I saw thrones, and they sat upon them, and judgment was given unto them: and I saw the souls of them that were beheaded for the witness of Jesus, and for the word of God, and which had not worshipped the beast, neither his

image, neither had received his mark upon their foreheads, or in their hands; and they lived and reigned with Christ a thousand years. But the rest of the dead lived not again until the thousand years were finished. This is the first resurrection. Blessed and holy is he that hath part in the first resurrection: on such the second death hath no power, but they shall be priests of God and of Christ, and shall reign with him a thousand years. And when the thousand years are expired, Satan shall be loosed out of his prison, and shall go out to deceive the nations which are in the four quarters of the earth, Gog and Magog, to gather them together to battle: the number of whom is as the sand of the sea" (*Rev. 20:1*).

What can be said about this passage and its doctrine of the Millennium?

First, the emphasis here, interestingly, is less on the presence of Christ and more about the non-presence of Satan. The drama of the Millennium here begins with the appearance of an angel with the key of the bottomless pit and a great chain in his hand, who then lays hold on the dragon, the old serpent, which is the Devil, and Satan, and binds him a thousand years. It is interesting to note, in Enoch's vision it is Satan, not any binding angel, who is described as having "a great chain in his hand, with which he veils the whole face of the earth" (*Moses 7:26*). One might say, then, whereas the Book of Moses account of the Millennium is deeply positive and optimistic, (it is the period of the coming of the Son of Man, in connection with a meeting up of the heavenly and earthly Zions). The Book of Revelation account of the Millennium is deeply negative and pessimistic. It is the period of the temporary binding of the dragon, who otherwise causes widespread destruction and misery. This sharp distinction between the optimistic Enoch and the pessimistic John repeats itself. Whereas the righteous in the Book of Moses are those who "gird up their loins and look forth for the time of the coming of the Son of Man" (*Moses 7:62*). The righteous in the Book of Revelation are those who "were beheaded for the witness of Jesus, and for the word of God, and which had not worshipped the beast, neither his image, neither had received his name upon their foreheads, or in their hands" (*Rev. 20:4*). In Enoch's vision, the righteous are those who train their vision on the glorious coming of the Son of Man; in John's vision, the righteous are those who are martyred for not worshiping the beast. This "martyrdom of those who did not worship the beast" leaves a lot to be understood (*Rev. 20:4, Rev.13:15*).

Second, a less stark difference, but an important one nonetheless, is the Book of Revelation focuses on those who reign during the Millennium, whereas the Book of Moses was interested instead simply on He who dwells during the Millennium. While Enoch's vision provides a picture of Christ dwelling among the people, but there is nothing said about government or the like, John's vision provides a picture of the true martyrs reigning with Christ, apparently over the rest of the world. Here in Revelation there is a picture of government. Moreover, this difference is related to yet another comparison of those who dwell with Christ in the Enoch Millennium. This seem to be those who, on the one hand, in the earthly Zion, happen to be alive and faithful at the coming of the Son of Man and those who, on the other hand, in the heavenly Zion, were translated with Enoch and so never tasted of death. In the John Millennium, however, those who reign, not dwell, with Christ during the thousand years are those faithful martyrs who make up the first resurrection, while the rest of "the dead lived not again until the thousand years were finished" (*Rev.20:5*). Thus, in Moses, it is the still living righteous and the translated, who makes up the community surrounding Christ, but in Revelation, it is the uniquely resurrected martyrs, who make up the community.

Of course, all these differences do not necessarily mean Enoch and John have irreconcilable doctrines of the Millennium. One could certainly reconcile the two accounts, assuming simply, each emphasizes different aspects of what will take place (perhaps even suggesting Enoch has given an account of who will be governed during the Millennium, while John has given an account of who will govern during the same).

What is interesting is while the Book of Moses commits the believing Latter-day Saint to a conception of a millennium characterized by the earth's rest and the presence of the Christ at the intersection of the earthly and heavenly. The Book of Revelation commits the believing Latter-day Saint to a conception of a millennium characterized by respite from the untrammeled reign of Satan and the exaltation of the persecuted. The Book of Moses seems to commit the believing Latter-day Saint to a kind of postmillennialism, while the Book of Revelation seems to commit the believing Latter-day Saint to a kind of premillennialism

However, it is time to see what revelations from this dispensation have to add.

D&C

Only a handful of revelations in the Doctrine and Covenants have anything to say about a millennium, and only two of them are substantial. The three references to the Millennium with which will not even dealt with, since they are too brief and uninformative to deserve comment here: D&C 43:28-31; D&C 88:110; D&C 130:16). There are two substantial revelations taken in the order given: D&C 29:8-13, 22-23 and D&C 77:12, and later a smattering of D&C verses and Prophetic thoughts.

The first revelation concerning the Millennium came in connection with the first general conference of the Church, a few months after the Church was organized. Without speculating too much, there is good reason to suggest the Saints, who were very few in numbers, had their attention directed to the question of the Millennium by the revelations of Hiram Page had been receiving through his stone. It is interesting to note, the vision of Enoch had not yet been produced in the early work on the JST. It would come a couple of months after this revelation. It seems clear, at any rate, Page's revelations had made some claims about the location for the building of a New Jerusalem, and it is not too wild a guess to suggest, that there was something said about the proximity of the Millennium as well. At any rate, section 29 introduces the Millennium to modern revelation. Here is the passage and here again there are no significant textual variants.

"For the hour is nigh, and that which was spoken by mine apostles must be fulfilled; for as they spoke so shall it come to pass; for I will reveal myself from heaven with power and great glory, with all the hosts thereof, and dwell in righteousness with men on earth a thousand years, and the wicked shall not stand. And again, verily, verily, I say unto you, and it hath gone forth in a firm decree, by the will of the Father, that mine apostles, the Twelve which were with me in my ministry at Jerusalem, shall stand at my right hand at the day of my coming in a pillar of fire, being clothed with robes of righteousness, with crowns upon their heads, in glory even as I am, to judge the whole house of Israel, even as many as have loved me and kept my commandments, and none else. For a trump shall sound both long and loud, even as upon Mount Sinai, and all the earth shall quake, and they shall come forth—yea, even the dead which died in me, to receive a crown of righteousness, and to be clothed upon, even as I am, to be with me, that we may be one. . . . And again, verily, verily, I say unto you that when the thousand years are ended, and men again begin to deny their God, then will I spare the earth but for a little season; and the end shall come, and the heaven and the earth shall be consumed and pass away, and there shall be a new heaven and a new earth" (*D&C 29:8-13, 22-23*).

What should be said about this modern take on the Millennium?

Here, as in the Book of Moses, what launches the Millennium is the arrival of Christ from heaven to dwell in righteousness on the earth for a thousand years, though here there is an emphasis on the power and great glory with which He comes. Also unique to this passage is the arrival of

Christ with all the hosts of heaven—with, a multitude of angels. Here also the power and glory, coupled with the presence of the hosts of heaven, which seem to have a direct effect on the wicked. The phrase, the wicked shall not stand, immediately precedes verses drawing on the language of Malachi 4, suggesting, the very appearance of Christ and His followers will do what, burn up the wicked. This passage slightly echoes the Book of Revelation, where there is some kind of focus on the destruction of the wicked, but with a difference: the Book of Revelation seems to suggest the destruction of the wicked and righteous. This goes on until the coming of Christ, which everything to an end; here it appears almost as if the very appearance of Christ brings about the destruction. From the very start, then, this passage positions itself elsewhere than either of the two ancient texts: bearing some connections with each but adding entirely new elements, this revelation forges yet another understanding of the Millennium.

Also unique to this passage is the heavy emphasis on the apostles. "For the hour is nigh, and that which was spoken by mine apostles must be fulfilled; for as they spoke so shall it come to pass;" (*D&C 29:10*), so that all that is here said will be to the fulfillment of what the apostles said. Still more, the apostles themselves are a part of the drama: the moment of the arrival of Christ and the legions of angels, here described, Is the moment when the apostles will, exalted, level judgment on the house of Israel—Israel here defined, it seems, as those who have loved the Lord. Accordingly, the coming of Christ is here associated with a massive resurrection, something not unlike what in the Book of Revelation is described as the first resurrection, the resurrection of the faithful. Nevertheless, whereas those resurrected in the Book of Revelation seem to be specifically the Christian martyrs, here they are all the faithful making up Israel. Therefore, while yet again there seem to be some echoes here of other passages dealing with the Millennium, there are unmistakably new elements as well.

The language of the words of the Lord, concerning the introduction of the Millennium to the Saints, frames a distinctly third take on the Millennium. D&C 29 presents it as a time when all the faithful will be resurrected to dwell with Christ, who has come with the heavenly hosts in order to bring an end to wickedness on the earth, and who has thus established the possibility of a judgment of Israel undertaken by the original Twelve.

The other substantial revelation dealing with the Millennium, came a year and half-later (early in 1832). It came, curiously, in the form of a question-and-answer session regarding the Book of Revelation. Here is the text:

Q. What are we to understand by the sounding of the trumpets, mentioned in the 8th chapter of Revelation?

A. "We are to understand that as God made the world in six days, and on the seventh day he finished his work, and sanctified it, and also formed man out of the dust of the earth, even so, in the beginning of the seventh thousand years will the Lord God sanctify the earth, and complete the salvation of man, and judge all things, and shall redeem all things, except that which he hath not put into his power, when he shall have sealed all things, unto the end of all things; and the sounding of the trumpets of the seven angels are the preparing and finishing of his work, in the beginning of the seventh thousand years—the preparing of the way before the time of his coming" (D&C 77:12).

Here, as with every other passage on the Millennium, the emphasis is on the moment of its beginning, of how it is launched and with what aim. Here again, an entirely distinct picture is presented. The vision of things provided here is quite general, indeed so general there is no mention of Christs coming. Something, though differently characterized, featured prominently in each of the other passages. The emphasis here is first on the parallel between the Millennium and the seventh day of creation, and then on exactly what that implies about the overarching purposes and aims of the Millennium. In addition, what are they? "To sanctify the earth, and complete the salvation of man, and judge all things, and . . . redeem all things" (D&C 77:12). Note, the sanctification of the earth might echo the Book of Moses, or the judgment of all things might echo D&C 29, but the rest of this is new. What is meant by the completion of man's salvation? In addition, what is meant by the redemption of all things? Perhaps still more perplexing, what does it mean when the passage goes on to say, all things are limited to what God has put into Christ's power? What has putting into Christ's power to do with the sealing of all things?

Clearly, this passage is doing its own thing, and so rather than finding here a kind of synthesis of the other approaches to the Millennium, There is a distinctly fourth understanding. Arguably, in the end, there is more emphasis here on what precedes the Millennium than on the Millennium and its inauguration. The sealing of all things means whatever; it clearly is associated with the angels who undertake the preparing and finishing of his work. In these last stages, Joseph clearly would have associated this with the last dispensation and his own work. Here, then, the Millennium seems to be something like the capstone laid on the latter-day work, a finishing off of what is undertaken in the last days. Put another way, this passage almost serves to turn the Saints from any obsession with what is to come from verse 29, focusing them on the work they have to do in preparation for what is to come: The Saints are to get to work on the preparations, the work of sealing up everything until the end.

It is worth saying; the D&C, between these two passages discussed, and reproduces the tension between Enoch and John. D&C 29 presents a kind of premillennialist vision of things: The Christ is to come rather suddenly to destroy the wicked and to introduce a massive resurrection and judgment. D&C 77, on the other hand, presents a kind of postmillennialist vision: where the coming of Christ is not even mentioned, and the emphasis is clearly on the work needed to be finished, the Millennium's dawn marking the finishing off what had already been going on. Here again, it seems, the Saints are summoned to occupy the space between the traditional pre- and postmillennialist understandings of things.

Because of the destruction of the wicked at the Savior's Second Coming, only righteous people will live on the earth at the beginning of the Millennium. They will be those who have lived virtuous and honest lives. These people will inherit either the Terrestrial or the Celestial kingdom.

Previous texts have been looking at the Millennium mostly from a scriptural point of view but there are some things, latter day Prophets can almost clarify the subject, so let us cover some of them.

During the Millennium, mortals will still live on earth, and they will continue to have children as is done now (D&C 45:58). Joseph Smith said immortal beings would frequently visit the earth. These resurrected beings will help with the government and other work. (Teachings of the Prophet Joseph Smith, sel. Joseph Fielding Smith [1976], 268)

People will still have their agency, and for a time many will be free to continue with their religions and ideas. Eventually everyone will confess Jesus Christ is the Savior.

During the Millennium, Jesus will "reign personally upon the earth" (Articles of Faith 1:10). Joseph Smith explained, Jesus will "reign over the Saints and come down and instruct" (Teachings of Presidents of the Church: Joseph Smith, 258).

There will be two great works for members of the Church during the Millennium: temple work and missionary work. Temple work involves the ordinances necessary for exaltation. These include baptism, the laying on of hands for the gift of the Holy Ghost, and the temple ordinances—the endowment, temple marriage, and the sealing together of family units.

Many people have died without receiving these ordinances. People on the earth must perform these ordinances for them. This work is now being done in the temples of the Lord. There is too much work to finish before the Millennium begins, so it will be completed during this time. Resurrected beings will help correct the mistakes made while doing research concerning dead ancestors. They will also help find the information needed to complete their records. (See Joseph Fielding Smith, Doctrines of Salvation, comp. Bruce R. McConkie, 3 vols. 2:167, 251–52.)

The other great work during the Millennium will be missionary work. The gospel will be taught with great power to all people. Eventually there will be no need to teach others the first principles of the gospel because "they shall all know me, from the least of them unto the greatest of them, saith the Lord" (*Jeremiah 31:34*).

    a. How can people prepare now for work in the Millennium?

    b. In what ways will life during the Millennium be different from life on the earth now?

The Prophet Joseph Smith taught, during the Millennium, "the earth will be renewed and receive its paradisiacal glory" (Articles of Faith 1:10).

During the Millennium, Satan will be bound. This means he will not have power to tempt those who are living at this time (*see D&C 101:28*). The "children shall grow up without sin unto salvation" (*D&C 45:58*). "Because of the righteousness of [the Lord's] people, Satan has no power; wherefore, he cannot be loosed for the space of many years; for he hath no power over the hearts of the people, for they dwell in righteousness, and the Holy One of Israel reigned" (*1 Nephi 22:26*).

Peace on the Earth

During the Millennium, there will be no war. People will live in peace and harmony together. Things used for war will be turned to useful purposes. "They shall beat their swords into plowshares, and their spears into pruning hooks: nation shall not lift up sword against nation, neither shall they learn war any more" (*Isaiah 2:4; see also Isaiah 11:6–7; D&C 101:26*).

Righteous Government

President John Taylor taught: "The Lord will be king over all the earth, and all mankind literally under his sovereignty, and every nation under the heavens will have to acknowledge his authority, and bow to his scepter. Those who serve him in righteousness will have communications with God, with Jesus, will have the ministering of angels, and will know the past, the present, and the future; and other people, who may not yield full obedience to his laws, nor be fully instructed in his covenants, will, nevertheless, have to yield full obedience to his government. For it will be the reign of God upon the earth, and He will enforce His laws, and command obedience from the nations of the world which is legitimately his right" (Teachings of Presidents of the Church: John Taylor [2001], 225).

No Death

During the Millennium, there will be no death, as experienced in mortality. When people have lived to an old age, they will not die and be buried. Instead, they will be changed from their mortal condition to an immortal condition in "the twinkling of an eye." (*D&C 63:51; 101:29–31*)

All Things Revealed

Many things have not been revealed to us. All things will be revealed during the Millennium. The Lord said He will "reveal all things—things which have passed, and hidden things which no man knew, things of the earth, by which it was made, and the purpose and the end thereof—things most precious, things that are above, and things that are beneath, things that are in the earth, and upon the earth, and in heaven" (*D&C 101:32–34*).

Other Millennial Activities

In many ways, life will be much as it is now, except everything will be done in righteousness. People will eat and drink and will wear clothing. (Teachings of Presidents of the Church: Brigham Young, 333) People will continue to plant and harvest crops and build houses (Isaiah 65:21).
At the end of the 1,000 years, Satan will be set free for a short time. Some people will turn away from Heavenly Father. Satan will gather his armies, and Michael (Adam) will gather the hosts of heaven. In this great struggle, Satan and his followers will be cast out forever. The earth will be changed into a celestial kingdom. (*D&C 29:22–29; 88:17–20, 110–15*)
Additional scriptures
    a. Zechariah 14:4–9; 1 Nephi 22:24–25 (Jesus to reign on earth)
    b. Daniel 7:27 (Saints to be given the kingdom)
    c. D&C 88:87–110 (conditions during the Millennium)
    d. 1 Nephi 22:26 (Satan to be bound)
    e. D&C 101:22–31 (enmity to cease; no death; Satan to have no power to tempt)
    f. Isaiah 11:1–9 (wolf and lamb to dwell together)
    g. D&C 43:31; Revelation 20:7–10 (Satan loosed for a little season)

However, let me step back from all this work on texts to say a few things by way of general reflection.

A Few Concluding Thoughts.

What has been presented here is a minimalistic view of the doctrine of the Millennium. It should be noted, the scriptures (ancient and modern) present a rather sketchy uneven picture of the Millennium. Only a few times does it even surface as a topic in scriptures, and each time it does it is presented with a drastically distinct emphasis and focus. Not even an emphasis on the coming of Christ can be said to be constant among the relevant passages. Each looks at the event in a different way. Other than a few brief references, nowhere in any of these scriptures is there any focus or detailed explanation on what takes place during the Millennium, only on its inauguration. One thing, though, is constant: the emphasis is always on the very moment in time when the Millennium begins. What is unique about each passage is the distinct way it understands and presents the significance of a radical break in the thing called TIME. Each passage attempts to make sense of the Millennium's dawn, apparently because the dawn of the Millennium is a kind of rupture of time as it is currently experienced, Most believe these scriptures represent the end of time, albeit very little is known about what TIME really is. To understand the reasoning behind this belief, refer to (D&C 43: "with crowns upon their heads, in glory even as I am, to judge the whole house of Israel". (Revelations 20: "And I saw thrones, and they sat upon them, and judgment was given unto them", seem to imply the final judgement has begun. To further explain, it is known, when the final judgement happens it is a demarcation point in the Plan of Salvation; the period of testing is complete, the time for repentance is over, in other words TIME, as explained by Alma, is no longer relevant. D&C 84; 100 is referring to the binding of Satan and time is no longer. D&C88; 109-10 is also referring to the binding of Satan during the millennium and saying, there shall be time no longer. People will have to decide on this for themselves. However, all in all this gives people something to theological reflect on rather than all this speculation about the details. The main focus should be on the way the Millennium, as such, affects time and what a rupture of time implies about the way mortals should experience the use their time right now. Enoch experiences time as a time to identify with the suffering earth, anticipating redemption. John experiences time as a time to endure intense suffering, persecution, and catastrophe, anticipating an exalted respite. The early Saints experience time as a time of waiting for the fulfillment of promises made anciently, anticipating the redemption of the faithful. Joseph experiences time as a time of undertaking the preparatory work the Millennium serves to complete, and anticipating the arrival of those who can complete it. Perhaps what is to be learned from these scriptures, concerning the Millennium, is time will end and the opportunities afforded to mankind by this grace of time will end. Is the personal use of time dedicated to following the way of the Lord, or is personal time spent in selfish pursuits?

New and Everlasting Covenant

A great key to understanding the New and Everlasting Covenant and the reason it was restored is given in the first section of the D&C. "For they have strayed from mine ordinances, and have broken mine everlasting covenant; They seek not the Lord to establish his righteousness, but every man walketh in his own way, and after the image of his own God, whose image is in the likeness of the world, and whose substance is that of an idol, which waxeth old and shall perish in Babylon, even Babylon the great, which shall fall, wherefore, the weak things of the world shall come forth and break down the mighty and strong ones, that man should not counsel his fellow man, neither trust in the arm of flesh- but that ever man might speak in the name of the Lord, even the Savior of the world; That faith also might increase in the earth; that mine everlasting covenant might be established" (*D&C 1:15-22*).

Similar words are used in the old and new testaments: "... Behold, the days come, saith the Lord, when I will make a new covenant with the house of Israel and with the house of Judah: Not according to the covenant that I made with their fathers in the day when I took them by the hand to lead them out of the land of Egypt (the carnal Law of Moses); because they continued not in my covenant, and I regarded them not, saith the Lord. For this is the covenant that I will make with the house of Israel after those days, saith the Lord; I will put my laws into their mind, and write them in their hearts: and I will be to them a God, and they shall be my people: and they shall not teach every man his neighbor, and every man his brother, saying, knowing the Lord: for all shall know Me, from the least to the greatest. For I will be merciful to their unrighteousness, and their sins and their iniquities will I remember no more. In that he saith, a new covenant, he hath made the first old. Now that which decayeth and waxeth old is ready to vanish away" (*Hebrews 8:8-13*).

The fullness of the gospel of Jesus Christ, The New and Everlasting Covenant, is discussed in D&C 66: 2. It is new every time it is revealed anew following a period of apostasy. It is everlasting in the sense it is God's covenant and has been enjoyed in every gospel dispensation where people have been willing to receive it and the promises made therein are everlasting. Jesus Christ revealed the new and everlasting covenant again to men on earth through the prophet Joseph Smith. It contains sacred ordinances administered by priesthood authority—such as baptism and temple marriage—that provide for man's salvation, immortality, and eternal life. When people accept the gospel and promise to keep God's commandments, God covenants to give them the blessings of his new and everlasting covenant. There are numerous scriptures related to this commandment,

"I will establish my covenant between me and you", (*Gen. 17: 7*). He shall have the covenant of an everlasting priesthood, (*Num. 25: 13*). "The people changed the ordinances and broke the everlasting covenant", (*Isa. 24: 5, D&C 1: 15*). "I will make an everlasting covenant with you", (*Isa. 55: 3, Jer. 32: 40*). "It shall be an everlasting covenant", (*Ezek. 37: 26*), "The Lord made a new covenant, and the old passed away", (*Heb. 8: 13*). "Jesus is the mediator of the new covenant", (*Heb. 12: 24, D&C 76: 69*). "This is a new and an everlasting covenant", (*D&C 22: 1*). "I have sent my everlasting covenant into the world", (*D&C 45: 9), (D&C 49: 9*). "The Lord sent the fullness of his gospel, his everlasting covenant", (*D&C 66: 2, D&C 133: 57*). "In order to obtain the highest degree in the celestial kingdom, a man must enter into the new and everlasting covenant of marriage", (*D&C 131: 1-2*). "The new and everlasting covenant was instituted for the fullness of the Lord's glory", (*D&C 132: 6, 19*). Joseph Fielding Smith taught:

"The new and everlasting covenant is the fullness of the gospel. It is composed of 'All covenants, contracts, bonds, obligations, oaths, vows, performances, connections, associations, or expectations' that are sealed upon members of the Church by the Holy Spirit of promise, or the Holy Ghost, by the authority of the President of the Church who holds the keys. . . Marriage for eternity is a new and everlasting covenant. Baptism is also a new and everlasting covenant, and likewise ordination to the Priesthood and every other covenant is everlasting and a part of the new and everlasting covenant which embraces all things" (*D&C, 132*).

Revelation given through Joseph Smith the Prophet, at Nauvoo, Illinois, recorded July 12, 1843, relating to the new and everlasting covenant, including the eternity of the marriage covenant D&C,1–6. Exaltation is gained through the new and everlasting covenant; D&C,7–14, The terms and conditions of this covenant are set forth; D&C,15–20, Celestial marriage and a continuation of the family unit enable men to become gods;

1 Verily, thus saith the Lord unto you my servant Joseph, that inasmuch as you have inquired of my hand to know and understand wherein I, the Lord, justified my servants Abraham, Isaac, and Jacob, as also Moses, David and Solomon, my servants, as touching the principle and doctrine of their having many wives and concubines—

2 Behold, and lo, I am the Lord thy God, and will answer thee as touching this matter.

3 Therefore, prepare thy heart to receive and obey the instructions which I am about to give unto you; for all those who have this law revealed unto them must obey the same.

4 For behold, I reveal unto you a new and an everlasting covenant; and if ye abide not that covenant, then are ye damned; for no one can reject this covenant and be permitted to enter into my glory.

5 For all who will have a blessing at my hands shall abide the law which was appointed for that blessing, and the conditions thereof, as were instituted from before the foundation of the world.

6 And as pertaining to the new and everlasting covenant, it was instituted for the fullness of my glory; and he that receiveth a fullness thereof must and shall abide the law, or he shall be damned, saith the Lord God.

7 And verily I say unto you, that the conditions of this law are these: All covenants, contracts, bonds, obligations, oaths, vows, performances, connections, associations, or expectations, that are not made and entered into and sealed by the Holy Spirit of promise, of him who is anointed, both as well for time and for all eternity, and that too most holy, by revelation and commandment through the medium of mine anointed, whom I have appointed on the earth to hold this power (and I have appointed unto my servant Joseph to hold this power in the last days, and there is never but one on the earth at a time on whom this power and the keys of this priesthood are conferred), are of no efficacy, virtue, or force in and after the resurrection from the dead; for all contracts that are not made unto this end have an end when men are dead.

8 Behold, mine house is a house of order, saith the Lord God, and not a house of confusion.

9 Will I accept of an offering, saith the Lord, that is not made in my name?

10 Or will I receive at your hands that which I have not?

11 And will I appoint unto you, saith the Lord, except it be by law, even as I and my Father ordained unto you, before the world was?

12 I am the Lord thy God; and I give unto you this commandment—that no man shall come unto the Father but by me or by my word, which is my law, saith the Lord.

13 And everything that is in the world, whether it be ordained of men, by thrones, or principalities, or powers, or things of name, whatsoever they may be, that are not by me or by my word, saith the Lord, shall be thrown down, and shall not remain after men are dead, neither in nor after the resurrection, saith the Lord your God.

14 For whatsoever things remain are by me; and whatsoever things are not by me shall be shaken and destroyed.

15 Therefore, if a man marry him a wife in the world, and he marry her not by me nor by my word, and he covenant with her so long as he is in the world and she with him, their covenant and marriage are not of force when they are dead, and when they are out of the world; therefore, they are not bound by any law when they are out of the world.

16 Therefore, when they are out of the world they neither marry nor are given in marriage; but are appointed angels in heaven, which angels are ministering servants, to minister for those who are worthy of a far more, and an exceeding, and an eternal weight of glory.

17 For these angels did not abide my law; therefore, they cannot be enlarged, but remain separately and singly, without exaltation, in their saved condition, to all eternity; and from henceforth are not gods, but are angels of God forever and ever.

18 And again, verily I say unto you, if a man marry a wife, and make a covenant with her for time and for all eternity, if that covenant is not by me or by my word, which is my law, and is not sealed by the Holy Spirit of promise, through him whom I have anointed and appointed unto this power, then it is not valid neither of force when they are out of the world, because

they are not joined by me, saith the Lord, neither by my word; when they are out of the world it cannot be received there, because the angels and the gods are appointed there, by whom they cannot pass; they cannot, therefore, inherit my glory; for my house is a house of order, saith the Lord God.

19 And again, verily I say unto you, if a man marry a wife by my word, which is my law, and by the new and everlasting covenant, and it is sealed unto them by the Holy Spirit of promise, by him who is anointed, unto whom I have appointed this power and the keys of this priesthood; and it shall be said unto them—Ye shall come forth in the first resurrection; and if it be after the first resurrection, in the next resurrection; and shall inherit thrones, kingdoms, principalities, and powers, dominions, all heights and depths—then shall it be written in the Lamb's Book of Life, that he shall commit no murder whereby to shed innocent blood, and if ye abide in my covenant, and commit no murder whereby to shed innocent blood, it shall be done unto them in all things whatsoever my servant hath put upon them, in time, and through all eternity; and shall be of full force when they are out of the world; and they shall pass by the angels, and the gods, which are set there, to their exaltation and glory in all things, as hath been sealed upon their heads, which glory shall be a fulness and a continuation of the seeds forever and ever.

20 Then shall they be gods, because they have no end; therefore, shall they be from everlasting to everlasting, because they continue; then shall they be above all, because all things are subject unto them. Then shall they be gods, because they have all power, and the angels are subject unto them.
21 Verily, verily, I say unto you, except ye abide my law ye cannot attain to this glory.

There is not very much that can be added to this discussion since these scriptures cover it all.

Obedience and Atonement

When religion is boiled down to the very basics, it is clear, in all the God based faiths in the world today there is a common objective that runs through each and every one of them, and through their tenets, doctrine, scriptures. The clerics, through their teachings, are endeavoring to help individuals in their congregations change their behavior so their character will be more closely aligned with the will of their God. To be sure, there are numerous religions, each with different Gods and different viewpoints on what correct behavior is and just as many opposing theories on where or how they came by these particular convictions. In the three Abrahamic religions, Islam, Judaism, and Christianity, God is the source of all doctrine, which guides human behavior. These religions believe God has given laws to structure behavior in a certain way and if all submit to his will, God will reward them, if they do not, He will not. Make no mistake about it, God gave out His Laws to be obeyed, and if any offend them, they fall into the hands of this His eternal justice, and so must suffer under His wrath. Even though His wrath will be merciful and just, it is still His wrath. Boiling down Christianity a little further, it is found, this behavior, which is pleasing to God, is represented by two actions and they are, obedience and service. This is known because of two laws or commandments found in Luke.

25" And, behold, a certain lawyer stood up, and tempted him, saying, Master, what, shall I do to inherit eternal life?
26 He said unto him, what is written in the law? How readest thou?
27 And he answering said, thou shalt love the Lord thy God with all thy heart, and with all thy soul, and with all thy strength, and with all thy mind; and thy Neighbor as thyself.
28 And He said unto him, thou hast answered right: this do, and thou shalt live" (*Luke 10: 25-28*).

What is gleaned from this scripture is, mortals must love God completely, but how can mortals demonstrate their love of God, since nothing in this mortal structure is of any use to God? The only way known, is through obedience to His laws, after all, this is how children express their love of their parents. In addition, service is the only way people can show their neighbors they care for them. The text above has already talked about the problems of disobedience and the problems therein, but it is necessary to understand that all mortals have been disobedient in some way at one time or another. As descendants of Adam and Eve, all people inherit, not the sins of the fall, but the effects of the fall. In this fallen state, all mortals are subject to opposition and temptation. When giving into temptation, mortals alienate themselves from God, and if they continue in sin, they experience spiritual death, and thus, separated from His presence. The only way for them to be saved is for someone else to rescue them. In their mortal state, mortals are not, and cannot ever be on a righteous par with God, and since mortality is such a short period, it is impossible to acquire sufficient virtuous qualities, which would enable anyone to have equivalence with God, therefore mortals cannot save themselves. What is needed is a Savior who can satisfy the demands of justice—standing in a person's place to assume the burden of the fall and to pay the price for the sins committed. In these three Abrahamic religions only Judaism and Christianity believe in the concept of a Savior. The Savior of the Jews is a Messiah believed to come sometime in the future, but Christians believe that Jesus is the Savior of the world. The Mormon religion teaches Jesus Christ has always been the only one capable of making such a sacrifice, an atonement.

"Atonement" as used in the scriptures means to stand place of another and suffer the penalty for his or her sins, thereby removing the effects of sin from the repentant sinner and allowing him or her to be reconciled to God. Those who fully repent and obey His gospel will receive the gift of eternal life with God. The spiritual act of atonement and indeed all spiritual acts are hard for a mortal understand or to visualize. For instance, the judgment, which is totally a spiritual circumstance, is perceived by some as a great courtroom in Heaven where they must stand at the bar, with shameful posture, and answer for their sins to an angry judge sitting above them. While others see it as a walk in the park, with the Savior's arm around them, where He tells them their sins are forgiven. It seems, humans need these visual images to facilitate understanding, but the fallacy in doing so is they are trying to visual a spiritual circumstance within a mortal framework, which is all they are capable of understanding. It must be realized, all spiritual things, which include prayers and the answering thereof, giving of blessings, all ordinances (the sacrament, baptism and temple and so on) are of a vicarious nature. Why is this so? Because God and all others involved in giving of blessing are spiritual and cannot act directly upon a mortal but can only act in a vicarious way, which is, acting through the spirit of a person (sometimes referred to as the "soul").

All the concepts mentioned above are not only of a vicarious nature but for the most part pertain to the spiritual person living inside the mortal framework. When a prayer is answered the answer is given vicariously, meaning, the blessing comes from a spiritual God to the Holy Ghost, who is spiritual, and then from the Holy Ghost to the spirit, wherein, and then the mortal being, benefits. (Pay attention to the wording of the last sentence). If a person can grasp the concept of prayer and understand the vicariousness of it then it is a small step mentally to understand how all blessings work. D&C 130: 21 teaches, blessings are obtained on the condition of obedience to the law the blessing is predicated on. Therefore, the mortal is the one who is either obedient or disobedient but the blessing is given to the spirit. How does this work? The spirit receiving the blessing must be clean in the eyes of the Lord in order to receive. If the Mortal is disobedient, he is damaging his soul, making the spirit unclean and therefore the blessing giver cannot attend the soul, thus, no blessing. The mortal then repents which is the act of repairing the damaged soul, and then blessings can flow. Now move to the Atonement--- If the mortal is disobedient he is damaging his soul and therefore the Atonement giver cannot attend the soul, thus, no atonement. The mortal then repents which is the act that repairing the damaged soul, now the atonement can take place. Even then, the atonement can only cover the sins where repentance is complete. Therefore, it is vicarious both ways. Remember ---all spiritual things have a vicarious essence---sin and all.

To be in a position to fully participate in the atonement a person's behavior and the ability to fully repent requires a very high level of commitment regarding obedience to the commandments, while membership in the church requires a lessor level of commitment. This can be illustrated by the story of the chicken and the pig. The chicken and the pig were in the barnyard discussing the contributions each of them was making to the farmer's breakfast table. The hen bemoaned having to donate her eggs for breakfast. The pig replied, yes, but for you, it is just a small sacrifice. For me, it's a total commitment!"
This anecdote contains some obvious lessons for members of the church. Having read the story of the pig and the chicken, members might ask themselves:

1- Will God be satisfied with the kind of member who feels, giving an occasional egg or two toward the effort of salvation is adequate?

2- Will God be satisfied with those who consecrate their all to God's cause and wish to receive all He has to offer?

In conclusion, always, always remember the chicken and the pig. The church today requires members to give up a small portion of their earnings, a little of their time on Sunday for services and occasionally some time for a calling. Members are ask to be the chicken but if anyone of them is serious about participating in the atonement, the individual must take every opportunity, on their own, to increase their commitment to the Lord and become the pig.

The PATRIARCHAL ORDER of the PRIESTHOOD
(The third priesthood)

Just before the temple was finished in Nauvoo Ill., the Prophet Joseph Smith said to a group of members the following, "The third Priesthood is Patriarchal authority. Go to and finish the temple, and God will fill it with power, and you will then receive more knowledge concerning this priesthood" *(Joseph Smith, Teachings of the Prophet, Section Six 1843B 44, p.323)*. Later he again referred to this same higher priesthood; "There are three grand orders of priesthood referred to in the Epistle to the Hebrews, the Melchizedek, the Patriarchal, and the Aaronic" *(TPJS, p. 322-23; HC 5:554-55)*. In the Doctrine and Covenants he recorded this revelation concerning this highest order of the priesthood: "Fullness of the priesthood, which is the highest order of priesthood, is attained only through an eternal union of male and female, sanctified by the sealing ordinances in a temple of the Lord and ratified by the Holy Spirit of promise" *(D&C 132:18-19)*.

A good many members of the church have absolutely no knowledge of this priesthood order nor have they ever heard anything about it. So what is the essence of this priesthood and what is known about it? While this Priesthood is unquestionably connected the temple experience, as many things in this religion are, this is not a discussion of any specific ordinances of the temple or anything concerning the temple, considered sacred or holy. Those who qualify for this Priesthood will be in an "ordered" or organized as sons, daughters, fathers, and mothers in the eternal family (this is explained later) made possible by Christ, and the Priesthood will be held and exercised in this family structure, which will be very different from the "church government" structure present today. Today, as members live their lives in the church they can get a small taste for the ordering of this Priesthood in the eternal realm by their participation in the temple and in the structure and workings of families and homes.

It is important, at the beginning of this discussion to clarify the difference between the spiritual patriarchal order mentioned by the Prophet Joseph Smith, called the Patriarchal Order and the temporal or social patriarchal order mentioned in the Old Testament, where both called by the same name. This spiritual patriarchal order, correctly known as "The Patriarchal Order of the Priesthood" refers to the order of the eternal family in the eternal realm. The temporal or social patriarchal order was practiced during the early times in the bible and we read about this practice in Abraham through Ephraim, a time referred to as *the time of the patriarchs*. During this time in biblical history, the patriarchal order was not the

Patriarchal Priesthood Order but a temporal order, which influenced the social intercourse dealing with family's economic wealth and the duties of the first-born male child in the family and his inheritance and birthright. These rights and conventions were followed by all families, regardless of whether the family members themselves held any priesthood authority but patterned after the religious orders of the day. During these times there was not a centralized organization of the church, as is known it today, so the Priesthood itself, both Aaronic and Melchizedek, was passed down through the family from father to son, as was the inheritance and birthright. It is easy to confuse the two, since both orders, with the same name, were passed down through the family and oft times there is not any distinction or clarification given in the scriptural text.

Now that this is cleared up, and while discussing the Patriarchal Order of the Priesthood. it will be helpful to start by comparing and/or contrasting all three of the priesthood orders in order to gain a fuller understanding of how they operate and their similarities. There are similarities between the Aaronic Priesthood and the Melchizedek Priesthood orders, such as, how they are obtained. Those with the proper authority conferred the priesthood upon a person then ordained them to an office. It does not appear the Patriarchal Priesthood is conferred upon a person in this manner, but the patriarchal priesthood is an order of the priesthood received through completion of the process called the new and everlasting covenant and, of course, this all happens starting with baptism and reaches its conclusion with the ordinances in the temple. By way of comparison then, the Aaronic Priesthood and Melchizedek Priesthood are both conferred only upon men by the laying on of hands but the Patriarchal Priesthood is conferred upon a man and his wife jointly when they are sealed in the temple for time and all eternity. There are no quorums in the Patriarchal Priesthood but there are only families. There are some striking similarities between the functions of the quorum and the family (more about this later).

The Aaronic and Melchizedek Priesthoods held only by male members of the church while functioning in the administrative structure of church government. The Patriarchal Order of the Priesthood does not offer the holders any administrative responsibilities in the church. Women do not hold the Aaronic Priesthood or the Melchizedek Priesthood in the Church, but they do hold the Patriarchal Priesthood in the family in eternity. "The ordinances of the temple are distinctly of priesthood character, yet women have access to all of them, and the highest blessings of the temple are conferred only upon a man and his wife jointly". (*John A. Widtsoe Program of the Church 1938 page 81*) We often hear the phrase Priest or Priestess used in connection with eternal rewards and obligations. When members hear these words, it is important to know, no person can be a Priest or Priestess in the eyes of God without holding some form of priesthood ordained by God.

Remember, when the eternal family is mentioned in the scriptures it is referring to the time when people and, possibly, the members of their earthly family are adopted into the family of Abraham, which is the family of Christ. The word possibly is used in this context, because the eternal family is organized or ordered in a very different manner than an earthly family. The organizing or ordering of eternal families is not fully understood at this time; however, it is believed; participation in an earthly family is God's way of preparing His children for their role in an eternal family. It is not known if the uniqueness of an earthly family will, or even can, represent the needs of an eternal family since the eternal family, is organized in a spiritual manner around the family of Christ. With the completion of the ordinances of the new and everlasting covenant, individuals are adopted into the family of Abraham, whether as a couple or individually are also unknown. This is the first glimpse of an eternal family. This entire issue of The Patriarchal Order of the Priesthood revolves around, the Abrahamic Covenant, the Priesthood and family of Christ, participation in the New and Everlasting Covenant, and the ability to obtain salvation through obedience to the Devine Laws of God.

In order to tie all of this together, an understanding, of the Abrahamic Covenant, and how it came about is needed. Abraham first received the gospel by baptism, which is the Covenant of Salvation; then he had conferred upon him the higher priesthood, and he entered into celestial marriage, which is the Covenant of Exaltation, gaining assurance, thereby, of having eternal increase. This was, of course, after marrying Sarah and learning of his lineal right to the Patriarchal Order of the Priesthood as disclosed in the Records of the Fathers (Abr. 1:2-4, 26, 31;2:2; Jubilees 12:27; cf. D&C 107:40-57), Abraham traveled to Haran, where he apparently received his ordination (Abr. 2:9-11; WJS, pp. 245, 303). Finally, he received the promise that all of these blessings would be offered to all of his mortal posterity. (Abraham 2:6-11; D&C 132:29-50). Included in these divine promises to Abraham, was the assurance that, Christ would come through his lineage, and the assurance, his posterity would receive certain choice, promised lands as an eternal inheritance. (Abraham 2; Gen, 17; 22:15-18; Galatians 3). All of these promises lumped together are called the Abrahamic Covenant. This covenant was renewed with his son, Isaac (Gen. 24:60; 26:1-4, 24) and again with his grandson, Jacob. (Gen. 28; 35:9-13; 48:3-4). Those portions of it, which pertain to personal exaltation and eternal increase, are renewed with each member of the house of Israel who enters the order of celestial marriage. Through this order, the participating parties become inheritors of all the blessings of Abraham, Isaac, and Jacob. (D&C 132; Romans. 9:4; Galatians 3; 4, Bruce R. McConkie, Mormon Doctrine, pg. 13) This Abrahamic Covenant or the promise thereof, was also renewed with Joseph Smith "For whoso is faithful unto the obtaining these two priesthoods of which I have spoken, and the magnifying their calling, are sanctified by the Spirit unto the renewing of their bodies. They become the sons of Moses and of Aaron and the seed of Abraham, and the church and kingdom, and the elect of God" (*D&C 84: 33&34*). Here it is explained, certain people can become airs to the seed of Abraham and inherit the highest kingdom, even though they have not yet received the Patriarchal Order of the Priesthood. D&C 131 explains how this accomplished. "In the celestial glory there are three heavens or degrees; and in order to obtain the highest, a man must enter into this order of the priesthood [meaning the new and everlasting covenant of marriage]; and if he does not, he cannot obtain it. He may enter into the other, but that is the end of his kingdom; he cannot have an increase." (*D & C 131:1-4*).

Couples enter into the Patriarchal Priesthood Order when they get married in the temple, which a man shares with his wife, but neither have any governing position in the Church, only over their own family. The Patriarchal Priesthood is given only to a man and his wife and it is inexorability intertwined with the family in eternity. Remember Joseph Smith said, all priesthood is Melchizedek, but there are different degrees or orders of it. The Patriarchal Priesthood Order, man and woman enter into when sealed in the temple, is part of the Melchizedek Priesthood. It is an order within the Melchizedek Priesthood. The Patriarchal Order of the Priesthood is the fullness of the Melchizedek Priesthood. Joseph Smith said, "Those who receive the fullness of the priesthood are Kings and Priests...." (*Joseph Smith Documentary History of the Church Vol. 5 page 555*).

Upon completion of the temple ordinances, a man and a woman also receive a calling or it might said they hold the office of husband and wife in the Patriarchal Priesthood. Again, the order or organization of these higher callings is different from the structure and nature of contemporary callings of which members are familiar. They eventually will also become Father and Mother. It is interesting; God Himself, is referred to by His highest priesthood office as Father.

The Aaronic and Melchizedek Priesthoods are organized by quorum, in the Church, in mortality. The Patriarchal Priesthood is organized by family, in the home, in eternity. In the Mormon Church today, members do not specifically refer to callings in the Patriarchal Priesthood by any scriptural specific name. It is interesting to note, each one of the offices or callings related to the Patriarchal Priesthood is for both a man and a woman and is referred to in the following manner: Husband/Wife - Father/Mother - Priest/Priestess - Patriarch/Matriarch - King/Queen - God/Goddess.

When couples are married in the temple they have the power of eternal lives (yes lives) sealed upon them. This concept is pointed out in the following scripture.

"And again, verily I say unto you, if a man marry a wife by my word, which is my law, and by the new and everlasting covenant, and it is sealed unto them by the Holy Spirit of promise by him who is anointed, unto whom I have appointed this power and the keys of this priesthood; and it shall be said unto them - Ye shall come forth in the first resurrection; and if it be after the first resurrection, in the next resurrection; and shall inherit thrones, kingdoms, principalities, and powers, dominions, all heights and depths - then shall it be written in the Lamb's Book of Life, that he shall commit no murder whereby to shed innocent blood, and if ye abide in my covenant, and commit no murder whereby to shed innocent blood, it shall be done unto them in all things whatsoever my servant hath put upon them, in time, and through all eternity; and shall be of full force when they are out of the world; and they shall pass by the angels, and the gods, which are set there, to their exaltation and glory in all things, as hath been sealed upon their heads, which glory shall be a fullness, and a continuation of the seeds. Then shall they be gods, because they have no end; therefore, shall they be from everlasting to everlasting, because they continue; then shall they be above all, because all things are subject unto them. Then shall they be gods, because they have all power, and the angels are subject unto them. Verily, verily, I say unto you, except ye abide my law ye cannot attain to this glory. For strait is the gate, and narrow the way that leadeth unto the exaltation and continuation of the lives, and few there be that find it, because ye receive me not in the world neither do ye know me. But if ye receive me in the world, then shall ye know me, and shall receive your exaltation; that where I am ye shall be also. This is eternal lives - to know the only wise and true God, and Jesus Christ, whom he hath sent. I am he. Receive ye, therefore, my law" (D & C 132:19-25).

"We have not the power in the flesh to create and bring forth or produce a spirit; but we have the power to produce a temporal body; the germ of this, God has placed within us. And when our spirits receive our bodies, and through our faithfulness we are worthy to be crowned, we will then receive authority to produce both spirit and body. But these keys we cannot receive in the flesh...."(*Discourses of Brigham Young page 398*).

When couples, who are sealed, have children, these children are born in the covenant of their family. Being born in the covenant brings a special blessing of a promise of eternal parents to the child. regardless of the worthiness of their mortal parents before or after the child's birth.

A family in eternity is similar in this sense to a family quorum in the Church today. When a child is born in the covenant, the child becomes a quorum member of the family into which he or she was born. Similarly, when any person in the Church changes their residence, they just change quorums. They do not have to be re-ordained or have any new office or have any new priesthood conferred upon them. In this same since, God's children do the same thing when they move from their earthly family to their celestial family. Once they are born in the covenant or are sealed, whom the parents are does not affect them. If a parent becomes wicked and for some reason breaks up the family and the mother marries another man, even in the temple, the children just change families with her. They are not resealed into their mother's new family. It is just as if a priesthood holder changes quorums in the church he just changes quorums. The child does not need any further sealing or ordinance work; they are already born in the covenant. It is the same for members of the patriarchal priesthood order and the families they belong to, nothing is given to or take away from the priesthood order if a change is made, and they just change families. "They require no rite of adoption or sealing to insure them place in the posterity of promise" (*James E. Talmage 1977*). If the natural parents are wicked and cannot be parents in eternity, then the child will receive parents who are worthy, but does not need to be resealed to them. The child becomes a member of the new family just by joining their family as it was with the quorum change.

Patriarchal Priesthood is Melchizedek Priesthood but is organized by family and within the priesthood realm; this family priesthood has new powers, not privileged of those holding only a priesthood organized by quorum. Herein lies the power of eternal lives or the eternal power of procreation. Looking at life from the eternal perspective, it seems a miracle. Godhood is the greatest gift Father in Heaven has for us. In addition, in his wisdom, He has reserved procreation in eternity for those who have received the highest order of the Celestial Kingdom only; all others are denied this great gift and are servants or angels. Yet in his divine wisdom, He has allowed His spirit children to come here to this earth to receive a body and then empowered then with the knowledge of procreation for a little season to practice, as it were, being a God to see how they perform. Moreover, one need not look around the world very far to see one thing - the highest and most sacred gift of God, procreation, is the single most abused of all of God's gifts. Is it any wonder he takes it away and reserves it only for Kings, Queens and Priests and Priestess in eternity?

Why should people pay so much attention to all this, because, the order of Heaven, which everyone is striving so hard to achieve, is patriarchal. The endowments are patriarchal in nature. The ordinances to make those who worthily participate as first born unto God, worthy to inherit all the Father hath, to be encircled about eternally in the arms of His love is patriarchal. It is those, in the Lord's ritual embrace receiving the fullness of the Patriarchal power, who receives the blessings of the Father, the covenant of Abraham the great Patriarch: The Priesthood, unfolded into His posterity, and receives His inheritance. When reading Abr. 2:9-11, this is what those scriptures are conveying to us.

Principle of Promise

A principle is defined, as a fundamental truth or proposition serving, as the foundation for a system of belief or behavior or for a chain of reasoning. A promise is a statement one will definitely do, give, or arrange something; undertake or declare, something will happen. When making a promise a person may only make promises about his own behavior. Additionally, the promisor cannot request anything in return since all constraints on the promisor are self-imposed, but if he does make demands, and then this ceases to be a promise but subsequently is the beginning of the negotiating process of a contract where both parties receive gain. In the world today a promise is viewed as something leading to an obligation, rather than promises being the traditional way of guiding behavior. When a person combines these two words, principle and promise, they come up with a concept out of the ordinary, unusual, unique, and even special. Instead of expecting performance out of obligation, here is a principle establishing a foundation for a system of behavior conjoined with a promise declaring, something will definitely happen because of that behavior. This system of guidance is found in The Church of Jesus Christ of Latter Day Saints today and once made aware of the concept it is replete all through the scriptures; God has been using it all along.

1. God has promised to supply every need. The Bible says "But my God shall supply all your need according to his riches in glory by Christ Jesus" (Philippians 4:19).

2. God has promised access to His grace, according to Romans 5:2.

3. God has promised His children will not be overtaken with temptation. I Corinthians 10:13.

4. God has promised victory over death. "For I delivered unto you first of all that which I also received, how that Christ died for our sins according to the scriptures, and that he was buried, and that he rose again the third day according to the scriptures (*I Corinthians 15:3,4*).

5. God has promised, all things work together for good to those who love and serve Him faithfully, Romans 8:28.

6. God has promised those who believe in Jesus, and are baptized for the forgiveness of sins will be saved. Mark 16:16 and Acts 2:38.

7. God has promised His people eternal life. John 10:27, 28.

Promise keeping is directly mandated by virtue, in particular, those of honesty and justice, (as well as charity in cases of purely gratuitous promises). "First, the truthful man, not the man who keeps faith in his agreements, i.e., in the things pertaining to justice or injustice (for this would belong to another excellence), but the man who in the matters in which nothing of this sort is at stake is true both in word and in life because his character is such. However, such a man would seem to be in fact equitable. For the man who loves truth, and is truthful where nothing is at stake, will still more be truthful where something is at stake; he will avoid falsehood as something base, seeing that he avoided it even for its own sake; and such a man is worthy of praise. He inclines rather to understate the truth for this seems in better taste because exaggerations are wearisome". (Nicomachean Ethics, iv. vii, 1127a-1127b)

The Roman Jurists like Cicero and Gaius developed this sort of view further, crucially conceiving of a specific moral duty to keep promises, and a specific (and for Cicero particularly Roman) virtue of fidelity to promises How is it, one comes to have a moral obligation to do what which they promise? The question is particularly difficult because promissory obligations differ from other sorts of moral obligations in a number of ways. Unlike typical moral duties, the duty not to harm for example, promissory obligations are not owed equally to everyone, but rather only, those who have received the promised. For this reason, promissory obligations are often categorized as special obligations owed to family and friends.

Principles

As far as historical research can disclose, the Church of Christ of Latter-day Saints is the only church currently using, or has ever used, principles as a gospel teaching method. While people understand this teaching method is in use, it seems, Principles of the Gospel are somewhat misunderstood by the rank and file members of the church. How many times have members witnessed another member of church discussing a scriptural excerpt or a point of doctrine and incorrectly calling it a principle of the gospel? Principles are defined as; "a foundation of facts put into place for the purpose of learning" (*Bible Dictionary*), they are the basis of all scriptures, doctrine, and commandments. All principles are found within the scriptural text, both ancient and modern, including the voice of modern day prophets. Finding and recognizing these principles among the biblical text is often difficult since most, if not all, scriptures are comprised mostly of stories, events, parables, similitudes, and sayings. Never the less, all are given by God to his prophets in order to reveal the Gospel of Jesus Christ to mortal man, not given for the express purpose of revealing principles, although they are in there. These different means of presenting the gospel (stories etc.) came into being a result of the oral tradition, the custom for centuries and it continues to this very day. To be sure, in the various magazines published by the Mormon Church wherein the leadership of the church is revealing or reiterating the word of God to us, their orations are structured in the very same fashion as the scriptures, i.e. stories, events, parables, similitudes, and sayings. Also contained within these scriptural narratives, be they bibles, books, magazines or electronic media, is the Doctrine of Jesus Christ. Even though the Doctrine of Jesus Christ is noticeably different from the Gospel of Jesus Christ, the essence of all doctrine is derived from the same pages of scripture revealing the Gospel of Jesus Christ. The Doctrine of Jesus defines the Gospel of Jesus Christ in terms of personal behavior and the measure of personal behavior is predicated on the extent of obedience, to the commandments. Part of the Gospel of Jesus Christ includes the commandments and the Doctrine of Jesus Christ explains how members are to live them. Commandments, more correctly called "the Devine Laws of god", are also found in the scriptures and stand as the foundation of all doctrine. Here again, finding and recognizing how the biblical language defines a commandment is often difficult.

This rambling is probably as confusing as it can be, maybe clarity can be gained by analyzing a scripture in terms of, principles, doctrine, and commandments. In Matthew 5 Jesus is giving His disciples a lengthy lesson on His doctrine and in His Gospel. He is explaining to the disciples what their behavior should be as they live certain commandments, such as verses 27 & 28 where He instructs them about their behavior in living the commandment concerning adultery.

27 "Ye have heard that it was said by them of old time, thou shalt not commit adultery:

28 But I say unto you, that whosoever looketh on a woman to lust after her hath committed adultery with her already in his heart." This is the Doctrine of Jesus Christ.

In verses 27 and 28, Christ is talking about doctrine, which controls behavior. Just before this conversation for, instance, in verse 17 &18 He is enlightening His Disciples concerning His mission.

17 "Think not that I am come to destroy the law, or the prophets: I am not come to destroy, but to fulfil.

18 For verily I say unto you, till heaven and earth pass, one jot or one tittle shall in no wise pass from the law, till all be fulfilled". Within this text the Gospel of Jesus Christ and the Mission of Jesus Christ is laid out.

Next comes Matthew 5:48 "Be ye therefore perfect, even as Your Father which is in heaven is perfect."

This verse is different from all the other verses, here the teaching format changes, Jesus is not just explaining His mission, discussing behavior or preaching the gospel but actually giving a new commandment along with certain principles. Take a closer look at this verse; the first principle here, which is not new, is, God is the father of all. The second principle is, God is perfect, and the third principle is, God is in Heaven. None of these three statements, given as principles, is doctrinal since there is not any language contained in the principles, which would give direction to behavior. They are just foundations put into place for learning. Although, knowing these three things gives the opportunity to enlarge the knowledge of God, it requires certain doctrinal behavior to help build a relationship with Him and become like Him. The first part of the verse, "Be ye therefore perfect", is a commandment and the behavior required is to be obedient. The doctrinal part of this commandment is; Father in Heaven is perfect and all of His children are to become perfect even as He is. So there you have it, this scripture imparts principles, a commandment and a point of doctrine. This point of doctrine clearly defines a small but important part of The Gospel of Jesus Christ, which is, living the commandments is the process of gaining virtue; God's virtue is perfect, therefore if people live the commandments correctly they can become perfect like Father in Heaven.

Continuing analysis; in Matthew 5 the Lord is giving directions to his disciples concerning things in this life. In Matthew 5:48, Christ gives the command, and by the form of it implies, it shall be carried out to the fullest during mortality. However, the absence of a statement of time leads to the understanding that the conception, of a gradual development of love which, eventually, will mature to the state in which God's love has ever been, and is the true meaning of this scripture. This will not happen immediately and not before the completion of all Christ's work in us.

Conclusion.

1.   Spiritual Father is God --- foundation of the gospel, (a principle) no action required.

2.   God is perfect --- foundation of the gospel, (a principle) no action required.

3.   God is in Heaven --- foundation of the gospel, (a principle) no action required.

4.   Become as perfect as God is --- a commandment, Action required.

Now the question is; what action do we, as mortals, have to take to become perfect? This is where doctrine plays such an important part of people's lives. If anyone will study hard and learn the doctrine correctly, they will know how to become perfect and how to live every other commandment properly. However, this will require ever-changing behavior because, today, one may feel they did their best only to discover, today's level of obedience is not good enough for tomorrow. The doctrine of the Church of Jesus Christ of Latter day Saints is perfect and is one of the reasons this church leads the members directly to salvation. "Teach one another the doctrine of the kingdom. Teach ye diligently and my grace shall attend you, that you may be instructed more perfectly in theory, in principle, in doctrine, in the law of the gospel, in all things that pertain unto the kingdom of God, that are expedient for you to understand" (*D&C 88:77–78*). Therefore, members of the Mormon Church need to grasp the concept of principles to understand why they are so important to their salvation.

Purpose of Life
(Why are people here?)

People often ask, what is the purpose for this mortal existence, and, exactly what are the things God wants everybody to do? Since most of people do not have a checklist of the things God requires from them, they just continue on their way doing the best they can and hoping for the best. These questions also perplexed many people for many years. Research reveals there at least six purposes for being here:

1. To grow in knowledge and virtue, in the teachings of Joseph Smith, he says "If you wish to go where God is, you must be like God, or possess the principles which God possesses" (*TPJS p 216*). This concept of developing toward the nature of God has to do with using all knowledge, talent, and gifts to gain as much virtue in this life as possible. While here in mortality, mortals cannot gain all virtue, such as God possess, but this is where it all starts. This virtue building process is what commandments are all about. Each commandment is designed to advance the believer, through obedience, toward an understanding and behavioral adjustment of a certain virtue. For example, the commandment "love your neighbor as yourself" (*Mark 12:31*), helps to learn to love others in a small way, as God loves all mankind, in a large way. This advancement in the capacity to love is exactly the point the scriptures are trying to make, by being obedient to the commandments, mortals are becoming more like God. All commandments operate in this same way

2. To fill and fulfill the missions and callings, conferred and foreordained in the preexistence. The story of the spirit world, found in Abraham, tells a lot about the time, when we, as spirit children of God, sat in "the counsel in heaven" and those who voluntarily subscribed to the conditions of mortality made covenants having to do with their activities during their probation here on earth. Were such promises made, sure, they were or none of God's children would be on earth today. Think of it this way, if, while in the spirit world, those who desired to come into mortality had not promised to follow Christ and be obedient to his will, then, by default they would have gone with Satan. If none of God's spirit children, were willing to subscribe to Jehovah's plan then there would not be a second estate, everything would have come to a stop since no one could have kept their first estate. This is somewhat addressed in Abraham "And they who keep their first estate shall be added upon; and they who keep not their first estate shall not have glory in the same kingdom with those who keep their

first estate; and they who keep their second estate shall have glory added upon their heads for ever and ever" (*Ab 3:26*). Here is explained the importance of engaging in the work of the Lord while on this earth.

3. To be tried and tested. Why, are mortals, being tested? Well, while in the premortal state, spirit children promised to follow the Savior's plan, so now God is seeing if their earlier promise is being kept. To illustrate this, the record of Abraham says, "We will prove them herewith, to see if they will do all things whatsoever the Lord their God shall command them" (*Abraham 3:25*). --- Prove herewith, what does this mean, prove what? The actions of mortals will prove whether their promise, to follow Christ and keep His commandments, is being honored. Therefore, it is here, during mortality, mortals demonstrate their ability to live the commandments, as the means to gain the greatest reward and to be living as Gods, with God, in the Celestial Kingdom sometime in the future. Conversely, if mortals demonstrate, during mortality, their inability to live God's Devine Laws, they will have to accept a lesser reward.

4. To exercise agency. Mortals are to exercise this agency without memory of the premortal existence, thus, walking by faith is the essence of the test. Agency is an eternal concept and is nothing more than the capacity to choose who will be followed, whether it is Satan or Christ. Indeed, the way mortals exercise their agency can either direct them toward Christ or away from Him. Anytime there is movement away from Christ there is movement toward Satan. Indeed, such agency appears to be a condition of existence, as discussed in D&C 93: 30, 2Nephi2:11-13. Both Joseph Smith and Nephi say if agency did not exist all things known the creation, ourselves, even God would cease to exist. This explains the very serious nature of Satan's failed plan and his subsequent rebellion. Satan tried to erase agency, completely in the preexistence and failed but this effort is not over and will not be until sometime after the millennium.

5. To establish the foundations of an eternal family, first as sons and daughters, then as fathers and mothers. Reams of paper can be written on this subject and it can be discussed for hours but for the sake of brevity, the scriptures say the foundation of an Eternal Family is contained in participating in the New and Everlasting Covenant. Which is the process of being adopted into the Abrahamic covenant, through, which God's children become members in the Eternal Family of Christ.

6. God's children are here to receive a body. Why do they need a body? God is a resurrected being, and for His children to emulate him they are required to have also have a body (no body, ergo, no resurrection) and having this body enables them, as mortals, to have the necessary experiences that, in part, prepares them become like God. Those experiences, ultimate maturation, and eventual permanent resurrection, are essential to the perfecting of the soul. This is what Christ meant when he said, "Be ye therefore perfect even as you're Father which is in Heaven is perfect." (Matt. 5:48) "We came to this earth that we might have a body and present it pure before God in the Celestial Kingdom" (*TPJS, p.181*).

RELIGION DEFINED

Having taught many classes in the church, and while teaching these classes the question has often been ask the class members to define religion in one word. In many of these classes, there were church members, new to the church and others who had belonged to the church all their lives and even for them; this question is very difficult to answer. Part of this difficulty can be attributed to church culture, most teachers falsely assume that the members already know or have a good idea of how they look at or think about religion. If this assumption is true, what is the definition of religion? Not just a particular church but also all religions worldwide. The answer is the same for any and all of the nine major God based religions in the world. The correct answer to this question is very important. It is the rudder, which steers a religious person through the maze of questionable beliefs, misunderstood doctrine, copious amounts of difficult scriptures, and truthful information oft times mixed with mythology, inaccuracies, and false teachings. Members have said, "The spirit to sorts these things out for me". If asking the spirit alone were sufficient to determine truth, there would not be thousands of different religions. There are instructions on getting the spirits help in Doctrine and Covenants 9:8, "But, behold, I say unto you, that you must *study it out in your mind*; then you must ask me if it be right, and if it is right I will cause that your bosom shall burn with in you". It clearly says, a person must first study it out in their mind and then ask if it is right. If a person's rudder is broken or maybe nonexistent they cannot just "study it out" and get the answer accurate enough or complete enough for the spirit to tell them if they are right. Be aware, the spirit is not a Sunday school teacher; it only delivers the conformation of truth.
So what is the definition of religion? This discussion starts with the nine major religions in the world today.

Christianity: In everything, do to others as you would have them do to you; for this is the law and the prophets. (Jesus, Matthew 7:12)

Zoroastrianism: Do not do unto others whatever is injurious to yourself. (Shayast-na-Shayast 13.29)

Judaism: What is hateful to you, do not do to your neighbour. This is the whole Torah; all the rest is commentary. (Hillel, Talmud, Shabbat 31a)

Sikhism: I am a stranger to no one; and no one is a stranger to me. Indeed, I am a friend to all. (Guru Granth Sahib, p. 1299)

Hinduism: This is the sum of duty: do not do to others what would cause pain if done to you. (Mahabharata 5:1517)

Jainism: One should treat all creatures in the world as one would like to be treated. (Mahavira, Sutrakritanga)

Islam: Not one of you truly believes until you wish for others what you wish for yourself. (The Prophet Muhammad, Hadith)

Buddhism: Treat not others in ways that you yourself would find hurtful. (Udana-Varga 5.18)

Taoism: Regard your neighbour's gain as your own gain, and your neighbour's loss as your own loss. (T'ai Shang Kan Ying P'ien, 213-218)

There are two outstanding disclosures in the main tenets of these nine religions.

1. They all teach the same thing, treat everyone, as you would like to be treated.

2. All of these teachings have to do with your personal behavior toward fellow man.

Therefore, the answer to the question, what is the definition of religion is, the biggest part of religion is behavior. All clerics in these religions, including ours, are trying to get their congregations to modify their personal behavior to the way, which God desires, thereby becoming closer to God. It is simple, God wants people to behave in a certain way, which is prescribed by the commandments, and if people do this, He will reward them greatly but if they do not, He will not. The behavior, God wants mortals to employ provides them with a steering devise (a rudder) to help them return to Him. So, which way is your rudder (behavior) steering you, if it is steering you at all, is it toward God and His reward or away from God? Once people understand religion as behavior and what they are supposed to learn from this journey through mortality is, they were placed here to learn how God wants them to behave. Once this understanding is in place the scriptures, the doctrine and teachings become a lot clearer because people now have a rudder to steer them in the right direction. One might ask, how does a person change their behavior, or, is there any prophetic or scriptural evidence that supports the need, for a change of behavior? The answer is yes. Boyd K. Packer, in his talk, Little Children, said this "true doctrine, understood, changes attitudes and behavior. The study of the doctrines of the gospel will improve behavior quicker than the study of behavior" (*Nov. 1986 Ensign*). As far as the scriptural evidence goes, the entire New Testament is a witness to this change of behavior through doctrine. What was Jesus doing out in the wilderness with his disciples for two years? He was teaching them His doctrine so they would change their behavior and grow to be worthy enough to become His Apostles. The very way the Savior taught His disciples is the same way the Mormon Church is trying to teaching and for the very same reasons. It is interesting to see how the doctrine and the methodology employed there, effect behavior. First, it is crucial to understand commandments and doctrine go hand and hand. For each commandment, which is the overarching pronouncement, then there is a piece of doctrine explains in detail what people are supposed to do in their daily lives to live this commandment the way the Lord wants them to live. It is supposed, at one time the scriptures had the commandments spelled out with doctrine and blessings intact but over time the world is left with the only the overarching pronouncement and the doctrine can only be obtained through revelation, and the blessings can only be obtained from God by understanding the doctrine and live it throughout your life. Some churches believe the "cannon is closed" meaning, they do not possess the priesthood or have direct revelation so they must read the scriptures and determine, on their own, the intent and meaning of the commandment and then come up with their own ideas on how the Lord desires their congregations to behave and hope they have got it right. However, there is a church, the Church of Jesus Christ of Latter Day Saints, where the cannon is not closed; members have the Lord helping them understand certain revealed doctrine and how it applies to any particular commandment. This concept of obeying the commandments through correct behavior permeates religious life. As advances are made in the gospel, like baptism, the priesthood, or the temple experience, members go through a series of interviews wherein questions are ask, and answers are given. The interesting thing about these interviews is the questions are not about knowledge of the scriptures, or understanding of the gospel, not even, about how often the member attends church, but only about their behavior.

273

REPENTANCE

The Book of Mormon contains a very interesting account of a man named Nehor. It is easy to understand why Mormon, in abridging a thousand years of Nephite records, thought it important to include something about this man and the enduring influence of his doctrine. Mormon was seeking to warn us, knowing this philosophy would surface again in the latter day.

Nehor appeared on the scene about 90 years before the birth of Christ. He taught, "All mankind should be saved at the last day, for the Lord had created all men, and had also redeemed all men, and, in the end, all men would have eternal life" (*Alma 1:4*). About 15 years later, Korihor came among the Nephites preaching and amplifying the doctrine of Nehor. The Book of Mormon records, "he was the Anti-Christ, for he began to preach unto the people against the prophecies concerning the coming of Christ" (*Alma 30:6*). Korihor's preaching was to the effect "that there could be no atonement made for the sins of men, but every man fared in this life according to the management of the creature; therefore every man prospered according to his genius, and every man conquered according to his strength; and whatsoever a man did was no crime" (*Alma 30:17*). These false prophets and their followers and did not believe in the repentance of their sins. (*Alma 15:15*). As in the days of Nehor and Korihor, people today are living in a time not long before the great advent of Jesus Christ and the time of preparation for His Second Coming. Similarly, all do not often welcome the message of repentance. Some profess; if there is a God, He makes no real demands upon people (see Alma 18:5). Others maintain, a loving God forgives all sin based on a simple confession, or, if there actually is a punishment for sin, "God will beat us with a few stripes, and at last we shall be saved in the kingdom of God" (*2 Nephi 28:8*). Others, like Korihor, deny the very existence of Christ and any such thing as sin. Their doctrine concerning values, standards, and even truth are all relative. Thus, whatever one feels is right for him or her, cannot be judged by others to be wrong or sinful. This kind of life style sounds familiar to the people of today.

On the surface, such philosophies seem appealing because they give society license to indulge any appetite or desire without concern for consequences. By using the teachings of Nehor and Korihor, individuals can rationalize and justify anything. When prophets come crying repentance, it throws cold water on their party. However, in reality, the prophetic call should be received with joy. Without repentance, there is no real progress or improvement in life. Pretending there is no sin does not lessen its burden and pain. Suffering for sin does not; by itself change anything for the better. Only repentance leads to the sunlit uplands of a better life. In addition, only through repentance do people gain access to the atoning grace of Jesus Christ and salvation. Repentance is a divine gift, and there should be a smile on everyone's face when hearing this word spoken. It points to freedom, confidence, and peace. Rather than interrupting the celebration, the gift of repentance is the cause for true celebration.

Repentance exists as an option only because of the Atonement of Jesus Christ. It is His infinite sacrifice, which "bringeth about means unto men that they may have faith unto repentance" (*Alma 34:15*). Repentance is the necessary condition, and the grace of Christ is the power by which "mercy can satisfy the demands of justice" (*Alma 34:16*). Be the witness of this: "We know that justification [or forgiveness of sins] through the grace of our Lord and Savior Jesus Christ is just and true. And we know also, that sanctification [or purification from the effects of sin] through the grace of our Lord and Savior Jesus Christ is just and true, to all those who love and serve God with all their might, minds, and strength" (*D&C 20:30–31*).

Repentance is an expansive subject, but, for the sake of brevity, there are just five aspects of this fundamental gospel doctrine, if understood, will be helpful.

First, the invitation to repent is an expression of love. When the Savior "began to preach, and to say, Repent: for the kingdom of heaven is at hand" (*Matthew 4:17*), it was a message of love, inviting all who would to qualify to join Him "and enjoy the words of eternal life in this world, and eternal life itself in the world to come" (*Moses 6:59*). If people do not invite others to change or if they do not demand repentance of themselves, they fail in a fundamental duty, which is owe to themselves and others. A permissive parent, an indulgent friend, a fearful Church leader are in reality more concerned about themselves than the welfare and happiness of those they could help. Yes, the call to repentance is at times regarded as intolerant or offensive and may even be resented, but guided by the Spirit, it is in reality an act of genuine caring (*D&C 121:43–44*).

Second, repentance means striving to change. It would mock the Savior's suffering in the Garden of Gethsemane and on the cross for anyone to expect that, He should transform him or her into angelic beings without any real effort on their part. Rather, individuals must seek His grace to complement and reward their most diligent efforts (2 Nephi 25:23). Perhaps as much as praying for mercy, one should pray for time and opportunity to work, strive, and overcome. Surely the Lord smiles upon one who desires to come to judgment worthily, who resolutely labors day by day to replace weakness with strength? Real repentance, real change may require repeated attempts, but there is something refining and holy in such striving. Divine forgiveness and healing flow quite naturally to such a soul, for indeed, "virtue loveth virtue; light cleaveth unto light, and mercy hath compassion on mercy and claimeth her own" (*D&C 88:40*). With repentance, one can steadily improve their capacity to live the celestial law, for it is well known, "he who is not able to abide the law of a celestial kingdom cannot abide a celestial glory" (*D&C 88:22*).

Third, repentance means not only abandoning sin but also committing to obedience. The Bible Dictionary states, "Repentance comes to mean a turning of the heart and will to God, as well as a renunciation of sin to which we are naturally inclined" (*bible Dict,*), One of several examples of this teaching from the Book of Mormon is found in the words of Alma to one of his sons. "Therefore I command you, my son, in the fear of God, that ye refrain from your iniquities; "That ye turn to the Lord with all your mind, might, and strength" (*Alma 39:12–13; see also Mosiah 7:33; 3 Nephi 20:26; Mormon 9:6*). For the turning to the Lord to be complete, the turning must include nothing less than a covenant of obedience to Him. People often speak of this covenant as the baptismal covenant since it is witnessed by being baptized in water (*Mosiah 18:10*). The Savior's own baptism, providing the example, confirmed His covenant of obedience to the Father. "But notwithstanding he being holy, he showeth unto the children of men that, according to the flesh he humbleth himself before the Father, and witnesseth unto the Father that he would be obedient unto him in keeping his commandments" (*2Nephi 31:7*). Without this covenant, repentance remains incomplete and the remission of sins unattained. In the memorable expression of a prominent professor, *the choice to repent is a choice to burn bridges in every direction having determined to follow forever only one way, the one path leading to eternal life.*

Fourth, repentance requires a seriousness of purpose and a willingness to persevere, even while living through painful experiences. Attempts to create a list of specific steps of repentance may be helpful to some, but it may also lead to a mechanical, check-off-the-boxes approach with no real feeling or change. True repentance is not superficial. The Lord gives two overarching requirements: "By this ye may know if a man repenteth of his sins—behold, he will confess them and forsake them" (*D&C 58:43*). Confessing and forsaking are powerful concepts. They are much more than a casual "I admit it; I'm sorry." Confession is a deep, sometimes agonizing acknowledgment of error and offense to God and man. Sorrow, regret, and bitter tears often accompany one's confession, especially when his or her actions have been the cause of pain to someone or, worse, have led another into sin. It is this deep distress, this view of things as they really are, leads one, as Alma, to cry out, "O Jesus, thou Son of God, have mercy on me, who am in the gall of bitterness, and am encircled about by the everlasting chains of death" (*Alma 36:18*). Even though a confession is given to any priesthood holder this does not eliminate the need to confess the same sin to the Lord. With faith in the merciful Redeemer and His power, potential despair turns to hope. One's very heart and desires change, and the once-appealing sins become increasingly abhorrent. A resolve to abandon and forsake the sin and to repair, as fully as one possibly can, the damage he or she has caused now forms in a new heart. This resolve soon matures into a covenant of obedience to God. With a new covenant in place, the Holy Ghost, the messenger of divine grace, will bring relief and forgiveness. One is moved to declare again with Alma, "And oh, what joy, and what marvelous light I do behold; yea, my soul is filled with joy as exceeding as was my pain!" (Alma 36:20). Any pain entailed in repentance will always be far less than the suffering required to satisfy justice for unresolved transgression. The Savior spoke little about what He endured to satisfy the demands of justice and atone for sins, but He did make this revealing statement:

"For behold, I, God, have suffered these things for all, that they might not suffer if they would repent; "But if they would not repent they must suffer even as I" (*D&C 16: 16-17*). "Which suffering caused myself, even God, the greatest of all, to tremble because of pain, and to bleed at every pore, and to suffer both body and spirit—and would that I might not drink the bitter cup" (*D&C 19:16–18*).

Fifth, whatever may be the cost of repentance; it is swallowed up in the joy of forgiveness. In a general conference address entitled, The Brilliant Morning of Forgiveness, President Boyd K. Packer provided this analogy: "In April of 1847, Brigham Young led the first company of pioneers out of Winter Quarters. At that, same time, 1,600 miles to the west the pathetic survivors of the Donner Party straggled down the slopes of the Sierra Nevada Mountains into the Sacramento Valley, they had spent the ferocious winter trapped in the snowdrifts below the summit. Some survived the days, weeks, and months of starvation and the indescribable suffering is almost beyond belief.

Among them was fifteen-year-old John Breen. On the night of April 24, he walked into Johnson's Ranch. Years later John wrote: "It was long after dark when we got to Johnson's Ranch, so the first time I saw it was early in the morning. The weather was fine, the ground was covered with green grass, the birds were singing from the tops of the trees, and the journey was over. I could scarcely believe that I was alive. The scene that I saw that morning seems to be photographed on my mind. Most of the incidents are gone from memory, but I can always see the camp near Johnson's Ranch" (*Boyd K. Packer*).

President Packer commented: "At first I was very puzzled by his statement that 'most of the incidents are gone from memory. How could long months of incredible suffering and sorrow ever be gone from his mind? How could that brutal dark winter be replaced with one brilliant morning? On further reflection, I decided it was not puzzling at all. I have seen something similar happen to people I have known. I have seen some who have spent a long winter of guilt and spiritual starvation emerges into the morning of forgiveness. When morning came, they learned this": "Behold, he who has repented of his sins, the same is forgiven, and I, the Lord, remember them no more" (*D&C 58:42*). "I gratefully acknowledge and testify that the incomprehensible suffering, death, and Resurrection of the Lord "bringeth to pass the condition of repentance" (*Helaman 14:18*). The divine gift of repentance is the key to happiness here and hereafter. In the Savior's words and in deep humility and love, I invite all to "repent: for the kingdom of heaven is at hand" (*Matthew 4:17*). I know, in accepting this invitation, you will find joy both now and forever. In the name of Jesus Christ, amen".

All accountable persons have sinned and must repent in order to progress toward salvation. Only through the atonement of Jesus Christ can any repentance become effective and accepted by God.

Sin;

Why do mortals sin? Alternatively –What causes them to sin? (Mosiah 16:3) These traits, carnal, sensual, devilish, knowing good from evil, were inherited from Adam and Eve, meaning that, while living in this state, all have experienced a spiritual death. In other words, they have become a natural man" having not been spiritually reborn.

Repentance

Why is repentance essential?

1- All men are lost, (Mosiah 16:5)

2-It's a commandment, "And this is my doctrine, and it is the doctrine which the Father hath given unto me; and I bear record of the Father, and the Father beareth record of me, and the Holy Ghost beareth record of the Father and me; and I bear record that the Father commandeth all men, everywhere, to repent and believe in me" (*3Ne 11:32-34*).

What happens to mortals when they repent? (Mosiah 3:19)

Repentance is the progress toward Salvation, what does this mean and how is this accomplished? (Mosiah 16:4&6-11) When people truly take upon themselves the name on Christ the process of repentance is started.

What is the definition of Repentance?

Turning away from or forsaking sin by changing one's actions to obey the teachings of Jesus Christ.

What is the process of Repentance?

The process of repentance is for mortals the do all they can to reverse those bad characteristics inherited from Adam and Eve. By overcoming those characteristics, it is easier to avoid sin and the road to true repentance is clearer and shorter. Six Steps of Repentance:

1. Feel Godly Sorrow.
   A. "For I will declare mine iniquity; I will be sorry for my sin." (Psalms 38:18)
   B. The first step of repentance is to recognize you have committed a sin against God's commandments.
   C. Feel true sorrow for what you have done and for disobeying Heavenly Father.
   D. Feel sorrow for any pain you may have caused toward other people.
   "By this ye may know if a man repenteth of his sins—behold, he will confess them and forsake them" (*D&C 58:43*)

2. Confess to God.
   A. Pray to Heavenly Father and be honest with him.
   B. Tell him of your sin(s).
   C. If necessary, confess your sins to your local LDS bishop.
   "And it came to pass I did frankly forgive them all they had done, and I did exhort them they would pray unto the Lord their God for forgiveness" (*1 Nephi 7:21*).

3. Ask for Forgiveness
   A. Pray to God for his forgiveness.
   B. Forgive others who have hurt you.
   C. Forgive yourself and know God loves you, even though you have sinned.
   "And if it be stolen from him, he shall make restitution unto the owner thereof." (*Exodus 22:12*).

4. Rectify Problems Caused by the Sin(s)
   A. Make restitution by fixing any problems caused by your sin.
   B. Problems caused by sin include physical, mental, emotional, and spiritual damage.
   C. If you cannot rectify the problem, sincerely ask forgiveness of those wronged and try to find another way to show your change of heart.
   "He that covereth his sins shall not prosper: but whoso confesseth and forsaketh them shall have mercy." (*Proverbs 28:13*)

5. Forsake Sin.
   A. Make a promise to yourself and to God you will never repeat the sin.
   B. Recommit yourself to obeying God's commandments.
   C. Continue to repent if you sin again.
   "Behold, he who has repented of his sins, the same is forgiven, and I, the Lord, remember them no more." (*D&C 58:42*)

6. Receive Forgiveness.
   A. The Lord will forgive you when you truly repent with a sincere heart.
   B. Allow his forgiveness to come upon you.
   C. When you feel at peace with yourself, you can know you are forgiven.
   D. Do not hold onto your sin and the sorrow you have felt. Let it go by truly forgiving yourself, just as the Lord has forgiven you.

Here is a little test that might be fun. (Answers below)
1. True or False? According to the Doctrine and Covenants, people who repent of their sins forsake their sin.
2. True or False? True repentance involves keeping the commandments.
3. True or False? In order to live with Heavenly Father, people must repent.
4. True or False? True repentance means never repeating the same sin again.
5. True or False? A crucial test of repentance is abandonment of the sin.
6. True or False? If people hope to achieve exaltation, they must overcome their sins through repentance.
7. True or False? Partial repentance of sins never results in complete forgiveness.

(Answers)

1. TRUE: "Behold, he who has repented of his sins, the same is forgiven, and I, the Lord, remember them no more. By this, ye may know if a man repenteth of his sins--behold, he will confess them and forsake them" (*D&C 58:42,43*).
2. TRUE: "To make our repentance complete we must keep the commandments of the Lord" (*Gospel Principles, 1992 ed., p.125*).
3. TRUE: "Our Father in heaven does not sin, and He does not allow people who sin to live with Him. To live with Him, one must repent of their sins. To repent means to feel sorry for our sins and stop doing them" (*Gospel Fundamentals, p.67*).
4. TRUE: "The forsaking of sin must be a permanent one. True repentance does not permit making the same mistake again" (*Repentance Brings Forgiveness, an unnumbered tract published by the Church of Jesus Christ of Latter-day Saints, 1984*).
5. TRUE: "There is one crucial test of repentance. This is abandonment of the sin" (*Teachings of the Presidents of the Church: Spencer W. Kimball, p.39. Also cited in Doctrines of the Gospel Student Manual: Religion 231 and 232, p.40*).
6. TRUE: "Christ became perfect through overcoming. Only as we overcome shall we become perfect and move toward godhood. As I have indicated previously, the time to do this is now, in mortality" (*The Miracle of Forgiveness, p.210*).
7. TRUE: "…incomplete repentance never brought complete forgiveness" (*The Miracle of Forgiveness, p.212*).

Repentance gets Harder

"And now, as I said unto you before, as ye have had so many witnesses, therefore, I beseech of you that ye do not procrastinate the day of your repentance until the end; for after this day of life, which is given us to prepare for eternity, behold, if we do not improve our time while in this life, then cometh the night of darkness wherein there can be no labor performed. Ye cannot say when ye are brought to that awful crisis that I will repent, that I will return to my God. Nay, ye cannot say this; for that same spirit which doth possess your bodies at the time that ye go out of this life, that same spirit will have power to possess your body in that eternal world" (Alma 34: 33&34).

President Brigham Young said, "It is a hundred times easier to repent here on the earth than it is in the spirit world. So why would it be harder to repent in the next life" ((*Conference Report*, Oct. 1970, p. 74))?

This discourse starts with the circumstances found in mortality. There are varieties of constraints places upon people by God during their mortal probation, which helps or directs their actions. With the right help and direction, a person can seldom be in the position to have to repent. These constraints start with mothers and fathers shortly after birth. They teach their kids to do things, helpful to the family and they teach them not to do things, causing, themselves or others harm. For example, the home is where kids learn, punishment is unpleasant, and so punishment becomes a constraint with which they must be deal. Most of this early family training lasts all of their lives. Then, comes school, where students learn there are social rules of conduct and the concept of being sorry and thus, having to apologize for any bad behavior. Apologizing is the first step in repentance. This, like punishment, becomes a constraint. As schooling continues, friends contribute the constraint training as they approve or disapprove of the behavior of other student's activities when around them. A person can only mess up so much before he finds he does not have any friends left. Pier pressure is a great teacher of constraint. Then there is the job, where they also have rules of conduct and often one discovers, participating in some unacceptable activities can cause the loss of job. The fear of losing a job seriously advances the constraint training. When married and starting a family, spouses, and parents, have to constrain themselves and their activities more than they did when they were single because their family requires it of them. Those who cannot constrain themselves to such an extent will find they no longer have a family. Then there are the limitations of our bodies. A person can only participate in the sins of the world for so long before his body refuses to respond. A person can only abuse himself so much before he becomes ill. Then there is the constraint of money, sin is expensive, so your finances regulate how much sin you can do until payday. Another institution, known is the police department, offers some stern constraints to bad behavior, and if a person has conflict with them, they will find themselves involved with the Justice department, where the solutions are even more serious, and the constraints are very painful. Therefore, from mother making her child eat their vegetables to the prison system there are many constraints. Next, consider the church as an institution dedicated to the eradication of sin and the furthering of repentance. The teachings of the church advance the view, members must constrain themselves in accordance with the will of God. All these constraints are in place to keep people on the straight and narrow.

Now just imagine that, in spite of all of the training received while growing up, there are still people having a hard time living within the framework of civil society, and they are constantly in trouble due to their bad deeds and find themselves at odds with all those around them. Additionally, they never take the blame for the problems they cause, thus, they never gave any thought to obedience or repentance, and then--- they pass on to the next life. Is there any evidence supporting a belief, old iniquitous instincts would cease to make their demands? Surely, those bad habits and favorite sins will be right there alongside and the verses in Alma seem to support this idea. In these new circumstances, people find themselves functioning with all of their old bad instincts, attitudes, and habits but now, almost all of those constraints present during their mortal life are gone. There are not any teachers, vice-principles or even a brick and mortar school in the place. There is no job nor any police department to consider, there is no money, or the need thereof, to limit their behavior. No physical body to give up when they over-do it, no hunger, no pain, and under certain conditions they may not even be around their friends or family. The truth is, if, when people had all those loving and concerned constraints to help them, and they could not bring themselves to listen and learn how to live a moral civil life and repent when they did something wrong. How could anyone expect them to achieve any level of righteousness in the afterlife when most of their mortal constraints are gone? President Young was right, correcting any past behavioral problems or going through the repentance process would be much harder once a person leaves this mortal probation.

RESURRECTION

Resurrection of the dead is a common component of a number of theologies, most commonly in Christian, Islamic, Jewish and Zoroastrian tenets. The phrase refers to a specific event in the future. There are multiple prophecies in the histories of these religions asserting, the dead are brought back to life at some point in the future.

One of the most fundamental doctrines taught by the Twelve Apostles of old and the Apostles of today is Jesus was risen from the tomb, with His glorified, resurrected body, and thus offered resurrection to all, as in Acts 1:21–22, 2:32, 3:15, and 4:33. To obtain resurrection with a celestial, exalted body is the center point of hope in the gospel of The Church of Jesus Chris of Latter-day Saints. The Resurrection of Jesus is the most glorious of all messages to mankind.

The Resurrection consists in the reuniting of the spirit body with the body of flesh and bones of a mortal individual who has died, never again to be divided. The Resurrection shall come to all, because of Christ's victory over death. Although there are many scriptures saying, Jesus Christ was the first to be resurrected, none of them say He was the first person, mortal or being **ever** to be resurrected on this earth. In most cases the phrase, first resurrection is referring to Christ's resurrection being the first in the general resurrection of all mankind, such as (Matt. 27:52–54; Acts 26:23; 1 Cor. 15:23; Col. 1:18). Although others have been brought back from death but were restored to mortality (Mark 5:22–43; Luke 7:11–17; John 11:1–45), whereas a resurrection means to become immortal, with a body of flesh and bone.

All who are resurrected will not be raised to the same glory (1st Cor. 15:39–42; D&C 76), nor will all come forth at the same time (1st Cor. 15:23; Alma 40:8). Christ was first; the righteous have precedence over the wicked and come forth in the First Resurrection, whereas the unrepentant sinners come forth in the last resurrection (Rev. 20:5–13). The Prophet Joseph Fielding Smith and Apostle Bruce R. McConkie both stated, Jesus' resurrection was the first resurrection but they did not give any details concerning the phraseology or exact meaning of their statement. They both, then added, God has, over time, resurrected many to further His purposes, so members are kind of left in limbo here.

There are several lines of thought on the phrase first resurrection. Members have taken some of these lines of thought and converted them into doctrinal statements without checking to see if they can pass the doctrinal test for correctness. These converted or expanded statements, and therefore, the members themselves, without any thought, may be spreading false doctrine and passing incorrect beliefs around Sunday Schools and Priesthood meetings. Part of this thesis is to examining a couple of these beliefs and sees what issues they bring up and where they can go wrong. The most common of these inaccurate or incorrect beliefs, passed around, is that Christ is the first and only person ever resurrected. This is most concerting and therefore it must be discussed.

Before getting started, it is important to understand the meaning of the word "angel" since it germane to the discussion. In (D&C Section 129 1-3) it says, there are two kinds of beings in heaven called angels.

1- Those who are resurrected personages, having bodies of flesh and bones— For instance, Jesus said, Handle Me and see, for a spirit hath not flesh and bones, as ye see Me have.

2- Spirits of just men made perfect, they who are not resurrected, but inherit the same glory.

By these scriptures, it is clear, all angels are either non-resurrected beings who are still in spirit form and, of course, cannot be seen by mortals or, resurrected beings having physical form and can be seen and felt. When the Savior appeared to His Disciples, He was a resurrected being, therefore He could be seen and handled as would be any angel, as described in the first instance, and would have a physical appearance to any mortal. Obviously all this is very important to the discussion of resurrection.

To repeat, some say the words first resurrection means Christ was the first being ever resurrected. Does this statement pass the doctrinal test for correctness? The Old Testament tells of two angels, who physically visited Abraham and dined with Lot's family. These were called angels in the account of Abraham and were surely resurrected beings according to the 129th section of the Doctrine and Covenants. The New Testament tells that three days before the crucifixion of Jesus, He was involved in the transfiguration where Moses and others appeared alongside Christ, to his disciples. Those who appeared with Christ during this event were also called angels in the scriptural account. Given that they were clearly seen by the disciples, one can only presume they were resurrected mortals in the form of angels since,

1- It is clear from the scriptures, they, the angels of the transfiguration, all lived as mortals and it is recorded, they all had died prior to this event.

2- The explanation given by the Prophet Joseph Smith in the 129th section of the Doctrine and Covenants concerning the characteristics of angels.

Those who retain this, *Jesus being the first and only person resurrected*, belief are faced with three doctrinal issues;

1- Is the doctrine given in the 129th section of the Doctrine and Covenants concerning the status of angels incorrect? Or

2- Is the bible incorrect by calling the two who appeared to Abraham and those who appeared with Christ angels? Or

3- Does the phrase *first resurrection* convey something completely different than these people think it does?

There are others, who have defined the phrase first resurrection as the resurrection, which begins at the resurrection of Christ and continues until the first, general, resurrection associated with his Second Coming. Does this belief pass doctrinal test for correctness? This definition offers two doctrinal issues.

1- It raises the possibility, where saints are being resurrected as an on-going occurrence in the interval between those two great events. The following scriptures shed light on this. "The First Resurrection is yet future and will take place at the time of the Second Coming" *(Mormon Doctrine, p.639)*. "We have no knowledge that the resurrection is going on now or that any persons have been resurrected since the day in which Christ came forth except those associated with the restoration of the gospel" (*D&C 88:96-102*). These beings included, among others, John the Baptist, and Peter, James and John, who restored the Aaronic and Melchizedek priesthoods to Joseph Smith and his associates. Moroni was also a resurrected being, commissioned to give the golden plates to Joseph Smith, all of whom had special labors to perform in this day, which necessitated tangible resurrected bodies

2- It disregards the statement; "the second coming of Jesus Christ will trigger the first resurrection and the millennium" (*Gospel Principles 44*). By disregarding the above-mentioned definition, they are saying, resurrected beings have been living in the millennium for the last 2000 plus years.

The term, first resurrection is used to describe three separate circumstances.

1- To those who lived before the resurrection of Christ, the day of his coming forth from the dead was known as the first resurrection. Abinadi and Alma, for instance, so considered it. (See Mosiah 15:21-25; Alma 40) These people lived without the assurance, they would be resurrected, but with the belief, the Savior would bring the doctrine into being when He came in the flesh. His resurrection would usher in resurrection for them for the first time, hence "first resurrection".

2- To those who have lived since that day, the first resurrection is a future event and will take place at the time of the Second Coming. (D. & C. 88:96-102). This phrase first resurrection is associated with the resurrection of Christ as He was the first to be resurrected in the general resurrection which is made up of first, second, third and fourth separate resurrection events (See Mosiah15:20-23), and is the resurrection triggered by the Second Coming of the Lord (See D&C 76:64). The Lord is the first person of the first resurrection to be resurrected. This first resurrection will include a select group who will accompany Him later, thus the phrase first resurrection.

3- Jesus was the first mortal righteous enough to bring about his own resurrection and cause His resurrection to be the pathway for all mortals to gain immortality. As far as it is known, this is the first and only resurrection of this type, so in a since, this can be termed a "first resurrection"

Now a few words about the four separate resurrections

A general first resurrection will occur when Christ comes again to initiate his great millennial reign. In this resurrection all, the good and righteous people of the earth will be brought forth as eternal resurrected beings. The evil people who are living on the earth when the Savior comes will not be resurrected at this time, but will be remanded to the custody of Satan for a thousand years. Then, at the end of the millennium, they too will be resurrected. Thus every living being, without any exception, and without any regard for the kind of life they have lived, will be resurrected.

These categories of resurrection and the ultimate destiny of resurrected beings can be divided into four groups.

The first group comprises those who have known and loved the Savior, who has been baptized by requisite priesthood authority for the remission of their sins, and who have been true and faithful to all the covenants encompassed in the gospel of Jesus Christ throughout their mortal lives. Joseph Smith refers to the resurrection of these beings as the Resurrection of the Just (See *D&C 76:64*). They will be resurrected with Celestial bodies to a Celestial glory, and will live in a Celestial Kingdom with God and Christ forever.

The second group who will come forth in the first resurrection, are the good people of the earth. They chose not to follow the Savior as members of his kingdom on the earth, and thus, made no covenants with the Savior of obedience to the principles of his gospel. They will receive a Terrestrial resurrection, inherit a Terrestrial glory, and will live on a Terrestrial world, which is the type of a world this earth was before the fall of Adam and Eve.

The third group resurrected will be those wicked people who followed Satan rather than the Savior and were under Satan's power and dominance during the thousand years of the Lord's millennial reign on the earth. They are resurrected in Telestial glory and with Telestial bodies, and will inhabit a Telestial world. This world with be of the same nature of the earth where these people live now. However, the glory of this Telestial world will be so great as to surpass all understanding.

There is yet a fourth group resurrected. They are those who, having known the Savior by the ministrations of the Holy Spirit and having made covenants of obedience to his gospel, have then turned away and have become the enemies of righteousness. These will come forth at the end of the Millennium, the last resurrection. However, they will not inherit a kingdom of glory but are cast into outer darkness, where they will live in agony with Satan for the rest of never-ending eternity. These are spirits called, sons of perdition, (See D&C 76:32-33, 81-112).

Sacrament and Covenants

For Latter-day Saints, covenants are the foundation of eternal relationships with God and with beloved family members. Covenants are established by means of sacred rituals, performed by authorized priesthood officials. Covenants have associated members of the Mormon Church with specific codes of conduct. Those who live faithful to their covenants are promised blessings approximating the glorious conditions of heaven. Those who willfully reject their covenants, once made, are threatened with dire spiritual consequences.

The first covenant addressed here is the occasion when a nonmember formally becomes a member of the church. The rituals of baptism and confirmation symbolize the spiritual rebirth of individuals and their purification from sin as they take upon them the name of Jesus Christ and promise to remember him and keep his commandments. In turn, baptismal candidates receive the promise of the continuing influence of the Holy Spirit.

The details of this covenant are expressed not so much in the contents of baptism and confirmation per se, but in the weekly renewal of this covenant in another ritual called the sacrament, or communion as it is generally known in Christianity. The sacrament is the centerpiece of the Sunday worship services of the Latter-day Saints. In it, the emblems of the atoning sacrifice of Jesus Christ are blessed by the Priesthood and then distributed to the faithful. The prayers used to consecrate the emblems of the sacrament are two of only three fixed prayers in Latter-day Saint public worship. The other is the prayer of baptism. Reinforcing the crucial nature of their wording, the sacramental prayers are specifically defined in two separate scriptures, once in the Book of Mormon and another time in the Doctrine and Covenants (Moroni 4:3; 5:2; D&C 20:77, 79). In both sacramental prayers, the covenant obligations of the faithful are summarized in the verbs witness and remember. As an essential tenet of church membership, Latter-day Saints are expected to remember and to witness to certain essential truths.

The spiritual imperative for Latter-day Saints to remember is not confined to the sacramental prayers. In the Book of Mormon, for example, the verb remembers and its various cognates appear more than two hundred times, making remembering one of the most frequently repeated messages in this keystone of Latter-day Saint faith. Furthermore, in most instances, the message to remember appears as a spiritual imperative, as in the plea "remember, and perish not" (*Mosiah 4:30*).

Similarly, the importance of witnessing finds numerous applications in the standard works. Most often, witnesses are selected people who, because of their unique relationship to a gospel truth, can testify to the world of its eternal veracity. However, the law of witnesses is not restricted to the oral or written testimony of holy men and women. Latter-day Saint scriptures are replete with examples of places or things serving as physical, tangible witnesses of spiritual experiences or other divine realities. Finally, historical events often serve as witnesses of sacred truths, as in the following example from a revelation that is generally considered a kind of constitution for the church.

Section 20 of the Doctrine and Covenants defines basic organizational structures, operational processes, and spiritual principles for the church. In the formal introduction to this revelation, Jesus Christ accepts the church and Joseph Smith as its leader. The revelation then makes reference to two key historical events—the first vision and the emergence of the Book of Mormon—that prepared Joseph Smith to assume his duties as prophet (See D&C 20:5-12). The introduction concludes in terms reminiscent of other church covenants: "Therefore, having so great witnesses, by them shall the world be judged, even as many as shall hereafter come to a knowledge of this work. And those who receive it in faith, and work righteousness, shall receive a crown of eternal life; but those who harden their hearts in unbelief, and reject it, it shall turn to their own condemnation" (*D&C 20:13-15*). This passage suggests, the founding of the church was signaled by certain historical events serving collectively as a witness to the world of the central message of this religion. Namely, the fullness of the gospel of Jesus Christ is once again upon the earth and the church serves as a means by which all people can avail themselves of its blessings. Historic sites, historical collections, museum exhibitions, and other historical resources and products of the church serve as a witness in all three senses—human, material, and experiential—and preserve an institutional memory of those things central to the church's spiritual mission.

Importantly, there are some reflections on the role of memory in defining the historical beginning and central truth claims of the church, namely, Joseph Smith's first vision. These reflections address the theology of memory on two levels: the individual memory of Joseph Smith regarding this defining event in his life and the symbolic significance of this event in defining the religious identity of the Latter-day Saints.

Joseph Smith's first vision occurred in a grove of trees on the family farm in Manchester Township, New York, in the early spring of 1820. Four separate, firsthand, accounts of this experience, written or dictated by the Prophet between 1832 and 1843, and several other, secondhand, accounts exist, written by Joseph's contemporaries and based on his oral testimony. These various accounts are remarkably similar, given the differences in time, place, and context in which they were given. These accounts also differ from one another in significant ways. There are two, firsthand, accounts, the first one in 1832, and the one he wrote six years later, which are the only accounts of this experience, accepted as scripture by the Latter-day Saints.

Contemporary learning theory acknowledges, what and how people learn from life's experiences depend upon several factors, including personal, social, physical, and temporal contexts. Learning is not an abstract intellectual activity. It is a complex process by which consciousness, including memory, character, and worldview is constructed. Personal expectations and backgrounds, social relationships, environmental conditions, and subsequent experiences all play important roles in defining how people remember and interpret their experiences.

What does this have to do with Joseph Smith's first vision? In 1832, when Joseph wrote his first known account, he seems to have been concerned primarily with personal redemption, because the message from the heavenly messenger to him was; his sins had been forgiven him. By the time, he dictated the second official account of the first vision, which was some six years later; Joseph Smith had received most of the major revelations that would eventually, be published in his lifetime. These greatly expanded his understanding of his own prophetic mission, the divine destiny of the church he had founded, the plan of salvation, and the nature of God. As a result, he had come to understand the first vision within this more expansive religious context. Hence, the 1838 account not only emphasizes Joseph's personal struggle for his soul but also becomes an authoritative narrative of the historical beginnings, the doctrinal foundations, and, at a symbolic level, the spiritual destiny of the church. So what is the point? Additional experiences and more mature reflections after 1832 helped Joseph Smith to remember details and express the meaning of the 1820 vision in more profound terms in 1838 than he could have possibly done in 1820 or even 1832.

The first vision also operates within the collective memory of the Latter-day Saints. On this grander stage, the first vision is no longer purely a historical event or an isolated spiritual experience. It has become a spiritual archetype, or model for the identity and behavior of a body of believers transcends time, space, and cultural boundaries. This sacred story provides a spiritual paradigm for individual conversion, resistance to temptation, persistence in prayer, study of the scriptures, and similar processes governing the religious lives of Latter-day Saints. The archetypal significance of the first vision was not immediately apparent for the Latter-day Saints. However, once it was canonized in 1880 as a portion of the Pearl of Great Price, it received the authoritative status to become, eventually, a foundational sacred story for the Latter-day Saints.

To conclude, the process by which memories seem to be made, and refined within these spiritual contexts, at both the individual and collective levels. Memories are generated from a person experiencing some kind of event and become a meaningful experience as it is interpreted within the individual's consciousness. The interpretation of experience is based on four distinct but interrelated contexts. The personal context of interpretation reflects the particular background, interests, and expectations of the individual. In a word, the personal context for learning recognizes the old adage seeing-is-believing, is equally valid in the reverse, believing-is-seeing. There is at least a dynamic interplay between perception and conception in the process of interpreting experiences. The social context of the making of meaning considers the influence of a person's interpersonal relationships. Family, friends, colleagues, and other associates all influence how a person interprets life's experiences. The physical setting is a third dimension of the learning process: What else was going on at the time of the initial experience? Were there distractions? How familiar were the surroundings? The more unfamiliar or novel elements of the setting will likely be those which are the least memorable, at least initially and without some kind of subsequent reinforcement. Finally, the temporal context of memory acknowledges, the meaning of experiences, are transformed, refined, erased, or, in some cases, re-created by subsequent experiences and reflections. The meaning of a profound or life-changing experience is rarely if ever fully comprehended at once and it is not surprising because the memory of spiritual experiences is complex, elusive, and even ineffable. Nevertheless, for the Latter-day Saints, the spiritual experiences defining their individual and collective lives are hardly ever exclusively intrapersonal. Hence, Mormon Church members are counseled to share them with one another, where appropriate, in oral and written forms, in testimony meetings, in gospel discussions, in journals and family histories, and so on. And the church devotes considerable resources to preserve in perpetuity the memories of those actual, real-life experiences in written, material, electronic, and other media "for the good of the church, and for the rising generations" (D&C 69:8).

Sacrifice

This is one of the most misunderstood concepts in the gospel dictionary and indeed one of the most important so a little more time will be spent on it. To some members, it is generally supposed, sacrifice was entirely done away because of the Great Sacrifice. When the sacrifice of the Lord Jesus was offered up, and the sacrificing of animals and other worldly material was discontinued, they presume, there will be no need for the ordinance of sacrifice in the future. Those who are of this persuasion need to study the teachings of the Prophet Joseph Smith when he said. "A religion that does not require the sacrifice of all things never has power sufficient to produce the faith necessary unto life and salvation; for, from the first existence of man, the faith necessary unto the enjoyment of life and salvation never could be obtained without the sacrifice of all earthly things. It was through this sacrifice, and this only, that God has ordained that men should enjoy eternal life," (*Lectures on Faith, 69*). What does the Prophet mean by all this? He is saying, the Law of Sacrifice has not and will not, ever be removed from the earth and all who desire to reach the Celestial Kingdom, must succumb to the requirements of this law. Any religious group or church, not requiring absolute sacrifice from its members does not have the doctrinal depth to provide, to its members, the spiritual strength for absolute salvation. As the Prophet Joseph Smith said above and the law of sacrifice itself calls for the sacrifice of all things then he adds, the sacrifice of all earthly things, meaning, sacrificing only those things pertaining to the saving of the soul of the person (note, do not mistakenly substitute earthly material or earthly possessions for things of this earth). God wants people to give up all earthly, ungodly things. This higher practice of the law of sacrifice reaches into the inner soul of a person. People continue to think the object given up, is the sacrifice, NOT TRUE, sacrifice never was just the placing some material possession, such as an animal, on the altar. Instead, sacrifice is the, willingness, of a person to place the animal within them upon the altar and let it be consumed! So, how does a person show the Lord they have symbolically put themselves upon today's sacrificial altar? Matthew explains, people demonstrate their sacrifice by living the first great commandment: "Thou shalt love the Lord thy God with all thy heart, and with all thy soul, and with all thy mind" (*Matt. 22:37*). When people overcome their own selfish desires, by putting God first in their lives, and covenant to serve Him regardless of the cost, they are then living the law of sacrifice. How does one know, this is what God wants? The instructions on this are in Doctrine and Covenants. "Thou shalt offer a sacrifice unto the Lord thy God in righteousness, even that of a broken heart and a contrite spirit" (*D&C 59:8*). Add this to another scripture "Verily I say unto you, all among them who know their hearts are honest, and are broken, and their spirits contrite, and are willing to observe their covenants by sacrifice—yea, every sacrifice which I, the Lord, shall command—they are accepted of me" (*D&C 97:8*). Paul counseled, "I beseech you therefore, brethren, by the mercies of God, that ye present your bodies a living sacrifice, holy, acceptable unto God, which is your reasonable service" (*Rom. 12:1*). Finally, "Behold, I have seen your sacrifices, and will forgive all your sins; I have seen your sacrifices in obedience to that which I have told you. Go, therefore, and I make a way for your escape, as I accepted the offering of Abraham of his son Isaac" (*D&C 132:50*.

Conclusion, the decisions made by people and their ability or inability to fully commit themselves, concerning the topics above, determine the degree of glory they will obtain. Another way looking at it is, the trip, called the gospel journey is nothing more than an educational process of behavioral change, beginning in the preexistence, and carrying on into eternity. Knowledge is the foundation, virtue is the direction, obedience is the work, sacrifice is the test, and commitment is the speed control. The level of commitment is at its highest when the day-to-day progress of humility, refinement, obedience, sacrifice, and purification are at their peak. This is truly living the law of consecration and this, is the time when people feel the most gratification in their gospel journey of growth and change. Friends, always, always remember the story of the chicken and the pig. The church requires members to be the chicken but law of consecration encourages them to take the opportunity to become the pig.

Sealing

The few references in the biblical text (Old and New Testaments) mentioning sealing seem to imply, this act is something performed or accomplished by God or the Godhead, except in Matthew 16:19 where the word is "bind" is used and this act is brought about by Peter's use of the Keys he has been given. In the other four places the word seal is used; "And he received the sign of circumcision, a seal of the righteousness of the faith which he had yet being uncircumcised: that he might be the father of all them that believe, though they be not circumcised; that righteousness might be imputed unto them also" (*Rom. 4:11*). "Who hath also sealed us, and given the earnest of the Spirit in our hearts" (*2nd Cor. 1:22*). "In whom ye also trusted, after that ye heard the word of truth, the gospel of your salvation: in whom also after that ye believed, ye were sealed with that Holy Spirit of promise" (*Eph. 1:13*). "And grieve not the Holy Spirit of God, whereby ye are sealed unto the day of redemption" (*Eph.4:30*). In these instances further study is needed since it is unclear what this seal is or how it works, although people can gather, it is a spiritual experience. "And I will give unto thee the keys of the kingdom of heaven: and whatsoever thou shalt bind on earth shall be bound in heaven: and whatsoever thou shalt loose on earth shall be loosed in heaven" (*Matthew 16:19*). The word bind is taken by some to mean, to obligate or compel, while others think it means, sanction or ratify. In the Book of Mormon the same passage is recorded in "Behold, I give unto you power, that whatsoever ye shall seal on earth shall be sealed in heaven; and whatsoever ye shall loose on earth shall be loosed in heaven; and thus shall ye have power among this people (*Helaman 10:7*), but here word bind is changed to seal. The Book of Mormon also uses seal in the (act of God) sense. "Therefore, I would that ye should be steadfast and immovable, always abounding in good works, that Christ, the Lord God Omnipotent, may seal you his, that you may be brought to heaven, that ye may have everlasting salvation and eternal life, through the wisdom, and power, and justice, and mercy of him who created all things, in heaven and in earth, who is God above all, Amen" in (*Mosiah 5:15*). But it is, act of the Devil, in Alma. "For behold, if ye have procrastinated the day of your repentance even until death, behold, ye have become subjected to the spirit of the devil, and he doth seal you his; therefore, the Spirit of the Lord hath withdrawn from you, and hath no place in you, and the devil hath all power over you; and this is the final state of the wicked" (*Alma 34:35*)..

Sealing has both literal and figurative uses in the bible as well as in the lexicon of the LDS Church today. In the literal sense, a sealing is a symbol of formal ratification, a symbolic way of allowing someone else to act on your behalf with your authority. In the Church today, this is generally associated with Priesthood Keys and Authority but it is always understood, the Divinity of Christ has the final word. This is the case in Helaman, "Behold, I give unto you power, that whatsoever ye shall seal on earth shall be sealed in heaven" (*Helaman 10:7*), where Nephi is given permission to literally act on the Lords behalf. In a figurative way, sealing's are viewed as an act or token of authentication, confirmation, proof, security, or possession. This is seen in the Book of Mormon "Christ, the Lord God Omnipotent, may seal you his" (*Mosiah 5:15*), and in Alma 34: 35 where Satan is mentioned. This scripture in Alma is very interesting since it covers the entire figurative aspect of sealing. The scripture authenticates the veracity of repentance, confirms the reality of spiritual death, is proof of personal wickedness, and witnesses Satan's ownership/possession of non-repentant spirits.

In the church today, the subject of sealing is often shrouded in confusion and oft-times fosters deep concern, especially when it comes to children or spouses who have been sealed to a now wayward family member. It seems, those who harbor these concerns believe, when sealed to another as one, the two of them are somehow tied, or locked together, in a family relationship forever, which cannot be broken. This false notion is what causes all the anguish and it can only be characterized as narrow thinking and it is completely out of step with the way the Mormon Church presents the ordinance of sealing, or any other ordinance, and what is needed here is a much broader view. The key understanding is, there is an unbroken chain of sealing is required, to bind the whole world into a single human family. This narrow thinking essentially locks people into the concept of small discrete families rather than the broader concept of Family of Christ. Many parents think, when they have their children sealed to them the parents can have their children with them in eternity. While this is true, people cannot be interpreted this sealing promise to mean, any child or spouse is thereby locked into receiving any blessing in glory, or any degree of condemnation based on the righteousness, or lack thereof, of someone they are sealed to. Additionally, there is no one forced, by the sealing ordinance, into a relationship with anyone or left out of anything, in the future. Even though a child is sealed to the parents the child may, later, themselves be sealed to their spouse and then sealed to their own children, they must still receive their own endowments and live worthy enough to be adopted into the Abraham Covenant. If parent and children alike can accomplish all this, God will ratify all of the sealing ordinances, sealed by the Holy Spirit of Promise, and their eternal reward in Heaven will be given, as promised. Conversely, if anyone of the sealed parties is found unworthy and the Holy Spirit of Promise withdraws, the other party can continue their progression unabated, since the salvation of neither party is not dependent upon any other mortal in any way. All sealed by the Holy Spirit of Promise are sealed with the expectation; they will be together within the family of Christ, not together with their earthly family. Not all mortal families, which are made up of spirits in a fallen state, can, as a single-family unit, be saved together. Those family members can only save themselves individually. It is only through individual acceptance into the Family of Christ, through the atonement, that any fallen spirit can regain the presences of God. Extensive research has not found any scriptural or prophetic evidence of any kind of group acceptance into the family of Christ.

The sealing ordinance is part of a group of ordinances called "the New and Everlasting Covenant". In order to understand how sealing takes place along with the other ordinances a more complete understanding of the

New and Everlasting Covenant is necessary. According to the Apostle Dallin Oaks the New and Everlasting Covenant is, in its entirety, (from baptism to sealing) the process that enables a Latter Day Saint, along with their continuing righteousness, to be adopted into the Abraham Covenant which ushers that very same person into the Family of Christ. The sealing ordinance is a necessary part of that process, and like all ordinances, it is initiatory, meaning the mortal part is just the beginning and in a figurative way, it is conformation, sometime later, a sealed person, is to have the sealing ratified by the Holy Spirit. "the Holy Spirit is given to them to confirm them as belonging to God...God grants to them His Holy Spirit as the certain pledge that they are His, and shall be approved and saved in the last day"(*Eph. 1:13; Eph. 4:30*). This approval or ratification of ordinances and sealing's by God is predicated on the person's life of righteous living. In a larger sense, everyone must be adopted into the family of God in order to enjoy the fullness of his blessings in the world to come. Although all mortals are the spiritual offspring of God it is because of the fall they have lost their heirship and are doomed to inherit the consequences of their fallen condition. It is the Only Begotten of the Father in the flesh, Jesus, who is the natural heir. Therefore, He is the only one whose birthright is acceptable for the adoption of God's children into the kingdom of His Father. This adoption process, the New and Everlasting Covenant, qualifies participants as joint-heirs with Christ in his Father's kingdom, and through the ordinances of the gospel of Jesus Christ, we can become heirs of God. Again, as summarized in the Doctrine and Covenants, "individuals who enter into the covenant and magnify their calling are sanctified by the Spirit unto the renewing of their bodies. They become the sons of Moses and of Aaron and the seed of Abraham, and the church and kingdom, and the elect of God" (*D&C 84:33-34*).

While these dispensational keys had varied applications, the key to keep the world from being utterly wasted was sealing, because God's work of bringing to pass the eternal life of man cannot be accomplished without the welding link of members to members who have been sealed. They cannot be made perfect without each other. Exaltation, meaning eternal increase cannot take place without the fulcrum of the temple and its sealing ordinances.

Joseph's vision seems to follow a similar theme, but is much grander. Elijah will reconcile the different factions of humanity under the banner of the Gospel, thus qualifying all for salvation and restoration. What is exactly affected by sealing in such a scenario remains elusive. At the very least, it suggests, sealing is much more than <u>families can be together forever</u>.

Marriages ending in divorce

In the Latter Day Saint movement, the First Presidency is the highest governing body in the Latter Day Saint church established by the Prophet Joseph Smith. If a man who is sealed to a woman but later is divorced, he must apply for a, sealing clearance, from the First Presidency in order to be sealed to another woman. This does not void or invalidate the first sealing. It merely establishes he is indeed divorced from her. A woman in the same circumstances would apply to the First Presidency for a, cancellation of sealing, sometimes incorrectly called a temple divorce, allowing her to be sealed to another man. This approval voids the original sealing as far as the woman is concerned. Divorced women who have not applied for a sealing cancellation are considered sealed to the original husband. However, it should again be noted, the LDS Church teaches that even in the afterlife the marriage relationship is voluntary so it is evident no man nor woman can be forced into an eternal relationship through temple sealing or any other ordinance. On occasion, divorced women have been granted a cancellation of sealing, even though they do not intend to marry someone else. In this case, they are no longer considered as being sealed to anyone and are presumed to have the same eternal status as unwed women.

Sealed marriages ended through death

In the case where a sealed marriage ends through the death of one of the spouses, the requirements are different. A man whose sealed wife has died does not have to request any permission to be married in the temple and sealed to another woman, unless the new wife's circumstance requires her to obtain a cancellation of sealing. However, a woman whose sealed husband has died is still bound by the original sealing and is required to have to request a cancellation of sealing to be sealed to another man. In some cases, women in this situation who wish to remarry choose to be married to subsequent husbands in the temple for time only, and are thereby, not sealed to them, leaving them sealed to their first husband for eternity. Again, each of us must understand, a sealing has very little or no effect on any of other temple ordinances. It is a separate event and though it done in the same place and just following the marriage ceremony, the sealing is a separate ordinance, and in the eternal scope of things, it stands on its own. The text above, it is evident, members may be sealed many times in mortality, and if they choose, some can be unsealed and resealed, or sealed in the afterlife, without any ill effect on their righteousness. However, none can participate in the Abrahamic Covenant and inherit the highest level of the Celestial Kingdom if they are not sealed for time and eternity.

Shepard and his Flock

Many people have spoken of the old adage of the good Shepherd and his flock, this metaphor is generally use to illustrate some point the speaker is trying to make. The most notable of these people was the Savior when He referred to Himself as the "Shepherd of the flock". What can be made of this metaphor, who identifies as the Shepherd, what is the Shepherd supposed to do and how does one become the Shepherd. Also, examine the role of the flock and what, if any, is their responsibility.

Who is the Shepherd?

This statement made by the Savior to his disciples was referring directly to his relationship with the Father, in the preexistence He (the Lord) said "Thy will be done" (John 10; 11, 25-27). So what is the Father's will? In the book of Moses, the calling of the Father is "For behold this is my work and my glory -- to bring to pass the immortality and eternal life of man" (*Moses 1; 39*). When Jesus said, "I seek not mine own will, but the will of the Father" (*John5:30*), He took upon Himself the responsibility of bringing immortality and eternal life to all the people on the earth and possible other Spheres--- thus becoming the Shepherd. Calling Himself the Shepherd was His way of affirming to all, the work of salvation in His area of responsibility was now His. The Prophet of the Church has also entered in an agreement with the Lord and has accepted the responsibility of this work for those on this earth. Therefore, He is the Shepherd for this sphere. Additionally, those who are call to position of responsibility in the church are also "Shepherds" who are contributing to the work for the Lord within their calling. Stake Presidents in their stakes, Bishops in the wards, Auxiliary Leaders in their callings, Teachers in their classes, Missionaries, Home/ visiting Teachers in their routes, are all are Shepherds in their own way.

What is the Shepherd supposed to do?

In (D&C 50:10-14) the Spirit is instructing the Elders of the church on this responsibility. Here they are instructed to teach the truth. In (D&C 75:4) the scriptural meaning of truth is given. The Shepherd is to proclaim the truth according to the revelations and commandments as given the elders by the lord. Therefore, the Shepherds are to teach the flock the commandments. For the most part, the Church Leaders do exactly that. The church magazines, teaching manuals, and talks given by the General Authorities, are there to reinforce the commandments, and how they must be lived.

How does one become the Shepherd? Any person can become a Shepherd by accepting a calling.

What is the role of Flock?

The role of the flock is far more interesting than the role of the shepherd. The flock is every person who ever been born on this earth and every person who is going to be born on this earth. The Prophet is the Prophet of all those who live on earth and all who have pass on since the time of Adam. Hence, there is need for temple work--- the work of the Lord. What is the responsibility of the flock?

If the responsibility of the Shepherd is to teach the commandments, then the responsibility of the flock is to learn and obey the commandments. In (Abraham3:24-25) it says, the earth was created as a test to see if mortals will do all the things the Lord commands. So learning the commandments should be the focal point of the flock.

This is where the responsibility of the flock gets interesting as the examination of the concept of Commandments continues.

1 - What is the purpose of commandments?

2 - What are commandments?

3 - How many commandments do we have?

4 - Is there any special way people are supposed to deal with commandments?

What is the purpose of commandments?

To understand this, there needs to be some perspective about ourselves. All mortals are a couplet, meaning they consist of two parts, each depending on the other. One part is the temporal person (root word, temporary) or the mortal body, spoken of in the scriptures as the vessel. The other part is the spirit person housed in the vessel, referred to as the soul. By the way, this spirit person, is the real us, having lived with the Father before mortality and going on to eternal life while the mortal remains decay in the dust for a while. The point of all this is, mortals have a personal responsibility to return their soul to Heavenly Father in good, untarnished condition. All have heard or read the scripture "the Lord is no respecter of persons". This is understood to mean, no matter the personal circumstances -- rich, poor, -- young, old, -- healthy, sick, whatever the earthly situation, people's first responsibility as a mortal is to their counterpart, the spirit person residing with them. The concept of living the commandments is the only way a mortal can fulfill this responsibility and this brings about the next question.

What are commandments?

Commandments are those things mortals, do, or do not do. These actions cause the mortal's soul to be cleaned, and strengthened, or, the soul is will be damaged. God has set these rules out for his children to live by as discussed in (Abraham3:24-25) and our ability to do the things commanded has a direct connection to our salvation. You might say the commandants are the owner's manual for mortals to live by. If the earth was formed as a test bed and the reason mortals were placed here is to see if they will obey the commandments, this is the only method known for mortals to return to Heavenly Father.

Here is a question about commandments

How many commandments do we have? Now one would think, considering all the importance placed on the commandments, at a minimum a person should know how many commandments there are. Some will say ten, others will not know. Is ten all the commandments ever given? Here is a hint--- in the New Testament there are about thirty-eight commandments. Then there is the D&C, Pearl of Great Price and Book of Mormon and latter day revelations. The truth is most members do not know how many commandments there are. Some might think, with all this emphasis on commandments why doesn't the church just printing a book with all the commandments listed and two or three pages' explanation on how to live these laws. If a person were to go to Deseret Book looking for such a book, they would not find one published by the church. To understand the reason the church opts out on this it is important to review some history. During the time of Jesus, He was upset with the Jewish leaders and called them hypocrites. What were church leaders doing that Jesus did not like? The Jews lived by the laws of Moses, which was written about 400 years before Christ. The Jews did not obey the commandments by faith, they were taught to read the Torah and be obedient by law. Living by law rather than by faith upset the Lord and his teachings clearly illustrates this point. This brings about the next question.

Is there a special way to deal with commandments?

The answer is, yes. Referring back to Moses "For behold this is my **work** and my **glory** -- to bring to pass the immortality and eternal life of man" (Moses 1; 39). This article, so far, has talked about the work part of this scripture now it is time to look at the glory part. How many times has everyone heard, "study the scriptures", not read the scriptures, but study the scriptures? Members are commanded to study the scriptures, to search the scriptures to find out what is the will of God. Once found, study it out, ask questions of the church leaders, learn the doctrine associated with the commandments, pray about it, receiving a testimony of the gospel from the Holy Ghost, and then incorporate all this into their lives through faith. It is only living the commandments through faith that anyone can personally glorify God and only through this way can mankind hope to gain salvation.

Sin
(A Brief Explanation of Sin)

This concept called sin is probable the least discussed concept in the church. In order to start to understand this concept we need ask ourselves the following questions,
1. What causes mortals to sin?
2. Why is a sin a sin?
3. Is any thought, unto itself, a sin?
4. Is any action, unto itself, a sin?
5. What exact thing constitutes a sin? Moreover, if this "thing" constitutes sin---Why?
6. Have God's children always been the ability to sin?
7. Will God's children always be able to sin?

Question # 1- What causes mortals to sin?

Why can people not just live their lives, do the things God wants them to do, and never have to deal with sin? The answer is in Mosiah. "For they are carnal and devilish, and the devil has power over them; yea, even that old serpent that did beguile our first parents, which was the cause of their fall; which was the cause of all mankind becoming carnal, sensual, devilish, knowing evil from good, subjecting themselves to the devil. Thus all mankind was lost; and behold, they would have been endlessly lost were it not that God redeemed his people from their lost and fallen state. But, remember that he that persists in his own carnal nature, and goes on in the ways of sin and rebellion against God, remaineth in his fallen state and the devil hath all power over him. Therefore, he is as though there was no redemption made, being an enemy to God; and also is the devil an enemy to God" (*Mosiah 16:3-5*). What was gleaned from the previous scriptures is, as children of Adam and Eve, all mortals inherited these certain traits (carnal, sensual, devilish, knowing good from evil) from Adam and Eve. While living in this state (mortality), it very easy to fall into the temptations of Satan (being beguiled as our first parents were) and thus, will experience a spiritual death (fallen state). In other words, through sin a person becomes a natural man. Natural man is explained in Mosiah. " For the natural man is an enemy to God, and has been from the fall of Adam, and will be, forever and ever, unless he yields to the enticing of the Holy Spirit, and putteth off the natural man and becometh a saint through the atonement of Christ the Lord, and becometh as a child, submissive, meek, humble, patient, full of love, willing to submit to all things which the Lord seeth fit to inflict upon him, even as a child doth submit to his father" (*Mosiah 3:19*). This scripture tells, all will remain an enemy of God and as long as they continue to live in this fallen state, they cannot return to God because they have not been spiritually reborn. Thus, every human being will sin during their lifetime and must repent and cease being a natural man.

Question # 2 - why is sin a sin?

This has to do with the promises made in the spirit world. As Satan took 1/3 of the hosts of heaven away during the war of words, as explained in Revelations, "And there was war in heaven: Michael and his angels fought against the dragon; and the dragon fought and his angels, and prevailed not; neither was their place found any more in heaven. And the great dragon was cast out, that old serpent, called the Devil, and Satan, which deceiveth the whole world: he was cast out into the earth, and his angels were cast out with him" (*Rev 12: 7-9*). The rest of God's children promised to follow Christ and do all things required, if permitted to come to earth and start progressing through eternity to become as God. In Abraham, "And there stood one among them that was like unto God, and He said unto those who were with Him: We will go down, for there is space there, and we will take of these materials, and we will make an earth whereon they may dwell. And we will prove them herewith; to see if they will do all the things whatsoever the Lord their God shall command them" (*Abraham 3; 24&25*). This scripture explains the reason the earth was created and the spirit children, as referred to above as them and they, will dwell on this earth and will have to prove they will live all of the commandments as promised. Did each person make such a promise? Sure, they did or they would not be here. Think of it this way, if had each spirit had not promised to follow Christ and do what He said, then, by default, the spirit would have gone with Satan. Now those spirits are here, as mortals, the Lord is finding out if they really are willing to follow Him and He does this by simply watching what is being done every day. Abraham was talking about this test. So, why is a sin a sin? When one breaks a commandment, they have sinned because they promised, while in the preexistence, they would not do anything against the will of God.

Exactly how is breaking a commandment a sin, this will be explained in # 5.

Questions 2&3 will be discussed at the same time.

Is any thought or action unto itself is a sin?
Thought- Satan uses thought as a temptation tool, but, any thought, by itself, cannot be a sin, but when a thought is coupled with an unrighteous plan or desire, then a sin has occurred, even though all this takes place in the mind. Actions- Although it is difficult for some to believe, no action, unto itself, is a sin with the possible exception of blaspheme against the Holy Ghost. Explanation, an action such as taking another person's life cannot always be defined as sin since death itself is not a sin. Also during the act of self-defense, death due to an accident and death during the act of war, and so on, these are not considered sins. Now if a person says murder is a sin the statement would be correct, understanding the word murder is a special kind of act, resulting in a person losing his life. Therefore, it is not the act itself but the circumstances involved in the act that causes the sin.

Question #5- What exact thing constitutes a sin?
If this thing constitutes sin---Why?

If thought, unto itself, is not a sin and action unto itself, is not a sin, what defines the act of sinning? The exact thing causing a thought or an action to be a sin is DECEIT. This is when a person knows the thing he or she is thinking about or doing violates the promise made to God and they continue anyway, they are being deceitful to God. The ability sin in this manner starts round the age of eight when children start to understand right from wrong. Of course, children generally do not understand the complex nature of Satan and his involvement in their thoughts or actions; they see these things from the standpoint of good and bad. The portrayal below shows the relationship between thought and action with deceit as the joiner.

303

1. Thought---deceit ---action required

2. Thought alone--- no sin

3. Thought taken to action --- sin

4. Thought with no action but accompanied with inappropriate desire--- sin. The addition of the inappropriate desire is the same as action.

Action --- Action alone cannot produce a sin. Take, for example, a person stumbles and accidently hurts another, this kind of action, done without any previous thought, is not considered sinful. There are many actions preceded by thought, when a person lets, their thoughts turn into action knowing the action is against the will of God; their contempt for His law is the sin. Therefore, the deceit lies between thought and action that causes the problem.

Why is deceit a sin? As mentioned above, while in the spirit world, and indeed in some instances here on earth, All people born on this earth made promises not to do things considered to be bad by the Lord, so when they do them they have broken their promise, thus they have sinned.

Question # 6&7 - Have people always had the ability to sin.
Will they always be able to sin?

Everyone has had, since the beginning, and will continue, through eternity, to have this thing call "Agency". Did agency exist in the preexistence? Yes, it did and was exercised it during the "war of words". Regarding the promises mentioned above, as long as God' children have agency they are responsible for their actions whether in the preexistence, in mortality or beyond. Even God has to be responsible for His actions, as seen in Alma 40: 12-26, God had to handle the Plan of Redemption with justice and mercy in a correct way, or He would cease to be God. Doing things in a correct way is God, Himself exercising His agency. Now, mortals are hoping to follow God's example, but if they do not or cannot handle themselves correctly during mortality, they can lose the opportunity to become Gods. While finding the way through this test period mortals must avoid sin for it is unsightly in the eyes of God.

Six Days of Creation

Everyone can clearly see the fulfillment of the creation which God imparted to Moses: "In six days the Lord made heaven and earth, the sea, and all that in them is, and rested the seventh day" (*Ex. 20:11*). It is of the creative events taking place on each of these days and the meaning of the word, day, people do not comprehend and this dilemma has caused a raging debate between the "young-creationist" and the" old-earth creationist". "Young" meaning the earth is young (6 thousand years or so) and "old" meaning the earth is much older (10's of thousands of years or more). How young or old the earth is depending on who you talk to.

First, what is a day? It is a specified period of time; it is an age, an eon, a division of eternity; or is the time between two identifiable events? In addition, each day, of whatever length, has the duration needed for its purposes. One measuring rod is the time required for a celestial body to turn once on its axis. For instance, Abraham says, according to Lord's time a day is one thousand years long. This is one revolution of the distant planet of Kolob, he says, and it is after the Lord's "manner of reckoning" (*Abr. 3:4*). Some ingenious fellow read this and joined this phrase with the six days of creation from Moses, assuming the six days was Lord's Time and came up with six thousand years of creation and then went one-step further and said the earth was only six thousand years old, thus feeding the Young-earth creationist's claim. Archaeological findings and dating processes, of course feeds the Old-earth creationist's claims. President Brigham Young, discussing the six days of creation, said, six days is a mere term, but it matters not whether it took six days, six months, six years, or six thousand years. Clearly, the creation occupied a certain period of time. So far, no one has had the authority to say, what the duration of these days was, and it cannot be known whether Moses actually penned these words, or whether the translators of the Bible have given the words their intended or unintended meaning. However, God created the world. God brought forth material out of which He formed this little terra firma upon which all roam. How long had this material been in existence, forever and ever, in some shape or another, and in some condition or another as indicated by the scriptures?

Second, there is plenty of information in the original language of the Old Testament entangled in this dilemma. In ancient Hebrew the word used in the Old Testament Scriptures for day is (yôm) with a number placed before it. In this case, the number is six. Hebrew scholars acknowledge the word translated "day" (yôm) has several literal meanings: daylight, day, time, moment, or long era of time. The question is which definition of yôm did the Genesis author intend? Biblical Hebrew has a very limited vocabulary–approximately 3,100 words compared to over 4,000,000 English words. In English, there are many words to describe a long period of time. However, biblical Hebrew has no word other than yôm to denote a long time-span or a short period of time. Some claim yôm attached to a number i.e., first, second, third, etc. requires a 24-hour-day interpretation. However, Bible scholars dispute that. For example, noted Hebrew scholar Gleason L. Archer states, this simply defines a symbolic unit of time and serves as no real evidence for a literal 24-hour day concept on the part of the Biblical author. Archer also points out, the days of creation do not bear a definite article in Hebrew, i.e., the first day, the second day, etc.. He states, "In Hebrew prose of this genre, the definite article was generally used where the noun was intended to be definite... Thus they, the days of creation, are well adapted to a sequential pattern, rather than to strictly delimited units of time."(*Glen L. Archer. A* Survey *of* Old Testament *Introduction1994*).

It should also be noted there are instances in Scripture where yôm used with a number does not restrict its meaning to 24 hours. Take the scriptures referring to the resurrection of Israel for example, "He will revive us after two days; He will raise us up on the third day" (Hosea 6:2), referring to Israel's ultimate restoration some hundreds or thousands of years in the future. Zechariah 14:7, describing the Day of the Lord, contains yôm echad (translated as unique day), which is identical to yôm echad of Genesis 1:5 (translated as one day). The context of Zechariah 14:7-8 suggests yôm echad will be a period of time spanning at least one summer and one winter, obviously longer than a 24-hour calendar day.

Third, Evening and Morning

Young-earth creationists claim "day" (yôm) accompanied by the phrase "and there was evening and there was morning" indicates the creation days were normal 24-hour days. However, there is lack of unanimity on this point. For example, The Wycliffe Bible Commentary states, "These are not ordinary days bounded by minutes and hours, but days of God... The beginning of each act of creation is called morning, and the close of that specific divine act is called evening."

In biblical Hebrew, the word, evening ('ereb) has several meanings, including sunset, night, or at the turn of evening and conveys a sense of gradual cessation or diminishing of activity. The word, morning (bōqer) also has several meanings, including the point of time at which night is changing into day... the end of night, daybreak, dawn, or beginning of day and conveys a sense of a new starting of creative activity. Thus, neither term restricts the meaning of day to a 24-hour period.

Much of the confusion comes from the King James Version, which combines evening and morning together, (the evening and the morning were the nth day). As Collins notes, grammatically, the AV [Authorized King James Version] compresses the two events into a sum, namely, (the evening plus the morning were a day). This is incorrect. A more accurate translation is found in the NASB and ESV: (And there was evening and there was morning, the nth day). Note the time period from evening to morning brackets only the night. As Collins states: This means any effort to find this as defining a 24-hour days runs counter to the author's, Moses' own presentation. The terms evening and morning can be used to represent long periods of time is evident in Psalm 90, which is attributed to Moses, the writer of Genesis. In the Psalm, morning, defines the beginning of life and evening, the end of life. Thus, morning and evening brackets the entire human lifespan. As Hebrew scholar Gleason Archer states, "Concerning the recurring evening and morning formula at the end of each creative day... there were definite and distinct stages in God's creational procedure... it serves as no real evidence for a literal twenty-four-hour day concept on the part of the biblical author" (Gleason Archer).

A statement concerning the term, day, should be made at the outset about biblical chronology of the six days of creation. Any attempt to correlate the biblical text with scientific knowledge must necessarily understand the term, day, to mean a phase or a period in the development of the world, rather than a time interval of twenty-four hours.
The Mormons weigh in on the debate,

There is no revealed recitation specifying, each of the six days involved in the creation consisted of the same duration or any specific duration. The three accounts of the creation are the Mosaic, the Abrahamic, and the one presented in the temples. Each of these stems back to the Prophet Joseph Smith. The Mosaic and Abrahamic accounts place the creative events on the same successive days, so let us analyze these scriptural recitations. The temple account, for reasons apparent to those familiar with its teachings, has a different division of events. It seems clear the six days are one continuing period and there is no one place where the dividing lines between the successive events must, of necessity, be placed. The Mosaic and the temple accounts set forth the temporal or physical creation, the actual organization of element or matter into tangible form. They are not accounts of the spirit creation.

The days of work listed below is Abraham giving a blueprint as it were of the creation but one cannot discern from this account whether he is talking about the Spiritual creation or the Physical creation. He tells the plans of the holy beings who wrought the creative work. After reciting the events of the "six days", he says, "And thus were their decisions at the time that they counseled among themselves to form the heavens and the earth" (*Abr. 5:3*).

It matters not whether the Abrahamic account is one of the Spiritual creation or the Physical creation, when he says they performed as they had planned means anyone can, by merely changing the verb tenses and without doing injustice to the sense and meaning so the narrative can work in both instances. In addition, if you supplant the word day with a long era of time as the Hebrew language would allow the timing problem goes away.

The First Day—Elohim, Jehovah, Michael, a host of noble and great ones all these played their parts. The Gods created the atmospheric heavens and the temporal earth. It was without form, and void; yet it could serve no useful purpose with respect to the salvation of man. It was empty and desolate; life could not yet exist on its surface; it was not yet a fit abiding place for those sons of God who shouted for joy at the prospect of a mortal probation. The waters of the great deep were present, and darkness reigned until the divine decree: Let-there-be-light. The light and the darkness were then divided and one was called Day and the other Night. Clearly, the planet earth was then formed, as a revolving orb and placed in its relationship to the sun (See *Moses 2:1–5; Abr. 4:1–5*).

The Second Day—on this day the waters were divided between the surface of the earth and the atmospheric heavens surrounding it. A firmament or an expanse called Heaven was created to divide the waters, which were under the expanse from the waters, which were above the expanse. Thus, as the creative events unfold, provision seems to be made for clouds, rain, and storms to give life to that which will yet grow and dwell upon the earth (*Moses 2:6–8; Abr. 4:6–8*).

The Third Day.—this is the day, when life began. In it, the waters under the heaven were, gathered together unto one place, and the dry land appeared. The dry land was called Earth, and the assembled waters became the Sea. This is the day in which the Gods organized the earth to bring forth grass and herbs and plants and trees; and it is the day in which vegetation in all its varied forms actually came forth from the seeds planted by the Creators. This is the day when the decree went forth, grass, herbs, and trees could each grow only from its own seed, and each could in turn bring forth only after its own kind. Thus, the bounds of the plant and vegetable kingdoms were set by the hands of those, by whom each varied plant and tree was made (See *Moses 2:9–13; Abr. 4:9–13*).

The Fourth Day—After seeds in all their varieties had been planted on the earth; after these had sprouted and grown; after each variety was prepared to bring forth fruit and seed after its own kind—the Creators organized all things in such a way as to make their earthly garden a productive and beautiful place. They then organized the lights in the expanse of the heaven so there would be seasons and a way of measuring days and years. It cannot be known what changes then took place in the atmospheric placements in heaven, but during this period the sun, moon, and stars assumed the relationship to the earth, which, now is theirs. At least the light of each of them began to shine through the lifting hazes enshrouding the newly created earth so they could play their parts with reference to life in all its forms, as it soon would be upon the new orb, (See Moses 2:14–19; Abr. 4:14–19).

The Fifth Day—next came fish, fowl, and every living creature whose abode is the waters. Their Creators placed them on the newly organized earth, and they were given the command: Be fruitful, and multiply, and fill the waters in the sea; and let fowl multiply in the earth. This command—as with a similar decree given to man and applicable to all animal life—they could not then keep, but they soon would be able to do so. Appended to this command to multiply, was the heaven-sent restriction, the creatures in the waters could only bring forth after their kind, and every winged fowl could only bring forth after his kind. There was no provision for evolvement or change from one species to another (*Moses 2:20–23; Abr. 4:20–23*).

The Sixth Day—the crowning day of creation is at hand. In its early hours, the great Creators made the beasts of the earth after their kind and cattle after their kind, and every, creepeth thing upon the earth after his kind. Moreover, the same procreative restrictions applying to them apply to all forms of life; they too are to reproduce only after their kind.

All that has been recited is now accomplished, but what of man? Is man found upon the earth? He is not. Therefore, the Gods, having so counseled among themselves, saying, let us go down and form man in our image, after our likeness. … So the Gods went down to organize man in their own image, in the image of the Gods to form they him, male and female to form they them." They then did as they had counseled, and the most glorious of all the creative acts was accomplished. Man is the crowning creature to step forth according to the divine will. He is in the image and likeness of the Eternal Elohim and to him is given dominion over all things. And then, finally, His purposes shall roll everlastingly onward, God blesses the male and female, which He has created and commands them: Be fruitful, and multiply, and replenish the earth, and subdue it, and have dominion over the fish of the sea, and over the fowl of the air, and over every living thing that moveth upon the earth. As the sixth day closes, the Creators, viewing their creative labors with satisfaction, see all things, which they have made are very good (See *Moses 2:24–31; Abr. 4:24–31*). Such is the revealed account of the creation of all things and this summary has combined elements from the Mosaic, the Abrahamic, and the temple accounts. At this point in the Mosaic record the scripture says, "Thus the heaven and the earth were finished, and all the host of them. The Lord then rests on the seventh day" (*Moses 3:1–3*).

Mormon theology takes the creation event one-step further.

Having come this far in the analysis of the creation it is important to ask, why did the Lord give mortals these revealed accounts of the creation? What purposes do they serve? How does the knowledge in these accounts help people work out their salvation, or to center their affection in Him? It is self-evident; the Lord does not deliver useless and unneeded revelations. All the Lord does has a purpose and serves a need. He expects mortals to treasure up his word, to ponder in their hearts its deep and hidden meanings, and to understand its full import. Those who have done so know the revealed accounts of the creation are designed to accomplish two great purposes. Their general purpose is to enable people to understand the nature of their mortal probation, a probation in where all men are being tried and tested "to see if they will do all things whatsoever the Lord their God shall command them." (*Abr. 3:25*) The specific purpose, of all things ever revealed, is to enable mortals, to understand the atoning sacrifice of the Lord Jesus Christ. The infinite and eternal Atonement is the very foundation upon which revealed religion rests.

It is only fair to say, a mere recitation of what took place during the six days and of the Lord's resting on the seventh day do not of themselves set forth with clarity the purposes of the creation accounts. Therefore, the Lord, as recorded in chapter 3 of the Mosaic account, proceeds to explain the purpose and nature of the creation. He comments about the creation. He reveals some facts and principles without which readers cannot envision what the true doctrine of the creation is. His statements inserted into the historical account, gives it true depth, meaning and import. They are not chronological recitations, but are commentary about what He had already set forth in its sequential order.

The Lord introduces His commentary about the creation by saying, the events of the six days, which He has just recited, "are the generations of the heaven and of the earth, when they were created, in the day that I, the Lord God, made the heaven and the earth" (*Moses 3:4*). Thus, all things have been created; the work is finished; the account is revealed; but it can only be understood if some added truths are set forth. These deal with the premortal existence of all things and with the paradisiacal nature of the earth and of all created things when they first came from their Creator's hand. Both of these concepts are interwoven in the same sentences, and in some instances, the words used have a dual meaning and apply to both the premortal life and the paradisiacal creation.

Therefore, the Lord says He created "every plant of the field before it was in the earth, and every herb of the field before it grew. ... And I, the Lord God, had created all the children of men; and not yet a man to till the ground; for in heaven created I them" (*Moses 3:5*). Clearly, He is speaking of the premortal existence of all things. This earth, all men, animals, fish, fowls, plants, all things—all lived first as spirit entities. Their home was heaven, and the earth was created to be the place where they could take upon themselves mortality.

"For I, the Lord God, created all things, of which I have spoken, spiritually, before they were naturally upon the face of the earth" (*Moses 3:5*). Apply these words to the spirit creation, if you will, and they will be true in such a context. However, these words have a much more pointed and important meaning. This statement then follows them. "For I, the Lord God, had not caused it to rain upon the face of the earth; ... and there was not yet flesh upon the earth, neither in the water, neither in the air; But I, the Lord God, spake, and there went up a mist from the earth, and watered the whole face of the ground" (*Moses 3:5–6*). The Lord is here telling about the events of which he has spoken, about the events of the six days, about the account of the physical, tangible, or temporal creation set forth in chapter 2 of Moses. He says the things so made were spiritually created and were not naturally upon the face of the earth, for the reasons quoted.

At this point, insert a statement from the tenth article of faith: "We believe ... the earth will be renewed and receive its paradisiacal glory" (*A of F 1:10*). When the earth was first created, it was in a paradisiacal state, a state in which there was no death. In addition, when the Lord comes again, and the millennial era is ushered in, the earth will return to its paradisiacal state and be renewed. It will be made new again; it will become a new heaven and a new earth whereon dwelled righteousness. "There shall be no sorrow because there is no death" (*D&C 101:29*).

Thus, the initial creation was paradisiacal; death and mortality had not yet entered the world. There was no mortal flesh upon the earth for any form of life. The creation was past, but mortality lay ahead. All things had been created in a state of paradisiacal immortality. It was of this day, Lehi said, "And all things which were created must have remained in the same state in which they were after they were created; and they must have remained forever, and had no end" (*2nd Ne. 2:22*). If there is no death, all things of necessity must continue to live everlastingly and without end.

Continuing the divine commentary about the creation Moses said this. "And I, the Lord God, formed man from the dust of the ground, and breathed into his nostrils the breath of life; and man became a living soul, the first flesh upon the earth, the first man also; nevertheless, all things were before created; but spiritually were they created and made according to my word" (*Moses 3:7*). How filled with meaning are these words! The physical body of Adam is made from the dust of this earth, the very earth to which the Gods came down to form him. His "spirit" enters his body, as Abraham expresses it (*Abr. 5:7*). Man becomes a living, immortal soul; body and spirit are joined together. He has been created spiritually, as all things were because there is yet no mortality. Then comes the fall; Adam falls; mortality, procreation, and death commence. Fallen man is mortal; he has mortal flesh; he is "the first flesh upon the earth." In addition, the effects of his fall pass upon all created things. They fall and they too become mortal. Death enters the world; mortality reigns; procreation commences; and the Lord's great and eternal purposes roll onward.

Thus, all things were created as spirit entities in heaven; then all things were created in a paradisiacal state upon the earth; spiritually were they created, for there was yet no death. They had spiritual bodies made of the elements of the earth as distinguished from the mortal bodies they would receive after the fall when death would enter the scheme of things. Natural bodies are subject to the natural death; spiritual bodies, being paradisiacal in nature, are not subject to death. Hence, the need for a fall, mortality and the death resulted out of it.

Thus, as the interpolative exposition in the divine word explains, "I, the Lord God, planted a garden eastward in Eden, and there I put the man whom I had formed" (*Moses 3:8*). Adam, the first father, dwelt in the Garden of Eden. He was the first man of all men in the day of his creation, and he became the first flesh of all flesh through the fall. Because of the fall, "all things" changed from their spiritual state to a natural state. "And out of the ground made I, the Lord God, to grow every tree, naturally, that is pleasant to the sight of man; and man could behold it. And it became also a living soul. For it was spiritual in the day that I created it" (*Moses 3:9*).

Also, consider the Greek take on the Six-Day issue, Philo, in On Allegory, rejected simple and literalistic interpretations of the Bible, including the creation story as told in Genesis 1. "It is quite foolish," Philo wrote, "to think that the world was created in the space of six days or in a space of time at all." Six, as he saw it, represented to Moses (Philo assumed Moses to be the author of Genesis), not a number of days, but a perfect number signifying the perfection of God's creation. No one, not even Moses, could ever give expression in an adequate manner to the beauty of God's ideas respecting the creation of the world. Therefore, the author of Genesis did the best he could. Although "it is in the nature of God to create all things simultaneously," the number six is "the most suitable for creation," (Philo contended). The reasons for adopting a six-day creation story rather than, say, a five-day or nine-day creation, might seem more compelling to a mathematician than the average Christian today. Philo pointed out, the number six is unique among numbers in that it is equal both to the product of its factors ($1 \times 2 \times 3$) and to the sum of its factors ($1+2+3$). He also attached sexual significance to the choice of six, arguing, it is the product of an even (female, he believed) number and an odd (male) number. Seeing a symbolism likely to escape the notice of most, Philo wrote, because creation required birth from couplings it was necessary it should be shaped to correspond to the first mixed (odd-even) number, which has the characteristics of the male who sows the seed and the female who receives it. One can say what one will about Philo's theory of numbers, the key point is, the Biblical text, as Philo saw it, was just a departure point for exploration of God's purposes. Most Biblical scholars today believe the author of Genesis chose a six-day creation because it fit best with the Sabbatarian, an early sect of Jews who shaped most of the Jewish doctrine. Beliefs, which had developed in the Jewish community, by the time of the Books writing in the sixth-century B.C.

When Moses wrote, the world was created in six days, Philo argued, he did so to show God's love of order. Philo declared, the law corresponds to the world and the world to the law. Philo believed the creation, in fact, happened all at once, not in external action but in thought. God thought, therefore everything is. The great Moses, as Philo explained, thinking that a thing, which has not been created is as alien as possible from everything, which is visible before our eyes…have attributed eternity to that which is invisible and discerned only by our intellect. From the simple fact, Philo concluded, "this world is visible, it must have been created." Moses wrote the creation story of Genesis, according to Philo, to give a very venerable account of God—a God who modeled the physical universe to reflect the forms first conceived in his own unfathomable mind. Philo argued, when God created the universe, he also created time, before the world, time had no existence. So when Moses wrote, in the beginning, he meant, in Philo's view, in the beginning of time. God existed before the beginning—as did the idea, the universe represents.

Suffering

This section will be a comparison of the Jewish view if suffering, the Christian's view of suffering, and the Mormon's view of suffering.

The Jews of the Old Testament thought suffering was the result of sin, sin being violations of Mosaic Law. They tended to judge their relationship with God by their circumstances in life. There are many examples in the scriptures of Jews describing their situation as punishment for sin or reward for faithfulness, both individually and collectively. Here are two of the many scriptures used to support this: In God says, "I will punish them for their ways, and reward them for their doings" (*Hosea 4:9*). Isaiah states, when God was angry with his People, the Jews, He put them under the care of Babylon. However, Babylon "did not show them mercy" (*Isaiah 47:6-14*). According to the Torah, the Covenant at Sinai, in which the Israelites agreed to abide by the commandments and they would be rewarded if they followed God's ways. Yet, suffering often seems to be meted out randomly. Righteous people suffer and wicked people prosper. Early Jewish literature conceives of God as all-powerful, good, and knowledgeable. As early as Moses the population was asking questions such as; why do bad things happen to good people? If God is so powerful, why does not God prevent misfortune? If God knows everything, then God knows about all evil. If God is all-powerful, then God can prevent all evil. If God is perfectly good, then God should prevent all evil. Yet, evil exists. How can this be true? Those questions are still asked today by some Jews and all many others. Jewish thinkers have always been bothered by the existence of suffering and but it was not until the time of Daniel, who is believed to be the last Prophet who lived before Jesus, in the Jewish scriptures the devil or Satan is associated with the misfortune and suffering of the Jews. A person could ask, how about Job, Adam, and Eve, surely, the Jews knew what happened there concerning Satan.

In the prologue to the Book of Job, where Satan appears, replying to the inquiry of God as to whence he had come, with the words: "From going to and fro in the earth, and from walking up and down in it" (*Job 1:7*). Both question and answer, as well as the dialogue which follows, characterize Satan as having the evil purpose of searching out men's sins and appearing as their accuser. He is characterized as a kind of celestial prosecutor. In verses 8-12, Job is considered only for a limited test by permission of God.

The Jews believe it is evident from this prologue; Satan has no power of independent action, but requires the permission of God, which he may not transgress. Therefore, he cannot be regarded, as an opponent of God. The Jews believe this view is also retained in Zech. 3:1-2, where Satan is described as the adversary of the high priest Joshua. In both of these passages, Satan acts only under permission.

In the Adam and Eve Story there is not any direct reference to Satan or the Devil but only to a serpent. The Jews believe in a literal interpretation and do not associate the serpent with Satan or the devil.

This problem still exists today in Jewish communities and it results from the unique relationship between God and the Jews who occupied early Jewish literature, mainly The Covenant at Sinai.

To this very day, there are people who are suffering from some dilemma saying, *what have I done to God to deserve this punishment*. This is not just a problem for Jews, but for anyone who conceives of God in a certain way. They tended to think God blesses the wealthy and God curses the poor and suffering.

To illustrate this disassociation between Satan and suffering; the word Satan occurs eighteen times in the Old Testament, 14 of those in Job.

However, where did Satan come from? The stories of Satan's rise to power is nowhere explained clearly in the Old Testament, although there have been some rather unconventional interpretations made in this regard. In Isaiah 14, there is a lament for and against the king of Babylon for his deeds against Judah. In the midst of this passage it says, "How you are fallen from heaven, O Day Star, son of Dawn! How you are cut down to the ground, you who laid the nations low" (*Isaiah 14.12*). The phrase, O Day Star, is a translation of the Latin word Lucifer and has become known, by some, from this lone passage, as the proper name for Satan, but in fact, it is the just Latin word for the morning star. How did this Latin word get into Isaiah's narrative, who lived and died long before there were Romans or the Latin language? Historians do not really know, anyway, from this passage rose the story; Satan was once an angel who went bad. Further passages used to support this notion include Daniel, "It threw down to the earth some of the host and some of the stars" (*Daniel 8.10*).

So the Jews have somewhat reconciled the issue of Gods punishment by bringing Satan into the picture and by the time Christ appeared the subject of Satan and suffering was general known and accepted by only a few Jewish sects. This led early Christians to closely examine the doctrine of suffering.

Christians, from the very start, viewed suffering from a completely different angle. Satan occurs thirty-six times in the New Testament. Twenty-eight of these times, it is accompanied by the definite article. There is no question that in the New Testament, Jesus Himself predicted His followers would experience trouble, heartache, and even persecution. Why? Well, Satan of course and they looked upon the Romans as Satan. The early Christian movement had a lot of documentation to show, suffering is of the devil and it is all biblical. After all Satan had even tried to tempt Jesus and destroy his sacred mission. They believed all sickness, sin, suffering, pain, and death are of the devil. They would admit, Satan tempts people to sin and God judges them, but in the end, it is all of the devil and his legions who have been loosed on earth causing all these problems. This is the world in which everyone is called to follow the Master and share His suffering. Whether they recognize it or not, the hearts and minds of the Christ-rejecting world are not only under the control of Satan, but in fact, they are in a war where Satan and Christ are contending over their spirits.

Listen to the Lord's own words in John, "If the world hates you, keep in mind it hated me first. If you belonged to the world, it would love you as its own. As it is, you do not belong to the world, but I have chosen you out of the world. That is why the world hates you. Remember the words I spoke to you: 'No servant is greater than his master.' If they persecuted me, they will persecute you also. If they obeyed my teaching, they will obey yours also. They will treat you this way because of my name, for they do not know the One who sent me. If I had not come and spoken to them, they would not be guilty of sin. Now, however, they have no excuse for their sin. He who hates me hates my Father as well if I had not done among them what no one else did, they would not be guilty of sin. Now they have seen these miracles, and yet they have hated both me and my Father. But this is to fulfill what is written in their Law: They hated me without reason" (*John 15:18-25*). "All this I have told you so that you will not go astray. They will put you out of the synagogue; in fact, a time is coming when anyone who kills you will think he is offering a service to God. They will do such things because they have not known the Father or me" (*John 16:1-3*).

During the time when these passages were written the early Christians, being hunted and killed by Romans, could easily see Satan as the root of all of their problems.

However, Christians of today still ask the same question and the Romans are long gone: Why do sad and bad things happen to innocent and good people? This question is often followed with an attempt to judge God as was seen with the Jews: If God is truly loving, good and kind why would He allow such things to happen. This indictment is of God has dangerous consequences; it disallows the person to reconcile the pain and suffering of mortals with the kind and loving nature of God. Oft time those in this situation lose faith in God and His plan for them and embrace the secular notion, God caused this pain and suffering for no reason. Orson Pratt dealt with this indictment and answered this question when he explained, when God created Man, specifically Adam and Eve they were not created as mortal beings. It would be contrary to His great goodness to make man mortal, subject to pain, subject to weakness, subject to death. When He made those two intelligent beings and placed them upon this creation, He made them after His own likeness and his own image. He did not make them mortal, but He made them immortal like unto Himself. If He had made them mortal and subject to pain, there would have been some cause to say, the Lord subjected man, without cause, to afflictions, sorrow, death, and mortality. However, He could not do this: it is contrary to the nature of His attributes, contrary to the nature of the infinite goodness, which dwells in the bosom of the Father and the Son, to make a being subject to any kind of pain. So, now, a Mormon scholar has spoken, what do the Mormons themselves believe? Do they believe the Jewish doctrine or any part of it? Do they believe the Christian doctrine or any part of it? Do Mormons have their own doctrine?

Mormon Doctrine presents an understanding of suffering completely different from any other religion; the belief is suffering is inherent in mortality. Physical bodies are subject to pain and discomfort from hunger, disease, trauma, violence, and exposure. As a social being, man is vulnerable to emotional suffering, which often rivals physical pain— anxieties, rejection, loneliness, despair. Among the sensitive there are also other levels of profound suffering. They may relate, for example, to the awareness of the effects of sin or the anguish of the abuse or indifference of one's loved ones. In addition, there is vicarious suffering in response to the pain around one and the sense of the withdrawal of the Spirit. Modern day Christians, including some Mormons, attempt to explain the necessity of suffering in a verity of ways:

1. It is an essential element in testing and building moral character,

2. It is the unavoidable side effect of agency,

3. It is illusive or utterly mysterious.

Whatever partial consolations these attempts provide, suffering remains. LDS doctrine provides two explanations, uncommon in the Judeo-Christian tradition.

First, all mankind chose to enter mortality with full knowledge of the great price, which would be required of the Christ and of discipleship in his name.

Second, one's suffering is to be in the image of the Lord, whose suffering was requisite "that his bowels [might] be filled with mercy…that he might know according to the flesh how to succor his people according to their infirmities" (*Alma 7:12*). For Latter-day Saints, Jesus' words on the cross "My God, my God, why hast thou forsaken me?" is a measure of the depth of his suffering (*Matt. 27:46*). In no other way, could the redemption of the universe and the unleashing of authentic love and compassion be achieved. Jesus described his own mission almost entirely in terms of healing. "To bind up the brokenhearted, to proclaim liberty to the captives, and the opening of the prison to them that are bound; ...to comfort all that mourn; to appoint unto them that mourn in Zion, to give unto them beauty for ashes, the oil of joy for mourning, the garment of praise for the spirit of heaviness" (*Isa. 61:1-3; Luke 4:18-19*).

Only in the life to come amid the glories of the New Jerusalem will the full effect of Christ's mission "wipe away all tears from their eyes; and there shall be no more death, neither sorrow, nor crying, neither shall there be any more pain" (Rev. 21:4). Even so, for Latter-day Saints the embrace of his messiahship and the proclamation of his gospel was intended to relieve needless pain and suffering. They do so in many ways.

First, they provide a foundation for hope, through the Atonement of Jesus Christ one may find reunion with God.

Second, they offer continuous access to the Holy Ghost, the Comforter, and, through this, to an inner peace "passeth all understanding" (*Philip. 4:7*).

Third, they teach the law of the harvest where many blessings follow naturally from obedience to the laws, which govern them and much unhappiness, can be avoided, including sin and its accompanying pain, shame, and spiritual bruising.

Finally, they establish a community built on kinship, a society of mutually supportive and protective fellow believers whose charge is to "bear one another's burdens, that they may be light; yea, and are willing to mourn with those that mourn; yea, and comfort those that stand in need of comfort" (*Mosiah 18:8-9*).

Concerning such things as natural disasters, this world is a living organism and in its natural course of working, humans just get in the way by living to close to a river or under a volcano or some such thing. The decisions people make in these areas can and often do cause suffering but are the consequence of exercising their free agency.

The concept of Satan in both the Jewish and early Christian doctrine is somewhat different from LDS doctrine. In terms of the Jewish belief, Mormons understand Satan and his legions run amuck on this earth but they do not believe Satan operates with permission from God but he operates with permission from mankind. The early Christian idea where everything bad is Satan's fault releases them from any personal responsibility in terms

318

of their own suffering. Mormons, simply do not believe in the phrase "Satan made me do it".

Latter-day Saints do not believe pain is intrinsically good. However, when suffering is unavoidable in the fulfillment of life's missions, one's challenge is to draw upon all the resources of one's soul and endure faithfully and well. If benefit comes from pain, it is not because there is anything inherently cleansing in pain itself. Suffering can wound, embitter, and darken a soul as surely as it can purify and refine and illumine. Everything depends on how one responds. At a time of terrible desolation and imprisonment, the Prophet Joseph Smith was told, "My son, peace be unto thy soul; thine adversity and thine afflictions shall be but a small moment; and then, if thou endure it well, God shall exalt thee on high…. Know thou, my son, that all these things shall give thee experience, and shall be for thy good. The Son of Man hath descended below them all. Art thou greater than he? Therefore, hold on thy way, fear not what man can do, for God shall be with you forever and ever" (*D&C 121:7-8; 122:7-9*).

There is an old Chinese tale about the woman whose only son died. In her grief and suffering, she went to the holy man and said, "What prayers, what magical incantations do you have to bring my son back to life?" Instead of sending her away or reasoning with her, he said to her, "Fetch me a mustard seed from a home that has never known sorrow. We will use it to drive sorrow out of your life," The woman set off at once in search of a magical mustard seed. She came first to a splendid mansion, knocked at the door, and said, "I am looking for a home that has never known sorrow. Is this such a place? It is very important to me." They told her, "You've certainly come to the wrong place," and began to describe all the tragic things recently befallen them. The woman said to herself, "Who is better able to help these poor unfortunate people than I, who have had misfortune of my own?" She stayed to comfort them, and then went on in her search for a home that had never known sorrow. However, wherever she turned, in hovels and in palaces, she found one tale after another of sadness and misfortune. Ultimately, she became so involved in ministering to other people's grief, she forgot about her quest for the magical mustard seed, never realizing it had in fact driven sorrow out of her life

The Symbolism of David and Goliath

Many believe all of the stories recounted in the scriptures are there to symbolically, help people understand their situation today. When reading and understand the biblical stories, Christ's followers will gain an advantage in the fight against Satan during their lives. Some of the stories are very strait forward, it is easy to see symbolism, the intent of the writer, and the message is plainly there for everyone to see. However, some are not so easy to get a grip on, such as the story of David, and Goliath. To understand the story, one must examine the features of the story to see what caused this story to be included in the bible. The complete story is in the New Testament, Samuel 17, but for now, just a summary the story will do.

The Philistine army had gathered for war against Israel. The two armies faced each other, camped for battle on opposite sides of a steep valley. The custom of those days was, each opposing army would send out their best man to fight. These two men would engage each other in a one on one battle, and the winner of the fight would decide the outcome of the entire war. The Philistines sent out a giant measuring over nine feet tall, wearing full armor, and for forty days he stood mocking, and challenging the Israelites to fight. His name was Goliath. Saul, the King of Israel, and the entire Israeli army were terrified of Goliath. King Saul would not, nor could he get any of his men to, meet the challenge. One day, Jesse sent David, his youngest son, to the battle lines, to bring back news of his older brothers. David was probably just a young teenager at the time. While there, David heard Goliath shouting his daily defiance, and he saw the great fear stirring within the men of Israel. David responded, "Who is this uncircumcised Philistine that he should defy the armies of God?" David went to the king, and volunteered to fight Goliath. After some persuasion, a reluctant King Saul finally agreed to let David fight against the giant. Dressed in his simple tunic, carrying his sling, and a pouch of just five stones, David approached Goliath. The giant cursed at him, hurling threats and insults. David said to the Philistine, "You come against me with sword and spear and javelin, but I come against you in the name of the Lord Almighty, the God of the armies of Israel, whom you have defied ... today I will give the carcasses of the Philistine army to the birds of the air ... and the whole world will know there is a God in Israel ... it is not by sword or spear that the Lord saves; for the battle is the Lord's, and he will give all of you into our hands" (*1st Sam. 17: 45-47*). As Goliath moved in for the kill, David reached into his bag, and slung one of his stones at Goliath's head. Finding the weakest spot in the armor, the stone sank into the giant's forehead, and he fell face down on the ground. David then took Goliath's sword, and cut off his head. When the Philistines saw their hero, killed, they turned, and ran. The Israelites pursued, chasing and killing many of them, and then returned to the battle lines, and plundered the Philistine camp.

Most Christian churches teach this legend as a typical, underdog victory against overwhelming odds, kind of story, but for LDS members this interpretation does not work well, since they do not feel they are an underdog of any kind. So what are LDS members to take out of the story to fortify their lives? --- Well, to start, David represents the righteous element of the world, and Goliath represents the evil of the earth. Aside from this, the readers of the story have the difficult task of understanding the symbolism of Goliath's size, armor and weaponry, the reason it is related in such detail, the significance of David's refusal to wear Saul's armor, left only to be clothed in the armor of God, and the significance of the five smooth stones.

Beginning with presentation of Goliath, whose height was six cubits and a span, which is about 9 ft. 9in, and he had an helmet of brass upon his head (weight unknown), and he was armed with a coat of mail. The weight of the coat was five thousand shekels of brass, which is about 157 pounds, and he had greaves (boots with shin guards) of brass upon his legs, weight unknown. A target of brass between his shoulders, which is a javelin slung onto his back, and the staff of his spear was like a weaver's beam, which is about 2-2 ½ inches in diameter, and his spear's head weighed six hundred shekels, (about 15 pounds) made of iron. An armor bearer, carrying the shield, went before him. Goliath was carrying a large sword, length, and weight unknown. Therefore, he was bigger than life, extremely well-armed, and well protected, except for his face. Amazingly, this is much more detailed than any other biblical story in memory. If all this is a metaphor for evil of today, it is spot on. The evil seen here is certainly huge, and does seem to be unstoppable. Nevertheless, the message, this story is conveying is, evil is conquerable, and this can even be accomplished by a seemly unarmed boy. While reading this story the reader is supposed to uncover the vulnerability of the adversary, and discover the way to be victorious over evil, in their lives. When analyzing Goliath, it is hard to see any vulnerability, and how those, who read about it, can be victorious over evil. Maybe, the answer is in David's side of the story.

David, presented here as a young shepherd, who is a musician and, in most people's mind, would be the last person on earth to confront Goliath. The people involved in this battle reiterate this underdog image. Saul, his troops, and David's family, also seem to think David would not have any kind of a chance against Goliath, and since the outcome of this one on one confrontation decides the winner of the war, and the fate of their country, the king and his military commanders are not too keen on David doing battling with Goliath. On the other hand, David does not see himself as an underdog at all. He is convinced, if the Lord could help him prevail over a lion, and a bear in the wilderness there is not any reason he, along with the Lord's help, could not beat Goliath. At any rate, in the end, Saul allows David to take on Goliath because he nor, any of his men will agree to fight

Goliath, and he has no other options available. Saul gives David his armor to wear in the battle, but after trying Saul's armor on, David rejects the offer, and goes to face Goliath in his every-day clothing, and instead of using Saul's weapons he takes only his sling. On the way to the spot where the battle is to take place, David picks up five smooth stones from the brook, and puts them in his pouch. As the battle begins, David, running toward Goliath, slings one of the stones, which struck Goliath in the forehead, and killed him instantly. Well, so far, no information concerning the vulnerability of the evil has arisen and not much insight gained by David's victory, which would help anyone be victorious over evil in the future.

Most people understand, all biblical stories, and the elements contained within are metaphors for the battle between Christ and Lucifer and the claiming of souls, which started during the War in Heaven, and continues today. All of these descriptive terms such as the armor, the size of Goliath, and the five stones of David are symbolic of things in people's lives. So, what do these terms symbolize, and what does each of them mean? The Philistine war against Israel is representative of the war between good, and evil, still going on today. The steep valley represents mortality, where evil and righteousness reside side, by side. The physical size of Goliath represents the enormities of the evil, people are confronted, with today. The armor of Goliath represents the deceitfulness, hatefulness, and viciousness in which evil people cloak themselves, in order to protect themselves, and, of course, to intimidate those, who they wish to oppress. The weapons of Goliath (spear, sword, and javelin) represent the methods, which evil people use to attack, and overwhelm their foes. Today these methods are things, such as, the media, the entertainment industry, political ideology, and political correctness, which, as Goliath's shield bearer exemplifies, are willing facilitators for the truly evil ones. The cursing, and denouncing of God, is significant of the anti-religion sentiment, and attacks on religion, happening right now. On the other hand, David's size and demeanor, nowadays, represents the Lord's small, but confident army of righteous folks, who feel they do not need any exterior armor since they are not trying to oppress anyone, and truly believe the meek will inherit the world. In today's world David's weapon, in particular the sling, is represented today by the word of God, (scriptures) and the five smooth stones are symbolized by faith, obedience, prayer, service, and the gift of the Holy Ghost, outlined by Dallin Oaks, in his talk, five smooth stones. King Saul is symbolic of a church leadership, Bishoprics or Stake Presidencies who are failing in their calling since the King, nor any of his generals seem willing to confront the evil at their door. The reluctant army of Saul is comparable to the Christian congregations of today who are slothful in their callings, and cannot bring

322

themselves to convey God's message, to their neighbor. David's aggressive defense of his religion against the philistines is symbolic of the Church of Jesus Christ of Latter Day Saints, and the church member's missionary efforts around the world.

There, in a bible story, thousands of years old, the malevolence, and godliness is metaphorically describing the way the world is today, and with great accuracy. Now, the last thing left to do is identify the weakness of evil, and the strength of righteousness, which, by the way, have to be the same thing. Some say, weakness v/s strength can only be one thing---AGENCY, and the use thereof. This was the crux of the War in Heaven, and is still the prevailing enterprise on both sides of the conflict, even today

In an effort to illustrate and clarify, the concepts of using agency to defeat evil refer to the movie Driving Mrs. Daisy, as an example. In this movie, Mrs. Daisy is a narcissistic wealthy Jewish widower who is advancing in age, to the point, where she cannot drive any longer. Her only son, who is managing the family business, employs an elderly black man as her driver. The new driver, unknowingly, walks into a prejudicial situation; Mrs. Daisy is tremendously distressed about losing her driving privileges. She also is extremely prejudice, and does not want a black man as her driver, but her son will not relent. She is also an unbearable complainer, an elitist, she is appallingly vain, and since her son will not hire a suitable driver, she decides to take out all her resentments, on her new driver. She utilizes all the deceitful, hateful, and vicious means she can think of, to get even with her son, and force this black Man to leave. This is classic evil at work. In terms of agency, this decision of brutality is Mrs. Daisy using her agency incorrectly. The evil, as represented by Goliath, initiated by Mrs., Daisy, came into existence by the improper use of her agency, just as it was in the preexistence by Satan. On the other hand, this poor unfortunate driver is a humble; God loving, and a patient man, who can see the pain Mrs. Daisy is suffering, from the roll changes, and disruptions in her life, is willing to forgive her for her indiscretions, immediately. It is not to say he takes all this lying down, but he always corrects her in a loving way. He will not play into her hands by saying, or doing anything she could use against him, but at the same time, he makes his point, and retains his dignity. Over the years, the two of them go through many difficult clashes, but eventually, the unreserved love shown by this man, starts to have its effect on Mrs. Daisy. He goes from being some distasteful thing she would not allow, to sleep under her porch, to becoming, tolerated as her driver. He is soon, accepted as her assistant, later to become her confidant and adviser, and then becoming her best and only friend. The driver in this story is using the same tools David used, symbolically, in the David and Goliath story, and in doing

323

so demonstrated the correct use of his agency. It is as if this, unwanted driver slung the stone of loving service, straight into the unprotected forehead of Mrs. Daisy, where all the decision of brutality was made and defeated her evil thoughts forever. When taking this David and Goliath story out of its metaphorical format and applying it to daily life, inappropriate agency use is the culprit of evil. Agency is evil's vulnerability, wherein, even a young boy with the proper tools, obedience to the gospel, can defeat evil.

The Three Perspectives of God

The Church of Jesus Christ of Latter Day Saints has a very unique view of the institution of God but, for the most part, the rank and file members either cannot or do not desire to examine or discuss it in any depth. If you ask, any member to explain the three purviews of God you would undoubtedly get this as an answer, the father, the Son, and the Holy Ghost. These are not perspectives, these are the three members of the Godhead, unfortunately, most member would be unable to expound further on the subject.

The word God is used in the scriptures in three different ways, giving rise to three specific perspectives where God's influence is felt. These areas are defined as,

1. God the Calling,

2. God the Man

3. God the Office,

Take *God the Office* first. In Genesis, where God is involved in the creation, which is the entire chapter one and two, what is being described here is God administering the duties of His office. This is much like the office of a Stake President or the office of a Bishop where they are making things happen within the limitations of their callings. These administrators, along with the help of others, and within the range of their authority are appraising situations, considering the use of materials, analyzing talent at their disposal, issuing callings, and evaluating the results. This is exactly what is occurring in the first two chapters of Genesis.

God the Calling, In the Pearl of Great Price, God is explaining the continuum of His creations. He was telling Moses the purpose of His labors, and why He will continue, i.e. He is fulfilling His calling. "And as one earth shall pass away, and the heavens thereof even so shall another come; and there is no end to my works, neither to my words. For behold, this is my work and my glory—to bring to pass the immortality and eternal life of man" (Moses, 1: 38&39). Verse 39 spells out the calling of God and as He explains to Moses, He will continue in this calling eternally. This calling has enormous consequences for mortals and is not just unique to God the Father. Jehovah took on this very same calling for the universe He had created, when presenting His plan during the war in the preexistence when He said "Thy will be done and the glory be thine forever" (*Moses 4:2*). The Prophet of the Church of Jesus Christ of Latter Day Saints takes upon himself the same calling for the earth with a small caveat; the immortality of man has already taken care of by Christ. Additionally, the Stake President takes on this came calling for his stake and the Bishop takes on this same calling for his ward. Both the Stake President's and the Bishop's, administration of their office reflects their efforts to bring eternal life to their congregations. In addition, missionaries take on this calling for the area of their labor, every person who accepts a calling in the church takes on this calling for the position they accept and all people baptized take on this same calling for themselves. Therefore, this same calling is taken on by almost everyone in the church, indeed, their work, their glory, their eternal life, and their reward in Heaven is based, on their success in this calling.

God the Man, this is probably the most interesting part of the institution of God as advocate by the Church. The First Vision was, for many, is the beginning of their understanding of this concept, but the portion of the King Follett discourse where Joseph Smith spoke of God as a man cemented this image in the mind of many people, forever. This portion reads as follow.

God an Exalted Man. "I will go back to the beginning before the world was, to show what kind of a being God is. What sort of a being was God in the beginning? Open your ears and hear, all ye ends of the earth, for I am going to prove it to you by the Bible, and to tell you the designs of God in relation to the human race, and why He interferes with the affairs of man. God himself was once as man is now, and is an exalted man, and sits enthroned in yonder heavens! This is the great secret. If the veil were rent today, and the great God who holds this world in its orbit, and who upholds all worlds and all things by His power, was to make himself visible—I say, if you were to see him today, you would see him like a man in form—like yourselves in all the person, image, and very form as a man; for Adam was created in the very fashion, image and likeness of God, and received instruction from, and walked, talked and conversed with Him, as one man talks and communes with another. In order to understand the subject of the dead, for consolation of those who mourn for the loss of their friends, it is necessary to understand the character and being of God and how He came to be so; for I am going to tell you how God came to be God. We have imagined and supposed that God was God from all eternity. I will refute that idea, and take away the veil, so that you may see. These ideas are incomprehensible to some, but they are simple. It is the first principle of the gospel to know for a certainty the character of God, and to know that we may converse with Him as one man converses with another, and that He was once a man like us; yea, that God himself, the Father all, dwelt on an earth, the same as Jesus Christ Himself did; and I will show it from the Bible" (*The Teachings of Joseph Smith*). Below are a few extracts of The Prophet's comments for the purposes of further understanding. They read as follows,

Of the kinship between God and man, Joseph Smith taught, "If men do not comprehend the character of God, they do not comprehend themselves" (*TPJS, p. 343*). "It is the first principle of the Gospel to know for a certainty the Character of God, and to know that we may converse with him as one man converses with another" (*TPJS, p. 345*). Echoing his first vision, the Prophet taught what he called the great secret: "If the veil were rent today, and…God…[were] to make himself visible, if you were to see him today, you would see him like a man in form-like yourselves in all the person, image, and very form as a man" (*TPJS, p. 345*). Creation, he taught, was not by mere fiat or ex nihilo. God's role was to bring harmony to primal, unorganized elements and to "institute laws" whereby weaker intelligences might have the privilege of advancing like himself (*TPJS, p. 354*). Of man's potential, the Prophet said that even as God is eternal and self-existent, so the intelligence of man is also eternal. The Father has become what he is through eternities of progress. Christ, who did nothing but what he had seen the Father do (see John 5:19), followed identical paths and patterns. Since all mankind have a divine Father, they are potential "heirs of God and joint-heirs with Jesus Christ" (*TPJS, pp. 346-47, Romans 8:17*). In this sense, all the children of God are embryonic gods or goddesses. Obedience to the fullness of the gospel is the perfecting process through which they may go "from one small degree to another and from a small capacity to a great one, from grace to grace, from exaltation to exaltation…until [they] arrive at the station of a God" (*TPJS, pp. 346-47*).

Members, learn from all this, callings in the Mormon Church have a parallel in all other spheres. In mortality, the administrative callings are somewhat like the callings of deity. In other words, the calling of a Prophet, Bishop, Stake President, etc. is the Calling of a Man to an Office, which is similar to the all of the calling made by God. These three parts are present in all callings and are necessary and intentional because they, for the most part, are where God's influence is felt.

True meaning of True
(Is the book of Mormon true?)

All of us, at one time or another, have been sitting in a fast and testimony meeting and heard someone, while bearing their testimony, say, I know every word in the Book of Mormon is true, or something to that effect. These kinds of statements are somewhat misguided since the person making the statement may not be able to understand the entire spiritual perspective, or probably cannot remember every word contained in the Book of Mormon in order to know they all are true. So, the members who hear this statement have to ask, where did this person get such a notion? Well, they most likely got it from the many church publications, or the talks given by the General Authorities at conference where words such as true, correct, historicity and verisimilitude, which are given without any explanation of the exact meaning of these words or the context in which they are being used. Are all these sources misguided? The answer is, NO, they are not. When the General Authorities use these words they know what they are saying but many times the meaning is something very different than many members understand. To get up in a meeting, without any insight of how these words fit into the context what you are saying, and using any of these words in the context of your personal testimony of the Book of Mormon, is risky.

It's important to take a look at the usage of these words and what they mean so there can be some understanding of how the words true, correct, historicity, and verisimilitude, apply to the Book of Mormon.

In the context of this discussion and in most conference talks the word, true refers to the spiritual nature of the Book of Mormon, not the vocabulary or vernacular of the text. In the same vain Joseph Smith said, "I told the brethren that the Book of Mormon was the most correct of any book on earth, and the keystone of the Mormon religion" (*TJS Chapter 4*). Some critics claim the word correct, in this context, means perfect and the book should not contain any type of errors. This is a silly argument and only use to discredit the Book of Mormon. Joseph obviously understood the book did contain errors because

(a) He corrected many errors in later editions and

(b) The original Book of Mormon prophet and writer himself expressly stated the likelihood of errors (*Title Page and Mormon 9:31-32*).

The word *correct*, in the context used by Joseph, is related to word *true*. The Book of Mormon teaches those correct and/or true principles, which can lead people to God. Is the Book of Mormon the word of God? Does following its precepts draw one closer to God? These questions can be answered only on a spiritual level -- through faith, humility, personal study, and prayer but surely not by simply repeating what you hear someone else say.

Some archeologist say the historicity of the Book of Mormon does not fit with their findings, meaning, when anyone uses the events in the Book of Mormon as historical commentary, the archeological evidence might not back it up, indicating, the Book of Mormon is not as advertised. LDS scholar Ben McGuire explains historicity this way: Did the events described in the text really occur to real people at a certain time and place? There are two ways to approach this question. The first way is a general approach: Were there really Nephites and Lamanites who lived somewhere in the ancient Americas? Most people will say yes, even though they may use many different names for these groups of people, it is obvious they were there. The second way is a limited approach: Did every event in the Book of Mormon happen in precisely the way, place and time as recorded? While Latter-day Saints believe, stories contained in the Bible are primarily based on actually events but they do not necessarily believe all things related in the Bible happened precisely as described. They believe, for instance, biblical authors often used hyperbole, metaphorical and poetic language to convey their ideas. For example, the creation of Eve from Adam's rib is viewed figuratively. Most do not believe the earth is shaped like a dish or the sun goes around the Earth, as described by Old Testament authors. Not all LDS Church members believe the sun stood still (Joshua 10:13) or Noah's flood covered every inch of the entire planet. Members recognize, while there really was a Jesus, Moses, Abraham and Adam, they also recognize the ancient authors wrote from within their own world-views, from their own perspectives and understandings of their beliefs, and they wrote according to "their weakness, after the manner of their language" (*D&C 1:24*). The same principle applies to the Book of Mormon. Nephite prophets wrote from their own perspectives, their own understanding of history and the world around them, as well as their proclivity to take hyperbolic and poetic license in their writings. Accepting the historicity of actual Nephites and Lamanites does not necessarily mean everyone believes that everything single thing written, was recorded with historical perfection. Latter Day Saints believe in the Book of Mormon is a book recording the spiritual journey of those particular people and was never intended to be a manuscript for historical verification. If these records were to be accurate in every way, Mormon would have never abridged the writings, since any abridgement means, some things had to be changed or left out. When members say they believe the overall history of the Book of Mormon is correct -- Lehi and his family fled to the New World, fought with others, taught by revelation, and visited by Christ -- they are actually talking about the verisimilitude of the Book of Mormon. The verisimilitude refers to how close the written record approximates the actual events that took place. No record -- even by the best scribe or historian in the entire world -- will get all details right on all things.

Therefore, everyone must be careful when making broad statements about knowing the exactness of things, especially the scriptures, when they were, intentionally written to have several layers of meaning. They were, written in ages past where the vernacular and connotation of certain words was different, and in some cases have been, interpreted several times where the true meaning of some sections has been lost. However, it perfectly ok for a person to say they believe or they have a testimony of the truthfulness of the Book of Mormon.

Virtues of God
(Taken in part from the lectures on faith)

The purpose of this article is to draw a parallel between the need to gain as much virtue as can be gained while in mortality and the benefits of obtaining total virtue equivalent of God while progressing through eternity. "We here observe that God is the only supreme governor and independent being in whom all fullness and perfection dwell; who is omnipotent, omnipresent and omniscient; without beginning of days or end of life; and that in him every good gift and every good principle dwell; and that he is the Father of lights; in him the principle of faith dwells independently, and he is the object in whom the faith of all other rational and accountable beings center for life and salvation" (*Second Lecture on Faith*). "Had it not been for the principle of faith the worlds would never have been framed neither would man have been formed of the dust. It is the principle by which Jehovah works, and through which He exercises power over all temporal as well as eternal things. Take this principle or attribute -- for it is an attribute -- from the Deity, and He would cease to exist. He is a saved being, and if we should continue the interrogation, and ask how it is that He is saved, the answer would be -- because He is a just and holy being; and if He were anything different from what He is, He would not be saved; for His salvation depends on His being precisely what He is and nothing else; for if it were possible for Him to change, in the least degree, so sure He would fail of salvation and lose all His dominion, power, authority and glory" (*lectures on faith*). He is the font of all virtue and all virtue is essence of His perfect being as He sits at the head of the worlds that He created and the family that inhabits His creations. In the record of Abraham, mortals are the literal offspring of God and it is His profound wish for us, His children, is to grow and progress in faith and virtue to become like Him. He created the universe and the Plan of salvation as a space and a probationary time, where His children, while out of His presence, could learn and be tested. As God's children traverse through the various spheres associated with the plan of salvation, they are constantly being placed in certain situations or given certain trials, where they are taught the virtues of god in order to gain the necessary faith, to return to His presence and regain His glory. The Bible instructions are, "Be ye therefore perfect, even as you're Father which is in heaven is perfect" (*Matthew 5:48*). Here the followers of Christ learn that during this time of their probation they must advance, as far as mortally possible, to the point of perfection, even as Father in Heaven is perfect. This idea of being perfect seems to be an overwhelming task when looking at it from a mortal perspective but then one must realize mortals are only two spheres into this time of probation (the preexistence and mortality), and have four or five spheres to go. As they grow and progress in their knowledge, obedience, and faith the undertaking of being perfect, will be less daunting. Children may be intimidated by the thought of growing into adulthood, just give them a few years and they will find it does not look so quite bad. Therefore, it is the same with us, the prospect of becoming like God will be a little intimidating at first, then it will start to seem probable, then possible, then attractive, then certain as one gain more knowledge and faith. This concept of developing toward the nature of God has to do with people using all knowledge, talent, and gifts to gain as much virtue in this life as possible. Most people realize, while here in mortality they cannot gain total virtue such as God possesses but it is important to know, if He was to lose any of the virtue, He now possesses, God could cease to be God. Conversely if any individual fails in their final effort to gain the requisite virtue they will not be accepted in the Celestial Kingdom with God. They will have to accept a lesser reward. As we are barreling headlong toward eternity, trying to put God in our everyday lives, here is an outline the some of the attributes of the God, His followers want to emulate.

A. He was God before the world was created, and is the same God after it was created.

B. He is merciful and gracious, slow to anger, abundant in goodness, and He is from everlasting, and will be to everlasting.

C. He changes not, neither is there variableness with Him; but He is the same from everlasting to everlasting, being the same yesterday, today, and forever; and His course is one eternal round, without variation. He is consistent.

D. He is a God of truth and cannot lie.

E. He is no respecter of persons: but in every nation, he who fears God and works righteousness is accepted of Him.

F. He is love," (Lectures on faith).

If people are to make a major effort to develop God's virtues in their lives, they should have an idea of how many virtues there are.

Here is a partial list,
Acceptance, Assertiveness, Authenticity, Caring, Charity, Cleanliness, Commitment, Compassion, Confidence, Consideration, Contentment, Cooperation, Courage, Creativity, Determination, Dignity, Enthusiasm, Ethical, Fairness, Faithful, Forgiveness, Friendliness, Generosity, Gentleness, Graciousness, Gratitude, Harmony, Helpfulness, Honesty, Honor, Hope, Humility, Integrity, Joyfulness, Justice, Kindness, Love, Loyalty, Moderation, Modesty, Optimism, Orderliness, Passion, Patience, Peace, Perseverance, Preparedness, Purposefulness, Reliability, Respect, Responsibility, Reverence, Self-discipline, Service, Sincerity, Tact, Temperance, Tenacity, Thankfulness, Tolerance, Trust, Truthfulness, Understanding, Unity, Wisdom, Wonderment.

Now, the true nature of God has been introduced, some of His attributes, and some of the virtues He possess, one can only say, WOW, how can anyone master all this? The answer is; follow Christ in all things of your life and live the commandments to the fullest. This is one of those times where the answer is simple; but the performance is difficult. "Be ye therefore perfect, even as you're Father which is in heaven is perfect" (Matthew 5:48). People find a means of applying the second part of the answer, living the commandments, into their lives. So where do one start? They start right here on earth by learning about and living the commandments. By living the commandments, individuals start learning how to handle themselves in virtuous situations under the rules of God. Now, a person cannot just wake up one morning and fully live all the commandments, no, they have to sort of ease into the process, but most of this they start learning at an early age. You might say, at the beginning of this process, people are kind of, practicing, to handle things in a small way, as God handles things in a big way. So how does living commandments help in the effort to gain even a small amount of virtue? Take for instance, the commandment "love you neighbor as you love yourself" this helps to learn, in a small way, the virtue of extending love beyond ourselves. It is necessary for people to cultivate an expansion of their love, similar to the expanded love God has for all his children. When living the commandment, thou shall not steal, people increase their virtue by not forsaking others and by being honest, as God said He would never forsake anyone or never take anything from them, but rather, He offers all he has. This offering is the virtue of charity, which also needed by mortals in order to progress to a Celestial state. It is the same with all commandments or laws given to by God, commandments are designed to help start the process of attaining all the virtues of God. So when reading, "His lord said unto him, Well done, thou good and faithful servant: thou hast been faithful over a few things, I will make thee ruler over many things: enter thou into the joy of thy lord" (*Mathew 25:21*). Adding this to Joseph Smith's statement, "As man is, God once was; and as God is, man may become" (*Lectures on Faith*). It is clear; life in mortality is a condensed version of celestial life. During their mortal state people are to learn, as Nephi said, "line upon line, precept upon precept, here a little and there a little" (*2 Nephi 28:30*) how to be like God. In other words, people are given a small amount of knowledge and power now, to practice with, to see if they can handle the glory and power inherited later. The greatest test of a mortal's life is to live the commandments and develop the virtues necessary to be, next to God or one with God. As was stated above, mortals are just starting the process, so as they progress from sphere to sphere they advance their ability and understanding of the quality of righteousness acceptable to God. Through this entire process, there is a constant need of support. To this end, God has provided mankind with the Savior, access to the Holy Ghost, the Church, the scriptures, and their families.

Now, back to the question, how is anyone ever going to master all this, and look at the first part of the answer; follow Christ in all things of life. It is important to realize the mission of the Savior was, and still is, to bring the fullness of the gospel to the earth for the benefit of God's children. A good portion of His teachings centered on this process of gaining virtue through obediently living the commandments. In the scriptures, this is referred to as being, one with Christ. If each of person can make Christ, the center of their lives they can start to understand repercussions of what Jesus said. "Neither pray I for these alone, but for them also who shall believe on me through their words; that they all may be one; as thou, Father, art in me, and I in thee, that they also may be one in us; that the world may believe that thou hast sent me. And the glory which thou gavest me I have given them; that they may be one, even as we are one: I in them, and thou in me, that they may be made perfect in one; and that the world may know that thou hast sent me, and hast loved them, as thou hast loved me" (*John;17: 20-24*).

The scripture above tells the whole story of gaining perfection of virtues by living his example. It says; "neither pray I for these alone, but for them also who shall believe on me, that they all may be one, as thou, Father, art in me, and I in thee" (*John 17:20&21*). This means Jesus became one with his father by believing on Him and His father became one with Him due to His obedience. Then it says they also may be one in the Father and Son, meaning if the saints follow His example, they will be in unison, or have this oneness with Christ and God the Father. Then it says the world may believe, thou hast sent me, meaning, the restored gospel will testify to the world of Him. In addition, He said, "the glory which thou gavest me I have given them" (*John, 17:22*), meaning, the glory which Christ gained from His Father will be extended to those who believe on Him and have this oneness with Him. Then He says, "they may be one, even as we are one: I in them, and thou in me" (*John, 17:23*), meaning, this oneness can only be gained in this specific manner - God to Christ and Christ to mankind. Next, "they may be made perfect in one", meaning, this oneness with Christ will lead to perfection. Then, "the world may believe that thou hast sent me", meaning, those who are one with Christ will, through His example lead the world to believe in Christ. Lastly, "the world may know that thou hast sent me, and hast loved them, as thou hast loved me", meaning, as this conversion happens the world will know of Christ's mission and that God's love for His children is equal to the love that He has for Christ (*17 John; 20-24*).

What Causes a Sin to be a Sin?

Have you ever asked yourself---what causes a sin to be a sin? This is an important question since everyone is trying to avoid or mitigate sin in his or her lives, but seldom is there a meaningful discussion about this subject. Mortal sin is inseparably, connected to three unique pieces of LDS doctrine, Covenants, Commandments, and Agency. The following is a briefly discussion each of these doctrines separately and then tie them together as they relate to a sin being a sin.

Covenants:

Perhaps no doctrine has had greater impact on Latter-day Saint theology than the doctrine surrounding covenants made by in the pre-existence, and man's potential godhood being eternally connected to the oaths, promises and vows made with the Lord prior to coming to earth .

In 1975, President Kimball said this: "We made vows, solemn vows, in the heavens before we came to this mortal life. We have made covenants. We made them before we accepted our position here on the earth. We committed ourselves to our Heavenly Father, that if He would send us to the earth and give us bodies and give to us the priceless opportunities that earth life afforded, you and I made a solemn commitment, that we would do all things whatsoever the Lord our God shall command us. This was a solemn oath, a solemn promise, a covenant. When you think about it, this very covenant is the source of most of our sins." Did we make such a promise? Sure we did, look at it this way, if we had not made such a promise we would have, by default, gone with Satan. This will be discussed a little further when we get to agency" (*conference talk, Be Ye Therefore Perfect*).

Commandments:

Commandments were ordained in the preexistence and were given spiritually before the earth was formed, but even though they are spiritual they are in full force here during mortal probation and they will carry on into the eternities. From a mortal perspective, a person may not understand the concept of stealing or false witness or parenthood as they relate to the eternal realm. Commandments are those things, which mortals either do, whereby they strengthen the soul, and kept it clean. Or, they do not do thus, damaging their souls, and in some cases causing irreparably damage. God has set these rules out for his children to live by as related in Abraham,
"And there stood one among them that was like unto God, and he said unto those who were with him: We will go down, for there is space there, and we will take of these materials, and we will make an earth whereon these (meaning His spirit children housed in a mortal body) may dwell; and we will prove them (meaning us) herewith, to see if they will do all things whatsoever the Lord their God shall command them; and they who keep their first estate shall be added upon; and they who keep not their first estate shall not have glory in the same kingdom with those who keep their first estate; and they who keep their second estate shall have glory added upon their heads for ever and ever" (*Abraham3:24-26*).
Members can be certain, considering the statement of President Kimball and this proclamation from the record of Abraham that sometime after the war in heaven and before entry into mortality, God's spirit children made a promise to keep all the commandments. Now, those spirit children are here and God is able to see if they are keeping their covenant. If living commandments is the reason this earth was formed and the reason mortals were placed here and living the commandments is the only way to can get

back to Heavenly Father, which is the greatest of desires, followers of Christ must answer this question.

How many commandments are there? Now, one would think, considering all the importance placed on the commandments, at a minimum, they should know how many commandments there are. Some of you will say 10, some will say more; here is a hint--- in the New Testament there are 38 commandments or 42 depending on how you read them. Then we have the D&C, Pearl of Great Price and Book of Mormon and latter day revelations concerning Priesthood, Temples and so on. The truth is most people simply do not know how many commandments there are.

A person might ask, "With all this emphasis on commandments, why doesn't the church just print a book listing all the commandments and then two or three pages of explanation on how to live that law". However, if you were to go to Deseret Book looking for a book of that nature you would not find one published by the Church. The General Authorities are smart enough not to fall into that trap. They only have to look at history to see the Jews have such a book, called the Laws of Moses, which was written about 400 years before Christ and this manuscript contains the written instructions on all the rituals associated with each and every commandment, 644 in all. Jews believed then and still believe today, by perfectly living these laws they are assured salvation, they did not need faith, and they just needed to obey the law. Because of these written instructions, which completely usurp the notion of personal revelation, the Jews did not need a Savior. Now they wanted a Savoir to chase the Romans away but not to tell them how to live. It seems like, the Jewish population was worshiping the Law, as for the Lord if they acknowledge Him at all, He, is just directing traffic. Today every person carries the full responsibility of learning the commandments and must rely on the Lord to help them obey each commandment correctly. So, how can this be accomplish? Members, repeatedly have been, and still are, told to study the scriptures, not to just read them, but study them---for what--- to find the scriptures teaching them the commandments and learn how to live them through personal revelation. One might say that the commandants are the owner's manual for mortals to live by, but how many times has someone bought a new appliance or car and the owner's manual, remains, never read. Why do people ignore these documents? Because they do not have to—they have agency, which leads to the next piece of LDS Doctrine.

Agency:

Without the gift of agency, mortals would absolutely be unable to demonstrate, to their Heavenly Father they are doing all things, which He commanded. The word, agent, saturates the Doctrine and Covenants; therein the word agent most often appears as the Saints being a representative of the Lord. In Mormon theology, everyone has agency and everyone recognizes this phrase is as important as what it implies. Explained here in this scripture, "And it is given to them to know, good from evil: wherefore they are agents unto themselves" (*Moses 6: 56*). Here, when acting for oneself, they have the absolute freedom to decide how and when to represent themselves, and it is for sure, they are acting solely for themselves. Since having agency is the covenant making everyone, a representative of the Lord it is clear, making these choices places them in a position of responsibility, and any choice they make has liability attached, and they are making these choices with the understanding, the outcome governs any reward in heaven. A scripture in Helaman clearly explains this. "And now remember, remember, my brethren, that whosoever perisheth, perisheth unto himself; and whosoever doeth iniquity, doeth it unto himself; for behold, ye are free; ye are permitted to act for yourselves; for behold, God hath given unto you a knowledge and he hath made you free. He hath given unto you that ye might know good from evil, and he hath given unto you that ye might choose life or death; and ye can do good and be restored unto that which is good, or have that which is good restored unto you; or ye can do evil, and have that which is evil restored unto you" (*Helaman 14:30-31*).

Some, biblical gurus, claim there was complete free agency prior to the war in heaven. Now this is pure speculation since there is not much known about that time, but what is known, is when the war in heaven was over, agency, in spite of whatever it was before it changed. Agency was now a choice, only between Satan and Christ. This is known because there was not a Satan nor a Christ prior to the war in heaven episode, it was all still in the planning stages and only God knew the outcome. So, when people question the covenants made in the pre-existence before coming to this mortal life, there was not, and still is not a third choice. There was then and still is, only two choices and if the spirit children of God did refused to follow Christ, which is keeping His commandments and so on, they would have automatically sided with Satan.

So, now is the time tie this all together.

If mortals were never taught the Law, could they sin? The answer is no. Paraphrasing Romans 4:15, for where no law is, there is no transgression

If people did not have agency, could they sin? The answer is no. This is what Satan wanted to do---take away all agency, thus no sin—everyone makes it into heaven.

If a covenant was never made, could there be sin? The answer is no. No promise, no problem---of course--- no promise, no mortality.

It takes a combination of the three for sin to happen. So, what causes a sin to be a sin? It is only mortals, not keeping agency under control, and allowing themselves to break some or all of the commandments thus violating the covenant made with Heavenly Father before coming into this world.

It is clear, the correct use of agency, making and keeping covenants is what got mortals here, and the correct use of agency, and the continuation of making and keeping covenants is what will get us into the Celestial Kingdom.

www.ingramcontent.com/pod-product-compliance
Lightning Source LLC
Chambersburg PA
CBHW051814090426
42736CB00011B/1469